Praise for the original edition of
WHO RUNS CONGRESS?

"A good deal of meat and validity."
—former Senate Majority Leader Mike Mansfield

"A highly readable and often entertaining cataloguing of congressional sin, arrogance, ineffectiveness, and unresponsiveness."
—*The New Republic*

"A solid, competent work."
—Nicholas von Hoffman,
The Washington Post

"A useful . . . Everyman's Guide to What's Wrong with Congress."
—*Business Week*

"A valuable handbook for people action."
—*Seattle Times*

"The best book ever done on Congress—about ten billion light-years ahead of its nearest competitor. It amounts to a postgraduate course in the actualities of politics, should be memorized word for word by every citizen."
—Ferdinand Lundberg, author of
The Rich and the Super-Rich

YOU CAN MAKE A DIFFERENCE

"Some citizens, peering into the chasm between congressional potential and congressional failure, may understandably shrug their shoulders in indifference. But mixed among all the cases of sloth, corruption, insensitivity to injustice, and massive lobbying are remarkable instances of citizen power. Congress has been moved by men and women with no special wealth or influence, little or no political experience, and no uncommon genius, but with the modest combination of commitment to a cause and the facts to make a case. Not often, but enough to show the way, citizen advocates have taken on industrial giants, bureaucratic inertia, public indifference, antipathy to 'troublemakers'—and they have won, or at least made a difference."

—from *Who Runs Congress?*

Other books by Mark Green:

With Justice for Some (1971, edited with Bruce Wasserstein)

The Closed Enterprise System (1972, with Beverly C. Moore, Jr., and Bruce Wasserstein)

The Monopoly Makers (1973, editor)

Corporate Power in America (1973, edited with Ralph Nader)

The Other Government: The Unseen Power of Washington Lawyers (1975)

Verdicts on Lawyers (1976, edited with Ralph Nader)

Taming the Giant Corporation (1976, with Ralph Nader and Joel Seligman)

The Big Business Reader (1980, edited with Robert Massie, Jr.)

Winning Back America (1982)

Ronald Reagan's Reign of Error (1983, with Gail MacColl)

WHO RUNS CONGRESS?

Fourth edition completely revised
and updated by
MARK GREEN

with
Michael Waldman
Michael Calabrese
Lynn Darling
Bruce Rosenthal
James M. Fallows
David R. Zwick

Introduction by Ralph Nader

A DELL BOOK

Published by
Dell Publishing Co., Inc.
1 Dag Hammarskjold Plaza
New York, New York 10017

Dell ® TM 681510, Dell Publishing Co., Inc.

ISBN: 0-440-19676-0

Printed in the United States of America
First printing—January 1984

ACKNOWLEDGMENTS

Many friends and colleagues helped create and shape the editions of *Who Runs Congress?* The original 1972 edition grew out of the fertile editorial guidance of Jean Highland and Judy Knipe of Bantam Books, and Dick Grossman, Tom Stewart, and Julie Colmore of Grossman Publishers. Doug Cassell contributed to the Epilogue, "Taking on Congress: A Primer for Citizen Action." In addition, Joan Claybrook, Robert Fellmeth, Michael Pertschuck, and Harrison Wellford gave us valuable insights and comments.

The second edition in 1975 contained sections written by Lynn Darling and Bruce Rosenthal. Significantly contributing to the researching and writing of the third edition was Michael Calabrese—with assistance provided by Daniel Becker of Congress Watch. And on this fourth edition, Michael Waldman of the Democracy Project has proven to be an invaluable collaborator— and Robert Nelson, Bonnie Tenneriello, and Joel Berg were essential to the research and production of the book. Editor Gary Luke guided this fourth edition with patience and skill.

Finally, two people deserve special note. Publisher Oscar Dystel perceived a need for citizens to better understand Congress in the early 1970s, and helped develop the original concept for this book. And of course there is Ralph Nader, without whom this book wouldn't exist. In this effort, as in so many others, he exemplifies what Felix Frankfurter used to call the highest office in a democracy—the office of citizen.

MARK GREEN
New York City
August 1, 1983

To Deni and Jenya

Contents

Introduction
by Ralph Nader

Mark Green's *Who Runs Congress?* coauthored in this fourth edition with Michael Waldman, has endured for 12 years as the most widely read book in American history on the U.S. Congress. The reasons, I think, are its readability and prescience. Back in the original 1972 edition, Green (with James Fallows and David Zwick) warned us of the growing tide of special-interest money and lawlessness—and counseled specific changes in such debilitating traditions as the filibuster, seniority, and budget and war-authorizing processes. At the time, the book unsettled many in the congressional power orbit. President-to-be Gerald Ford denounced it. *Time* magazine congressional correspondent Neil McNeil said, in anger, "They're accusing some members of crimes!" What followed was a decade of PAC proliferation as well as Koreagate and Abscam (indeed, Abscam prosecutors tell how they read this book to learn about the way money and politics operate in Washington). Yet it was also a decade of important reforms in rules governing the filibuster, seniority system, and budget-and-war-authorizing processes. The authors foresaw how Congress might be taking a step back for every step forward.

11

In this fourth edition of *Who Runs Congress?* it would be facile to describe the transformations in our national legislature, since the first edition came out in 1972, by recycling the durable French observation that the more things change, the more they remain the same. Facile, and not sufficiently precise. True, the major organized power groups have an impressive way of adjusting both to new legislative procedures and to new legislators. They adjust only to conquer. But something deeper has occurred in the Congress that has reduced its stature in the midst of crises—those junctures when lawmaking bodies often rise to historic heights of performance. The word of self-criticism most heard on Capitol Hill is "paralysis." With overlapping subcommittees and committees in each house, with the severe loss of party discipline, with the members finding their own funding sources further aiding the recent procedural decentralization of Congress, the institution invites a metaphor of a herd of mules haphazardly digging in.

This paralysis extends to their output as well as to their procedure. The chasm between what Congress documents and what Congress decides has grown wider in recent years. In the past there was a higher correlation between congressional hearings and congressional decision making. What Congress did not want to decide, it usually managed not to hear. No longer. Elaborate hearings depict massive inequities in the tax laws and then both House and Senate pass further special privileges for the well-heeled. Facing serious safety and economic problems in the nuclear industry, Congress has disregarded the many reports of its own investigative arm, the General Accounting Office, and continued to fund prominent boondoggles like the Clinch River Breeder Reactor project. In the midst of a corporate crime epidemic ranging from illegal payoffs to toxic wastes, the federal legislature entertains a White House proposal to weaken the law against foreign bribery by U.S. corporations. With more bank failures than at any time since the Great Depression, Congress has rushed so fast into deregulation of that industry that even some financial specialists within the banking community have urged a slowdown. Confronted by massive corporate merger movements,

Congress has appropriated billions of dollars in direct and indirect corporate subsidies ("aid to dependent corporations" in the wry words of Public Citizen's Congress Watch) while impeding or defeating measures in auto, drug, pesticide, and food safety. This conduct is in a long tradition of shielding corporate misbehavior from the rule of law and turning Congress and the executive branch into a bustling bazaar of bonanzas—bonanzas that take the form of subsidies, tax privileges, protection from competition, inflated government contracts, and other assorted windfalls.

But is it too much to expect Congress, with its superior information sources and authority, to lead, to foresee and forestall, to mobilize the "felt necessities" of our time? Apparently the answer is often yes if one looks at examples of congressional inaction even when confronted front and center with abuse. For example, after the most intense experience with the executive lawlessness of Watergate, the Congress saw some of its members draw up a list of reforms in 1974 following the conclusions of those celebrated hearings. They remain on the shelf of congressional disinterest. To any close observers of Congress such withdrawals are not surprising. After all, some veteran members of Congress knew about the secret war in Laos and did nothing, in violation of their oath to uphold the Constitution. They knew much about the lawlessness of the CIA and did nothing, again in violation of their oath to uphold the Constitution.

There are many disincentives to engaging corporate power issues— not the least among them the threat to lay off workers and to close down or move plants and offices. But a major reason is surely the rise of political action committees. As this edition of *Who Runs Congress?* describes and documents, campaign funds, through the enormous growth of ever more special interest PACs (they gave $8 million in 1972 and $83 million in 1982), have transformed influencing Congress into a retail operation (with more money going to more hands) and ever higher economies of scale. Through the dispersion of authority into many congressional hands, the old way of concentrating on a few Senate and House committee chairmen cannot deliver the House or Senate the way a Wilbur Mills or a

Russell Long used to do. Also, subcommittee chairs, such as Representative Henry Waxman, can keep a chair like Representative John Dingell from delivering his committee during the struggle over the Clean Air Act amendments in 1982, thus requiring the influence of members' votes one by one.

As the costs of campaigning zoom upward, the PAC phenomenon creates entry barriers to less endowed players in the political arenas—starting with those who would run as candidates. PAC money influences, discourages, and punishes. Who says so? The legislators and their aides whose quoted remarks in *Who Runs Congress?* indicate they are more willing than ever to speak about the buying or renting of congressional behavior. The not so astonishing priorities that certain measures receive—like the legislative veto of the used-car rule, or the Alaska Gas Pipeline Guarantee bill—in contrast to the wandering attention paid to asbestos in schools or erosion of our farmlands are lucratively recurrent themes.

But the Age of PACs not only concentrates power in the lap of the corporate government; it also drains it away from others. Labor unions cannot keep up in campaign dollars and incumbents develop their own financial bases and organizations that eliminate any need to rely on party money and its disciplinary demands. Such individuation of the electoral process is reflected in the inability of the House and Senate leadership to tie legislative programs to voting support from party members. On several occasions I have seen Speaker Tip O'Neill beseech young Democratic members of the House to vote for a bill. They shrugged him off almost mockingly. Speaker O'Neill must be nostalgic for the days of Speaker Sam Rayburn and the Texan's stable of usable sanctions against such rebellions. This substitution of interested money for party cohesion has been one of the least noticed factors in the lively debate over the scope of PAC financing.

"Crowding out" further displayed itself in the relationship between the Reagan administration and Congress in the early eighties. "Money, money, money, that's about all we've been talking about," wailed Senator Russell Long (D.-La.). It is worse than that complaint

14

implies. As the House and Senate hurriedly passed President Reagan's budget reconciliation bills with few hearings and little debate, they were overriding the authority and scrutiny of standing committees, rewriting vast stretches of law. And when Congress became so mired in abstract budget discussions that it allowed most decisions to be made in a back-door process of omnibus legislation, it even let its own budget process atrophy.

The other casualty was the main task of Congress—deciding major policy issues for the world's most powerful society. Anyone who judges Congress to be power-hungry needs to explain why it is so consistently averse to treating the big questions that only the nation's legislature can handle. Here, personal constituent services are its reelection inventory. Broader visions and fundamental responses are its rarities. Congress as a whole has managed to avoid passage of responsive legislation to meet the problems of energy, taxes, health insurance, inflation, and unemployment. It has not faced up to the relentless concentration of multinational corporate power over the economy, nor is it seriously anticipating the consequences of computer controls and genetic engineering.

Over the past quarter century, for example, the principal social justice drives have found Congress lagging, not leading. Whether in civil rights, women's rights, consumer, environmental, or arms-control movements, Congress began moving only after it got on the bandwagon. This is not to say that Capitol Hill was without courageous legislators—they were there, heads held high—but it took an aroused populace to push Congress as a whole toward enactment of these programs. Were it not for the deep outpouring of citizen concern over the arms race, most senators and representatives might still be looking the other way from that momentous peril.

The Reagan years have shown Congress to be better at resisting the unraveling of the past than the reaching out toward the future. Even with a Republican-controlled Senate, the President has been unable to persuade either house to enact legislation that would straitjacket the ability of agencies that regulate business; weaken the pesticide, clean air, clean water, and food safety laws; or restrict the

Freedom of Information Act. None of these measures received any-where near the support that Mr. Reagan secured for his budget reconciliation bills during his first two years in office. While mem-bers of both parties were bellowing against "overregulation," fewer of these legislators were willing to abandon the preservation of substantive laws passed in the sixties and early seventies designed to defend consumers and the environment and to assist students and the poor. It is as if the Congress wished to save the laws while doing little to asure that they are enforced by the executive branch of government. This pattern persists into the 98th Congress, notwith-standing a remarkable turnover in membership since 1978. Most of the architects for these laws are gone (Muskie, Nelson, Magnuson, Moss, and Rosenthal), yet, with 43 of 100 senators in their first term and 210 of 435 House members in office for less than six years, their legacy remains largely unperturbed.

The elemental affliction of Congress is its chronic loss of stature as an institution. The national polls show a regular drop in public approval. And *Who Runs Congress?* shows Congress to have a higher crime rate than the general population, even though there is *not* a predisposition on the part of prosecuting authorities to devote many resources to that quest. From Koreagate to Abscam, the public sees only the outline of the problem on Capitol Hill. To many Americans, campaign contributions by lobbies, together with the wining and dining and other luxuries in kind, appear little more than institutionalized bribery. The exemption of Congress by Congress from many of the civil rights, freedom of information, and labor-safety laws it applies to the rest of government and society can agitate even normally tepid temperaments.

Still, nothing infuriates more people across diverse political spectra than the furtive, frantic late-session moves by congressional grown-ups to raise their own salaries or enlarge their own incomes by more indirect methods. (According to one homespun song played on radio and set to the tune of "The Battle Hymn of the Republic," "we'll remember in November when we vote.") Salary grabs have become customary features on the congressional landscape. They are not always successful— some have been rolled back, like the notorious tax break that Congress gave itself in late 1981. But even occasional losses do not stop the lawmakers from their deep dissatisfaction with earning only more than four times the average wage in their country. The present anomaly finds the representatives being paid $69,800 plus benefits, while the senators chose late in 1981 to revoke their limit on total speech income so trade groups and companies can supplement their salary of $60,662. All these self-seeking machinations—and they are constantly bubbling with intrigue and backbiting— have gone on at the same time Congress is telling workers to restrain their wage demands, accept cutbacks, and fight inflation. What is so dismaying is the dearth of recognition by so many elected representatives that being a model to the nation is their most enabling asset.

In this example as in others, members of Congress show themselves to be not very representative of the American people. Almost one third of the Senate are millionaires. Almost half the Congress is composed of lawyers, who make up less than one third of 1 percent of the population. Blue-collar workers may get to Congress, but usually as tourists passing through the guided tours. Women and minority groups are, for the most part, severely underrepresented.

In a democracy, ultimate governmental power is supposed to reside in the people. And in the interest of practicality and expertise, the people delegate much of the daily exercise of this power to elected legislatures, which on the national level means Congress. But delegation requires vigilance, and, lacking vigilance, delegation becomes abdication. One of the objectives of this volume is to make more people care about what they've lost to Congress so that they can take more of it back for the good of themselves, their fellow citizens, and their children. Less than half the adults polled back in 1965 knew the name of their member of Congress. Only 40 percent of the electorate voted in the November 1982 Congressional elections. As a result, without the participation of the people, Congress has surrendered its enormous authority and resources to special interest groups, waste, insensitivity, ignorance, and bureaucracy.

Americans do not spend much time doing something about Congress; they spend far more time worrying about their personal problems—taxes, school, health, pollution, energy, war, traffic, housing, inflated prices, crime, injustice, poverty, corruption. They worry about a steady slippage in the quality of American life—not about Congress. Yet these are the problems and abuses that Congress has the power to help them with—that is what Congress is *supposed* to be for. Its laws affect the price of meat and gasoline; decide how clean the environment is to be; permit or encourage warfare; feed massive military expenditures; shape huge government bureaucracies (which it alone can create); affect the size and quality of the economy; and spend over $800 billion of your money annually. Yet while the average television watch time by viewers is 25 hours a week, probably less than a hundred thousand people spend 10 hours a year watching Congress as citizens. At the same time, 15,000 lobbyists work on the congressional offices daily as employees of or advisers to corporate and other trade associations.

This edition of *Who Runs Congress?* still contains its original optimism that, although Congress is the Great American Default, it is potentially the branch most exposed to democratic demand. And so turning Congress around *for* the people is the most practical and immediate priority in improving the executive and judicial branches as well. The stakes are now so apparent and so mounting that accomplishing this transformation *by* the people must be viewed as an *obligation*, not just a right, of citizenship. This citizenship must be ingrained as part of the daily work and fun of America.

For the U.S. Congress, like the nerve center of a traffic control system, stands potentially as both reflector and initiator of democratic solutions. The word *potentially* is used deliberately—as both an expression of hope and of realistic possibilities—even though Congress in its past and in its present has been a continuous underachiever. It is the right and duty of every citizen to strive for such development. And it should not have to be the equivalent of reaching for the stars.

Traditionally, the political system in this country has led Americans to look to the presidency for inspiration and leadership. But the Congress can be an even more effective leader and shaper and receiver of democratic values and action. For some of Washington's old hands, such an aspiration might be taken as a bad joke, if not an explicitly bizarre goal. But it is not as bizarre as it sounds when one considers the number of flexible and decentralized options that are open to Congress. The constitutional authority given to Congress accords it an importance that far transcends the indentured status or chronic inaction presently woven into its fabric.

Who Runs Congress? offers some initial practical advice on what *you* can do about reclaiming it for American citizens. The rest is up to you—your sense of justice, your faith in people, your energy and imagination. If you want to do something about it, start now. It is the mark of our nation's fingertip potential, unprecedented in world history, that we are a generation of Americans who have to give up little in order to achieve much of lasting endurance for the earth's people. Two centuries of delegation have worn their course. It is time to grasp the labors of daily citizenship and assume more closely the responsibility of government.*

Washington, D.C.
August 1983

---

*Please turn to the last pages of this volume which describe how you can obtain useful materials to assist you in monitoring and contributing to congressional policies on the important issues of the eighties.

1

Who Owns Congress?

Congress is the best money can buy.
—Will Rogers

The influence of big money on government has been a theme of critics ever since the founding of the Republic. Were it not for the sordid tales of bribery and payoffs regularly floating out from behind the Capitol Curtain, scandal columnists might long ago have gone on unemployment compensation. But for all their titillating impact, the crudest forms of bribery are vastly overshadowed as a corrupting influence by a much more sophisticated and widespread practice. Instead of going into the congressman's pockets, the money is put in the campaign coffers for the next election.

Of course, when a big campaign contribution is given in return for an assurance of receiving special treatment, it doesn't matter what the transaction is called. It's still nothing more than good old-fashioned graft in a very thin disguise. But who needs to extract a promise from a politician if spending enough money at election time can put a "reliable" man or woman into office? Or better yet, if spending enough money at nominating time can ensure that *all* the surviving candidates by the time the general election rolls around are "reliable"?

Expensive Merchandise

Part of the problem is inflation. As the cost of U.S. political influence has soared, casual buyers have fled the market and left it to the truly rich or the corporate purchasers. Expenses weren't always so high. In the election campaign of 1846 friends of Abraham Lincoln collected a fund for his first try for Congress. The $200 they scraped together would barely cover one week's phone bills for a modern candidate. But at the end of the campaign Lincoln returned $199.25 of it. The rest had gone for his one campaign expense, a barrel of cider for local farmhands.

Honest Abe might have spent the rest of his life splitting rails if he'd tried the same thing much later. The turning point for campaign expenses came with the Civil War. As the newly powerful corporate empires began to buy political favors—and as the politicians of the time showed themselves willing to be bought—competition pushed the prices up. The mounting expense, however, did not curb demand, since the companies saw the hard business advantage of friendly politicians. In 1903 a Standard Oil agent (who was himself a member of Congress), screening a "loan request" from a senator, wrote to the company's vice president John Archbold, "Do you want to make the investment?"

The return on such investments was a Congress increasingly populated with men like Senator Boies Penrose. Penrose was a Pennsylvanian, a Republican, and a devoted glutton. (He weighed 350 pounds and kept in condition with meals like the following: one dozen oysters, pots of chicken gumbo, a terrapin stew, two ducks, six kinds of vegetables, a quart of coffee, and several cognacs.) But his deepest allegiance was to the welfare of Corporate America. He candidly explained his philosophy of economy and life to a group of his business beneficiaries: "I believe in a division of labor. You send us to Congress; we pass laws under . . . which you make money; . . . and out of your profits you further contribute to our campaign funds to send us back again to pass more laws to enable you to make more money." A good operating guideline, he once confided to an associate, was to work on "legislation that meant something to men with real money and let them foot the bill"—as when Archbold of Standard Oil gave him $25,000 on one proven occasion. Penrose was merely an Americanized version of the Medici family, whose slogan was "Money to get power, power to protect money."

Today's politicians can afford neither Penrose's candor nor his appetite, but his mottoes live on. In 1955, for example, the Texas oil industry noted that congressional proposals to change the industry's tax subsidies had not been killed as quickly as usual. Anxious to set things right, the president of the Texas oil trade association told his fellows that "it seems only fair to tie a few strings to the contributions we make to political organizations and candidates." When, in 1958, the oil depletion tax loophole was up for its biennial round of criticism in Congress, a staff member of the Democratic senatorial campaign committee went to see some candidates from the Western states. "I was informed that if I could get some of these fellas out West to express their fealty to the golden principle of 27.5 percent [depletion allowance], there might be a pretty good piece of campaign change involved," he later told Ronnie Dugger of the *Texas Observer*. Oklahoma senator Fred Harris fondly recalls his baptism in this old style of campaign spending when, in the 1954 Oklahoma Senate race, incumbent oil millionaire Robert Kerr squared off against another oil millionaire, Roy Turner. Harris, who worked for Turner, says:

> Some [people] wanted to be country or town campaign managers for whichever candidate would pay the most. An unprincipled preacher offered to bargain away supposed influence with his unsuspecting congregation. An Avon saleswoman was willing to consider—for a price—adding a pitch for a candidate to her usual sales promotion to regular-route customers. And there were the ubiquitous importunings of hundreds of poll haulers and hangers-on. They wanted everything from $25,000 to carry a county to a half pint of whiskey to make the day. From fifty

dollars for "gas and expenses" to get to the district church conference, to a thousand dollars to pay back taxes to keep a weekly newspaper publishing. . . .

One young man in the Turner headquarters had as his principal duty running to the Federal Reserve Bank every day as soon as it opened to bring back a thousand or so dollars in cash to be doled out to those who came in declaring that victory in their counties required a little money "to put on a barbecue" or "to hire some woman to pick up old folks on election day."

But Darwin rules in politics as in nature, and the richest survive. Turner ran out of money midway through the campaign and had to quit. Kerr kept his seat.

If Turner were running his campaign in the 1980s, the daily money deliveries would have to be closer to ten thousand than to one. As election techniques have risen from barbecues and preacher-bribing to the higher technologies of electronic advertising and computerized direct mail, the demands on candidates to raise funds has exponentially increased. And many don't like it one bit. "Campaign financing is a curse," said the late Hubert Humphrey, who had been through enough campaigns to know. "It's the most disgusting, demeaning, disenchanting, debilitating experience of a politician's life. It's stinky, it's lousy. I just can't tell you how much I hate it." Representative Mike Synar, a Democrat from Oklahoma, says that "if you ask 100 Congressmen, 99 would say the worst part of the job is raising money. We'd rather be caught in an elevator with an insurance salesman." This objection is not a partisan one. To conservative Republican Senator Paul Laxalt, our system of fund-raising is "cruel and barbaric—too expensive and too intensive."

But they do it—and, indeed, are raising and spending more and more money.

The first million-dollar congressional race occurred in 1978. By 1982 there were races where *each* of the two candidates spent a million dollars or more. In 1974 John Culver and David Stanley together spent $807,037 in their Iowa Senate contest; when Culver ran for reelection against Charles Grassley in 1980, they spent $3,933,708—or a 487 percent spending increase in just one term. While all congressional candidates spent $72 million in 1974, by 1982 spending swelled to $300 million. The average House candidate spent $54,000 and the average Senate candidate spent $437,000 in 1974—yet by 1980 these figures were $157,000 and $1.1 million, respectively. Of course, the average *winners* spent a good deal more. In 1982 the median winner of a Senate race spent $1,746,230, a 69 percent jump from 1980's figure of $1,031,277; in the House the median for winners increased from $145,292 to $214,767.

Why the rise? First, costs have risen. In 1974 a thirty-second TV spot cost $1,100 in Baltimore and a stamp went for 8 cents. Today the spot costs $3,000 and the stamp 20 cents. But second, the price of running for office has been bid up by special interests who have encouraged a kind of feverish arms race where each candidate feels the pressure to spend not merely *enough*, but *more*. For the odds strongly favor the candidate who spends the most money. A study by Public Citizen's Congress Watch of 1978 "open seat" races (i.e., where there's no incumbent) found that winners outspent losers in four races out of five; twenty-seven of the thirty-three successful Senate candidates in 1982 spent more than their unsuccessful opponents. Out-fund-raising your opponent doesn't guarantee success, but it apparently doesn't hurt.

As costs have risen to the point where even the millionaires must borrow, so, too, rises the certainty that politicians must turn to rich special interests for help. President Eisenhower, in an era of what now looks like small-change campaigns, was appalled by the "outrageous costs of getting elected to public office." Later, Robert Kennedy agreed that "we are in danger of creating a situation in which our candidates must be chosen from among the rich [like the Kennedys] . . . or those willing to be beholden to others."

Few congressmen would admit that they can be "bought," but their protest is like that of a free-living woman who decides she might as well take money for what she enjoys, but insists she is not for sale. With their more sympathetic view, they can open up the range of government favors to private interests: subsidies, lucrative contracts, tax exemptions, toothless regulatory laws, restraints on overeager regulating agencies, protective tariffs, foreign policies to protect private investment. Those who suffer when the favors are passed out—the taxpayers, the purchasers of overpriced goods—never get a chance to sit down with the politicians in the same chummy atmosphere.

A Case of Milk

A striking historical example of the corrupting influence of special interest campaign contributions involved nothing more complicated than a quart of milk. Early in 1971 the dairy industry demanded that the government raise the guaranteed price it paid farmers for "manufactured milk"—raw milk used to make many dairy products. The increase they wanted would raise retail food prices by hundreds of millions of dollars, at a time when inflation was beginning to worsen. It would also, U.S. Department of Agriculture officials predicted, lead to serious milk surpluses piling up in government warehouses—an extra burden on a strained federal budget.

Weighing these disadvantages and finding no cost justification for an increase, Secretary of Agriculture Clifford Hardin announced on March 12, 1972, that the price would not go up. But not for long. Dairy representatives swung into action, and by March 25—less than two weeks later—the administration had caved in. Citing "new evidence," Secretary Hardin announced a 6 percent price boost, just what the milk men had asked for. The cost of the decision to the American eater, who spends one out of every seven food dollars on dairy products, was an estimated $500 to $700 million per year (one cent extra per quart, plus large increases in other dairy prices).

What did the milk men have going for them that the housewife didn't? They had a lot of pure homogenized Grade A cash, milked from consumers in inflated prices. Like the shrewd John Archbold of Standard Oil, they invested their money wisely; by putting it into politics, they earned the legal right to bilk the consumer of more money, a small portion of which they could again invest in politics. The dairymen had hit on the tactic several years earlier, when—as William A. Powell, president of Mid-America Dairymen, explained in a letter to one of his organization's members—they learned "that the sincere and soft voice of the dairy farmer is no match for the jingle of hard currencies put in the campaign funds of the politicians by the vegetable fat interests, labor, oil, steel, airlines, and others."

The obvious remedy was to make sure the farmers could match the other jingles with an ample jingle of their own. In their first two years of political fund-raising, they put together a war chest of $1 million. More than $500,000 of this they sunk in the congressional elections of 1970.

The investment paid off. Within a week of Hardin's first announcement, the industry had drafted a bill that would have taken the price decision out of the Agriculture Department's hands by making an increase mandatory. In the House, 116 members—fifty of whom had received dairy contributions—jumped on the milk wagon as cosponsors. There were 29 sponsors in the Senate, including even consumer advocate (and Wisconsin's) Gaylord Nelson. Twelve of these senators had run in 1970—eight of them with dairy contributions.

But another dairy beneficiary, the Nixon administration, beat Congress in making the move. Helping enamor Richard Nixon were thousands of dollars the farmers sent to his election fund. Of this, $35,000 was a down payment, funneled into Republican campaign committees only days before Hardin announced the price rise. The rest was paid out in installments, stretching several months past "delivery." The first of these, a $45,000 installment, was paid on April 5, just four days after the new price went into effect.

What happened just before Hardin's turnabout announcement is revealing. The first big contribution was on March 22. It got quick results. The next day, President Nixon invited sixteen dairy and farm representatives to the White House. Their audience with the President— the ultimate in purchased political access—lasted nearly an hour, twice as long as scheduled. The meeting with the President was later described by William Powell, president of the Mid American Dairymen, in a letter to one of his members:

> We dairymen as a body can be a dominant group. On March 23, 1971, along with nine other dairy farmers, I sat in the Cabinet room of the White House, across the table from the President of the United States, and heard him compliment the dairymen on their marvelous work in consolidating and unifying our industry and our involvement in politics. He said, "You people are my friends, and I appreciate it."
>
> Two days later an order came from the U.S. Department of Agriculture increasing the support price of milk . . . We dairymen cannot afford to overlook this kind of economic benefit. Whether we like it or not, this is the way the system works.

The only thing unusual about the dairy campaign was the publicity it received. Fresh off the farm, the dairymen at first made the "mistake" of filing a candid set of financial reports. An amazed Democratic campaign hand told Frank Wright of the *Minneapolis Tribune*, "My God, we've been doing that sort of thing for years, and we've never, never had it reported so publicly." The milk men's efforts at concealment may have been a bit rough around the edges, but they had learned their basic lesson well: they paid their money and patiently waited for the dividends.

After the 1972 election the dairy co-ops continued their monetary influence-peddling. Between election day 1972 and May 31, 1974, one of every seven members of the Senate and House had received a dairy contribution. But by 1974 the walls began to crash in on the cooperatives. The publicity revealed not only their massive influence but also cast a shadow of illegality on some of the campaign donations: $222,450 in illicit corporate donations arranged by the former special counsel of the American Milk Producers, Inc. (AMPI), David L. Parr; $330,000 in illegal corporate contributions over a six-year period arranged by former AMPI general manager Harold S. Nelson. AMPI was fined $35,000 and Parr and Nelson were each fined $10,000 and sent to jail for four months.

The Rise of PACs

"I'm scared," says Representative Barber Conable, the eight-term Republican from upstate New York. "I'm scared," he softly repeats, anxiously pacing around his high-ceilinged office in the Cannon House Office Building. "These new PACs [Political Action Committees] not only buy incumbents, but affect legislation. It's the same crummy business as judges putting the arm on lawyers who appear before them to finance their next campaign."

James Shannon, a thirty-year-old Massachusetts Democrat and member of the Ways and Means Committee, has his office down the hall. "During the tax bill," he says, "lobbyists asked me to help their cause because 'it will be good for the party,' which meant that business PACs would contribute money to the Democratic party if Democrats cooperated. One lobbyist who saw me in my office said of a client, 'He makes good PAC contributions to the party.' At this point I exploded, saying, 'I'm tried of hearing appeals based on money.' And you know what he said? 'You think I like this any more than you do?' "

And when five representatives of stature retired after the 97th Congress in 1982—Richard Bolling, Henry Reuss, Jonathan Bingham, Millicent Fenwick, and William Brodhead—all said in their separate valedictories that the growth of special interest PACs threatens, in Bolling's phrase, "to destroy the democracy of the United States."

PACs are groups of like-minded people with an internal means of communication—corporations, trade associations, labor unions, ideological groups—who raise funds among themselves to give to candidates. They are allowed to give a candidate up to $10,000 per election cycle, $5,000 for a primary and $5,000 for a general election. PACs are a new rendition of the old melody sung by

Penrose and his nineteenth-century business supporters—except on a louder scale.

Next to home computers and video games, PACs are the biggest growth industry in America. There were six hundred of them in 1974 and thirty-five hundred by 1983. They come in all sizes, shapes, and names—so long as the suffix is PAC. There's the Dr Pepper PAC, Bake PAC, American Motorcyclist PAC, Snack PAC, Sierra Club PAC, PeacePAC, the American Tax Reduction PAC, and the Brewers' SixPAC—not to mention the better known corporate, labor, and trade PACs.

PACs gave $8.5 million to congressional candidates in the 1972 election cycle, $12.5 million in 1974, $35 million in 1978, $55 million in 1980, and $83 million in 1981–82—for a tenfold increase in ten years. Corporate PACs have enjoyed the greatest growth of all, nearly doubling their contributions in two years—from $9.8 million in 1978 to $19.2 million in 1980. By 1982 business PACs generally (corporate and trade associations) were outspending labor union PACs nearly three to one. And there is plenty of room for growth: forty percent of *Fortune*'s 500 largest industrial corporations have not yet even established a PAC.

Individual business PAC giving indicates their exponential progression. The Realtors PAC gave $6,700 in 1970, $1.6 million in 1979–80, and $2.5 million in 1981–82. Oil and gas PACs doubled their giving from 1978 to 1980, and their $7 million in 1982 exceeds what the Democratic National Committee raised for all its candidates. Then there's the Builders' PAC. Spending $38,000 in 1977–78 and $600,000 in 1979–80, it gave $2 million in 1982, and, says spokesman Pat Collins, will spend $4 million next time.

This proliferation won't slow down soon, since every lobbying group feels the need to keep pace in the PAC race. Woe to the bowling alley without Pac-Man, or the lobby group without PAC-men. Announcing Wheat PAC, for example, Carl Schwensen, executive vice-president of the National Wheat Growers Association, said, "Wheat growers are aware of the trend toward more and larger political action committees. That is now a part of the political scene.''

Despite their large number and variety, PACs usually have several things in common. First, they like winners, which means they like incumbents, who have won 92 percent of the time in recent House elections. So two thirds of their funds go to incumbents, and the rest to challengers and candidates for ''open seats.''

Second, PACs like committee chairmen and the ''money'' committees (Ways and Means, House Appropriations, Senate Finance, Senate Appropriations) for reasons Willie Sutton once famously explained. It makes sense for business PACs to help out those in the best position to benefit their constituencies. Representative Al Gore, Jr., of Tennessee calls such gifts ''smart bombs.'' Hence, the chairmen of the House and Senate Banking Committees in 1980 received contributions from 36 and 35 financial PACs respectively; the chairmen of the House and Senate Energy Committees got funds from 34 and 37 energy PACs respectively. The members of House Ways and Means raise twice as much from PACs as those who sit on Judiciary. Or as one Southerner remarked, ''If I didn't sit on Ways and Means, I wouldn't raise a dime.''

Third, PACs like each other. Those of similar inclination pool information on which races are hopeless and which are hopeful. The U.S. Chamber of Commerce, for example, held a pre-election ''teleconference'' where some two hundred PAC managers heard regional reports about important races. So a long-shot candidate may find himself or herself PAC-less, while a credible challenger, or better yet a committee chairman, gets support from dozens of PACS he's never heard of. Some PACs, like BIPAC (Business Industry Political Action Committee), are a kind of credit survey whose ratings can make or break a candidacy by their imitated blessing.

In at least one way, however, PACs differ radically. Labor PACS prefer Democrats by a 13 to 1 margin, while business PACs give two thirds of their funds to Republicans, usually conservative Republicans. It was not always so. When Democrats formed an overwhelming majority in Congress, business PACs chose incumbency over philosophy and split their gifts evenly between the parties, an evenhandedness that infuriated ideological conservatives. "We found that our 'friends,' the *Fortune* 500, were, playing both sides," complained Nevada Senator Paul Laxalt in 1978. "When you push water for them as long as we have, that's a little hard to swallow." Ronald Reagan, then a private citizen, told a conference of corporate public affairs officers that year, "I don't think the Republican Party has received the kind of financial support from corporate PACs that its record deserves. Why does half the business PAC money go to candidates who may not be friends of business?"

Soon thereafter, business PACs began showing a pronounced Republican tilt. In the last few weeks of the 1978 campaign, 71 percent of their funds went to Republicans. Of the Chamber of Commerce's 99 "opportunity races" recommended for business contributions in 1982, for example, the Republican was preferred in 98. In that year's Senate races with a Republican incumbent, business PACs favored the incumbent by 56 to 1.

So although labor PAC spending rose in 1982, and although liberal issue groups are now giving PAC contributions (NOW, National Abortion Rights Action League, Sierra Club, Friends of the Earth, Human Rights Campaign Fund), the future of PAC gifts will be overwhelmingly written on business checks to Republicans. And as they swell, the role of the small individual donor correspondingly declines.

Are Conable, Shannon, Bolling, Reuss, Bingham, Fenwick, and Brodhead right in believing that the rise of PACs threatens democracy? That the link between PAC contributions *to* candidates and PAC lobbying *of* congressmen is corrupting? PAC managers invariably protest that their gifts merely enable them to gain "access" to members of Congress. And an annoyed Bernadette Budde, for twelve years with the Business Industry PAC, argues, "No one has ever shown me one body—not one—who has sold his vote for a contribution."

Admissions of vote-buying, which is a felony, are usually as rare as cherry blossoms in November. But for the first time members of Congress began talking in interviews in 1982 and 1983 about specific (if often anonymous) instances when a colleague admitted that a PAC gift procured a vote, or tried to:

—In the mid-1970s a labor union that gave Representative Leon Panetta (D.-Calif.) a $1,500 contribution asked for support of pending "cargo preference legislation." When Panetta asked about the substance of the bill, he was told, "I don't have to tell you anything substantively—we gave you money. We support the bill, and we expect you to." Panetta kicked the lobbyist out of his office, and voted no.

—Republican Representative Claudine Schneider of Rhode Island tried to persuade a Republican colleague to oppose more funding for the Clinch River Breeder Reactor. He declined, explaining, "Yes, but Westinghouse is a big contributor of mine."

—Another Republican Representative, Jim Leach of Iowa, tells how he once suggested to an urban Democrat with no dairy constituency that it would be wisest for him to oppose a dairy price support measure, and was told, "Yeah, but their PAC gave me money. I have to support them."

—Also according to Leach, "Bill Moyers [of CBS] told me that he had three signed affidavits indicating that if enough members of one political party supported the Alaska Gas Pipeline project, that party's congressional campaign treasury would be well rewarded in the 1982 elections. It was no accident that many so-called [congressional] consumer activists cast silent votes in favor of legislation which represents what one member described as the biggest rip-off in history."

—A New York Democrat admitted that he voted for the Alaska Gas Pipeline, even though he opposed it on the merits, because "I didn't want the construction unions contributing to my opponent."

—According to one PAC manager, a certain liberal Democratic representative, unsure how to vote on the recent Reagan tax increase, was told by a business PAC that if he supported the bill, "the slate would be wiped clean" between them. The Democrat voted for the bill, for reasons having nothing to do with the business lobby. Yet when the PAC sent him a $500 check, he angrily returned it, telling the PAC manager, "It was like leaving a twenty-cent tip." The PAC then doubled the contribution, which the Congressman accepted.

—When Representative Dan Glickman (D.-Kan.) asked a colleague in 1982 to join him in opposing a measure that would forbid the FTC regulating auto dealers, he was told, "I'm committed. I got a $10,000 check from the National Automobile Dealers Association. I can't change my vote now." (In a separate incident the Iowa Beef PAC began a letter asking for Glickman's support on a bill by noting, "As we trust you will recall, the Political Action Committee of Iowa Beef Processors, Inc., has heretofore supported your candidacy. . . ." Glickman sent back their $250, and then voted for the measure, as he had originally intended to.)

—A drug industry lobbyist in 1982 told an aide to Democratic Representative Barney Frank of Massachusetts that if Frank could cosponsor an industry-sponsored Drug Patent Act, the lobbyist would come to Frank's first fund-raiser in Washington, D.C. Frank's response: "Tell him to go fuck himself."

—Retiring Representative Millicent Fenwick recalls, "I wasn't down here but two months [in 1975], at a dinner for Alvin Toffler, when I sat down next to a reformer in Congress and asked if he'd be overriding a President Ford veto. He said, 'Are you kidding? I took $58,000 from labor and they want it.' "

—Senator Charles Mathias (R.-Md.) reports that shortly before a crucial and close vote in his Judiciary Committee, he received a message through an intermediary from a Bristol-Myers lobbyist. "You tell Mathias if he doesn't vote my way on 'Illinois Brick,' he won't get any of my PAC money."

—Representative Mike Synar (D.-Okla.) says, "I go out on the floor and say to a member, 'I need your help on this bill,' and often he will say, 'I can't do that, I got $5,000 from a special interest.' So I no longer lobby congressmen. I lobby the lobbyists to lobby the congressmen."

Are these admitted incidents of PAC influence typical or aberrational? According to studies by Public Citizen's Congress Watch and Common Cause, PAC contributions invariably correlate with legislative results. When specific economic interests invest substantial amounts in many members before key votes, the dividends roll in.

In August 1982, of those voting who received $3,000 or more from five corporations supporting the Clinch River Breeder Reactor, 100 percent voted for the reactor; but of those receiving no contributions, only 29 percent voted for it. In 1981 representatives who voted for higher dairy price supports received ten times more money from three large dairy PACs than those who voted against the supports. In the two months before a crucial July 1981 vote in the Ways and Means Committee affecting commodities traders, commodity industry PACs gave contributions to 22 members of the panel. They voted 19 to 3 for the commodities tax break; the rest of the committee voted 8 to 5 against. Out of the 50 representatives who received the most contributions from the AMA's PAC in 1979, 48 supported the AMA's position by voting against President Carter's health-cost containment plan. Of the 58 representatives receiving over $2,500 from oil and gas PACs in 1978, 55, or 95 percent, favored the industry-sponsored amendment on the windfall profits tax.

This volume of congressional admissions and vote correlations renders denials of PAC sway as persuasive as denials that Niagara falls. It is getting increasingly difficult for supporters of the current campaign finance system to keep claiming that all PACs do is secure access and reward good government. An article on PACs in *Inc.*, a magazine for small businessmen, argued that PACs were not a moral issue. "If politicians want to sell and the public wants to buy, there is not much you can do to stop the trade." To Justin Dart, the chairman of Dart Industries and a close friend of President Reagan, "Talking to politicians is fine, but with a little money they hear you better." One White House aide, speaking of coordinating spending by PACs and the Republican National Committee for 20 vulnerable Republicans in the 1982 campaign, was quoted in *Newsweek* saying, "If we can't buy half these races, we don't know our business."

Such explicitness should permanently bury the view that, ultimately, we have to trust members of Congress to disassociate money and votes. An earlier and colorful version of this sentiment was Harold Ickes's remark in the 1930s that "if you can't take their money and drink their booze and screw their women and then vote against them, you don't belong here." By that standard Congress would be a lonely place. The point is not that members of Congress are corrupt. Few are. It's the system that's corrupt—a system that provides nearly irresistible temptations to public office-holders. For PAC gifts cause substantial and predictable behavior modification even in conscientous elected officials.

"We are the only human beings in the world," says Representative Frank, "who are expected to take thousands of dollars from perfect strangers on important matters and not be affected by it." Before his retirement, Richard Bolling asked, "If you had two phone calls at once, and your secretary said one was a constituent, the other a PAC that gave you $10,000 last election, which phone would you pick up?" When he was in the House, Toby Moffett (D.-Conn.) described how large PAC contributions affected even well-meaning colleagues: "It paralyzes people politically. It takes the edge off their sense of urgency. It makes 'em take a walk on a lot of issues. I talk to these guys every week, different members of the House who won by 52 or 53 percent. They're facing opponents who already have half a million dollars (in March), and they've raised $70,000. Now, how would you react? You'd get desperate. You've got to raise money, you don't know how you're gonna do it, and maybe you sit on a Ways and Means Committee and these guys come in with the big bucks, who want your vote on things. It's a tremendous temptation."

In these circumstances normally functioning human beings are predictably a) affected by thousands of dollars from strangers given at their moment of electoral peril, b) will take the $10,000 phone caller, and c) tend to bend over backward not to dissatisfy a watchful and perhaps vengeful lobbyist with a PAC.

Of course, such legislatively interested money doesn't invariably

36

buy a member's vote or even attention. No amount of money, obviously, could alter Senator Kennedy's views on national health insurance or Senator Helms's position on busing for integration or Senator Proxmire's support for high milk price supports from lactate Wisconsin. Issues of conscience or constituency can easily outweigh particular PAC gifts. Or the amount of unfavorable publicity given large PAC gifts—such as maritime money for "cargo preference legislation" in 1979 or AMA money for an FTC exemption in 1982—can be so substantial as to make a vote in favor of the PAC position more politically costly than it's worth. But on issues which are neither in the headlines nor on voters' minds, which is most issues, our elected officials may search diligently for any plausible rationale to justify a position that protects access to future contributions.

Adding insult to injury is the way candidates have to seek PAC funds. Many business PACs require a candidate either to submit to a personal interview or answer a questionnaire, and it doesn't take a genius to calculate the cost of a wrong answer. When the National Education Association asks, "Please explain your position on the following: a.) Tax credits for tuition paid to private . . . schools," it's what one Republican senator in an interview called "the $10,000 question," which he answered incorrectly. Randall Moorhead, of the Realtors PAC survey, says, "Sometimes candidates call me and plead with me to give them the correct answers so they can fill out the questionnaire to our satisfaction."

Consequently, many candidates surrender to the temptation to pander to PAC prejudices. Even a moderate, thoughtful Republican like New York's Benjamin Gilman, who was redistricted into a successful race with his Democratic colleague Peter Peyser, wrote to PACs saying, "I am fighting for my political life against an ultra-liberal Democratic congressman. . . . Can I count on you for commitment to the free enterprise system, to America, and to my reelection?" Kent Jones, who lost to Democratic Representative Byron Dorgan in North Dakota, wrote to the pharmacists' PAC: "The opponent is best known for his vigorous efforts to win substantial tax settlements against large corporations and has capitalized on the image of being a 'champion of the people,' fighting 'Big Business'. . . ." Then there was Republican John Beuchner, challenging Tim Wirth in Colorado, whose standard solicitation letter left little to the imagination. After asking for funds, he concluded, "What do you stand to gain? You stand to gain my support of pro-business legislation once I am elected."

Not only candidates but parties feel the pressure to court the PACs. Even Democrats, or rather especially Democrats. For Republicans quite naturally are attracted to the positions of corporate and trade PACs, while Democrats have to try harder to win approval from this greatest sector of PAC growth. For example, Representative Tony Coehlo (D.-Calif.), head of the House Democratic Campaign Committee, told PAC officials they would be receiving a list of "pro-business" candidates deserving business support. "As far as your companies are concerned, there are many Democrats in the House who are doing a better job than some Republicans. We will give you their names."

In interviews other Democrats understood the need for such an effort even though they lamented the need. After all, with the Republican party out-fund-raising the Democratic party seven to one in 1979–80 and 1981–82, it's predictable that Democratic party leaders would want to avoid a Republican-PAC merger. Still, the unseemly result is that business PACs now are in a position to co-opt both "the party of wealth" *and* "the party of the people." The embarrassing bidding war on Reagan's tax bill in 1982, with Democrats trying to buy business support with preferential tax breaks, is one example of how money distorts political behavior. And it is why commentator Bill Moyers, after many Democrats supported the big-energy-firm position on a 1982 vote for the Alaska Gas Pipeline, said, "The Congress is not up for grabs, it's up for sale."

This process has offended at least fourteen members to the point that they refuse to take any PAC money or accept only limited amounts. These include senators Proxmire and Boren, and representatives Archer, Bafalis, Beilenson, Bingham, Conable, Gradison, Jacobs, Leach, Natcher, Pritchard, Synar, and Whitten. (Gary Hart,

Walter Mondale, and Reuben Askew refused all PAC contributions in their race for the Democratic presidential nomination.) Some of these members lack serious races and some can help fund their own campaigns—but a few have run the risk of losing their seats. Former Representative Millicent Fenwick (N.J.) continued to refuse PAC funds in 1982, despite having a wealthy opponent in her New Jersey Senate race; she lost. And Andy Jacobs (D.-Ind.) still declined PAC funds even after redistricting forced him into a primary with another Indiana Democrat in 1982. Jacobs, who first won in 1964 but tasted defeat in 1972 before returning in 1974, was outspent two to one—yet he won.

Jacobs's epiphany on PACs came in the summer of 1976. "A lobbyist whose organization contributed to my 1974 campaign approached me after I cast a vote on the Ways and Means Committee and literally began twisting my arm—a post-vote twist," Jacobs recalls. "I believe I said something along the lines of 'Take your hand off this suit, creep,' and decided never to accept a contribution from anyone having a special interest in national legislation."

Jacobs recalls something important his father, who was a one-term congressman, once said: "All this country needs is more members of Congress who would be willing to lose." What it has instead is a process in which, Jacobs says, "campaign contributions are not terribly different from a bribe. The only reason it's not bribery is because Congress defines what bribery is."

There is occasional evidence that even some PAC managers are beginning to object to this process. One said in an interview, "I feel like a pimp in a medium-class whorehouse." Others complain about the tedium and effort involved in running between several fund-raisers an evening during the political season, since the lobbyist himself might as well be seen personally by the member if he's making a contribution. "It's beginning to be like a shakedown," believes Tom Railsback, a House incumbent Republican defeated for reelection in 1982. "It could reach a point where the PAC people themselves are going to want some controls."

No doubt the system involves much physical and ethical wear-and-tear on both givers and takers. But PAC-men are not about to surrender voluntarily the system that gives them their power. Indeed, PAC managers and supporters have developed an array of arguments to defend their activities against growing criticism in the past few years. Some brief arguments and rebuttals follow:

• *$5,000 or $10,000 is too insignificant a sum to buy a congressman.* To which Representative Tom Downey (D.-N.Y.) quipped, "you can't buy a congressman for $5,000. But you can buy his vote." In fact, a maximum $10,000 PAC gift, which could swing on one key vote, may involve a $20,000 variable, potentially both a loss of $10,000 to a member and a gain of $10,000 by his opponent. Also, there is the fact that PACs run in packs, as Representative David Obey (D.-Wis.) explains. "When a large number of groups which have made substantial contributions to members are all lobbying on the same side of an issue, the pressure generated from these aggregate contributions is enormous and warps the process. It is as if they made a single, extremely large contribution."

• *PAC money rewards past votes, rather than buys future votes.* Then why do many PACs cross-examine candidates in questionnaires and in person about their positions on pending matters? To Jay Angoff, an attorney at Public Citizen's Congress Watch, "whether a member votes for legislation . . . because he has received some money from [a certain] group, or receives money because he has voted for legislation sought by that group, it makes no difference to the consumer. Either way, people continue to get elected who vote to further the interests of the business lobbies that contribute to their campaign."

• *PACs on both sides of an issue cancel each other out.* Senator Bob Dole of Kansas remarked, "Poor people don't make campaign contributions. You might get a different result if there were a PoorPAC up here." On an array of economic issues, such as those involving used cars, oil and gas, dairy price supports, housing, maritime and trucking policy, funeral homes, and antitrust exemptions, specific economic interests have PACs while the consuming public does not.

• *PACs are just voluntary associations of politically like-minded people*. So is a monopoly. This issue is—does it serve the interests of associating members in such a way as to injure some public interest? Also, both business and labor PACs are *not* simply free associations, for the start-up and overhead costs of both can now be subsidized by their respective treasuries. Finally, it is not clear how voluntary some PACs are. Sterling Drug, Inc., applying a means test, asks its top 525 executives to give at least one half of one percent of salary, up to a ceiling of $200. "Specifically, we're asking for a *voluntary* contribution from you," the letter says, "for a political fund to be allocated to those legislators . . . whose . . . election is *important* to our industry and to *Sterling Drug, Inc.*" (emphasis in original). Over at Litton Industries, an employee told *The Wall Street Journal,* "I know it isn't mandatory to give. But the word around the water cooler is that if you don't give or if you give less than the amount expected based on your salary, you're liable to be called in for a pep-talk from the divisional president."

• *PACs are thousands of people giving small gifts*. That's true, but the donating is done in one voice and in fairly sizable amounts. If PACs allowed their small givers to specify whom they want to receive their small contribution, that would be far more democratic and defensible. But PACs don't allow such designation precisely because it would deny them their raison d'être—leverage over legislators by giving money with strings attached.

PACs And The FTC

The earlier milk-fund case-study showed how special interests use cash to pry desired results from the President and Congress. Has the subsequent introduction of PACs changed the way special interests persuade Congress to do their bidding? The problem has only gotten worse—genuinely a case of old wine in a new bottle. The attempts by used-car dealers and doctors to avoid regulation by the Federal Trade Commission are perhaps the most graphic examples of how the new push-button Congress works.

That Congress votes at all on FTC regulations is due to the exertions of well-funded economic interests. In 1979 business foes of the activist FTC had attempted to get Capitol Hill to curb the "rogue agency's" powers to regulate and investigate. Instead, after a hard-fought battle, FTC allies warded off these restraints, only to see Congress give itself the power to cancel specific regulations by use of the legislative veto. As a result Capitol Hill became a court of last resort, voting on technical rulings of great financial importance to well-funded interests—fertile grounds for PAC distortion of the process. Thomas J. Campbell, the FTC's top enforcement official, complained to the *National Journal* that businessmen, when faced with regulation or prosecution, now threaten to "go to Congress," where a PAC gift would speak louder than a lawyer's brief.*

In September 1981 the FTC issued a ruling that required used-car dealers to put a sticker on the car window listing any defects they know about. (The rule did not even force the dealers to actually *inspect* the cars.) The requirement was so mild that it was backed by the Republican majority on the FTC and by President Reagan's consumer advisor, Virginia Knauer. Once the rule was promulgated, Congress had 90 days in which to veto it.

The used-car dealers swung into action with what *The New York Times* called "one of the best orchestrated, best financed lobbying campaigns seen on Capitol Hill in a long time." Used-car dealers across the country stopped hawking long enough to pull out their checkbooks. During its 1981–82 assault on the used-car rule, the National Auto Dealers Association (NADA) PAC contributed $919,795 to members of Congress, making it the fourth largest in the country, behind the American Medical Association, (more about which below), the United Auto Workers, and the National Association of Realtors.

In September 1981 the FTC issued a ruling that required used-car

---

* The practice of Congress voting or specific regulations was ruled unconstitutional by the Supreme Court in June 1983 in its overturning of the legislative veto. See Chapter 4 for a discussion of this decision.

dealers gathered in Washington to round up cosponsors for the veto bill of Representative Gary Lee (R.-N.Y.). PAC manager Frank McCarthy told the assembled dealers that if the congressman from a dealer's district had received NADA PAC money, "I can almost assure you he will at least give you a chance to talk. We can do it if you do your job." The dealers then fanned out across Capitol Hill, and they did not come back empty handed: the first day they garnered 90 House and 20 Senate cosponsors. The numbers continued to swell, although for months the names were a secret, closely held between Representative Lee and his favorite PAC.

The pace of the donations and members signing on did not abate as the vote approached. From January 1982 to the May 25 vote, or a half year before the next election, the PAC gave members of Congress $75,000. Fully sixteen congressmen jumped to cosponsor the veto within ten days of receiving the campaign gift.

The results surprised no one when the vote finally came. The rule was vetoed in the House by a vote of 286–133 and in the Senate by 69–27. Of the 286 representatives who voted to kill the bill, 242 had received money from NADA. Elizabeth Drew of *The New Yorker* said it "was almost a caricature of what happens" when PAC money is wisely deployed in a lobbying campaign.

A white-smocked, utterly respectable doctor is a far cry in the public imagination from an overreaching used-car dealer—but in Congress they had in common the desire to escape FTC regulation by PAC-aided legislation. Beginning in January 1979, the doctors lobbied to eliminate *all* FTC jurisdiction over doctors and other professionals. In the 97th Congress, after scrounging the House of Representatives to find a friend of the physician to introduce their bill, they discovered none other than Representative Gary Lee.

The next lesson they learned from the used-car dealers was the steady application of cash. From January 1979 until the 1982 election, especially as the vote on Lee's bill approached, the doctors and dentists PACs gave $2,796,551 to members of the House of Representatives. (The American Medical Association's funding arm, AMPAC, also spent heavily in other ways, helping candidates with gifts of polling and with independent expenditures. Representative Richard Gephardt (D.-Mo.) was the beneficiary of a $38,515 poll for his 1982 race. Yet Gephardt voted against the doctors, prompting Congress Watch to label him a ''Profile in Courage.''

In fact, the majority of Gephardt's colleagues on Energy and Commerce voted against the doctors. Here we see how PACs can bypass established centers of congressional power and buy wholesale. For when the physicians could not get committee approval for the exemption, they simply took their effort to the full House, taking care to distribute gifts to scores of members rather than just those on the committee. (Such mass expenditures are one reason PAC contributions have risen in volume so rapidly.)

At first their tactics seemed to pay off. The exemption passed the House in October 1982, and again during the lame-duck session in December. But the doctors' luck began to run out when they shifted their attention to the Senate. One reason was institutional. Because House members run every two years and because all PAC or a particular PAC's gifts comprise a higher percentage of their fund-raising, they tend to be more responsive to the legislative needs of PACs. And with only 100 senators as compared to the much larger House, it becomes harder for senators to cast quiet votes for special interests. The other reason was publicity. Nurses, public-interest groups, and the media pounded a drumbeat of criticism. *Time* magazine, *The New Yorker*, and *The New Republic* all devoted major stories to PACs, giving the doctor exemption as a case study. And while liberal Democrats had opposed the bill in the House, in the Senate free-market conservatives also took up the standard. ''I get excited when I see someone trying to perform a frontal lobotomy on the free-enterprise system,'' said Senator Warren Rudman (R.-N.H.). On December 16, 1982, the Senate voted 59–37 against the exemption. The representatives on the conference committee could not persuade the senators to put the exemption back in the omnibus money bill to which it was added, and the legislation died with the 97th Congress.

So had Gary Lee, politically. Lee's constituents came to wonder if he remembered whom he was working for: the doctors, the used-car dealers, or them. They reminded him the best way they knew how. Lee lost a Republican primary to another incumbent over this issue, leading *The New York Times* to editorialize, "Opportunistic congressmen who flack for special interests may wind up paying with their jobs."

The case studies of milk and auto dealers and doctors demonstrate how PAC money changed the way special interests work. In the milk case, lobbyists concentrated on winning over the executive branch with gifts of campaign money to a president. Then public financing of presidential campaigns greatly curtailed the ability of special interests to buy favor with the White House. But like a balloon squeezed at one end, business money has traveled to the other end of Pennsylvania Avenue—Congress. Reforming presidential campaign financing has served to worsen the crisis of a Congress for sale.

"Dishonoraria"

Congress itself has recently cleared yet another path for business control of elected officials, by stripping away limits on hefty honoraria for speaking engagements. Honoraria had been limited in 1977 as part of the ethics bill, but some members chafed at the restriction. In October 1981, House leaders of both parties tried to pass a measure doubling to $18,200 the amount a representative could make from honoraria, but were beaten, 271–147. A month and a half later they tried again—and this time they did not make the mistake of allowing open debate. Late one afternoon, when Representative Robert Walker (R.-Pa.), who had led the fight against raising the limit, was off the House floor, Speaker O'Neill took the chair. He recognized John Murtha (D.-Pa.) to introduce an unheralded and unnamed resolution. The clerk began to read the bill, but thirteen words into its text—before any mention of "honoraria" or speaking fees—he was interrupted by Murtha. The Pennsylvania Democrat asked for "unanimous consent," a procedure in which a bill is considered to be passed if no one objects. No one raised a voice, so in less than thirty seconds the limit was doubled. Former Representative Millicent Fenwick recalls, ''It happened in seconds, and I didn't have any idea of what it was about. It was absolutely maddening.''

Also in October 1981, the Senate voted to lift altogether its cap of $25,000 per senator and thus allow unlimited honoraria. The limit was to be restored in January 1983, but in the lame-duck session at the end of the 97th Congress the Senate refused a pay raise and instead opted for unlimited speaking fees. (The House took the raise, and its limit on honoraria jumped automatically to $20,940.)

Special-interest spending on honoraria for senators and representatives has ballooned accordingly. In 1981, for example—even though the cap was lifted for only three months—senators received $1,742,172 in speaking fees. Like PAC funds, honoraria from business groups flow uphill—to party leaders and committee chairmen. Senators heading standing committees or holding party leadership posts averaged $27,208 in 1981 while other senators averaged $15,835.

1982 was the first full year of unlimited Senate honoraria, and the amount senators received jumped 37 percent to $2,381,104. Republican senators garnered nearly $1 million more than they had two years before. Both houses together took in $4,454,444. When the 1982 financial disclosure forms were filed, figures like Senator Rober Dole's 1982 take of $135,750—more than double his public salary—prompted a new look at what was becoming an institutional embarrassment. For the first time public and editorial attention focused on the issue, and angry rank-and-file House members threatened to bring the issue to a vote. On June 9, 1983, the Senate voted 51–41 to accept Senator Henry Jackson's (D.-Wash.) amendment recapping outside income. Opponents of unlimited honoraria breathed a sigh of relief—a sigh quickly sucked back in a week later, when the Senate (raising its salary to the House's $69,800 level) postponed the cap until January 1984. Given the Senate's record on the matter, all critics could do was hold their breath, while the honoraria continued to pour in.

Some members of Congress feel that these fees are even more

pernicious than PAC contributions, in part because honoraria money goes directly from the lobbyist into the congressman's pocket. Congressman Dave Obey, calling the payments "the most dangerous thing that's happened since I've been here," warns that a caste system may be developing in which senior members who attract fees will have higher private income than public income and far higher income than their junior colleagues; and that they'll spend their time hopping from speech to speech instead of doing committee work. And, as ever, honoraria money is interested money. So much comes from groups with legislation before Congress that Representative Andy Jacobs dubbed the payments "dishonoraria."

Frequently the very industries under a committee chairman's jurisdiction are those that tender him the most money. Richard Conlon, staff director of the Democratic Study Group, an organization of House Democrats, says half in jest, "I'm going to do a study of honoraria to find an honorarium that is *not* trying to influence legislation." Senate Banking Committee Chairman Jake Garn (R.-Utah) in 1981 made—and kept—$48,000, much of the money coming from speeches to banking groups like the United States League of Savings and Loan Associations, Citibank, and the American Bankers Association. There is a $2,000 limit per speech, but there is no limit on how many times a senator can speak to a group in a year. (One California group had the ingenious idea of paying Senator Paula Hawkins (R.-Fla.) $2,000, and paying her husband *$3,000*.) And there are of course no restrictions on how many groups from a single industry may invite a speaker. Some lawmakers, like Hawkins, even accept honoraria for speaking to groups in their own state. The entire practice repels some members of the old school like Senator John Stennis (D.-Miss.), who refused honoraria, according to an aide, because "he views giving speeches as part of his job."

Few current members of Congress are thrilling orators. But even if a lawmaker's speech is a cross between John F. Kennedy's inaugural and George Washington's farewell, schoolchildren of the future may be unable to commit it to memory—because few of these talks are delivered from prepared texts. Chatting with a couple of trade association representatives at a Washington lunch is more typical of these ''speeches.'' Former Representative William Brodhead, who quit the House in part because of the fee spree, recounts his introduction to the world of honoraria: ''If somebody invites you to go up to New York, a few months from now, you think, 'Hey, that's great.' You think about what you want to say,'' he recalls in an office suite crammed with packing crates that signify his voluntary retirement. ''Then you go up there and it's just a few guys who want to rap, and then they bring up a piece of legislation that's before your committee—and you know what's going on.'' After several such encounters members of Congress stop preparing speeches. In one lucrative jaunt to Minnesota in 1982, Indiana Senator Richard Lugar made $8,500 by speaking extemporaneously to a bank holding company, a mail-order firm, a financial firm, senior executives of General Mills, and the employees and PAC of Pillsbury—all in a throat-numbing thirty hours.

If judges earned as much in fees from defendants as they did from their public salaries, it would be scandalous. So why should legislators be allowed to sell their offices for private gain? As Richard Conlon of the Democratic Study Group put it: '' 'Lecture fees' has the connotation of someone going around to ladies' tea clubs and colleges. The press has to call them what they are: They're special-interest payments.''

The Struggle for Reform

We have come a long, long way since 1677, when the House of Commons passed a standing order that if anyone should spend above ten pounds before election in order to win ''it shall be accounted bribery'' and the seat vacated. Based on the checkered history of campaign finance reform, it's unclear whether we can ever return to purer eras.

In 1907, under pressure from President Theodore Roosevelt, Congress enacted the Tilman Act banning corporate contributions to candidates; individual businessmen could contribute, but not businesses. Then in 1925 Congress enacted the scripture of modern politics, the Federal Corrupt Practices Act of 1925, with deficiencies so obvious that Lyndon Johnson called it "more loophole than law." For a start the law did not even apply to primaries—where so much of the spending goes on, particularly in one-party states. For everything after the primaries Senate candidates were required to file spending reports with the secretary of the Senate, and House candidates with the clerk of the House. Just how seriously the law was taken is indicated by a few of the filed reports. In his 1968 Senate reelection campaign in South Dakota, George McGovern's total expenditures were "none." The explanation was that the candidates must only report funds used with their "knowledge and consent." McGovern's executive assistant kept McGovern in blissful ignorance by being "very careful to make sure that Senator McGovern never saw the campaign receipts."

Another clause provided that all donors of $100 or more must list their names and addresses. Witty contributors then made as many $99.99 donations as they wanted to various campaign committees working for the same candidate. The most important loophole in the 1925 law, however, was its provision that campaign committees would have to report their contributors only if the committee operated in two or more states. There was ample office space in the District of Columbia for thousands of campaign committees, and *none* of them had to report their activities. Along with the cherry trees, another rite of election-year springs in Washington was the flowering of campaign committees for candidates all over the country. To give one illustration among many: James Buckley took in $400,000 in 1970 toward his New York Senate seat through a series of false-front D.C. committees. More receptive to the spirit of the law than many deadpan candidates, Buckley's staff invented names like "Committee to Keep a Cop on the Beat," "Neighbors for Neighborhood Schools," and "Town Meeting Preservation Society" for their groups. "We made a game of it," staffer David Jones said.

Figuring that even a good joke may get stale after forty-seven years, the public pressured Congress to enact a new law, which was signed by President Nixon in February, 1972. The saga of this reform actually began a decade before, when the Commission on Campaign Costs, appointed by President John F. Kennedy in 1962, reported that "individuals and organizations providing substantial gifts at critical moments can threaten to place a candidate in moral hock." The eventual Federal Election Campaign Act extended coverage to financing of primaries, runoff and special elections, party caucuses, and nominating conventions. A candidate could no longer feign ignorance of funds spent by others on his behalf.

But Congress, determined to have the last laugh, relented at the last minute and left in a few saving provisions. The least subtle of these was the "grace period"—the two-month delay between the bill's passage in February and the date when candidates would first have to report contributions. With a joyous, free-for-all spirit not seen since the Oklahoma Land Rush, candidates from all parties scrambled to pack their campaign chests before the April 7 deadline. Led by President Richard Nixon—whose chief fund-raiser, Maurice Stans, and others openly exhorted (some say extorted) businessmen to get their money in on time—many congressmen lost all inhibitions in their eagerness to make the most of the remaining time. The only barrier was fatigue; one lobbyist, hand presumably sore from reaching for his wallet, complained to Arizona Representative Sam Steiger that he had to attend 162 fund-raising parties between February 23 and April 7.

With such freewheeling times behind them, private interests still have to rely in the future on the bill's more restrained loopholes. The 1972 act made a minor revision of the $99.99 clause by providing that only contributions of "more than" $100 must be reported—contributions identified by name, address, occupation, and principal place of business. This at least gave voters a fighting chance to find out who was contributing to campaigns and identify any possible special interests; unfortunately, sizable contributions could still be, and have been, poured into campaign coffers immediately prior to election day, or weeks or months after the election, giving the voter no opportunity to view a contributor list before he or she casts a ballot.

For years even the old law was openly and massively violated, yet Justice never acted. Then in 1968, newly elected House Clerk W. Pat Jennings surprised everyone by sending a list of violations from the 1968 campaign over to the Justice Department. President Nixon's new attorney general, John Mitchell, fresh from firsthand experience with campaign contributors during his year as Nixon's campaign manager, was fascinated by Jenning's list; he and his colleagues at Justice kept it so close that it seemed to have disappeared. Jennings, slow to get the message, sent other lists in 1969 and 1971—each time with the same result.

The 1972 act received roughly similar treatment. One day after President Nixon signed it into law, Ralph Nader and his organization, Public Citizen, tried to sting Justice into action by filing a lawsuit demanding strict enforcement. Their complaint included a ninety-two-page list of hundreds of unprosecuted campaign finance violations (for example, candidates who had waited to file until after the election, "thus defeating the purpose of preelection disclosures," or who had failed to file reports at all).

In June 1972, Common Cause asked the clerk of the House to investigate ninety-one candidates from Alabama, Indiana, Ohio, Pennsylvania, and the District of Columbia who had ignored the reporting requirements of the new law. As of September 1972, the Justice Department had never prosecuted a single candidate for breaking the campaign finance laws. (In 1974 the prosecutions of campaign finance violators were carried out by the Watergate Special Prosecutor's office, not the Justice Department.)

A final change in the 1972 law had little immediate consequence, but was a time bomb of explosive potential. The act modified the flat ban on the use of corporate and union treasuries. It allowed the establishment of a separate fund—a political action committee, or PAC—to make campaign contributions. But the ban still applied to entities with government contracts. And since so many companies -

had government business, they shied away from the contributions game. Help would be forthcoming.

The Federal Election Campaign Act of 1974 continues to illustrate Congress's inability to reform adequately the system of campaign financing. The law was a direct outgrowth of the Watergate scandal and a public shocked at the volume of large secret gifts to Richard Nixon's Committee to Reelect the President.

To be sure, the 1974 act contained several significant advances. Individuals couldn't give more than $1,000 to any federal candidate per election (for a total ceiling of $2,000 for a primary and a general election). Also, a wealthy person could not give more than $25,000 annually ($50,000 per married couple) to all candidates combined. This law not only sets a limit, but forbids an individual to contribute to numerous separate committees all supporting the same candidate. A $5,000 limit was placed on special-interest groups and those few PACs that existed; so if a group gave to a candidate in both the primary and general elections, the ceiling was $10,000. A Federal Election Commission (FEC) was created to enforce the provisions of the act—and despite significant limitations, the FEC has proven a more capable overseer than the House and Senate clerks. And the 1974 law provided for a system of matching public funds for the presidential primaries, and full public financing for the presidential election.

Congress also put a ceiling on what candidates could spend of their own money, on the total expenditures a campaign could make and on the amount that "independent expenditure" groups, not coordinating with the candidate, could expend to promote or criticize a candidate.

Despite some of its worthy provisions the 1974 act has failed in three ways. First, the Supreme Court in the *Buckley* v. *Valeo* decision of 1976 found these last three sections to be unconstitutional on the theory that in this instance money was tantamount to speech. Limits on contributions were fine since contributions could corrupt; but the amount a candidate gave himself could not corrupt him. Second, Congress, with more than a hint of hypocrisy, refused to apply to itself the public financing system it applied to presidential campaigns. And last, it was a largely unheralded and now forgotten amendment that gave birth to the modern PAC movement, an amendment that now threatens to subsume all else these acts attempt.

Ever since 1940, Section 611 of the U.S. Code had prohibited corporations with government contracts from creating PACs; and since most large corporations had important federal contracts, most of them didn't have PACs. When TRW, Inc., tried to create one in 1972, Common Cause sued and forced the firm, which had government contracts, to end it.

But Common Cause found itself with a Pyhrric victory. Fred Wertheimer, now president of Common Cause, recalls, "Labor was concerned that this rule might jeopardize COPE [the AFL-CIO's Committee on Political Education], since their manpower training contracts could be considered 'government contracts' under Section 611." So labor and business closed ranks to lobby for an amendment to end the restriction. "This was war," Wertheimer says. "The stakes could not have been higher. The fight left hard feelings." On one side were Senator Proxmire, Senator Robert Stafford of Vermont, Common Cause, and substantial editorial opinion. (*The Washington Post* called the amendment "another loophole to more corruption in American politics.") On the other side were the U.S. Chamber of Commerce, the National Association of Manufacturers, and the AFL-CIO, all eager to continue or establish PACs.

The result was that on July 27, 1973, the Senate voted 51 to 38 to eliminate Section 611, which the House had already done. As the *Congressional Quarterly* reported at the time, "In an unusual coalition, conservative Republicans with business ties and liberal Democrats loyal to labor teamed up" to change the law.

Among those supporting the repeal were Senators Kennedy, Mondale, and Cranston, who today decry the rise of special-interest PACs and whose votes that day helped burst the dam holding back the surge of business PAC money in federal elections. With Section

611 out of the way, labor PACs grew 75 percent in the next nine years, and business PACs 1,750 percent, a ratio of 1 to 23.

Some critics of all campaign finance efforts argue that this proves the "law of unintended consequences." Not quite. The business community and its supporters intended exactly what happened. Common Cause predicted what would happen. Labor and its allies simply miscalculated.

The growing influence of PAC money has created a movement to alter the campaign finance laws. There are several possible ways to diminish the sway of special-interest contributions and enhance the role of individual gifts:

—*Matching public funds.* First proposed by Teddy Roosevelt in 1907, public financing would assume some campaign costs, relieving part of the pressure on candidates to take special-interest gifts. The most prominent public financing measure is the "Clean Campaign Act of 1983," introduced by Representative David Obey in the 98th Congress. It would provide matching funds up to $90,000 for gifts of $100 or under, *if* the candidate agrees to three conditions: limit the amount he/she accepts from PACs to $70,000; limit the amount of personal contributions to $25,000; and limit expenditures to $240,000. A candidate is free to reject the entire package of matching funds plus PAC and personal limits, but then an opponent who agrees to the program gets not a one-to-one match but a two-to-one match.

Supporters argue that public financing has worked to clean up presidential campaigns—so why not Congressional campaigns? Since we would never tolerate PACs paying for the election day process and machinery, why permit them to pick up the tab for so much of a candidate's expenses? And while the plan would cost millions of taxpayer dollars to implement, it would save billions of taxpayer dollars in averted special-interest breaks, loopholes, subsidies, and favors. Lobbyists certainly know how to spend a little to yield a big return. Critics attack the idea as, in the words of Representative Bill Frenzel (R.-Minn.), "an incumbent's protection act." If so, one wonders why Congress, comprised only of incumbents, hasn't enacted it long ago—and why the first two times it was tried at the presidential level, both incumbents (Ford, Carter) lost.

—*Free TV and radio*. In a report released in September 1982, the Democracy Project detailed a "Voter Access Plan" to provide minimal guaranteed TV and radio time to all Congressional candidates in general elections at a cost of $21 million, or a dime per citizen, with funds coming out of the existing surplus in the tax check-off fund for presidential campaigns. (For urban areas where there are many congressional districts in one media market, a qualified candidate would have the option of "cashing in" the air time for any equivalent mailing.) Great Britain, France, West Germany, and Sweden, among other countries, routinely provide some free air time to candidates. Because this approach is inexpensive, involves voluntary taxpayer funding, and does not require more federal bureaucracy, it has the potential to attract bipartisan support.

—*A PAC cap per candidate*. The Obey-Railsback bill of the 97th Congress sought to limit the amount a House candidate could accept from all PACs to $70,000 per election cycle and to reduce the allowable PAC contribution from $5,000 and $5,000 (primary and general) to $3,000 and $3,000. Nearly 200 candidates got more than $70,000 from PACs in 1980. Supporter Jim Leach calls it "a kind of domestic SALT agreement between big business and big labor, an agreement which is likely to be disliked by each." A version of it passed the House 217 to 198 in 1979, but was not acted on by the Senate.

—*An increased tax credit*. At present $50 of the first $100 contributed to congressional candidates can be taken as a tax credit. Instead, if all taxpayers were entitled to a tax credit of say, $100, then thousands of individual citizens would be motivated to contribute to favored candidates up to that amount, since there is no cost to them. Although this approach is a form of public financing, since there is a consequent revenue loss, it has political appeal because it involves small subsidies to many small contributors rather than a large subsidy to a particular candidate. It is a "democratic" way of funding the campaigns of candidates who lack the wealth of New York multi-millionaire Lewis Lehrman or the Builders' PAC.

—*Discounted TV/radio.* Candidates can now buy time on the electronic media at the "lowest unit charge" for commercial advertisers. If a "Voter Access Plan" cannot be enacted, the rates could be further discounted so stations don't lose money, but don't profit, either, from public elections—a mild precondition, imposed every other October, for the granting of a lucrative public license.

—*Abolish subsidized PACs; permit voluntary PACs.* Political Action Committees are now allowed to begin operations by using general treasury funds of their corporation or labor union. But since such spending is tax deductible to the corporation (and union dues are tax deductible), all taxpayers are in effect paying to help finance some PACs. Instead, all PACs should be "voluntary" in that participants have to pay up-front costs and not depend on the deep pocket of treasuries that were created for different purposes.

—*Constitutional Amendment.* Led by Representative Jonathan Bingham, twelve representatives in 1982 proposed a constitutional amendment to enable Congress and the states to "enact laws regulating the amounts of contributions and expenditures intended to affect elections. . . ." The amendment, requiring two thirds of the Congress and three fourths of the states for approval, would overturn *Buckley* v. *Valeo's* conclusion that independent spending, expenditure caps, and a candidate's contributions couldn't be limited.

Can any of these approaches become law? People ranging from Fred Wertheimer to conservative commentator Kevin Phillips and the corporate Public Affairs Council agree the question is not whether but when. A backlash to recent trends appears to be building—trends such as the tripling of campaign expenditures in ten years, the doubling of corporate PAC spending in two, and the growing share of campaign fund-raising accounted for by PACs: Ed Roeder's *PACs Americana* calculates that PACs accounted for an average of 43 percent of the campaign treasuries of incumbents in the past Congress.

Already in a recent Roper poll, the public thought that PACs were undesirable by a margin of 2.5 to 1. Even *Business Week* in 1982 editorialized strongly in favor of congressional public financing. People understandably wonder why we had national elections in 1982 that cost $300 million, while the British held theirs in 1979 for $3 million—and why we're the only country on the planet considering itself a democracy that virtually requires its candidates for federal office to raise a half-million dollars from people with specific economic interests in legislation. This process is a quadruple threat: it Balkanizes the Congress into many minorities each backed by PACs, frustrating legislative majorities on behalf of PAC-less public interests; at the same time it "nationalizes" districts with the result that landlocked farm districts see their members vote for maritime subsidies and energy-consuming states have senators who are pro-oil; it discourages able citizens of modest means from running for federal office—the "silent casualties . . . defeated before they start" in Judge J. Skelly Wright's words; and it tempts most elected officials to genuflect to outside advocates with more money than merit.

For in Washington today Pac-Man is not a video game for kids. It is a cynical business affecting the behavior of adults who govern us, and it takes, not quarters, but $5,000 checks to play. Unless Congress institutes the public financing of congressional campaigns as the best way to cleanse the epidemic of purchased politicians—or at least establishes free and equal access to television, radio, and the mails for bona fide candidates—the jingle of corruption and veiled bribery will continue to be heard in its halls.

2

Who Influences Congress?

Suppose you go to Washington and try to get at your government. You will always find that while you are politely listened to, the men really consulted are the men who have the biggest stake—the big bankers, the big manufacturers, the big masters of commerce. . . . The government of the United States at present is a foster child of special interests.

—Woodrow Wilson

When the dairy industry was looking for its 1971 price rise, it had the advantage of having warmed up dozens of congressmen with campaign contributions. If the milk men had done no more, the quart of milk might simply have risen with the consumer price index. Only through *lobbying*—direct persuasion of legislators—was the industry able to convert its half-million line of credit with Congress into a half-billion extra income. As Congress is being bombarded by big money, the lobbyists act as the special interest's infantry.

In its broadest sense "lobbying" is anything but sinister. A lobbyist is, by definition, anyone who works to influence decisions by public officials—including a concerned citizen who writes his congressman urging a vote for stricter air pollution laws. This right to "petition the Government for a redress of grievances" is firmly grounded in the Constitution's First Amendment. But the way the armies of special-interest agents have dominated this process has made "lobbyist" synonymous with corruption and improper influence. "Lobbyists are on that awkward plateau shared by chiropractors and sex therapists," wrote Bill Keller in the *Washington Monthly*, "who believe in their own worth yet still are surrounded by agnostics."

As might be supposed, the lobbyists first got their name from hanging around the lobbies of government buildings, waiting to launch their pitch for government favors. By the middle of the nineteenth century, high-paid panhandlers swarming all over Congress prompted James Buchanan to write Franklin Pierce: "The host of contractors, speculators, stock-jobbers, and lobby members which haunt the halls of Congress all desirous . . . on any and every pretext to get their arms into the public treasury, are sufficient to alarm every friend of the country." The power of many lobbyists who have worked in Washington through the years is legendary. Wayne B. Wheeler, the legislative counsel for the Anti-Saloon League during the days of its prohibition successes, "controlled six Congresses, dictated to two Presidents . . . and was recognized by friend and foe alike as the most masterful and powerful single individual in the United States," said his administrative assistant, who would watch him maneuver.

In the late 1940s and early 1950s brazen influence-peddlers and so-called "5 percenters"—those who introduced friends to powerful people in government in exchange for a percentage of any resulting business—got the Truman administration in trouble and reinforced lobbying's odious connotation. Clark Clifford, for example, when he left the White House for private practice in 1951, felt it necessary to tell the press, "I have not and will not register as a lobbyist, for that is not the kind of work we do. We run a law office here."

By 1950 lobbyists had so increased their strength in Washington that the House Select Committee on Lobbying Activities declared lobbying "a major industry." Then there were an estimated 2,000 lobbyists—and today there are an estimated 15,000 (or thirty for each member of Congress), spending $2 billion a year. "They come at you in relays," said a weary Senator Daniel Patrick Moynihan, expressing the conventional Senate lament. "It's like the human-wave approach to legislation. They never stop." Eighty percent of the nation's thousand biggest corporations already have representatives in Washington. In 1983 *Fortune* magazine estimated that "92,500 people—6 percent of the entire Washington labor force—are employed in one way or another by the business lobby."

How Lobbies Work

Beyond the fundamental technique of delivering substantive analyses in submitted materials or face-to-face meetings with legislators, lobbyists can work in very inventive ways. On behalf of a business client, Abe Fortas once got a minister to call a senator to give a pitch—a tack which infuriated the legislator, who hung up. While Senator William Proxmire was taking his morning jog to his Capitol office, a Pan Am pilot ran alongside, uninvited, and explained to an irritated Proxmire why the government should bail out his floundering corporation. When Mother Teresa met with her old friend Senator Mark Hatfield on Capitol Hill in 1982, she startled Hatfield by asking (after being primed by "pro-lifers"), "Tell me, are you for abortions?" Usually, though, the organized lobbies have developed and refined more conventional techniques. Five of the most important follow:

INFORMATION CONTROL. Lobbies derive their strategic advantage by controlling the flow of information in and out of Congress. By this, lobbyists serve two functions; they take and they give. They constitute, in effect, an informal intelligence network that can pick up advance and often confidential information, and use it to good advantage. When lawyer-lobbyist Thomas Corcoran was asked why he was so successful, he said, "I get my information a few hours ahead of the rest." Or as Senator Alan Cranston told a meeting of lobbyists, "Lobbyists are in fact an extension of our congressional staffs, providing information and ideas that are vital to the molding of legislation."

As any industrialist can tell you, he who controls the source of supply can control the product. During the "energy crisis" in 1973–74, for example, the government continued to rely heavily on, of all disinterested observers, the oil companies and their lobbyists for data on oil and gas supplies; tough subpoenas for cost data were never issued by interested committees—but then, congressional committees have rarely been eager to demand information from our giant corporations. This reliance by public authority on private interests is a consequence of congressional weakness. As Allard Lowenstein complained when he was a congressman:

> How much can anyone do with limited staff and all the mail and what not to cope with? If you aren't independently wealthy, you can't have a staff that is capable of putting things together much beyond what you can come up with from the sources available to everyone—the executive departments, the lobbies, the staffs of congressional committees, the Library of Congress. That's one reason why the lobbies are so influential. They have people who are able to spend all their time collecting data on why pollution is good for River X. What congressmen can match that?

None can. That's why congressmen so often have to depend on the superior manpower of the lobbies to suggest solutions to problems, draft legislation, provide the evidence for it, help develop legislative strategy, persuade the rest of Congress to go along, and even raise the problems in the first place. With the lobbies' pressure bearing in from all sides, Congress ends up, for the most part, responding to the heaviest push. Senator John Kennedy once said, "Lobbyists are in many cases expert technicians and capable of explaining complex and difficult subjects in a clear, understandable fashion," which makes them all the more persuasive.

WINING AND DINING. "I've never known a lobbyist who wasn't a nice guy" is a familiar refrain. Which should be expected, for savvy lobbies understand Marshall McLuhan and politics: the context is more important than the content, and an amiable delivery can camouflage bias.

To develop a congenial ambience, lobbyists for large economic interests come equipped with the traditional expense accounts to make life more pleasant for select congressmen. The sweeteners can range from imported perfumes to Christmas gifts "carted in by the cartload" according to one Senate aide. *Washington Post* reporter Ward Sinclair described the atmosphere during a recent Christmas: "It is Christmas season on Capitol Hill, the one time of year when the flow of goodies is reversed. Instead of dishing it out, the legislature scoops it up. Wreaths and flowers, liquor, cheese, pens, datebooks and calendars, small appliances . . . are among the holiday remembrances flooding the hill." GE sends around small deep-fat fryers; 3M, kits of cellophane tape; and Kraft Food, cheese packets. Nor does the giving stop on December 26. Atlanta Congressman Wyche Fowler, Jr., tells how he three times told Atlanta-based Coca-Cola to stop plying his office with cartons of free Coke—but each time the Coke kept coming. Fowler, a strong-willed and independent representative, bowed to the inevitable. If you visit his office, more likely than not you'll be offered a free guess-what.

Then there are the parties. Come the spring, the large party rooms off the corridors of the Rayburn Building are full of lobby groups, making the end of the day a little more pleasant for hard-working representatives. The Grocery Manufacturers of America, for example, invited all 535 national legislators and their families to a carnival and picnic at a fashionable local country club just before a crucial vote on the consumer protection agency bill, a bill the GMA vigorously opposed. "Certainly senators and congressmen have been entertained on a small scale," the Freight Forwarders' Washington representative Stanley Sommer concedes, "but it's nothing more than a three-hour cruise down the Potomac."

Former Senator Paul Douglas has explained the process:

> The enticer does not generally pay money directly to the public representative. He tries instead, by a series of favors, to put the public official under such a feeling of personal obligation that the latter gradually loses his sense of mission to the public and comes to feel that his first loyalties are to his private benefactors

and patrons. . . . Throughout this whole process the official will claim—and may, indeed, believe—that there is no causal connection between the favors he has received and the decision which he makes. He will assert that the favors were given or received on the basis of pure friendship.

The Ways and Means Committee, at both the chairman and staff level, graphically demonstrate the point. Ted Gup of *The Washington Post* wrote a series in mid-1982, "Golfing No Handicap for Rostenkowski," explaining in detail how numerous companies with interests before Ways and Means spent thousands of dollars to put up chairman Dan Rostenkowski (D.-Ill.) at various golfing resorts. Legislatively interested companies don't restrict their lavishness to members. Ways and Means senior staffer James Healey, Jr., his wife and two children spent five days at Lake Tahoe in 1980, paid for by Harrah's, one of the largest casinoes in the world. At that time there was a bill pending to repeal the occupational tax on wagering. Healey was at least candid about the process: "I knew [the casinoes] had legislation before the committee and Rostenkowski was on the committee. I'm generally considered to be his senior employee. Everyone knows I'm close to Danny . . . it's a safe assumption that everyone knows my connection with him and hopefully they could make their case better known to him through me. I think that's a very, very justifiable reason for having me or anybody else go out there." Later John Sherman, Rostenkowski's press secretary, explained that "Washington is a casual sort of 'let's-have-lunch, let's-go-to-New-Orleans' kind of town."

Many staffers don't have to worry about forgetting their lunch money, as companies stand in line to take them to favorite dining places. This thoughtfulness eventually makes its point. "You begin to look forward to those three or four lunches a week with the lobbyists at the good restaurants," one committee aide said, "to the $25 bottles of Scotch, the football tickets, the occasional junkets, and if you don't watch out, you get pulled into the lobbyists' frame of reference." Or as super-lobbyist Samuel Ward put it a century ago, "The way to a man's 'aye' is through his stomach."

GOING TO THE "GRASS ROOTS." Rather than simply buzzing in the legislator's ear in Washington, the aim of "grass-roots" lobbying is to subject him to mass appeals from people back home. According to Hilton Davis of the Chamber of Commerce, "We really put a lot more stock in what people at home can do to influence members of Congress than what we can do by talking to congressmen. We don't vote in their districts." A House subcommittee in 1978 estimated that business lobbyists spend up to a billion dollars a year generating such grass-roots "support" for their issues.

The oil industry has always excelled at this lobbying tactic, particularly when the large companies pool their efforts. In one carefully orchestrated industry effort in the 1970s on behalf of the depletion allowance, for example, an oil company asked its stockholders to write to Congress; another worked at mobilizing its retired employees; another aimed at service-station operators; a fourth mailed off brochures to its credit-card holders. Intent on preserving an impression of spontaneous revolt emanating from the hinterlands, the Washington coordinators of oil's campaigns have on occasion remained conspicuously silent while the letters and requests to testify flooded in.

A decade later AT&T refined the technique in its successful drive to frustrate a communications act it considered onerous. After Representative Tim Wirth's H.R. 5158 had cleared his telecommunications subcommittee 15–0, AT&T, the world's largest corporation, with $137 billion in assets, went to work. It spent $850,000 to correspond with its three million shareholders ("Your investment, your savings are at stake") and to provoke them in turn to write their elected officials; $200,000 more went into advertisements in twenty major newspapers in swing districts; and regional Bell affiliates spent an additional $500,000 on local activities to rally support among employees, shareholders, and customers. The result: half a million letters poured into Congress and Wirth had to surrender since he couldn't muster a majority in full committee. (For examples of consumer and environmental grass roots drives, see epilogue, "Taking on Congress: A Primer for Citizen Action.")

Such inspired mail campaigns are a major component of grass-roots efforts. If letters appear original and personal, they are extremely influential—and particularly American. Compared to the hundreds of letters a week representatives receive and thousands a senator gets, writes Elizabeth Moynihan, "a long-term member of Parliament [England], a member of the shadow cabinet, receives only about 150 letters a week. And in Sweden, one of the best-known and respected members of the Riksdag, the Swedish Parliament, gets only about 10 letters a week from individuals and seldom more than 25 from business firms." But if identical and obviously choreo-graphed letters flood a member's office, the impact is often marginal. "A whole pile of computer-written letters or postcards wouldn't impress me as much as a single handwritten letter," said Representative Norman D. Shumway (R.-Calif.). Another office has its computer programed to begin some replies with "Thank you for your form letter" and "Thank you for your preprinted postcard."

PERSONAL ASSOCIATIONS. One day in 1926, Pennsylvania Senator David Reed—whose father had been a key member of the Gulf Oil controlling syndicate—went to lunch with the president of the Mid-Continent Oil and Gas Association. The Mid-Continent man told Reed of the heavy burden that drilling costs were forcing on the industry. The senator was so moved by this complaint that he rushed to tell his colleagues on the Senate Finance Committee of the oilmen's desperate plight. Out of that discussion was born the oil depletion allowance.

It was, of course, natural that Reed, raised under the roof of Big Oil, would be dining out with another oilman. Men in Congress obviously have social acquaintances and former business acquaint-ances outside of Congress—"know who" rather than "know-how." In the words of Robert Keith Gray, a leading lobbyist and cochair of President Reagan's inaugural committee, "I'm making the most of my connections." That simple fact gives the business lobbies one of their most important conduits into the Congress.

The danger arises because the average congressman is not the average American. Allard Lowenstein once commented that "the House in some ways isn't very representative. There's almost never anyone here under thirty. . . . And, of course, there are only nine blacks [in 1969, though in 1984 there were 21] when proportionately there should be about fifty." This disproportionate representation is even more skewed for women and blue-collar workers. The fact that members of Congress come almost exclusively from professions that serve mostly business clientele or from business itself gives the corporate community a several-step head start over other citizens in making Congress work for them.

The average citizen gets little opportunity to see lobbying operations in action, as they are seldom covered in the news media. One that did make the news occurred in connection with the 1970 lobbying effort of the banking industry on one-bank holding-company legislation. The American Bankers Association wrote to the officials of three banks asking them to get in touch immediately with three key members of the relevant House-Senate conference to ask them to oppose stringent controls. The three members happened also to be large stockholders in the respective banks. The banker asked to contact Representative J. William Stanton of Ohio also happened to have been Stanton's campaign treasurer in the previous election. The Bankers Association letter stressed an important point: "If at all possible, please make your contact in person."

Senator Tom Eagleton showed that blood is thicker than politics by his surprise vote in mid-1972 to bury no-fault auto legislation in the Judiciary Committee. He had been lobbied by a group of his trial-lawyer father's colleagues, men whom the senator, by profession and by upbringing, had come to respect. He explained ingenuously that his father had been a trial lawyer and would have "rolled over in his grave" had he voted against the tort system.

Finally, as perhaps the ultimate in intimate association, a third of the American Medical Association's district lobbying representatives happen to be the general practitioners who delivered either the congressman or his/her children.

CONTRIBUTIONS. Voluminous information, expensive dinners, personal associations, and grass-roots drives are important to the successful lobbyist. Still, ultimately, the giving or providing of substantial campaign contributions to members is the best way for a lobbyist to command their attention legislatively. As Chapter One explained, costs have so escalated that a lobbyist who is known to be able to channel several PAC donations attracts receptive congressional audiences. Consider, for one example, the House Armed Services Committee. Twenty-three of the largest twenty-four military contractors give hundreds of thousands of dollars to committee members. Panel member Pat Schroeder (D.-Colo.) describes the process. "Every year the Armed Services Committee gives the Department of Defense more weapons than they ask for. Spare parts, readiness, and pay have no PAC; big weapons systems have PACs"—with the result that committee hawks talk about maintenance, readiness, and pay but end up voting for the weapons systems contractors lobby for.

There has been a long linkage between lobbying and contributing, but the ties are far tighter—and more expensive—now. For any economic interests still unsophisticated in the ways of Washington, there is Washington lobbyist Robert McCandless, who said, "I won't even take a client now unless he's willing to set up a political action committee and participate in the process." One Washington, D.C., lawyer told Elizabeth Drew, "Ninety-nine percent of lobbying in this city is now fund-raising."

Sometimes overeager advocates don't even bother with the legal formality of establishing a PAC. Occasionally lobbyists come to congressional offices to drop off cash in envelopes, ostensibly for "campaign contributions." Representative Richard Ottinger saw the process happen to him, he said in an interview, and he rejected the offer. (Ottinger concluded, from his experience, that a seat on the

House Energy and Commerce Committee was worth a substantial amount of money.) Former Representative Pete McCloskey said he "was upset to find lobbyists leaving behind envelopes with $100 bills." He is convinced that straight cash from lobbyists in the form of campaign contributions is a subterranean corruption of great significance in terms of its influence on the behavior of recipient congressmen. But at least one such recipient disagrees. This congressman willingly took $250 in cash at a Washington bar from an industrial lobbyist, and then turned to a Washington reporter and indignantly protested, "That son of a bitch thinks he can buy me for $250." But he kept the money.

There is little need any longer for such brazen bribery, not after the Senate lifted its lid on "honoraria," as noted previously. Now if a special-interest lobby wants to give an important legislator money, it need only invite him to lunch, chat, call it a "speech," and write out a check for up to $2,000.

A Who's Who of Lobbying

Despite the lobbies' awesome impact on the law, the public retains only a cloudy picture of who the lobbyists are and what they do. For the economic interests who run the lobbies have hidden behind vague, institutional titles like the sugar lobby and the highway lobby. What follows are specific descriptions of major lobbying influences in Washington:

BUSINESS ORGANIZATIONS. "The defenders of American business had it pretty easy in 1955," lamented the National Association of Manufacturers in its magazine *Enterprise* in the mid-1970s. "There were, in those days, no self-ordained public-interest lobbyists to cope with; and the Eisenhower administration in league with the conservative leadership of Congress championed the interests of business whenever those interests were threatened." To the nostalgic executive, political conditions may never seem quite as favorable as during the quiescent 1950s. Still, the record of the big-business lobbies in the late 1970s led *Fortune* magazine to conclude that "the business community has become the most effective special interest lobby in the country. Suddenly business seems to possess all the primary instruments of power—the leadership, the strategy, the supporting troops, the campaign money—and a new will to use them."

More recent evidence, indeed, supports the view that major business lobbies appear to be able to exercise a de facto veto over measures they oppose. If business lobbies don't object, reform measures can become law; if they do, they can't. A united business community defeated the labor law reform bill, consumer protection agency, consumer class actions, and tax reforms; it got enacted the greatest corporate tax cut ever; a largely uninterested big-business community allowed airline deregulation, a bank for consumer cooperatives, and civil service reform to pass.

The leading general-membership business lobbies responsible for this record are the U.S. Chamber of Commerce and Business Roundtable. Operating out of a marble-and-limestone palace near the White House, the Chamber's $20 million budget, 70,000 corporate members, more than 1,300 professional and trade associations, and 2,500 local Chamber affiliates give it unusual leverage in Washington. It sends out a weekly newsletter, *Congressional Action*, to each of its members, describing the substance and timing of upcoming legislation. Its legislative department follows up with "Action Calls"—requests to their 1,200 local Congressional Action committees (with some 100,000 members) to contact their congressmen. These communications ultimately reach 7 million people sympathetic to its causes, says the Chamber.

Finally, the Chamber operates a backup communication process for critical bills or surprise votes. It activates its field force of Chamber representatives spread throughout the country. In each congressional district, field representatives develop personal contacts called key resources people (in Chamber jargon, KRPs). KRPs have close personal relationships with their representative, or senator, whether from their college fraternity, law firm, country club, or church.

The Chamber's organizational strengths are somewhat undercut by its primitive leadership under Richard Lesher, its president. A practitioner of personal smears, he said of Esther Peterson, President Carter's Consumer affairs advisor, during a consumer battle, "Hell hath no fury like a woman scorned" and charged that the 1980 effort called Big Business Day "is run by socialists" (it wasn't).

A less militant and less visible counterpart to the Chamber is the Business Roundtable. Founded in 1972 and with a $2 million budget, it is a group of 190 chief executive officers (CEOs) of the nation's largest corporations. While groups like the Chamber issue alarms to their memberships, the Roundtable emphasizes the personal visit from a prominent CEO, the supportive study, the legal analysis. While few lobbyists can get direct access to a senator, no one in Congress is likely to turn away the head of GM or Du Pont. As one congressional aide observed, "A visit from a CEO has an unbelievable impact, as perhaps it should. It shows a commitment."

Consequently, in a short time the Roundtable has become an influential, more genteel version of the Chamber. It has helped defeat the consumer protection office, negotiate a compromise Arab-boycott bill, and weaken the 1976 antitrust improvements act. All this despite the fact that its members almost never testify in public hearings, preferring instead to deal with staff and officials behind the scenes. In fact, the Business Roundtable won't even issue a list of who its 190 members are. It is the most influential secret lobby in Washington.

INDEPENDENT BUSINESS LOBBYISTS. These lobbyists, retained for their expertise or entrée on particular bills, are an important part of the lobbying process—and are growing in number. With power redistributed from a few committee chairs to many subcommittee chairs and the rise of public interest lobbyists, business lobbyists have to work harder to get their way. What used to take a few phone calls to acquiescent chairmen and leaders now requires fleets of retained lobbyists who meet weekly and collaborate in coalitions with discreet names like the Carlton Group (to lower business taxes), the Clean Air Act Working Group, the Emergency Committee for American Trade.

One of the flashiest, if not most influential, of business advocates on Capitol Hill is Charles Walker, deputy secretary of the Treasury under President Nixon and founder of his own "economic consulting" firm. A cigar-smoking Texan, he has a large stable of blue-chip clients such as General Electric, Ford, Du Pont, Bethlehem Steel, and Proctor and Gamble. The telephone, three-martini lunch, chauffered Cadillac limousine, flip-chart, and personal association are his primary tools of trade. He dines or plays golf regularly with cabinet secretaries, senators, journalists, and banking and business leaders. He claims to phone Russell Long, ranking minority member on the Senate Finance Committee, two or three times weekly before breakfast. It didn't hurt his efforts on an energy bill in 1978 to be godfather to Energy Secretary James Schlesinger's youngest child and close family friends with Thomas (Lud) Ashley (D.-Ohio). (Not even Walker could hedge all bets. When the Senate went Republican, Walker's influence at Senate Finance plummeted—because Long was a buddy and Dole has made disparaging public reference to the "Charlie Walkers" that lobby his committee.)

Walker claims that much of his influence comes simply from understanding the motivations and professional problems of key legislators. Like a good attorney Walker marshals only the facts that best suit his case. There is a difference, however, between being selective and being wrong; to mislead a congressman or his staff is potentially suicidal to a lobbyist's reputation and, hence, his effectiveness. He told Elizabeth Drew of *The New Yorker*, "If they know you and trust you, they'll listen to you and they'll tell someone else you're a good guy, and you reach a point where if you put a piece of paper in a member's hand, he knows he's not going to be blind-sided."

Finally, Walker appreciates how members of Congress "spend most of their time taking care of their constituents' problems with the government—so it becomes difficult to do good legislative work. So to an extent we become an extension of the staff. A member of the House said in the cloakroom the other day that he needed an amendment for part of the energy bill in conference, so we drafted it for him.''

Although it is nearly impossible to tell whether a lobbyist is changing the course of legislative events or merely choosing to represent the side with the upper hand, Walker in the 1970s helped persuade Congress to increase the investment tax credit from 7 to 10 percent; saved some eastern railroads from bankruptcy by persuading a reluctant Nixon administration to pour federal funds into Conrail; won big tax breaks for the nation's five largest airlines and for the Cigar Association of America, and helped lead the business effort to discredit President Carter's plans to introduce major tax-law reforms in 1978.

Walker achieved his greatest successes with the advent in Washington of the Reagan administration, many of whose leaders were close to Walker and sympathetic to his view that cutting the business taxes of his clients would promote "capital formation" and hence economic growth. ("I think about capital investment the way Mark Twain did about good bourbon whiskey," Walker has said. "Too much is barely enough.") In 1981 and 1982 Walker became the man to see. He was the head of the influential American Council for Capital Formation at the same time that he headed the Reagan transition task force on tax policy. (A conflict, he was asked? "That's a nonproblem, I think. It seems to assume that the only people that you can have in those sorts of positions are either college professors or monks.") He later sat on President Reagan's Economic Policy Advisory Board, and with the *National Journal* ran a conference where 100 foreign business leaders met with top Reagan officials for three days—which was ironic since the *Journal* had earlier chided his firm as an example of how "influence peddlers flaunt their access to government officials."

In 1981 Walker led the successful drive for the largest business tax reduction in history, which included an enlarged investment tax credit, an accelerated depreciation schedule, and a system of "tax leasing" that allowed Walker's clients to get cash for tax breaks they couldn't use. Later Robert Kaus would write in *Harper's*, "It would not be too much of an overstatement to say that through the elaborate corporate tax breaks he has promoted both as a lobbyist and as a Reagan advisor, he is more responsible than anyone for the current budget deficit."*

LABOR LOBBYISTS. Pushing Congress from another ideological vantage point is the labor lobby. The linchpin of labor's effort is the AFL-CIO's lobbying arm, for a quarter century headed by the well-known Andrew Biemiller until his retirement in 1978. (He recalled how George Meany told him just three things when he began lobbying: "Don't beg, don't threaten, and don't think you are always 100 percent right.")

The golden age of labor's social-progress lobbying was in the mid-1960s, when the Leadership Conference on Civil Rights—an alliance of labor, religious, civic, and civil rights groups, which counted labor as its most powerful member—pushed through civil rights legislation and, finally, over longtime AMA opposition, Medicare. The "liberal-labor" coalition in Congress also rose to challenge successfully Nixon Supreme Court nominees Carswell and Haynsworth. "On issue after issue" in the fifties and sixties, wrote political analyst Michael Barone, "almost every non-Southern Democrat . . . followed organized labor on almost every roll-call vote. Labor set up and enforced the agenda for the Democratic party . . . not because of its prowess in campaigns but because of its skills as a lobby."

---

*Perhaps weary from the pejorative nature of his lobbyist's label, Walker has gone so far as to propose a lobbyist's Code of Ethics and an "American League of Lobbyists"—a lurch toward respectability and professionalism by means of imitating the AMA and the ABA. In the tenth amendment of his draft code, a lobbyist would promise to "preserve the public's trust and safeguard the lobbying profession by promptly and fully reporting all violations of these principles to the designated officials of the American League of Lobbyists."

In recent years, however, labor has been stymied on many strictly "labor issues," such as the labor law reform, common situs picketing, cargo preference, and "domestic content" legislation. These losses are variously attributed to a declining union membership (now barely 20 percent of the labor force), the growing sophistication and expenditures of the business lobby, and, until his death, George Meany. "A picture of George Meany on the front page of an American newspaper," said William Winpisinger, the outspoken head of the International Association of Machinists, "has the same kind of impact a picture of Jay Gould or J. Pierpont Morgan once had: that of a cigar-smoking, affluent patriarch."

Organized labor hit bottom in 1980, when so many of its favored candidates lost and when Ronald Reagan gained the votes of 43 percent of working families. Since then the AFL-CIO seems to be rebounding from its long decline, for at least four reasons. First, Reagan's antiunion program and the 1980–82 recession reminded many workers that, in Ben Franklin's phrase, either they would hang together or hang separately; as is often the case, being out of power forged unity and activism. Second, Meany successor Lane Kirkland has begun to escape the long shadow of his powerful predecessor. It was he who thought up and labeled Solidarity Day in 1981—the first mass protest against Reagan's domestic policies. Third, especially after the retirement of crusty Al Barkan as the head of COPE (Committee on Political Education), labor seems more willing to work in alliances with allied groups (women, consumer, environmental, anti-PAC). Finally, there has been a political maturation under Barkan's successor, John Perkins. A fifty-year old former carpenter from Indiana, he is guiding labor into the high-tech politics of the eighties and nineties: the AFL-CIO now has the capacity for repeated in-house polling; its direct mail can specify name and union; a test of a computerized precinct-by-precinct computer system in 1982 proved successful; there is a new Public Affairs Institute to improve labor's public image and make better use of TV.

"Too many people have written labor's obituary, and that's crazy," said labor consultant Vic Kamber in 1982. "Labor is still the largest single-interest constituency in America.'' Politicians were reminded of this in November 1982. COPE orchestrated 10 million phone calls to union households on or near election day. Also, union PACs significantly increased their contributions, and labor-backed Senate candidates, successful only 34 percent of the time in 1980, won 65 percent of their races in 1982.

SINGLE-ISSUE LOBBYISTS. Ideological single-issue groups often lobby on just one subject, are uncompromising, and have long memories. They have been heralded as a new and dangerous political genre, though they have obvious antecedents. From the Anti-Masons of the 1830s to the Prohibitionists a century later and the Vietnam protestors of the 1960s, there is a long history of groups that organize around not a party or a person, but a cause. The key to such lobbies today—e.g., antiabortion, anti-ERA, antigun control, anti-busing, or pro-choice and pro-freeze—is *intensity*. They adhere to the political axiom that a group's power is based less on who it votes for than what it pickets for. The political implications of such intensity are obvious when one listens, for example, to Howard Phillips, the pugnacious national director of the Conservative Caucus: ''We organize discontent. We must prove our ability to get revenge on people who go after us.'' Thus members of Congress understand well how one outraged group can easily overwhelm several mildly pleased ones. The 1978 election defeats of Senators Dick Clark in Iowa and Thomas McIntyre in New Hampshire are widely attributed to their respective positions on abortion and the Panama Canal.

Single-issue groups are achieving some success because they link up their intensity with computerized mailing lists. Richard C. Viguerie is the king of right-wing mailing lists, having spent fourteen years collecting the names of 5 million conservatives. ''Any special-interest group that has a better mailing list than you, owns you,'' says Representative Charles Rose (D.-N.C.). ''It can reach your constituency better than you can.'' Single-issue groups can be considered new political parties doing what the old parties used to do—reach constituents and generate funds.

76

Perhaps the paradigmatic special-interest lobby is the two-million-member National Rifle Association, spokesman for the nation's rifle and gun owners. The NRA operates out of an eight-story building in downtown Washington and has a staff of 250 and an annual budget of $8 million. Supported by gun owners, gun manufacturers, and gun dealers, it claims the ability to trigger hundreds of thousands of letters on forty-eight hours' notice for its pro-gun causes. After each of the political assassinations of the sixties, it was mainly the NRA that discouraged Congress from passing tough gun-control laws. Although twelve national polls in the past twenty years have shown majorities of two thirds of the public favoring strict gun control laws, and although 20,000 Americans a year die from guns, senators and representatives still fear that organized gun interests will electorally retaliate against their perceived enemies.

The NRA, consequently, succeeds because two million motivated gun owners count for more politically than the other 238 million unmotivated non-gun owners. Apparently the love of guns by a few exceeds the fear of crime by the many. So when President Carter's Treasury Department studied the idea of centralizing gun record sales to facilitate tracing weapons used in criminal conduct, 350,000 letters of protest stopped the proposal dead. When Congress considered a "Keep Away from Children" warning on a box of Devastator (explosive) cartridges, the NRA stymied the effort. And a NRA film "It Can't Happen Here," characterizing the Bureau of Alcohol, Tobacco and Firearms as "a jack-booted group of fascists," was part of an abortive campaign to persuade President Reagan and Congress to abolish the agency.

THE NEW RIGHT. Many of the conservative single-issue causes have been bundled together by New Right groups into a powerful political force. The most prominent New Right group, one with a "better mailing list," in Representative Rose's phrase, is the National Conservative Political Action Committee (NCPAC, pronounced "Nick-pack"), which tries to influence Congress by electoral intimidation rather than the gentle persuasion of more smoothly honed lobbyists. An "independent committee," NCPAC makes use of a gaping hole in the 1974 election law created when the Supreme Court allowed unlimited spending in an election if the PAC doing the spending is independent of the candidate it helps. NCPAC can thus spend huge amounts on advertisements attacking liberal incumbents while not mentioning the conservative challenger. As NCPAC head Terry Dolan put it, "A group like ours could lie through its teeth and the candidate it helps stays clean."

Founded and led by Dolan, a moustachioed thirty-two-year-old with a penchant for outrageous statements (relishing his bad boy image, he once bragged NCPAC "could elect Mickey Mouse if we wanted to"), NCPAC's biggest success was the 1980 election. Raising substantial funds by hyperbolic direct-mail campaigns and spending $1.2 million against six incumbent Democratic senators, the committee played an active role in defeating four of them— George McGovern, Birch Bayh, Frank Church, and John Culver.

A week after the 1980 election, a confident Dolan stood before a thicket of microphones and told a crowded press conference that NCPAC would target twenty Democratic senators in 1982. But when the votes were counted two years later, only one intended victim had been beaten, and NCPAC was counted the big loser. It entered 1983 on the defensive and $800,000 in debt. What had happened? Apart from the deepening recession and the increasing unpopularity of the Reagan administration, NCPAC was itself faced with a powerful backlash. Its tactics antagonized even its friends. Conservative Republican Jake Garn (Utah) accused Dolan's group of using "fear tactics"; then-Republican chairman Richard Richards warned that it had the potential to make "all kinds of mischief." Members of Congress were also angered by the group's strong-arm lobbying techniques; Dolan sent Representative Stephen Neal a letter threatening to campaign against him if he voted against the tax cut, but leave him alone if he voted for it. In addition the ads themselves were often inaccurate—John Melcher was listed as voting to "give away" the Panama Canal, even though he voted against the treaty (Dolan: a "typographical error"); Dennis DeConcini was listed as supporting abortion even though he voted against it 28 out of 29 times (Dolan: "If a senator votes once for busing or abortion we think it's justified to list him as probusing or proabortion"); indeed, they were so inaccurate that many television stations refused to show them.

Ultimately, NCPAC itself became the issue rather than aid to Nicaragua or school prayer, helping its target more than hurting him. By condemning Daniel Patrick Moynihan as the "most liberal" member of the Senate, for example, NCPAC helped him avoid a possible challenge in the Democratic primary. But the biggest back-fire was in Maryland, where NCPAC spent $650,000 to unseat Paul Sarbanes—who proceeded to run against out-of-state "extremist groups" and win with 63 percent of the vote.

The NCPAC phenomenon has subsided to a lower level. Adjusting, the group intends to spend more of its funds on *positive* independent ads in 1984. And any group that can raise $9.5 million, as it did in 1981–82, will obviously have an impact on wary lawmakers.

THE OIL LOBBY. When fully mobilized, the oil lobby can send into action lawyers from the most highly regarded law firms, public relations consultants, numerous ex-government officials, newsmen who serve as "advisers," company executives, corporate legal departments, admen from advertising agencies, government officials in several of the executive departments, trade association representatives, and—though only a small fraction of the total—men who actually register as lobbyists. Whenever legislation affecting oil is on the docket, the oilers can easily afford to have a corporate vice-president or similarly impressive official assigned to persuade every member of every relevant committee. If reinforcements should be needed, the industry can call on a vast reserve of sales agents, filling station operators, and other small businessmen. In other words, they are different from you and me.

Presiding over these far-flung legions are the oil trade associations, with the most powerful being the American Petroleum Institute. The API is generally regarded as the spokesman for the "majors"—including Exxon, Mobil, Gulf, Arco, Texaco, Shell, Standard

Oil of Indiana, and Standard Oil of California—although its membership roster runs on to include some 350 other companies. One of the API's subsidiaries, the American Petroleum Industries Committee, operates in virtually every state capital, augmenting the work of individual oil companies and a formidable array of state and regional trade groups. Organized to the grass-roots level, the industry also has committees with extensions reaching into local and county governments.

API has an annual budget of $46 million, with much of it, according to the API, spent on "research." This goes to support a staff of 580, working in Washington, D.C., plus offices in Dallas, New York, and several states. API is joined in its efforts by the Independent Natural Gas Association of America, the National Oil Jobbers Council, the National Petroleum Refiners Association, the American Gas Association, the American Public Gas Association, and the Association of Oil Pipe Lines. These reinforcements proved helpful in the 1973–74 period when the energy shortage provoked consumers—who waited hours at gas stations and spent small fortunes to heat their homes—to write members of Congress to let them know the full measure of their anger.

Whatever API and its companion lobbies spend has been, for them, a very worthwhile investment. For the fifteen years of the oil import quota, according to a much downplayed 1970 White House study, a bonus $5 billion annually shifted from the pockets of consumers to the bank accounts of Big Oil. The oil depletion allowance and foreign tax credits—until they were scaled down in 1975 by a Congress finally suspect of the industry's swollen profits—would save oilmen another $5 billion every year. The added profits from the legislated deregulation of natural gas rates in 1978 and oil prices in 1979 are expected to be many times $5 billion.

To protect these investments, the oil lobby is spending even more in political races. "We came to the decision that the only way we could change the political fortunes of the petroleum industry was to change Congress," said Harold Scroggins, a Washington lobbyist for the Independent Petroleum Producers Association. Big Oil doubled its PAC contributions from 1978 to 1980, with five sixths of the money going to Republicans. It worked: the two Senate challengers getting the most oil money won and now sit on the influential Finance Committee (Grassley and Symms); the 10 House challengers who received the most oil PAC money were all GOP freshmen in 1981.

FORMER CONGRESSMEN AS LOBBYISTS. A more subtle form of compensation to the legislator for his labors on behalf of a lobby is the potential of a high-paying job when he retires from Congress. Not that congressmen *expect* to be out of office in the near future, but the unhappy possibility can never be entirely out of their minds.

In fact, later employment in the lobbying sector is a popular career path for retired politicians. They charge higher lobbying fees than others, but their clients know they are worth it. Former members of Congress have a number of built-in advantages as lobbyists. They already know dozens of members and staff and they are schooled in the nuances of congressional rules and bargaining. They retain their rights to use the recreational and dining facilities reserved for members of Congress, they retain their former titles of "Senator" or "Chairman," and they have lifetime visiting privileges in the private cloakrooms and on the floor of the chamber in which they served. With these credentials and accustomed to the big time— "Negligence work or divorce work is just not appealing to me," said Herb Harris after his 1980 defeat—most stay on in Washington to sell their expertise.

Intent on losing no time after his 1974 election defeat, Indiana Republican Roger Zion sent out solicitations to prospective lobbying clients on his congressional stationery before he vacated his office. He explained that he would continue to be active in congressional social activities, and thus would "maintain contact with my good friends who affect legislation." A tasteful Senate custom holds that the former senator turned lobbyist should not appear on the floor when a measure affecting his client comes up—a custom, however, occasionally honored in the breach. But such excesses are really not necessary, for the normal prerogatives and contacts of former members are usually more than adequate to make their views known and to convince clients they are worth their keep.

This role offended former senator Albert Gore. ''As a member of the Senate, I felt resentment when a former colleague took advantage of our friendship and association to lobby for some special interest,'' he said. But obviously many of his former colleagues disagree. Fully 124 former members have registered as lobbyists under the 1946 lobbying act; but given the widespread noncompliance with that law, it is likely that more than 124 former members return to Congress to lobby their earlier colleagues. Between 1946 and 1966 an average of nine former congressmen and senators formally registered as lobbyists after an election. Of the 85 legislators leaving after 1980, however, 20 registered and another 15 joined law firms, consulting firms, or interest groups in D.C.

Neatly every big lobby has at least one (and often more than one) ex-member of Congress on its staff. The road from the floor of Congress to the lobby is so well worn that only a few of many examples can be given:

• Frank Ikard was a protégé of House Speaker Sam Rayburn and served with him as representative from Texas from 1952 to 1961. In 1961, Rayburn died, Ikard resigned, and the American Petroleum Institute got a new lobbyist, one who headed their Washington office until 1979. Ikard said that his change of job was ''a question of economics.''

• Former Senators Thurston Morton and George Murphy lobby for tobacco interests and Taiwan, respectively.

• Wayne Aspinall, representative from Colorado for twenty-four years and chairman of the House Interior and Insular Affairs Committee, made a rapid comeback following his 1972 primary election defeat. On a $1,750-a-month retainer for AMAX, Inc., a large mining firm, lobbyist Aspinall easily buttonholes former colleagues on mining legislation. During House debate on a strip mining bill of key concern to AMAX, Aspinall strolled onto the House floor in apparent violation of House rules which forbid former members to be on the floor during debate in which they have an interest. When asked about this inprudent move, the former chairman complained of "this new rule," though the rule in its basic form was passed in 1880. Apparently trying to avoid any further embarrassments, Aspinall told a reporter, "I'm trying to stay my distance"—although this determination did not prevent Aspinall from then asking a page to tell the House speaker he would like to see him "for a few minutes at his convenience."

• On an antitrust bill that would immunize a handful of companies found guilty of price-fixing from hundreds of millions of dollars in possible damage awards, the affected firms took no chances and in 1982 retained three former members of the Senate Judiciary Committee: Sam Ervin, Joe Tydings, and Birch Bayh.

• Liberal Democrat James Corman now lobbies for the drug, tobacco, and oil/gas interests he previously opposed. (He used to have a sign in his home that thanked people for not smoking.) "I have never taken a client who wanted me to lobby for something that was against my ideals," says Corman, adding, "People don't hire lawyers to work on the things I worked on when I was in Congress."

• Harold Cooley has dealt with sugar for a long time—for sixteen years as Democratic representative from North Carolina and chairman of the House Agriculture Committee (where he was known as the "sugar king"), and more recently as lobbyist for sugar interests in Liberia and Thailand. Joining him in the sugar contingent is a relative novice in sugar questions, former California senator Thomas Kuchel. Despite his inexperience Kuchel has earned $200 per hour as a lobbyist.

One of the sugar lobbyists—Thomas Hale Boggs, Jr.—illustrates yet another variation on the congressman-as-lobbyist theme. Young Boggs is the son of the late House majority leader Hale Boggs and of successor Lindy Boggs, and the inheritor of his father and mother's network of congressional associations. Understanding this, several private interests have made use of young Boggs's legal services: Texaco, Boeing, Armco Steel, Chrysler, *Reader's Digest*, and the state of Louisiana, among others. He charges $250 an hour, earns a half million dollars annually, and played a pivotal role in the Chrysler bailout bill. After the 1980 campaign his law firm hired two top political operatives: one worked for Ted Kennedy and the other for Ronald Reagan. "The Boggs firm," said one Washington insider to *The Wall Street Journal*, "looks more like a fusion government than a law firm."

LOBBYISTS AS STAFF/STAFF AS LOBBYISTS. Sometimes, outside lobbyists can operate as extensions of inside staff—and sometimes, the reverse.

The tradition of lobbyists drafting legislation is a long one, the result of overworked staffs looking for a shortcut and lobbyists looking for impact. So in 1937 a law partner of Senator Millard Tydings, who represented the National Association of Retail Druggists, drafted the Federal Fair Trade Act to allow price-fixing between suppliers and dealers. Never discussed on its merits on the Senate floor, the measure passed as a rider to the District of Columbia appropriations bill. The next year Congress was vigorously debating a new food and drug act, much of which was drafted by a young lawyer in Covington & Burling named H. Thomas Austern. The bill and his language became the 1938 Food and Drug Act.

More recently, business lobbyist Peter Nyce used to have such a clear pipeline into the Senate Interior and Insular Affairs Committee that he often sat in on closed meetings, was allowed to question other witnesses at hearings, and reportedly wrote two Senate bills on mineral leasing. Food lawyers played a significant role in drafting Senator Orrin Hatch's bill, S.1442, to amend the Delaney Amendment Amendment governing carcinogens in food. "At one point we had something like fifteen lawyers in one room, all screaming at each other," recalls Hatch aide Steve Grossman of a 1981 meeting. "Our staffers finally had to walk out and let them settle it among themselves."

In other circumstances, some business lobbyists seem to assume that if you can't persuade 'em, join 'em. The American Institute of Merchant Shipping, for example, should get a warm reception from

Ralph Casey, former chief counsel of the House Committee on Merchant Marine and Fisheries. Casey came to the committee from his previous post as executive vice-president and lobbyist for the Institute. Peter Hughes was a congressional staffer for six years before joining the Boeing Company's Washington office in 1976. A year and a half later he left to become a staff assistant to the Investigations subcommittee of the House Armed Services Committee. There he is playing a significant role in the committee's work on the MX intercontinental missile, on which Boeing has three developmental contracts with the Navy.

The exchange can, of course, be reversed. The banking lobby, for example, counted no fewer than five alumni of the Senate Banking, Housing, and Urban Affairs Committee's staff among its staff during its successful 1970 effort to soften a Senate bill to regulate one-bank holding companies, a device which banks can use to take over other industries. Sometimes, though, this cultural exchange can get politically crass. When two former aides of Senator Abe Ribicoff (D.-Conn.) formed a consulting firm, they circulated a memorandum to prospective tax clients seeking fees of up to $200,000. They explained that they were "in an unusually good position to influence the outcome of the debate" on Senator Ribicoff's proposal on the taxation of Americans abroad because Jeffrey Salzman of the firm "has been the principle [sic] drafter of all variations of that approach. (He was, of course, formerly legislative assistant to the senator.)" Ribicoff says he was "shocked" by the memorandum—a memorandum unusual for the world of Washington lobbying only in that it became public.

WASHINGTON LAWYERS. When a lobbying assignment calls for the maximum in prestige, legislative strategy, and delicate dealing, as well as inside influence, the men who are often called upon to do the job are Washington lawyers, the aristocrats of powerlaw. Lawyer-lobbyists in Washington are often men of liberal persuasions who came to Washington in high posts with a Democratic administration and then stuck around to make the most of their well-developed contacts in government—people such as the late Thomas ("Tommy the Cork") Corcoran, former New Deal brain truster who was often retained by gas and airline clients. Today it is Lloyd Cutler, who, as hired lobbyist for General Motors, successfully had the criminal penalties section deleted from the 1966 Automobile Safety Act; and, most notably, Clark Clifford, adviser to Presidents from Harry Truman to Jimmy Carter, who saved Du Pont hundreds of millions in taxes with a special bill in 1962 dealing with the firm's court-ordered divestiture of General Motors stock. Until he was appointed secretary of defense in 1968, neither Clifford nor any of the other members of his firm registered. "We did no lobbying and never have." What he is doing is simply keeping his corporate clients "informed on policies and attitudes in government."

Michael Pertschuk, a veteran watcher of Washington lawyers and later chairman of the Federal Trade Commission, does not similarly understate their talents and impact. As he said in a 1974 article:

> The mischief lies with the lawyer-lobbyist who parks his conscience and personal moral accountability on Delaware Avenue outside the Old Senate Office Building. Far too many lawyers have conveniently lost sight of the origin of that peculiar societal role which permits the lawyer to suspend his own moral judgments. It is the *courtroom* not the *legislature* that frames the adversary system. When the State seeks to deprive a citizen of his liberty, it is proper that the lawyer undertake the defense of the accused without regard to the lawyer's own judgment or morality. . . . But imagine, if you can, a lawsuit which followed this bizarre scenario: Instead of a courtroom, the relevant events take place in floating forum. To be sure, there are several minor scenes played out in a Congressional hearing room, which displays the familiar props of a courtlike tribunal, such as witnesses testifying publicly upon a record. But the scene, and the forum, shifts abruptly:
> —now to the cramped enclave of a beleaguered junior staff counsel;

—next to the sixth hole at Burning Tree Country Club;

—back to a spare, obscure Committee room, packed with a curious amalgam of Administration bureaucrats and corporate lawyers and sprinkled with a handful of sympathetic Congressional staff;

—next a circuit of quiet, ex parte sessions in Senatorial offices;

—on to Redskin stadium, intermission of the Dallas game;

—and final argument over the diet special at the Federal City Club.

If this forum seems elusive, so do the parties. At least one party may be identified with certainty; a corporate entity with a heartfelt economic stake in the status quo. But the adversary party or parties appear in several guises, including "competition," "labor," "the consumer," "the environment," and "the public interest." These adversaries are as fairly matched as the New York Yankees and the Bushwick little league irregulars.

Other key lobbies now at work:

• The military contractors lobby is the instrument of what President Eisenhower memorably dubbed the "military-industrial complex." While at one time it relied on entertaining members and staff for long weekends in hunting lodges, such unsavory devices have given way to more traditional modes. First, the industry relies on an "iron triangle," in analyst Gordon Adams's phrase, of personnel between contractors, the Pentagon, and Congress. For example, more than 2,000 former military officers of the rank of major or higher were recently employed by military contractors. Second, they develop exhaustive information on weapons systems, emphasizing subcontractors and jobs per congressional district. Indeed, as the Lockheed C5-B and Boeing 747 rivalry showed in 1982, they are investing in splashy full-page ads in the major media that elected officials and procurement officials read. Third, the PACs of the top ten contractors are growing, from a half million dollars in 1976 to $1.7 million in 1980, which is still modest as compared to their $28 *billion* in contracts. Finally, there is old-fashioned buttonholing of key members, which can occasionally exceed legal bounds. A 1982 report by the General Accounting Office charged that a coordinated lobbying campaign for the C-5 air cargo plane by Lockheed and the Air Force violated the law prohibiting federally appropriated funds to be used to propagandize or lobby Congress. Explained a nonplussed Dan Daniel (D.-Va.), of the House Armed Services Committee, "I think that . . . if you didn't do that, you wouldn't get many bills through."

• The tobacco lobby has as its cornerstone the Tobacco Institute, a consortium of the leading companies which spent $4.5 million in 1977. Though their product is under criticism from government officials and health specialists for causing 325,000 premature deaths a year, "We have never lost anything" in Congress, boasts Jack Mills, its top lobbyist.

• The automobile lobby has mushroomed in the past several years in Washington to oppose tougher auto-safety standards and air-pollution requirements and to push for favorable tax privileges. Its repeated refrain is that federal safety and environmental controls cost consumers between $500 and $1,000 per car annually. Yet when the National Highway Traffic Safety Administration obtained data from the automobile manufacturers on how much cheaper a car would be if there were no federal standards, the answer was $80 a car.

• The American Bankers Association has a membership of 14,000 banks, 93 percent of all banks in the country. It maintains an extensive network of "contact bankers" in congressional districts. As one of their admiring staff aides observed, "Most of the members don't realize the reason they are hearing from bankers back in their district is that Mr. Lowrey [the head of the office] over on Connecticut Avenue has pressed the computer button." When the bankers in 1983 decided to go all-out to repeal a new law requiring that taxes on interest and dividends be withheld, they got over three hundred representatives and more than half the Senate to cosponsor their bill.

• The Religious Right aggressively lobbies Congress on so-called "profamily" issues like abortion, school prayer, and tuition tax credits for private schools. The Moral Majority, led by television evangelist Jerry Falwell, is only the best known of these fundamentalist groups. Falwell's biggest success was in 1981, when Congress—which has veto power over any bills passed by the Washington, D.C., city council—defeated local legislation that legalized homosexual relations. Representative Ron Dellums (D.-Calif.) correctly pointed out this was a ''cheap vote'' for congressmen, who would never favor such laws if they applied to the folks back home. ''They just wanted to get the Moral Majority off their backs. They didn't care one way or another about the District,'' complained one congressional aide.

This lobby's power and numbers were probably never as great as many people believed—for example, while much of the media has reported that Falwell's *Old Time Gospel Hour* program is watched by 25 million people, its actual viewership is 1.4 million—and it has been unable to persuade Congress to pass any of the major items on its agenda. It has also stumbled when straying from its social-issue base. When queried why the Moral Majority asked Congress to weaken corporate crime statutes, Falwell replied that the Chamber of Commerce had drafted his letter. He added, ''We do favors for each other. And perhaps we went too far in this case.'' Its tactics have even alienated some conservatives. For example, *Christian Voice* included among the issues in its ''Morality Index'' the 1981 budget vote, a tax indexing proposal, and aid to Taiwan. (The 1981 ''Morality Index'' also flunked 30 of 32 Jewish members of Congress.) But while conservative evangelicals have so far been unable to succeed with their agenda in Congress, their influence is high in two places that matter—with President Reagan and in many communities in the Sunbelt.

• The elderly lobby relies more on inexorable demographic trends than on campaign cash or backroom arm-twisting. The average age of Americans is creeping steadily upward (by 1983 there were 25 million retirees) and the political power of the elderly is increasing just as inexorably. One reason is that they are much more likely to vote than the rest of the population, and they have the time to write letters and work in campaigns. (Notes House Ways and Means committee chairman Dan Rostenkowski, recipient of much pressure on Social Security: "they're like paratroopers—they can drop in on you anytime.") They also are well organized—the American Association of Retired Persons has 14 million members kept on alert by a monthly newsletter and a telephone network to rival that of any lobbying group; the second largest senior lobby, the National Council of Senior Citizens, has 4 million members.

• The environmental and public interest lobbies began arriving on the legislative scene in the late 1960s. Before that time, conservation groups had largely refrained from lobbying in an effort to protect their tax-deductible status and, hence, their ability to raise money easily. Because it lobbied against Grand Canyon dams, for example, the Sierra Club was stripped of its preferred tax status in 1968. Now, having established affiliate organizations which are allowed to lobby, active environmental/conservation lobby groups include the Sierra Club, Environmental Action, Friends of the Earth, the Environmental Policy Center, League of Conservation Voters, Council for a Livable World, Wildlife Federation, and Wilderness Society. These groups have applied pressure on environmental issues as well as on a wider range of public problems.

They tallied their earliest victory in 1971, when Congress ended the taxpayers' subsidy for the SST—an aircraft whose saving of a few hours for transoceanic business travelers was far outweighed by its environmental costs. Environmentalists won passage of a strip-mining bill in 1977. Though weakened in its final form, it required that most strip-mined land be returned to its appropriate original contour, that certain land be off limits to strip mining, and that state and local governments jointly enforce these provisions.

But losses for a time equaled successes. The defeat of the environmental coalition's move in March 1972 to strengthen the industry-gutted House water-pollution bill signaled a hardening opposition to the movement for environmental change. In 1973, Congress authorized construction of the Alaskan oil pipeline, and prohibited any legal action to stall or bar the pipeline on environmental grounds.

Although ecology was fashionable in name and concept, converting it into legislative reality was another matter.

The environmental lobby hit stride in the 1980s, ironically just as the least environmentally interested President in recent memory took office. In part this movement was aided by the appointment of people such as Interior Secretary James Watt and EPA administrator Anne (Gorsuch) Burford, who were so openly disdainful of environmental values as to trigger a backlash among the public generally. Aided by such self-wounding figures, environmental groups did well in Congress because of their popularity *in* the polls and *at* the polls: public-opinion surveys showed the public strongly in favor of environmental laws such as the Clean Air Act; and the "Green Vote" turned out thousands of volunteers who helped reelect environmental allies such as Senator Robert Stafford (R.-Vt.) ("Without them . . . I would have lost") and the late Representative Phil Burton (D.-Calif.) ("If they had done the same thing for my opponent, he would have won"). Bob Chlopak of the Friends of the Earth PAC explained the theory: "After the 1980 election we were faced with a Congress that was unlobbyable. We had to change the players to get the kind of legislation we need and that every poll shows the people want."

Their success was soon apparent. In one week in August 1982 an overconfident business lobby in separate committee actions lost two of its major goals—weakening the Clean Air Act and the pesticide law that permits states to impose stricter limits than the federal government. *Fortune* magazine was sufficiently impressed to conclude that the environmental lobby has "become so much stronger and more sophisticated that it deserves to be ranked with the National Rifle Association and the right-to-life movement as a super lobby."

Completing this recent list of "public" advocates are young lawyers who strive to counter the private interests' well-connected Washington lawyer-lobbyists. Creating "public interest" law firms, they undertake court litigation and advocacy before the state and federal courts, the federal regulatory agencies, and the Congress. Together this array of public lobbyists—most notably Common Cause,

Public Citizen's Congress Watch, and the Consumer Federation of America— has been instrumental in the passage of laws involving public financing for presidential elections, auto safety, job safety, credit reform, better meat and poultry inspection, and a national bank to extend credit to consumer cooperatives. More defensively, these lobbies have helped prevent the Reagan administration from attaining all its desired budget cuts and deregulation. The "Fair Action Budget Coalition," for example, defended effective social programs; thirty-eight groups in the nutrition field formed the "Safe Food Coalition" to frustrate attacks on the laws against carcinogens in food; and the Equal Justice Foundation and Alliance for Justice led the counterattack that enabled the Legal Services Corporation to survive.

But compared to the silent successes of the business bloc—the declining corporate income tax, procurement cost overruns, regulatory nonfeasance, which endure uninterrupted—the successes of citizens' groups have been indeed modest. One problem is the overwhelming size of the opposition forces. Consumers' Union estimates that all annual consumer lobbying resources equal only .3 percent of business advocacy advertisements ($3 million versus $1 billion). While special-interest groups can keep their agents stationed at all the important pressure points in Congress, the public lobbyists are lucky to have among them the equivalent of a single person working full time on any major issue.

To a Congress accustomed to servicing private-interest lobbies— who have time, information, and potentially, campaign money—the public lobbies stand at the back of a long waiting line. "There's the twenty-three-year-old consumer lobbyist and the businessman who gives you $5,000," congressional aide Peter Kinzler says. "Whom are you going to listen to?" One environmental lobbyist recalls waiting outside a closed committee session, surrounded by milling lobbyists from numerous industrial interests, known and unknown. Seeking stringent pollution control measures, he was heartened when, during one of the breaks, a congressman walked out and said, "I got one of yours in." His elation was tempered when he realized that the same congressman was delivering what looked like similar good tidings to the other lobbyists clustered in the hall.

Case Studies of Lobbying Techniques in Action

LABOR LAW REFORM BILL. This 1977 bill was among the most heavily lobbied pieces of legislation in history. Labor and business groups representing millions of members together spent more than $8 million and strained the postal system with 20 million pieces of mail. George Meany called it a "holy war" and one business coalition called the bill "Big Labor's latest assault on the individual human rights of every wage earner in America."

"It's our macho vs. their macho," one lobbyist told *The Washington Post*. Each side, for example, commissioned a poll showing that a majority of Americans agreed with its position. Each side paid for expensive economic impact studies to show congressmen how a victory by the other side would damage the economy. Both labor and business warned that campaign endorsements and contributions for the 1978 elections would hinge primarily on this issue. Why this effort? Because in Washington, where the appearance of power is often as important as the ability to exercise it, both sides believed the outcome would affect not merely this bill but also their entire legislative program and industrial relations in general.

Easily forgotten was the substance of the legislation, which aimed to ensure prompt elections among unorganized workers on whether to be represented by a union. It included stronger penalties against business violators (including double back pay for fired union organizers) and required speedier decisions by the National Labor Relations Board on charges of unfair labor practices.

The Right to Work Committee opposing the bill said it sent out about 12 million pieces of mail during the six months preceding the June 1978, filibuster. They were joined by the more credible National Action Committee for Labor Law Reform, a business coalition led by powerful organizations such as the Chamber of Commerce, the Business Roundtable, the National Association of Manufacturers, and the National Federation of Independent Business. Right to Work mailings were done by mass mail specialist Richard Viguerie.

Even before the House approved the reforms by a wide margin in

October 1977, the AFL-CIO had raised an $870,000 lobby fund from its affiliated unions by a special tax. George Meany had placed eleven key staff people on a special Task Force on Labor Law Reform to lead the lobby battle in Washington. More than 2,000 local union leaders were brought to Washington for briefings on the bill. They left armed with a twenty-one-page manual to help them resume the lobby battle on the home front. This organization helped the unions send more than 3 million pieces of mail to Capitol Hill and put 1 million signatures on petitions in support of cloture (i.e., stopping the Senate filibuster).

This double mass bombardment by mail put many senators under political pressure, and their offices under administrative burdens just processing all the generated letters. Democrat Dale Bumpers of Arkansas was one of twelve uncommitted senators courted relentlessly by both sides during the series of cloture votes. There were 50,000 Right to Work solicitations sent into his state. Concerned by the business deluge, a labor union official appeared in Bumper's office carrying shoe boxes filled with 8,700 postcards supporting the reform. He even offered to send more if the 1,000 or so a day Bumpers was receiving were inadequate. "Labor felt senators were impressed by the volume of mail they were getting [from business] and so they felt they had to generate a like volume" Bumpers said afterward.

The protagonists sent in not only mail, but lobbyists. One Senate staffer estimates that he saw five hundred people on this one bill. After the Chamber of Commerce sent its predominantly small-business membership a newsletter headlined "Big Labor Versus Small Business," virtually every small business association in Washington joined the corporate giants like Sears and Firestone to aggressively oppose the legislation. The U.S. Chamber of Commerce began paying for delegations of businessmen to come and spend a week lobbying on the Hill to counter the AFL-CIO's local COPE presidents, who had also flown in to do some arm-twisting.

In the end labor needed only two more senators for cloture, but no one wanted to stick his neck out and be the sixtieth senator. Unable to find two more votes and unwilling to gut the bill in order to get something, labor capitulated. Majority Leader Byrd shelved the bill after nineteen days of filibuster and a record six cloture votes. So while a 60 percent majority vote in the House had been considered a smashing success, nearly the same margin in the Senate was a major defeat. "The biggest thing working against us," said a bitter Howard Paster, the UAW's chief lobbyist, "was an undemocratic system."

CONSUMER PROTECTION AGENCY. What can you say about a bill that passed the House or the Senate five times in seven years, that was endorsed by President Carter, Speaker of the House O'Neill, and 150 consumer, labor, elderly, and citizen groups, that the public supported by a 2 to 1 margin in Harris surveys—and yet was defeated 227–189 in February 1978?

For eight years consumer groups had pushed the idea of a small, nonregulatory advocacy office which would promote consumer interests before other federal agencies. As the fourteen Democratic and Republican members of the Senate Governmental Affairs Committee unanimously concluded in 1977, "At agency after agency, participation by the regulated industry predominates—often overwhelmingly. . . . For more than half of the proceedings there is no consumer participation whatsoever. In those proceedings where participation by public groups does take place, typically it is a small fraction of the participation by the regulated industry." The purpose of this consumer advocacy office was to make regulation work better by making the adversary process work better.

On one side stood a coalition of citizen groups, who visited every wavering member of the House and who organized a "nickel campaign" that generated the mailing of 40,000 nickels to 83 undecided representatives. (A nickel represented the average cost per citizen for this "costly" new agency.) Arrayed against them were big-business interests—such as the U.S. Chamber of Commerce, the Business Roundtable, the National Association of Manufacturers, Armstrong Cork, Procter and Gamble, and Sears—who made the bill a litmus-test issue of a representative's fidelity to their creed. Speaker O'Neill said that he had "never seen such extensive lobbying" in his quarter century in Congress.

For example, the Business Roundtable hired Leon Jaworski to lobby against the bill in early 1977, and later hired the North American Precis Syndicate (NAPS) to send canned editorials and cartoons against the consumer agency to 3,800 newspapers and weeklies. These prepared statements—statements that never acknowledged as their source a business lobby opposed to the bill—appeared approximately 2,000 times, according to NAPS. Identical hostile editorials appeared in ten newspapers around the country, newspapers not of the same chain (*Oxnard Press-Courier*, Calif.; *Thomasville Times*, N.C.; *Mount Vernon News*, Ohio; *Middletown Journal*, Ohio; *Ypsilanti Press*, Mich.; *Santa Paula Chronicle*, Calif.; *Greenwood Commonwealth*, Miss.; *Roseburg News-Review*, Ore.; *Kentucky New Era; Murray Ledger and Times*, Ky.).

The U.S. Chamber of Commerce conducted a national poll in 1975, which it cited often over the next three years, concluding that "81 percent of Americans are opposed to a new consumer agency." The Library of Congress, however, discredited this survey as biased and unfair because the key question was phrased as follows (italics added): "Those in favor of setting up an *additional* consumer protection agency on top of *all the other agencies* . . ." This poll led an outraged Senator Charles Percy to denounce it from the floor, saying, "The dissemination of useless poll information does nothing to help the image of American business, which is at an all-time low."

Finally, business opponents were able to parlay their financial resources into success. One California Democrat in a meeting with consumer advocates half-joked that he might vote for the consumer bill if their groups could throw him the "$100,000 fund-raiser" he was forfeiting by supporting their position. Two swing House members candidly told labor lobbyists that they had recently and for the first time raised $20,000 to $40,000 from small-business groups, who had been instructed by the Chamber of Commerce to be opposed. One representative was told by his campaign finance chairman that their major contributors were opposed to the bill—at which point, to his credit, the representative fired his finance chairman. One Florida representative told Ralph Nader that he had no objections to the bill, but added, "I'm afraid that the Chamber will run a candidate against me in the primary."

Ultimately the opposition lobby had the money and machinery to propagandize that the issue was "big government"—not consumer fraud, not consumer health and safety, not one-sided regulatory proceedings. Thus the repeated refrain that the Office of Consumer Representation was just more "OSHA-like" regulation stuck—even though there was no reasonable comparison between the Occupational Safety and Health Agency, with its $136 million budget and the power to order business to redesign its workplaces, and a $15 million nonregulatory advocacy office armed only with the power of an advocate.

As the vote neared, many members acknowledged that they supported the bill on its merits, but didn't, as one said, "want to explain five hundred times in my district why the consumer office wasn't just more government." One Southern Democrat who swam against the current and voted affirmatively said, with some bitterness, "If we had voted today on a bill to abolish the U.S. Government, it probably would have passed." Despite a fiery floor speech by Speaker O'Neill, the vote tally against the measure hit 227, at which point business lobbyists watching from the House galleries stood up and cheered and applauded. Chairman Jack Brooks of the Government Operations Committee, a major sponsor of the bill, was not pleased. "Those who want it all," he remarked, "will lose it all."

THE VOTING RIGHTS ACT. The fight to renew and strengthen the Voting Rights Act differs from the Labor Law and CPA fights in that civil rights lobbyists battled not a well-financed lobby group like the Chamber of Commerce but an unsympathetic President and key committee leaders. Advocates of a strengthened law overcame these obstacles through a careful, broad-based, and ultimately overwhelming grass-roots lobby campaign. "It used to be political suicide to support a bill like this," said Senator Russell Long (D.-La.), "but now it's political suicide not to support it."

Prior to 1965, black citizens in the South were prevented from voting by a variety of ruses, including literacy tests, poll taxes, and physical intimidation. The 1965 bill outlawed these forms of racism and decreed that any election law changes in southern states had to be approved by the Justice Department. Later revisions, in 1970 and 1975, expanded the law to cover some northern areas and mandated bilingual ballots in Hispanic areas. The law worked: From 1960 to 1975, a Census Bureau study found, the percentage of voting-age blacks who were registered to vote more than doubled to within 4.8 points of the percent for whites, and today more than 2,400 blacks hold elected office in the South. As Senator Ernest Hollings (D.-S.C.) said during the 1982 debate on extending the bill, "The cliché is correct. It is the most effective civil rights bill ever passed."

But success created backlash, and when Ronald Reagan and the Senate Republican majority took power in 1980, civil rights advocates were worried. The law was up for renewal in the 97th Congress, and the new chairman of the Senate Judiciary Committee was none other than Strom Thurmond (R.-S.C.)—the Old South personified, who had led a walkout of the "Dixicrats" from the Democratic party in 1948 in protest over a civil rights plank in the party platform.

Facing a hostile President and chairman, civil rights leaders made a crucial tactical judgment—they started organizing *early*, in December 1980. The vehicle for the civil rights lobbyists was the Leadership Conference on Civil Rights, a (usually) loose agglomeration of over 150 civil rights groups, unions, church groups, and even organizations like the Elks and the National Funeral Directors and Morticians Association. The Leadership Conference knew it had to maintain unity among factions, for in 1975 feuding between blacks and Hispanics almost derailed that year's bill. This time the glue held. In a Capra-esque scene, black and Hispanic leaders filed into a meeting with Attorney General William French Smith, who had refused to meet with the two groups together. Gesturing to a Hispanic

98

leader, an NAACP official said, "If she leaves, we all do." Encouraging such solidarity was the job of Leadership Conference director Ralph Neas, who acknowledged, "My principal role is just making sure that people keep talking."

Working with Democratic aides, the coalition arranged for forceful testimony on still-common abuses in a series of hearings throughout the South. In October 1981 the House easily passed a strengthened Voting Rights Act that outlawed discrimination, without a requirement that discriminatory intent be proven.

All eyes turned to the Senate. Hundreds of citizens lobbied full time or part time. Dozens of litigators—the lawyers who had actually fought voting rights cases in the nation's courts—were brought in to educate and visit lawmakers. Minimarches, symbolically resonant of the 1960s, were held. Key states, whose senators sat on the Judiciary Committee, were targeted. Barton Gellman, in an article in *The New Republic*, describes one effort:

> All the strategists in Washington could not have put . . . victory together without the likes of Mona Martin, the president of the Iowa League of Women Voters. Charles Grassley, an Iowa Republican who sits on a key Senate subcommittee, was wavering on an important vote [in March 1982]. The Leadership Conference in Washington sent Martin a list of local organizers from unions, church groups, black and Hispanic groups, farm and education groups, and Common Cause. Martin then applied the heat where it counted. The Church Forum—representing denominations from Catholic to Episcopal and Baptist to Presbyterian—sent out "minister advisories" suggesting sermon ideas on voting rights. A "media committee" held press conferences, distributed slick p.r. packages, wrote Op-Ed pieces, and took out a quarter page ad in the *Des Moines Register*. Borrowing a wats line phone bank from a local business, Martin organized "telephone trees," which work just like chain letters. Grassley got five hundred calls from constituents in one day alone. "We were just letting him know that we expected him to do the right thing," Martin says. He did.

Despite the pressure the Judiciary Committee was deadlocked on key provisions. Lobbyists turned their attention to Senator Robert Dole (R.-Kan.), a key committee member who was wavering and who had up to then paid little attention to the debate. Common Cause, the citizen lobby "in charge" of Kansas for the coalition, turned to its patented device for grass-roots lobbying: phone banks. "Night Callers" from the national office in the capital made hundreds of calls an evening urging Kansans to write Dole. The same array of tactics they used in Iowa were called out—sermons, press conferences, editorials. It worked. Dole stepped in and in three days negotiated a "compromise" that essentially duplicated the strengthened House bill. As he left the podium where he announced the compromise, Dole muttered audibly, "Now would you get the Wichita *Eagle-Beacon* off my back?"

With Dole committed, other conservative Republicans began to support the bill. President Reagan, who had denounced the House bill as "extreme," gave the Senate bill his "heartfelt support." It passed the committee 13–4 and the Senate by 85–8, with even Thurmond and John Stennis (D.-Miss.) voting aye.

While special-interest lobbies have a near-veto over legislation they don't like, they don't always prevail with legislation they desire—certainly not always when they're trying to grab a bit more power or profits—for at least three reasons. It's harder to win passage than stop passage; occasionally publicity over excessive PAC giving can create a backlash effect; and often the special interest has such a poor case as to embarrass even its allies. The AMA, for example, got to the brink of success in its 1982 effort to largely exempt doctors from FTC jurisdiction, only to fall short in the U.S. Senate because of its poor case and publicized PAC gifts. When the drug lobby sought to extend the life of patents on drugs from seventeen to twenty-four years, for an industry among the most profitable in the U.S., it failed and inspired articles like Jack Newfield's in *The Village Voice*, "The Drug Lobby Soaks the Sick."

Although organized interests may not always prevail, they tend to have a shaping interest over the laws that govern us all—lobbyists and laymen alike. Too often, however, they engage in their lobbying legerdemain largely free of public scrutiny, for Congress has only the flimsiest of lobbying disclosure laws, laws even more primitive than those in the campaign finance area. In Franklin Roosevelt's day, Representative George Tinkham (R.-Mass.) once introduced legislation which would have required that lobbyists register and that written certifications be renewed each month. The House debate on the bill went so far as to suggest that lobbyists wear conspicuous clothing or badges to identify themselves. One congressman only half-jokingly proposed that lobbyists be required to wear uniforms designed to reflect their rank, importance, and affiliation.

The current lobby law, instead, has its origin in the Legislative Reorganization Act of 1946, whose language is so ambiguous that courts have interpreted it as applying only to groups and individuals who collect funds for the principal purpose of influencing legislation through direct contact with members. This leaves three gaping loopholes: (1) groups which do not collect funds *specifically* for lobbying purposes are not covered by the law; (2) if the group's *"principal purpose"* is not lobbying, it does not have to file disclosure reports: (3) only *direct* contact with Congress (not mass mailings, phone calls, etc.) is covered by the act.

To ensure that citizens know who is pulling the levers of power in Congress, new lobbying legislation is needed to identify major lobby groups, the issues they work on, the monies they spend. Equally important are the ad hoc techniques for bringing the lobbies out into the open. TV documentaries, increased press coverage, congressional investigations, citizen-sponsored investigations, and countervailing lobbies exposing one another—all these need both institutional and informal encouragement.

But whatever is done to air the actions of the organized lobbies, a citizens' lobby must at the same time become a political counterweight, growing in numbers, resources, and sophistication. Public interest advocates can be created within the government itself, as in the recently defeated proposal for a Consumer Protection Agency. Or it can be encouraged by the government via tax credits for contributions to public interest lobby groups. But ultimately, the backbone of any citizens' lobby must be citizens—active, organized, and informed.

3

Who Rules Congress?

*More and more people are coming to understand
that the Congress doesn't work . . . not from the
point of view of either the issues or the individual
members.*
— Representative Richard Bolling

We all recall the neat textbook diagrams in our civics books
outlining "how a bill becomes a law," that very logical process
which is our legislative trademark. A congressman submitted a bill;
it went to a committee which refined it and then reported it to the
floor; if it passed, and if the other chamber had passed a similar
measure, it went to a "conference committee" to iron out any
differences; after repassage, the President signed it into law. Things
were so simple.

Unfortunately life does not imitate art. The diagrams don't show
535 local heroes and potential presidents jousting among themselves
for power and prestige. They don't at all show who holds the cards,
or how those who control the process control the law. They don't
explain the *dynamics* of power, the shift and flow of forces that
make our laws. To get a more realistic picture, we must look at the
ruling forces of Congress: the committee system, which gives disproportionate power to forty-odd men (not women); the seniority tradition
which, to an extent, still chooses the men who will exert the power; the
rules of secrecy and power-brokering, which can seal the system off
from the people.

Committees—"Little Legislatures"

"Congress, in its Committee rooms," Woodrow Wilson observed in his 1885 *Congressional Government*, "is Congress at work." Permanent congressional committees are a necessary outgrowth of the heavy and complex work of Congress. A division of specialized labor became necessary as far back as the early nineteenth century in order to handle proposed legislation. In the Third Congress (1793–95), the House created 350 ad hoc committees, one to handle each bill. This clearly would not do, so by 1825 Congress had trimmed the system to 43 standing (i.e., permanent) committees, each with a designated area of authority.

But, as often happens, neither house could control its creations. Committees began to proliferate, as each member wanted "his" committee to provide him with a platform. By 1913, at the system's grandiose height, there were 61 standing committees in the House and 74 in the Senate. Reforms in 1946 cut the numbers to 19 and 15 respectively, but a new form of committee growth emerged: subcommittees. By 1970, counting standing committees and subcommittees, there were a total of 305 in both houses; by 1980, 320.

Committee proliferation contributes to a frenetic if not paralyzed Congress. In the 95th Congress one computer study found eleven-thousand separate instances when House members were supposed to be in two or more committee meetings at the same time. According to Representative David Obey (D.-Wis.), on days when the House was in session from January through May 1977, there were an average of 33.5 committee and subcommittee meetings held *per day*. There are 21 subcommittees with jurisdiction over a power dam, for instance. And the sight of six separate committees and chairmen elbowing each other to investigate Anne (Gorsuch) Burford's EPA created some sympathy for that unsympathetic lady. The two chambers seem to be reverting to the 1913 era, as more than half the Democrats in the House, for example, chair at least one subcommittee, double the proportion of twenty-five years ago. "If the trend is not reversed," predicted House Judiciary chairman Peter Rodino in

1981, "the day is not far off when every majority member will head a subcommittee. Then we will have no leadership and no 'follower-ships.' Everybody will be a boss."

Periodically Congress recoils at its committee creations and vows abstinence, even reform. But it can't kick the habit. Within the past decade separate "committees on committees" led by Representative Bolling (D.-Mo.), Representative Obey, and then Representative Patterson (D.-Calif.) all failed to reduce their number because while all representatives were appalled by the overall system, few volun-teered to surrender *their* subcommittee. For example, the Demo-cratic leadership supported Representative Patterson's reforms, which included merging the many energy committees into one. But Interior chairman Udall wanted to keep his jurisdiction over nuclear energy, and Commerce chairman John Dingell worried that his energy sub-committee would be subsumed into a new entity. The result: a substitute amendment that merely added the word "Energy" to the existing Commerce Committee passed 300 to 111. Sighed Patterson, after 19 of 22 chairmen went against him, "I really thought it would be close. From now on I'm sticking to legislation, not reform."*

Committees vary in size and importance, and there is a distinct committee caste system. The House Ways and Means Committee and the House Appropriations Committee, with 37 and 55 members respectively, determine our tax structure and federal budget, which touch the pocketbooks of us all. These two, plus the House Budget Committee, the Senate Finance Committee, and the Senate Appropria-tions Committee, are the big five of Capitol Hill, the ones with the most power and, by Washington's perfect logic, the most prestige. When Professor Richard Fenno asked members of Ways and Means and Appropriations why they sought out their committee assignments, the overwhelming majority said they sought "power," "prestige," or "importance." "The Budget Committee is where all the action is

---

*But hope springs eternal. In April 1983 former senators Abraham Ribicoff and James Pearson produced an important report on ways to improve Senate efficiency. Among their major recommendations is to eliminate 7 of the twenty current committees.

in Congress,'' said Representative Geraldine Ferraro (D.-N.Y.) shortly after joining the committee. ''I didn't like the way the budget's been coming out.'' Another said proudly of his Ways and Means assignment, ''It's the top committee in the House of Representatives. The entire revenue system is locked into the committee.''

The appointment of freshmen to these committees is a matter for great care. Traditionally—with the notable exception of 1975—they rarely get on the best committees because, said one veteran, ''It would be too risky to put on a person whose views and nature the leadership has no opportunity to assess.'' A careful screening ensures that nonconformists do not slip through. Sam Rayburn and LBJ never let anyone sit on House Ways and Means or Senate Finance without asking what he thought about the oil depletion allowance. When a Maryland representative was being considered for membership on the House Interstate and Foreign Commerce Committee, he was asked by Kentucky's John Watts, ''What's your position on tobacco?'' The representative replied half-jokingly, ''I don't smoke''—and was not appointed to the committee.

Not only is the leadership careful in committee picks, but so too are outside interests. Ray Dennison, the chief AFL-CIO lobbyist, called the Speaker's office the day after the 1982 elections to remind O'Neill's aides that organized labor was very interested in the composition of the committee handling trade legislation. When freshman Harry Reid of Nevada tried for a seat on Energy and Commerce in 1983, *he* was besieged by lobbyists who promised to help him if he pledged to help them on their bills. Disgusted, he withdrew. Representative Henry Waxman (D.-Calif.), a subcommittee chair there, explained the stakes. ''A number of issues on the Energy and Commerce Committee, for instance, were decided by one vote or two votes. Millions, if not billions, of dollars are at stake for major industries in this country.''

Newcomers still want to get on the ''best'' committees possible and struggle as intensively as the old pols to get there. For they appreciate, as *The New York Times* once editorialized, that ''a good committee assignment can make the difference between a brief and obscure service in the House and the kind of influence that means tenure for decades." (Each party in each chamber has a committee of the committees to place congressmen on committees; the twenty-four-person Democratic Steering Committee, run by the speaker, took over this function from the House Ways and Means Committee in late 1974.) Freshman congressmen begin jockeying for choice posts immediately upon arrival, if not sooner. Representative-elect Herbert Harris, from a Virginia district with many civil servants, spoke to about two hundred members in 1974, including most of the Democratic Steering Committee, in his successful bid to be seated on the Post Office and Civil Service and the District of Columbia committees. Another imaginative member, returning to Congress after an absence, desired a seat on a prestigious committee. So he hired an investigator to uncover the vulnerabilities and desires of then speaker Carl Albert. Armed with this information, he was able to tailor his argument to Albert—successfully. Freshman Bob Mrazek (D.-N.Y.) didn't have to engage in such subterfuge, for it was his good fortune to have beaten a nemesis of Speaker O'Neill's, the overbearing John LeBoutillier. So when Mrazek tried for a coveted seat on Appropriations in the 98th Congress, he succeeded. Recalled one observer of the Steering and Policy deliberations, "As they were going through the ballots, Tip kept saying, 'This is the guy that beat LeBoutillier.' "

The appointment process is closely followed, if not shaped, by the special interests. Why? Because of the two crucial functions served by committees. First, of course, they are the workshops of lawmaking—the place where legislation is buried or where it matures to be reported to the full chamber. If a bill fails to get out of committee, it is usually dead. If it is reported out unanimously, it nearly always passes. This is not because committees are a representative sample of the whole chamber's views, but because legislators tend to follow the committee's judgment unless there's an unusual reason to doubt it.

"When internally unified and buttressed in parliamentary privilege by special rules," wrote Stephen Bailey, "[the committees] can almost at will dominate the business of the parent chamber.'' This is especially true after the reforms of the 1970s, according to R. D. Markley, Jr., for twenty years a major auto industry lobbyist. "The way Congress has been restructured, if a measure you don't like gets to full committee, forget it, you've had it. It's down here in the subcommittees where you've really got to do your work.''

Aside from processing legislation, the committees have a second important function: holding hearings to obtain information and publicize issues. The success and effect of the hearings, in turn, depend on two things: how carefully prepared and tightly focused the hearings themselves are, and how heavily the press covers them. Neither element alone is usually enough for public impact. When Representative Kenneth Roberts held a series of revealing hearings on auto safety in 1956, the press ignored them and Congress passed the issue by. Nine years later, Senator Abraham Ribicoff's, and later Senator Warren Magnuson's, auto hearings were front-page news; one of the results was the National Traffic and Motor Vehicle Safety Act of 1966. Colorful and well-covered hearings helped establish Senators George McGovern (Senate Select Committee on Hunger), Frank Church (subcommittee on Multinational Corporations), and Howard Baker (Watergate committee) as national figures and presidential contenders. "If the sound of congressional voices carried no further than the bare walls of the chambers,'' former representative Clem Miller wrote, "Congress would disband. . . . To the congressman, publicity is his lifeblood.''

The Rules of Congress

The committee system guarantees that *someone* will dominate Congress. An elaborate set of congressional rules determines just who those leaders will be and how they will work their will.

SENIORITY. Congress employs a seniority system to allocate power. Parodying Darwin, the system has simply ensured the survival of the survivors. No other federal legislature in the world selects its leaders by seniority. Yet under the seniority custom—enshrined neither in law nor in written rules—committee chairmanships have been automatically awarded to the members of the majority party with longest continuous service on the committee.

The seniority system itself is less antiquated than the chairmen it perpetuates. From 1910, when it took hold, until 1945, seniority determined only three of every four House chairmanships. But between 1945 and 1975, it guaranteed chairmanships to all ranking committee members—except Adam Clayton Powell, whose misfortune it was to be both spendthrift and black, a handful of ornery veterans who crossed party lines, and the four chairmen purged at the start of the rebellious 94th Congress in 1975. In the Senate, where seniority began in the 1840s, only five senior members in 125 years have been refused chairmanships, the last one 50 years ago. And those who become chairmen stay chairmen. Only after Senator Karl Mundt of South Dakota had lain in a hospital bed for two years, wholly incapacitated by a stroke, did Senate Republicans in February 1972 reassign his position as ranking minority member of the Foreign Relations Committee.

Mere antiquity, of course, is certainly no crime. Though occasional relics gain chairs, in what Jack Anderson hyperbolizes as the "Senility System," infirmity is not the chief vice of the seniority system. Its faults are more serious. A legislative branch encumbered by the seniority custom belongs in neither a republic nor a democracy: it bequeaths inherited congressional power to unrepresentative lawmakers in an undemocratic way.

In a country whose population is young, urban, and geographically dispersed, the seniority system historically turned over most positions of power in Congress to "representatives" who were old, rural, and southern. As long ago as 1859 a northern Democrat bewailed the seniority system which gave "senators from slaveholding states the chairmanship of every single committee that controls the public business of this government. There is not one exception." Southerners consistently held more than half of all committee chairs in Democratic Congresses from 1921 to 1966—because they came from one-party states, and once elected they were routinely reelected. In 1969 they headed ten of the sixteen standing Senate committees. They chaired the five most important in the Senate in 1977: Appropriations, Finance, Foreign Relations, Armed Services, and Judiciary. But then, in an unprecedented development, even the seniority system surrendered to the infirmities of age. Within a year John McClellan (D.-Ark.), chairman of Finance, died; and John Sparkman (D.-Ala.) and James Eastland, chairman of Foreign Relations and Judiciary respectively, announced their retirements. An unusually large number of defeated incumbents, coupled with the takeover of the Senate by Republicans has for the time being eased the problem of elderly, southern chairs. In 1983 only 6 of 22 committees in the House and 3 of 17 in the Senate have chairmen from the 11 states of the Old South.

Seniority is not without its supporters, mostly older congressmen. It assures, they argue, independent leaders who strengthen Congress's position relative to the dominant executive branch. But the price of using seniority as a way of insulating Congress from the President is to insulate certain members from the voters and the rest of Congress. Assertions are also often made that seniority places men of experience in power, thereby assuring competence and continuity. But if age implies talent, why was the average at the Constitutional Convention (even including eighty-one-year-old Ben Franklin) merely forty-three? Why did cabinet officers under President Nixon average twelve years younger than congressional committee chairmen? President Johnson's seventeen years younger? President Kennedy's nineteen years younger? As the adage goes, thirty years' experience may be no more than one year's experience relived thirty times.

The worst excesses of the seniority system were resolved in recent House and Senate reforms. In a significant shift in 1973 (discussed below), the House Democratic Caucus decided to *elect* chairmen. As a result, in January 1975, although sixteen panels had their most senior Democratic member as chairman, five did not. The Senate Democratic Caucus also decided to elect committee chairmen in 1974, though out of historical habit every chairman chosen was still his committee's longest serving majority member. Thus, the seniority custom still appears to be the most influential consideration in the selection of chairmen, though it is no longer automatic.

SECRECY. Congressional secrecy, especially secrecy in committees, began at the beginning of Congress. From 1789 to 1795 the Senate met and voted entirely in secret, fearing slanted newspaper coverage. Then it finally decided to open its doors for regular legislative sessions, but still held secret ("executive") sessions to consider all treaties and many nominations.

Committees have traditionally enveloped their activities in secrecy, though recently things have opened up more. In the 1970 Legislative Reorganization Act, committees had to make public their roll-call votes—which some chairmen avoided by simply not taking roll calls. Many committee sessions used to be closed altogether. In 1969, 36 percent of all committee sessions were held in secret; in 1972 it was 40 percent—despite the Legislative Reorganization Act, which tried to encourage open proceedings. Then, in 1973, the House voted to require all committees to meet in public *unless* the majority voted otherwise, and the Senate permitted each committee to set its own policies—as some adopted the 1973 House rule. The next year, as a result, only 25 percent of all Senate committee sessions and 8 percent of House committee sessions were closed to the public. Today nearly all are open to the public.

Beyond usual meetings and hearings, "conference committees" must also be public. Conference committees settle any differences between Senate and House versions of a bill. Calling them the "third house of Congress," Senator George Norris lamented in 1934 that "the members of this House are not elected by the people. . . . There is no record kept of the workings of the conference committee. Its work is performed, in the main, in secret. . . . As a practical proposition we have legislation then, not by the members of the House of Representatives, but we have legislation by the voice of five or six members." As he left the Senate in 1970, Tennessee's Albert Gore blasted the conference committees as "secret meetings often not even announced until the last minute [where] a few men can sit down and undo in one hour the most painstaking work of months of effort by several standing committees and the full membership of both Houses.'' At times the chosen conferees are hostile to the bill being negotiated, or unrepresentative of the views of their chamber. So in 1981, after the House voted to eliminate sugar and peanut support programs from an agriculture bill, the conference committee retained both because a disproportionate number of Senate conferees came from farm states. And when the overall farm bill went back to the House for an up or down vote (no amendments allowed), the House approved.

Secrecy here is used to twist the results. ''You certainly get some different attitudes in a conference than you would anticipate by listening to speeches on the floor,'' one member told the Brookings Institution's Charles Clapp. ''There is one senator, for example, who is known primarily for a particular position on foreign aid. Yet in conference I never saw anyone fight more ardently for a different position.'' In a memorandum that got into Jack Anderson's hands, a Ford dealer summarized a discussion an aide had had on auto safety with former Senator John Pastore: ''The senator . . . told Bob that when a consumer issue is before him and the cameras are on, he is not about to be anything but supportive of the issue.'' In 1978, even a conference committee as significant as the one handling the comprehensive energy bill often met in rump, secret sessions. Again, by 1982 nearly all conference committees were open.

When members have to be publicly accountable for their actions, however, the result can sharply differ from secret lawmaking. Before the advent of recorded ''teller voting'' in 1970 (previously votes on amendments, which make up the bulk of our laws, were never recorded), SST funding was easily approved, with only 188 members voting. But the first year that members had to go on public record with their SST vote, it was defeated 217–203. While recorded votes on amendments are desirable, what about votes in subcommittee, which can be among the most important cast in Congress since they can control whether a bill dies quietly or emerges into public light? Rarely are these votes recorded and published.

THE HOUSE RULES COMMITTEE. On paper the House Rules Committee makes sense. Before any bill moves to the floor for debate, this committee sets the agenda for its debate, for example, specifying how much time will be allowed and whether members can offer amendments. But in practice the Rules Committee can become a star chamber for bills which do not strike its members' fancy, for they have the power to block a proposal by simply not reporting it to the floor. As Representative Morris Udall wrote in a newsletter, "The Rules Committee has an almost complete power to determine on important issues *whether the rest of us can vote at all*" (emphasis his).

From the 1930s until the early sixties the House Rules Committee was dominated by a coalition of southern Democrats and conservative Republicans who frustrated much progressive legislation. A reform called the twenty-one-day rule was introduced in 1949. This allowed the committee which first considered a bill to force it out of the Rules Committee if it had lingered there for twenty-one days. Two years later the rule was repealed. Its power restored, the Rules Committee later showed that it could thwart the will of *both* houses. After President Eisenhower's proposal for federal aid for school construction had passed both the House and the Senate, the Rules Committee refused to send it on to a House-Senate conference, thereby killing it.

The new Kennedy administration had similar troubles and decided it could not tolerate this nest of obstructionist conservatives. With the cooperation of Speaker Sam Rayburn, the administration managed to increase the size of the committee from twelve to fifteen, and to stack it with enough liberals to get an 8–7 liberal majority. Subdued, the committee has flaunted its power less since then. Today, since the speaker appoints all the members of the majority party, it is he in effect who controls the committee—not unaccountable autocrats like Representatives Howard Smith and William Colmer, as was the case one and two decades ago.

THE FILIBUSTER. In 1808 a New York representative, Barent Gardiner, was shot and nearly killed by a Tennessee colleague who had become irate as Gardiner droned on week after week on some matter on the House floor. Probably not as a result, the House has adopted rules limiting debate, since it would be cacophony, not democracy, to allow any of 435 representatives to speak without limit on any issue.

The Senate, however, is a different story. Its tradition of allowing unlimited debate—known and ridiculed as the filibuster—is, like the seniority system, an unofficial custom which has acquired the durability of Divine Law. Senators can talk on the Senate floor until hunger, sleep, illness, nature, or cloture stops them. Cloture, as established by Rule 22 in 1917, was a two-thirds vote to stop debate. Between 1917 and 1975, 100 cloture votes were taken, and only 21 in those fifty-eight years were successful. The record for consecutive talking in the Senate is Strom Thurmond's twenty-four hours and eighteen minutes in August 1957, against the civil rights bill of that year. In second place, talking for twenty-two hours and twenty-six minutes on the tidelands oil bill of 1953, was the late Wayne Morse, who would pin a rose to his lapel and threaten to hold forth until the petals wilted.

Recently, filibusterers have not had to go through the ceremony of droning on and on and . . . Instead, when Majority Leader Howard Baker is apprised that a filibuster will ensue, he arranges for a cloture vote a reasonably short time after debate has begun, since he assumes one will come sooner or later.

To its supporters the filibuster is the highest example of the right of free speech. "I think it is of greater importance to the public interest, in the long run and in the short run, that every bill on your calendar should fail than that any senator should be cut off from the right of expressing his opinion," said Senator George F. Edmunds, expressing an unusual sense of proportion, in 1881. Governor Adlai Stevenson saw it differently. "Every man has a right to be heard," he said, "but no man has the right to strangle democracy with a single set of vocal chords." Speech may be sacred and valuable, but only if there are listeners. Ironically when filibusters begin, almost all senators leave. To cartoonists and comics, the filibuster is a gold mine, providing scenes of posturing politicians reading selections from the phone book, or favorite recipes.

But the filibuster is more than a caricature of itself; it is an offense to the concept of majority rule, a device which allows a minority to obstruct what it does not like. It has been used in a variety of situations, by southern conservatives against civil rights bills in the fifties, by northern liberals against Reaganite measures in the eighties, or by ideologues intent on catering to their hardcore supporters. While from 1917 to 1972 there were 60 filibusters, from 1973 to 1983 there were 101. Consider, for example, what columnist George F. Will called the "trivialization of the filibuster" by Senator Jesse Helms during his filibuster against the nickel-a-gallon gas tax in 1982. "But what epochal issue caused pent-up passion to spill from the recent Republican filibusters? Just a nickel tax on a gallon of gasoline. And what was the principle at stake? That taxes were yucky? Would Helms, East, Nickles, and Humphrey have filibustered about four cents? Three? What would they have done about ten cents—threatened to blow up the Washington Monument?"

Proposals to allow cutting off debate by majority or 60-percent vote rather than the two-thirds vote of the old Rule 22 have been periodically made—without success in 1958 and 1968. But 1975 witnessed the most important change affecting the filibuster since Rule 22 was established. For the first time the Senate (voting 51–42) and its presiding officer, Vice-President Nelson Rockefeller, agreed that the Senate could constitutionally change its rules at the beginning of each Congress by a simple majority vote despite the two-thirds cloture rule. But as Senate reformers, led by senators Mondale and Pearson, were patting each other on the back about a 60-percent cutoff, the late and wily Senator James Allen exploited obscure procedural rules to *filibuster* the reform against the filibuster. It seems that Senator Pearson's reform motion contained two parts, one of which was not debatable but one of which *was*. "Jim Allen is a very good practitioner of the rules and he caught a mistake we made," sighed a chagrined Mondale.

Several weeks of political stratagems and procedural minuets followed, which concluded in a compromise reform: to cut off a filibuster would require not two thirds of those voting but 60 senators no matter *how* many were voting. Thus, if 100 senators were on the floor, the new rule made it easier to end a filibuster, but if only 80 senators were there, the new rule would require a three-quarters cutoff rather than a two-thirds. It was a step forward—but how big a step?

One giant loophole in the filibuster reform soon became apparent— the postcloture filibuster. Once cloture is voted, debate on all pending amendments is strictly limited to one hundred hours, or one per senator—*except* that time-consuming roll-call votes, quorum calls, and other parliamentary procedures do not count against a senator's one hour. So early in the 96th Congress then Majority Leader Robert Byrd persuaded his colleagues to limit postcloture debate to 100 hours, with quorum calls and any votes on amendments coming out of those 100 hours. Still, even the threat of a serious filibuster at the end of a session of Congress, when so much of a session's legislation is processed, can stop a bill dead.

The Rulers of Congress

1. COMMITTEE CHAIRMEN. In the 67th Congress, during the 1920s, Rules Committee Chairman Philip Campbell of Kansas at times refused to report to the House resolutions approved by a majority of his committee. When they protested, he is reported to have said, "You can go to hell. It makes no difference what a majority of you decide. If it meets with my disapproval, it shall not be done. I am the committee."

Today's chairs are less blunt than Campbell, though still powerful. Congressional reforms in 1946, 1970, and 1973–75 have checked some of the worst excesses: regular meetings are to be held; a majority can force a meeting over a chairman's objection; and a majority of the House Democratic Caucus can eject a committee chairman—an ultimate sanction no chairman can entirely ignore.

Committee chairmen, nevertheless, can exercise their power in an impressive variety of ways. First, with some exceptions, they can set up subcommittees, or not. Once subcommittee heads are properly picked, a chairman can then refer a bill to whichever subcommittee he thinks will treat it best. Former Appropriations chairman George Mahon once simply transferred environment and consumer matters from one subcommittee to another dominated by his conservative allies.

A second tactic is adroit use of committee staff. Chairmen hire and fire committee staff; if the staffers are at all shrewd they learn to be loyal to the chairman rather than to the committee at large. Consequently the chairman can garner information the others lack, and the rest of the committee becomes even more dependent on him.

Third, powerful chairmen can offer bargains that regular congressmen can neither match nor resist. To get his way, the chairman can offer to set up a subcommittee, to pass a bill with the representative's name on it, to allow liberal traveling expenses, to sponsor hearings where the representative can make his name. He can usually decide when a committee will meet and what it will hold hearings on. He decides the agenda for meetings, chooses the floor manager of a bill, and helps the speaker or majority leader select delegates to the conference committee. Even strong chairmen may lose occasionally, said Richard Bolling in one of his farewell interviews in 1982, but most usually prevail with the right combination of "a strong will, good mind, good staff, knowledge of procedures and issues, and the use of experience and relationships to other committee members." So it was not entirely hyperbolic when a *New Yorker* cartoon saw one congressman saying to another on the House steps: "There are days, Hank, when I don't know who's President, what state I'm from, or even if I'm a Democrat or a Republican, but by God I still know how to bottle up a piece of legislation in committee."

Chairmen as a group are quite diverse in terms of personality, intelligence, stature, and drive. But they hold one thing in common: congressional power. Three who have this power follow:

• *Senator Robert Dole*—Rarely has a Capitol Hill reputation undergone so dramatic a transformation as has Robert Dole's.

His role as the "hatchet man" of a vice-presidential nominee in 1976—and especially his televised description of the World Wars, the Korean War, and Vietnam as "Democrat wars"—were roundly condemned and helped contribute to Gerald Ford's narrow defeat. Dole's 1980 presidential campaign was even more lackluster. Apparently power is an elixer, for when Dole unexpectedly became chairman of the Senate Finance Committee after the 1980 Republican gains, he blossomed. He is now widely considered the equal of his powerful predecessor, Russell Long. Moreover, as he moved to the center of power he moved to the center of the political spectrum, alienating some former allies but making himself the "liberals favorite conservative" in the process.

Dole's decathlon was the 1982 "Tax Equity and Fiscal Responsibility Act"—an election-year tax increase (itself oxymoronic) that plugged several dozen loopholes cherished by business interests of every pinstripe. The tax battle had not started out as a struggle for tax reform waged in the name of fairness, although that is what it became. Almost as soon as the 1981 tax cut had been signed by the President, looming deficits of unprecedented size sent businessmen and even conservative members of Congress into a panic. The President refused to even consider eliminating or reducing his tax cuts, so Dole and his staff were forced to look elsewhere in the tax code for sources of revenue. With a tax code laden with new loopholes from the previous year's "bidding war," in which Democrats and Republicans vied to bestow breaks to curry business support, the search was fruitful: Dole's 1982 bill eliminated "tax leasing," a ploy allowing corporations to buy and sell tax breaks; it imposed a "minimum tax" on several industries given huge tax breaks the year before; and it tightened the rules on depreciation of equipment by corporations. The bill also had provisions for years dreamt of by

118

Democratic tax reformers, including items forcing wealthy individuals to pay minimum tax and withholding payments from unearned income from stock, bonds, and savings accounts.

"Long a reliable friend of business," lamented a political analyst for Ford, Exxon, and other giants, "[Dole] has undergone a transformation this year, keeping business's representatives at arms length, personally and procedurally." The wry Kansan seemed to relish his newfound role as the little Dutch boy of the tax code. Caucusing with fellow Republicans late one night, he was told by an aide that lobbyists were lined up outside the room "Gucci to Gucci." "They'll all be barefoot by morning," he shot back.

Dole floated many policy ideas but kept his final intentions quiet, and was thus able to maintain the initiative and keep the lobbyists off balance. His brashest ploy was the proposed chopping of the "three-martini lunch" business deduction down to a "martini and a half." It was two A.M. and the Senate had just been pressured by the restaurant association into defeating a plan to withhold taxes for waiters' tips from restaurant receipts. That left the tax hikers two billion dollars short. Dole and two aides huddled intensely at the side of the chamber, and when he emerged it was to serve up the "martini-and-a-half" amendment. The drowsy Senate passed the provision, leaving the unprepared restauranteurs in a bind: if there was one thing they wanted less than tip withholding, it was an appetite depressant on the businessman's lunch. So in the conference committee they asked to have the tip provision reinstated in exchange for the restored three-martini lunch. Dole, triumphant, agreed. The bill passed the Senate, 50–47.

Dole's adept use of the legislative process forced the White House to accept a fait accompli. Reagan's acquiescence to a $99 billion tax increase over three years drew conservative fire (William F. Buckley mourned "the collapse of Reaganomics"). And Dole's rhetoric did little to dispel such criticism ("I never really understood all that supply-side business").

The tax bill was neither the first nor the last time that Dole followed this pattern: searching for the political center, staking out an independent position, gathering support for it, and then presenting it to the President to support or be embarrassed. His Voting Rights Act compromise in 1982 earned Dole the slightly awed praise of civil rights leaders. As columnist Mary McGrory wrote, "Dole . . . gave away nothing sought by civil rights activists. He cut the ground out from under the White House, which, under the guise of 'strengthening' the ten-year-old bill, was attempting to gut its key provisions." His prominent role in developing the Social Security package, and in eliciting President Reagan's participation in the process, followed a similar path.

Clearly Dole is at the epicenter of congressional activity in part because of the sheer number of important matters under the jurisdiction of his committee, which handles taxes, Medicare, Medicaid, and Social Security. He is also concerned that the Republican party may wither if it does not broaden its electoral base. At the same time, in the debate over whether there is a "new Bob Dole," he observes tartly, "Maybe I've just been noticed."

This is true, to some extent. Dole was born in the small town of Russell, Kansas, and there was always a streak of prairie populism in his rhetoric. In addition, his World War II wound, which almost killed him and left him flat on his back and seventy-five pounds lighter for two years, gave him firsthand experience with suffering. And in the 1970s, quietly, Dole had shepherded the growth of the food-stamp program, traveling around the country with former Senator George McGovern to investigate hunger. Dole recalls, "I sort of remembered there were a lot of poor people out there, and that just sort of spurred my recollection." So his deviation from ideological orthodoxy did not spring full-blown in 1982.

A final ingredient in his growing legislative clout is his wit, which he uses to soften up his enemies and smooth his path. When he first moved up from the House to the Senate in 1969, he suggested the move had "raised the intellectual level of both bodies." At the confirmation hearing of his wife, Transportation Secretary Elizabeth Dole, he told the committee: "I regret that I have but one wife to give to my nation's infrastructure. TV dinners are a small price to pay."

But whatever the reason, Dole has clearly shifted his focus. Sitting in an armchair of his huge white office in the new Hart Building, its sixteen-foot ceilings towering over the bust of Lincoln behind his desk, Dole reflects on his perspective. "I feel I'm a conservative member of the Senate, but I don't equate conservatism with the propertied class or somehow having a tilt against social programs that affect low-income people because they may not be voters, contributors, however people look at that." Gripping the armrest with his crippled right arm, Dole speaks slowly and pensively: "You've got some people, in very vulnerable groups, that are going to need help. And it's great to say, well, they ought to go out and get a job or they ought to go and do this . . . but there are some who can't."

• *Representative Dan Rostenkowski*—The archetype of the big-city machine politician and now the chairman of the House Ways and Means Committee, Dan Rostenkowski approaches the battle over tax rates and depreciation schedules the same way he would have approached a local ward fight: with an ideology of winning. "I never start a fight that I don't fight to win," he once told fellow committee Democrats.

"Rosty" (as the thirteen-term legislator is known) learned his brand of politics from Chicago Mayor Richard Daley, who elevated him from an alderman post to the state legislature at the age of twenty-four and to Congress four years later. He was a loyal cog in the Daley machine, even to the detriment of his House career. At the 1968 Democratic convention, on the orders of Daley and Lyndon Johnson, the six-foot-two-inch, 225-pound Rostenkowski wrestled the gavel from diminutive Speaker of the House Carl Albert and quieted an anti-Johnson demonstration rocking the amphitheater. (Albert was so incensed at this very public humiliation that he prevented Rostenkowski from getting a leadership position in the early 1970s.) To this day he hews closer to home than most of his colleagues, returning to the district nearly every weekend. He also

121

has retained his position in the Cook County Democratic Party, and thus keeps a hand on the local patronage till.

From his Chicago education Rostenkowski, now fifty-five, learned the value of accumulating thank-yous and personal politics. Once, after a legislative favor he performed, Rostenkowski sent Representative Richard Gephardt (D.-Mo.) a simple note: "I keep my word. Dan." Another congressman told *The New York Times*, "He's a very tactile politician. He moves in close, uses his hands—to gesture, put a hand on a shoulder. He makes it very personal." Like his deceased mentor, Rostenkowski also knows how to hold—and nurture—a grudge. Six years after the same Democratic convention, where Senator Abraham Ribicoff had denounced the Chicago police's "Gestapo tactics," Rostenkowski had a chance to go up against a Ribicoff tax bill in a conference committee. He devoted himself to the study of tax law, and startled his previously unimpressed colleagues by demolishing the bill.

Rostenkowski's accommodating approach continued once he assumed the Ways and Means Committee chairmanship upon the election defeat of Representative Al Ullman (D.-Ore.) in 1980. For example, he accommodated business by allowing them to lavish him with campaign gifts and honoraria. Although he had no Republican opponent in the 1982 election, PACs donated $295,000 to his campaign. During the "race," Rostenkowski held his first $500-a-head fund-raiser in Washington, D.C., a burden he had been able to avoid before becoming chairman of the tax-writing committee. He had been among those pushing hardest for a doubling of the $9,200 honoraria limit for House members—for understandable reasons. In 1981, the year the limit was raised, Rostenkowski garnered $53,000 in honoraria. In 1982 he took in $51,898. His fondness for junkets, corporate-financed golf tournaments, and "fact-finding trips" took him out of town ever more frequently.

But the skills of a ward heeler and an ideology of victory at all costs have made his tenure as Ways and Means chairman a difficult one.

In particular, after Ways and Means established a two-to-one ratio of Democrats to Republicans in 1981 (or greater than the House ratio as a whole), a nettled Barber Conable, the ranking Republican on the committee, said in an interview, "You know why Rostenkowski feels threatened by me? Because I know the tax code and he doesn't." Also, Rostenkowski was utterly unprepared to master the new political reality of a Republican President *equally* determined to win. When President Reagan first proposed a sweeping three-year tax-cut in 1981, Rostenkowski was the most eager of all the Democratic leaders for a win—regardless of what the final bill looked like. "It all depends on whether you want to lose courageously or to win. I want to win," he said. Seeking a compromise, he undertook negotiations with the White House in which he made a series of inglorious retreats: from a one-year cut to a two-year cut to a three-year cut. Reagan, noticing that the Democratic chairman had essentially adopted his plan, decided not to compromise after all.

Finally, in an effort to win conservative Democratic support for his bill, Rostenkowski began a "bidding war" with the White House for pro-business votes. The Democrats added "sweeteners"—a 1,000-barrel windfall profits tax exemption for the oil interests, a tax break for commodity traders, a slash in inheritance taxes. The Republicans added the sweetners to *their* bill, too. Representative Barney Frank (D.-Mass.) denounced the approach as the "Vince Lombardi school of politics, where winning becomes the only thing." But unlike Rostenkowski, Lombardi usually won. A few minutes before the climactic vote Rostenkowski got a standing ovation on the floor of the House—from the Republicans.

Not surprisingly, President Reagan feels more comfortable working with Rostenkowski than with other Democratic leaders. The burly Chicagoan, in turn, remains willing to break with his Democratic colleagues and stake out a more conservative position. In early 1983 he infuriated O'Neill by opposing any attempt to repeal the third year of the tax cut, just when O'Neill and Majority Leader James Wright were prepared to scuttle it. (O'Neill exploded privately, "You made me feel like a fool!")

Rostenkowski wants to be speaker, and of all the contenders for the job he is still the closest to his golfing buddy O'Neill (who has endorsed Majority Leader Wright). But House liberals would be unlikely to forget his performance in the face of Republican initiatives in 1981.

• *John Dingell* and *Henry Waxman*—Together these two men exemplify conflicting breeds in Congress—the strong-willed and domineering committee chairman, and the independent and powerful subcommittee chairman. Dominating the House Energy and Commerce Committee on its most important recent matter, the Clean Air Act, they took opposite positions—yet were similar in their enthusiastic use of power.

Energy and Commerce deals with a wide variety of topics, ranging from nuclear power to hospital-cost containment to the stock market to air pollution to telecommunications to industrial policy to consumer protection. The five subcommittee chairmen are all "Watergate babies" first elected in 1974, and, because of the scope of their jurisdiction and the authority delegated to them, they have as much power as many committee chairmen. Like a magnet in a room full of filings, such a committee attracts some of the brightest young congressmen (and staff) of both parties, as well as huge volumes of PAC money and lobbying effort. Not surprisingly, Energy and Commerce does not operate on consensus, a condition well captured by *Congressional Quarterly:* "Almost every member engages in political horse-trading, scheming, vote-counting, and coalition building." Until 1983, when committee ratios changed after the Democratic gains, Republicans and conservative Democrats came close enough to a majority to complicate matters further.

To straddle this contentious committee is no easy task, but six-foot-three-inch John Dingell (who brags he is no "pantywaist") is up to it. Known by many nicknames on Capitol Hill—ranging in affection from "Big John" to "Big Feet" (because, according to an aide, "he can step on anyone he wants")—Dingell's fierce determination is legendary. In language echoed almost exactly by many of his colleagues, Representative Ed Markey (D.-Mass.) asserts, "In the Darwinian world that is Congress, the one man you want on your side is Dingell, and the one man you don't want against you is Dingell." Dingell has suffered his share of defeats in recent years, having pushed hard but lost on proposals like the Energy Mobilization Board and the Alaska lands bill. But even the aura of power can be translated into real influence.

Among his successes was the way he maneuvered his committee's 1981 budget proposal, the only committee plan to survive relatively unscathed by the Reagan cuts. As congressional committees hammered their final budget plans into shape under the reconciliation process, Dingell realized that his panel would be evenly split on the Democratic plan. So he convened a meeting, looked around him, quickly announced that the committee was unable to agree to a package, slammed the gavel down—and sent the plan to the Budget Committee for a decision. The Budget Committee passed the buck to the Rules Committee, which allowed a separate floor vote. The White House realized it could not win, and quietly included Dingell's language in its own plan. So when the House voted for President Reagan's final budget on June 25, 1981, the Democratic proposal for the programs under Energy and Commerce's jurisdiction—including Medicaid and Home Fuel Assistance—passed on a separate vote.

The chairman's strongly held beliefs often seem contradictory to observers. He is a dogged foe of the oil companies, and supported Representative Tim Wirth (D.-Colo.) in attempts to break up AT&T. He achieved public prominence for spearheading the investigation of the Environmental Protection Agency in 1983. An avid hunter, he is a member of the National Rifle Association, and is antigun control.

But his main concern is always for the interests of his native Dearborn and Michigan's auto industry. So he deviates from his periodically proconsumer stand to oppose automatic crash protection standards for cars. He supported an FTC exemption for the auto dealers (but not for the doctors). He embarrassingly and publicly blamed the decline of the auto industry on "the little yellow people." And he pushes for the weakening of the Clean Air Act, especially loosened auto emission standards, and refuses to extend the automobile fuel efficiency law that he helped pass in 1975.

In the 97th Congress Dingell had his chance, for the Clean Air Act was due for renewal in his committee. The atmosphere seemed conducive to such a change. A new and popular President wanted a new bill. A wide coalition of business groups mobilized to weaken the act—businesses that came from many industries (like coal and oil) but all claiming that they had been harmed by the law. More likely, however, they were driven by a fundamental animus toward government, since documented damage from pollution standards is rare. "It's definitely ideological," a former National Association of Manufacturers lobbyist told journalist Frank O'Donnell. So these business groups were unusual allies for the traditionally liberal congressman. But he, his partners, and President Reagen were determined to push for a weakening of the law, which brought him into head-on conflict with Henry Waxman—the other archetype.

Waxman (D.-Calif.) is the House's "Mr. Health," inheriting that mantle from his predecessor as chairman of the subcommittee on Health and the Environment, Paul Rogers (D.-Fla.) The forty-four-year-old, mustachioed Californian shows that liberals can be adept at wielding power, not only issuing press releases. When still in the California legislature Waxman and Howard Berman created a potent political machine, which a decade later helped elect four new Democratic California congressmen in 1982—Berman, Esteban Torres, Marty Martinez, and Mel Levine. Waxman controls his own PAC which gives money to sympathetic candidates from other districts, including Energy and Commerce members. Critics charge that this election assistance helped create the atmosphere for Waxman's narrow election to the subcommittee chairmanship, when he defeated the immensely popular Richardson Preyer, his senior, by 15 to 12 in 1979.

Chairmen of these "minicommittees" are especially powerful in a sprawling committee like Energy and Commerce, where they have the power to hire their own staff. So business interests seeking legislation have to turn to people like Waxman. "He's becoming more and more powerful," one business lobbyist complained to *Fortune*, adding hyperbolically, "Nearly everything business wants ends up going through his subcommittee."

One such bill was the Clean Air Act renewal. Waxman chaired

what was in Capitol Hill parlance a "bad" subcommittee, meaning the majority of the members disagreed with the chairman. And when it was bad it was very, very bad—for over Waxman's objection it passed a version of the law that significantly loosened pollution-control requirements for a wide spectrum of industries. It then moved to the full committee level for markup. Waxman had prepared the ground for a full-committee fight: in June 1981, he had released a leaked copy of the administration's draft proposal to gut the act, generating so much protest that EPA never submitted a detailed plan; he brought in pollster Lou Harris to tell his subcommittee in September 1981, "Never in my public career have I seen such strong opinion on one side of an issue" as public support for an unchanged Clean Air Act.

The odds against Waxman were daunting, but as a black belt in legislative judo he used the very strength of his enemies against them. The strength—and flaw—was business solidarity (or alternately, as Waxman put it, "the greed of the industry"). Many industries (coal, for example) supported provisions that hurt them and helped their competitors in the name of a common lobbying front. So if even *one* industry were given reason to stop supporting Dingell's bill, the coalition would unravel as interests separately competed for committee favor. Waxman and his allies began submitting specific, technical amendments to the bill, actually wheeling them into the hearing room in shopping carts. One after another they were beaten down, until in April 1982, Dingell finally lost and Waxman won on an amendment reinstating tight air-standards in national parks (thus eliminating the provision desired by the western utilities). Things were beginning to come apart for Dingell, who two days later suspended the markup sessions.

The Michigan congressman was not to reconvene the panel until August, a delay that worked to Waxman's advantage. Environmentalists were able to light a fire of public opinion under the committee. Lobby days, rallies (at which protestors wore gas masks and "Dirty-Dingell" T-shirts) and letter-writing deluges were coordinated by the Clean Air Coalition. The much-vaunted business campaign, orchestrated by a public relations firm hired by the industry, was less successful than earlier lobby drives. Representative Thomas J. Bliley (R.-Va.) complained to a business group in October 1982, "About a year ago I asked several of the industries located in my district for some grass-roots support for H.R. 5252 to counteract the thousands of letters I was receiving from environmental groups. What I ended up with was two letters from the plant managers."

Still, when Dingell reconvened the committee in August 1982, he believed he had the votes to win. (One aide to another congressman explained that Dingell is so overbearing that timid representatives are afraid to tell him they will vote against him—so he is constantly surprised when he loses.) Immediately Waxman offered an amendment to force the EPA to act strongly to curtail toxic air pollutants, and it passed 21 to 20—as a result the chemical industry, a key element in the coalition, now had reason to oppose the bill.

Committee sessions were extraordinarily tense, as in the following encounter described by Ruth Marcus in *The Washington Post:*

> Dingell has complied [with Waxman's invocation of the rule that amendments be read aloud] by having the clerk read the amendments at tongue-twister pace, over Waxman's objection that the reading was incomprehensible.
>
> [On August 16], wielding his gavel with ear-splitting force, Dingell refused to let Waxman offer an amendment. After a wait of an hour and three quarters to try to assemble a quorum, Dingell was then forced to recess the session when Waxman objected to the absence of enough members to proceed.

In the end time truly was on Waxman's side. Dingell held up committee work on the other matters in hopes of passing the bill, but the session ended without the Clean Air Act being reported out. President Reagan's request that the act be one of Congress's top priorities during the lame-duck session was politely ignored.

That John Dingell—as personally skilled and powerful a chairman as there is in today's House—could be stymied on his chief legislative priority shows how far the pendulum of congressional power has swung toward subcommittee chairmen like Waxman, who through detailed substantive knowledge and adroit use of procedure can stop a bill dead in its tracks. Here, though, the personal conflict between the two men has left a residue of bitterness. Dingell expresses a hatred of environmentalists and what they stand for, while the more even-tempered Waxman has let it be known that he considers the chairman's frequent losses of temper "inappropriate" and his actions often "arbitrary." But as an "Ace in the Congressional Air Wars" (in Michael Barone's description), Waxman knows that both men were playing to win. And he is not apologetic for his dilatory tactics: "I thought that what I did was completely appropriate under the rules; I used the rules. It's not pleasant, but"—he pauses with a sly smile—"I didn't come to Congress just to make friends."

These and other chairmen obviously wield substantial power, though not quite so autocratically as they once did, due to events that came to a head in 1974. The reforms erupting at the start of the 94th Congress led even such veteran observers as Eric Sevareid and *The New York Times* to say, respectively, things like "a minor miracle" and "the House will never be the same again." Yet what happened was not a one-month phenomenon following an unprecedented election, but the culmination of more than a decade of committee reform drive that began with a ripple in the late fifties and ended with near tidal force in the seventies.

Ever since at least the 1920s the House had been ruled by committee chairmen who, selected by the divine hand of seniority, were accountable only to their longevity. After the Democratic landslide of 1958, leading Democrats were dismayed to discover that they still couldn't implement their program because entrenched and conservative committee chairmen were not responsive to the electorate. This conundrum gave rise to the Democratic Study Group (DSG), composed of reform-minded congressmen, founded by then Representative Eugene McCarthy. Their zeal, however, noticeably abated in 1961. "With a Democrat in the White House the need for change around here was not apparent," says Richard Conlon, now the DSG staff director. "This was especially true for LBJ, who could work magic with his old buddies, the southern committee chairmen." Or, the President proposes and Congress disposes.

Yet, as noted, President John Kennedy had to team with Speaker Sam Rayburn in 1961 to compel the obstructionist Rules Committee to add three members to give the administration a favorable majority. The sixties also heard from Representative Richard Bolling, a cerebral member who exposed the House's ineffective and authoritarian ways in two books, *House Out of Order* and *Power in the House*. "It is here [in the House Caucus] that methods should be adopted," urged the prescient Bolling, "to assure that reform Democrats rather than Tory Southern Democrats control the essential committees."

The concern of Bolling and the DSG founders came into full play with the election of Richard Nixon in 1968. No longer could congressional liberals lean on their president for succor and inspiration. They were on their own . . . and under the thumb of the same old committee chairmen. By 1969, according to a DSG study, one third of the Democratic committee and subcommittee chairmen were voting against Democratic programs *more* frequently than the average Republican! Alarmed, the DSG began to mobilize. Unable to do anything about the sitting President—impeachment, of course, was merely a historical curiosity in 1969—the DSG turned its attention to its own chamber—and to the largely moribund House Democratic Caucus as a forum to educate the members about seniority and to push ultimately for elective chairmanships. Their strategy was based on an irrefutable fact: though reformers did not have a majority of the House, they did have a majority of the House Democratic Caucus; and if that body could guide committees and committee selection, it could break the grip of the southern chairmen.

Even this proposal met resistance from traditionalists. "When [James] O'Hara would go around and tell colleagues that the Caucus had to be the instrument of party policy and power," recalls UAW lobbyist Dick Warden, "people would just stare at him and ask what he was talking about." DSG leaders nevertheless pushed ahead and asked Speaker McCormack to hold monthly caucus meetings. The kindly Boston octogenarian, perhaps seeing what was to come, initially refused, until then majority leader Carl Albert changed his mind. "It was to become a Greek horse," wrote reporter Mary Russell, "inside the walls of Troy."

The caucus began reforming things, slowly at first. In 1971 it decreed that members could not chair more than one subcommittee, a move that made some congressional elders grumble but opened up influential spots to more members. The caucus also, in a breach of the pure seniority system, permitted a vote on any committee chairman if ten caucus members publicly asked for it.

This was progress, but at best a half-step. House decorum being what it is, few thought it likely that members would publicly announce the need to challenge a particular chairman.

1974 did not promise to be the year the reformers had long been waiting for. Yet a confluence of events launched the House on its most drastic and far-reaching reform in sixty years. The preeminent event was the election of 75 freshman Democrats who would comprise over one fourth of the 291-member Democratic Caucus. Younger and more liberal than their colleagues, neither wedded nor indebted to the *status quo ante*, this freshman bloc would become, in the only partly hyperbolic phrase of *The Washington Post*, "the Red Guard of the revolution."

The freshmen provided the DSG reformers with the sine qua non of their strategy: the votes to control the caucus. With the election in December 1974 of former DSG head Philip Burton as caucus chairman— the canny Burton being the most liberal member of the House leadership within memory—the caucus completed its four-year transfiguration from cub to lion.

Its work would be aided by three developments. First, lobbying groups like the UAW, Americans for Democratic Action, Common Cause, and Public Citizen's Congress Watch had been pressuring Congress to alter its antiquated ways. Indeed, Common Cause, four days before the crucial vote on committee chairmen in mid-January 1975, sent every member a thirty-one-page "report card" documenting the abuses of several chairmen, a report providing crucial information for undecided members. Second, of course, there were the public antics of the usually staid Wilbur Mills, which not only toppled that pathetic man but cracked the aura of invulnerability around all chairmen; if even "the powerful" Mills was flawed, what about the others?

Finally, the freshmen developed an unprecedented maneuver. After the House Caucus had voted one morning in December to elect all Appropriations subcommittee chairmen, the freshmen recessed for a luncheon meeting. Suddenly Appropriations Chairman George Mahon appeared and lectured the uneasy though respectful newcomers on how they had made a dreadful mistake in discriminating against Appropriations subcommittee chairmen. Which gave Connecticut Democrat Toby Moffett an idea. "This shows why it's a mistake to listen to chairmen on *their* terms," he told his peers after Mahon had departed. "Let's invoke them on *our* terms." With Floyd Fithian (D.-Ind.) taking the lead in developing the concept, the freshmen began organizing sessions where chairmen would come to them to be questioned. One veteran television newscaster ridiculed their audacity. "You've got to be kidding. They'll never come."

But they did, in a congressional rendition of the mountain coming to Muhammad. On the mornings of January 9, 10, 11, and 13 a total of fifteen chairmen trekked into H-140, the august Appropriations Commitee chamber in the Capitol Building, to answer a series of prepared questions. Armed Services Chairman Hébert for example, was asked, "Would you be willing to make public the budget of the CIA?" and "Will you support keeping open all bill-drafting sessions of the Armed Services Committee?" Some of the committee chieftains were contrite, like Banking Chairman Wright Patman (D.-Tex.), who even brought along, and read in its entirety, a prepared fourteen-page statement lauding reforms and his committee; some inflicted wounds on themselves like Otto Passman, chairman of a Foreign Relations subcommittee of the Appropriations Committee, who was asked why we gave foreign aid money to countries that tortured prisoners, and who replied, "Well, there are troublemakers in every country." Others were more testy, like Chairman Hébert. Yet all were treated civilly and with deference. "We gave each one of them a standing ovation at the end," said Moffett.

With the applause still ringing in the chairmen's ears, the freshmen and the caucus began making their moves on January 15 against the more oppressive and unpopular chairmen:

• The imperial habits of F. Edward Hébert, chairman of the House Armed Services Committee since 1970, finally caught up with him. He had assigned committee members to subcommittees without obtaining their preferences; he would not refer bills to their relevant subcommittees if they were opposed by the Pentagon; he refused to hold hearings on controversial administration policies he supported, like the Cambodian bombing and military aid to South Vietnam. Nor did he impress the freshmen in their meeting. Hébert announced that, rather than withdraw from Vietnam, we should have sent *more* men and weapons in order to win the war. Nor did it help his cause when he referred to the freshman members as boys and girls. He was booted out of his chairmanship 150–133.

• What caught up with Wright Patman was not imperialism but age. By 1975 the Texas populist was eighty-one, had been in the House forty-six years, and had been chairman of the House Banking Committee for twelve years. Apparently, in the minds of a majority of the caucus, this unblinkable fact mattered more than his widely admired record.

Patman's first act as a representative in 1929 was to urge the impeachment of Treasury Secretary Andrew Mellon for conducting outside business while in office. For the next four and a half decades he fought high interest rates and the banks. Patman was instrumental in passage of the 1969 one-bank holding company act and in derailing the proposed Penn-Central bailout loan in 1970. In 1972 he successfully challenged Wilbur Mills's tax giveaways known as "member bills"; and he attempted to issue subpoenas to investigate Watergate *before* the 1972 election, but was overruled by his committee. "Patman was the only man in Congress since

133

Estes Kefauver to stand up to corporate power,'' James Ridgeway and Alexander Cockburn would write. But critics could acknowledge all that and still argue that he was out of touch, sometimes rambling, and incapable of effectively running his committee. Also Henry Reuss—intellectual, articulate, and ''only'' sixty-three—presented himself as an attractive alternative. Patman went down 152–117.

• Seventy-four-year-old William Poage of Texas marched to a different drummer from most of his Democratic colleagues. *Congressional Quarterly* voting studies showed that between 1968 and 1974, Poage voted with the Republican majority and against the Democratic majority fully 54 percent of the time. His penchant for ultraconservative candor could also be discouraging. He once intoned, ''I am in favor of establishing a university of thugs, mugs, and other hippies in the southwest corner of the walls of Huntsville''—which is the Texas state prison. During a hearing on food stamps Poage asked an Urban Coalition witness why he was ''so concerned in maintaining a bunch of drones. You know what happens in the beehive? They kill those drones. That is what happens in most primitive societies. Maybe we have just gotten too far away from the situation of primitive man.'' For such primitive wisdom Poage narrowly lost his House Agriculture chairmanship, 144–141, to Representative Tom Foley (D.-Wash.).

As the headlines reflected in early 1975, it was the House which did the most reforming, perhaps because it had the most to do. Still, not to be entirely outdone, the Senate stuck a toe in the Watergate-reform current. The sixty-one-member Senate Democratic Caucus routinely approved all chairmen by a voice vote. But the caucus agreed that whenever 20 percent or more of them, at the beginning of a Congress, indicated disapproval of a committee chairman by secret ballot, they would get an up or down vote on him within forty-eight hours. The key was the secret ballot. Previously any senator could publicly ask for a secret ballot of any chairman, but none ever had. ''There was a fear of retribution,'' confided one senator. This change situated the Senate where the House was in

1973: there was the potential to vote out abusive chairmen whenever the Democratic Caucus got the votes and guts to do so.

Mills. Hébert. Patman. Poage. The Senate rules changes on electing chairs. Since these developments in late 1974, no senior member of a major committee in either chamber has been denied the chairmanship though a handful of subcommittee chairs have not gone to the longest sitting member. But the change has still been profound. "It's totally different," concluded Representative Richard Ottinger (D.-N.Y.) "Chairmen bring up votes they don't like because they know *they'll* be voted on every two years. They can't afford to alienate members of the committee." Representative Udall perhaps put it best. "It used to be that when you met a chairman in the hall, you bowed low and said, 'Hello, Mr. Chairman,' " said the Arizona Democrat. "Now when you meet a chairman in the hall, *he* bows low."

2. THE LEADERSHIP. The "leadership" usually means the speaker of the House, the House majority and minority leaders, and the Senate majority and minority leaders. Yet the "leadership" has not always led. Jack Anderson wrote of John McCormack's speakership: "Under 'Old Jawn,' the office of speaker, formerly the second most powerful post in the country, has become Buckingham Palace—honored and respected, but more ceremonial than functional." And under Speaker Carl Albert, as well as Senate Majority Leader Mike Mansfield, this trend continued. Leaders became more buffers than bosses, elevated more because of inoffensiveness and general popularity than because of leadership abilities. (Majority Leader Howard Baker and Speaker Tip O'Neill are less passive than their predecessors, though still more likely to mirror their chamber's consensus than to shape it.) One representative accurately said of congressional leadership, "They want someone who will do them favors and speak at their fund raisers and not make too many demands of them." A House aide added in 1978: "They couldn't stand a Sam Rayburn again but they do want a certain amount of leadership without having bills shoved down their throat."

It was not always so. Henry Clay, a brilliant thinker and powerful orator, entered the House in 1811, at age thirty-four, and was promptly selected speaker. His power and charm were so abundant that soon he and his "War Hawks" had actively seized control of their chamber and were pressuring the hesitant President James Madison into declaring war on the British. One leading student of the speakership, Mary P. Follet, has concluded that Clay was "the most powerful man in the nation from 1811 to 1825."

Clay deposited some of his power and prestige in the office. Few of his successors have equaled his eminence, but others have exploited the job's potential power. James Blaine, chosen in 1869, "Czar" Thomas Reed in 1890 ("The only way to do business inside the rules is to suspend the rules"), and Joe Cannon in 1903 were some of the strongest. Cannon, for example, decided whether a congressman could speak after first finding out what he intended to say. Eventually this was too much for the rest of the House, and rebellious members stripped Cannon of many of his powers in 1910. The main blow was removing the decisive power of appointing committee chairmen. Since then speakers have had a harder time dominating, but one managed: Sam Rayburn. His central ability was that of forming coalitions by dint of his personal persuasiveness—a talent equaled in modern times only by his Texas protégé, Senate Majority Leader Lyndon Johnson. LBJ was both persuasive and imperial. Senator William Proxmire recalled in a 1983 interview the differences in eras. "The biggest institutional change in the Senate is that we now have an effective caucus on the Democratic side. When I came in [1957], Lyndon Johnson ran the Senate. We'd have one caucus a year and hear Lyndon's state of the union address."

With Johnson the one exception, strong leaders have been even rarer in the Senate than in the House. Woodrow Wilson observed in the late 1880s that a senator, "however eminent, is never more than *a* senator. No one is *the* senator. No one may speak for his party as well as for himself; no one exercises the special trust of acknowledged leadership. The Senate is merely a body of individual critics."

Even after the Senate created floor leaders in the 1920s, Wilson's observation remained largely true.

A number of key prerogatives have been retained by the top leadership positions in each house. The speaker presides over his chamber and has the right of recognition, decides points of order, refers bills to appropriate committees, appoints half of the Democratic Steering Committee, chooses all of the Democrats on the Rules Committee, can create ad hoc committees to handle significant bills, and selects House members of conference committees. When he is not presiding, the Senate majority leader can be recognized by the chair before all other senators, participates in handing out committee assignments, and can help determine which senators will get money (and how much) from the Senate Republican campaign committees. As a member of the Republican Policy Committee, the majority leader is well placed to shape his party's and the Senate's legislative program.

Institutional arrangements, however, often have less to say about the power of these offices than does the personality of the man in the office. Sam Rayburn and John McCormack held the same job, with the same strings to pull and hurdles to overcome. But Rayburn used it as a base for single-minded domination of the House, while McCormack listlessly observed events. A look at the present congressional leaders shows their strengths and weaknesses:

• *Thomas P. ("Tip") O'Neill*—Second in line to the presidency as the speaker of the House, the most important Democratic official in the country and the target of Republican barbs and television ads, the gregarious and genial Tip O'Neill is more at home playing poker in North Cambridge than he is at Georgetown dinner parties. His father was a Cambridge city councilor and later the city superintendent of sewers. So for the young Tip (named after a baseball player who consistently foul-tipped off strikes until he walked), politics was as much inherited as acquired. O'Neill ran a losing campaign for the Cambridge Council in 1932, while still in college. Since then his career has been a remarkably unopposed rise to the top.

The next year he won a seat in the State House and became the youngest speaker in Massachusetts history eight terms later, in 1949. As state speaker he demanded absolute party loyalty. On one occasion he locked the chamber doors to prevent a maverick Democrat from abstaining on a key vote.

His political stock rose further when he succeeded John F. Kennedy as the representative from Massachusetts's Eighth Congressional District. He became a protégé of Majority Leader John W. McCormack of South Boston, who urged O'Neill's appointment to the powerful Rules Committee early during his second term. Though it was unusual for a representative to straddle the leadership ladder so early in his career, O'Neill's position was strengthened when his mentor McCormack ascended to the speakership and his friend Kennedy occupied the White House.

In 1971, O'Neill supported Louisiana's Hale Boggs for majority leader over liberal Morris K. Udall. Boggs rewarded O'Neill with the whip position, and after Boggs disappeared in a plane crash over Alaska in 1972, O'Neill announced his intention to seek the leadership. His only opponent withdrew, saying O'Neill did not have "an enemy in the House."

And he did demonstrate strong leadership during much of the 95th and 96th Congresses—by winning passage of a tough new ethics code and most of President Carter's energy package. "Davey," O'Neill told Representative David R. Obey (D.-Wis.), chairman of the Commission on Administrative Review that was responsible for shaping the new ethics code in 1976, "if you're going to write one, go all the way. I want a damn good code I can be proud of. You produce it and I'll back it up." Obey did, and he did. To get the energy package passed he established a special rule governing floor debate that effectively frustrated technical amendments from crippling the bill. *The Washington Post* called it a "legislative miracle." And O'Neill was often called "Jimmy Carter's best friend in Washington" for his nearly paternalistic counseling of the novice President.

Yet even before the election of Ronald Reagan and the loss of effective Democratic control of the House, O'Neill became frustrated in his attempt to exert leadership. His efforts on behalf of legislation for a common situs picketing bill, a consumer advocacy agency, cargo preference, and public funding for House races failed to persuade a majority of his colleagues. He spent the last two years of Jimmy Carter's presidency in rearguard action moderating the extent of the budget cuts and defense increases sought by the president; "I did not become Speaker of the House to dismantle the programs that I've worked all my life for," he said in 1979, a year before the advent of Reagan. O'Neill's difficulties had many root causes—an antipathy to Rayburn-like arm-twisting, the decline of Democratic party funds for candidates, the noncoattails of President Carter, Republican cohesion fueled by strong party financial support. And, as he repeatedly told reporters, "In any other country in the world the Democrats would be five parties."

The speaker's problems of course worsened after the election of 1980. Though the House retained its Democratic majority, the Republicans gained 33 seats—depriving O'Neill of the cushion he needed to absorb the usual loss of southern Democratic votes on economic issues. It became apparent early that Democratic unity would not survive the momentum of the Reagan budget cuts. Democratic leaders faced a painful choice. They could attempt to compromise by offering a leaner budget that could attract conservative Democratic votes (the approach taken by House Budget Committee chairman Jim Jones), they could try to slow the Reagan steamroller (and risk being called obstructionist), or they could go down to defeat and hope that they would be vindicated in the future.

O'Neill chose the latter course, giving the Republicans de facto control of the House, a political judgment that has been historically vindicated. For O'Neill—like Ronald Reagan, but unlike many of his Democratic colleagues—had a coherent ideological vision that allowed him to think for the long run. This path had few other adherents at the time, as witnessed by the scathing criticism he received from younger members of his party. Representative Les Aspin (D.-Wis.) told his constituents in a newsletter that O'Neill was "reeling on the ropes" and "in a fog." Representative John Conyers (D.-Mich.) called on him to resign.

But O'Neill, while depressed at the fate that had befallen his beloved social programs, was far from befogged. "Listen, you think I don't know my guys are criticizing me? The walls have ears around here," he growled at one reporter. "But I've always known exactly where I'm going. Everything has been geared to the first Tuesday of November." He hammered away at the Social Security issue, delaying a necessary political compromise until after the 1982 elections; he began talking incessantly about "fairness" and "equity," slamming the President as a "Hoover with a smile," whose "Beverly Hills Budget" showed he had "ice water in his veins." As the size of projected deficits and unemployment figures became apparent, members of Congress began to question the faith they had placed in Reaganomics so wholeheartedly a year before. Finally, in order to win passage of the tax increase in 1982, President Reagan brought O'Neill and other Democratic leaders to the White House for a Rose Garden handshaking ceremony.

O'Neill's payoff came when the Democrats gained 26 seats, infusing enough liberal votes to give him a de facto as well as de jure speakership. Thus bolstered, O'Neill orchestrated moves to impose greater discipline on his party. "Boll Weevil" Texan Phil Gramm, who had introduced several Reagan budgets, was removed from the Budget Committee, prompting him to quit Congress and run again as a Republican. The caucus also voted to discipline any member who endorsed a GOP candidate. On matters of policy he used his new power to negotiate a compromise with the administration on issues like Social Security, and to force compromise on issues like the antirecessionary jobs bill that passed Congress in 1983. And in 1983 the House Budget Committee passed a budget that was virtually identical to O'Neill's, in marked contrast to earlier sessions, in which the committee was determined to show its independence of the speaker. Adversary Phil Gramm said what a lot of critics had come to understand: "This idea that the Speaker's old and he's out of it is a bunch of baloney. The Speaker is still easily the most politically astute member of the House leadership. Easily.''

For the Congress and the general public, though, O'Neill's most important feature has been that he is the one northerner, the one old-fashioned New Deal liberal, who has been in a position of real influence in domestic affairs in recent years. Although he was initially an adamant supporter of America's role in Vietnam, O'Neill broke with his friend Lyndon Johnson on the war issue in 1967, becoming the first congressional leader of either party to do so. (When confronted by LBJ, O'Neill supposedly responded, "Mr. President, those are *Democrats* who are getting killed over there!") More recently, O'Neill showed his priorities by assigning in the 98th Congress the Equal Rights Amendment "H.J.R. 1" and the nuclear freeze "H.J.R. 2." O'Neill's devotion to the traditional Democratic agenda sometimes pains younger Democrats; a top aide once admitted to a reporter that he couldn't think of any time the speaker had gone against the wishes of organized labor. He looks like an old pol. He *is* an old pol—but one who has not shed a progressive social-welfare philosophy that has carried him through forty-five years in public office.

• *James C. Wright, Jr.*—He is a fifteen-term incumbent who spent 1978 polling, shaking hands, doing favors, fund-raising for colleagues, giving out $300,000 from his own PAC to Democratic candidates for the House, and speech-making in over one hundred districts from coast to coast. No, he's not running for President. Jim Wright of Texas spent his first six years as House majority leader in a precarious position—for instead of standing firmly on the leadership ladder looking up, he had to keep looking over his shoulder.

If Wright appeared vulnerable, it's because his victory in the December 1976, Democratic Caucus elections was so narrow and unexpected. Democratic Caucus Chairman Phillip Burton was the clear front runner (he was lining up commitments for two years before the vote), with liberal elder statesman Richard Bolling of Missouri solidly in second. Yet Wright and a few friends felt that if

141

the liberal vote split enough for him to survive two ballots, he just might exploit the issues of Burton's and Bolling's hard-to-get-along-with reputations. The strategy worked. After Wright squeezed past Bolling in the second round by two votes, Representative Richard C. White of Texas emerged from ballot counting in the speaker's lobby holding one finger high. The final count: Wright, 148, Burton, 147.*

Wright is often described as a pragmatic conservative. Yet he can adeptly maneuver to port or starboard to ride out a political storm. He began his career as a liberal Texas state legislator in 1948, calling for abolition of the infamous poll tax and supporting an antilynching bill, integration of the University of Texas law school, and a strict law requiring lobbyists to register. Then he lost his seat, turned conservative, then more moderate when he needed labor support for a Senate race, and then finally in 1976 he veered left again. During the 94th Congress he voted with the conservative coalition of Republicans and southern Democrats 59 percent of the time. After he became majority leader, however, he voted with a majority of Democrats against a majority of Republicans 77 percent of the time in 1978. By 1981 and 1982 he was a rhetorical progressive excoriating President Reagan's tax program as a safety net for the "wealthy" *and* a conservative cosponsering a constitutional amendment requiring a balanced budget. He was, in a word, agile.

Wright entered Congress in 1955 and landed immediately on the Public Works Committee. His nearly thirty years on the committee have been the cornerstone of his legislative career. From the beginning he championed the kinds of pork-barrel defense and public

---

*With a one-vote margin, any of 148 could be argued to have made the difference. Much attention, however, focused on the vote of freshman Barbara Mikulski of Maryland, a liberal activist who demonstrated how so often in politics personal relations count more than ideology. "Congressman Wright was very helpful to me last summer in breaking the ice with the Baltimore business community," she said after the vote. ". . . they felt I was a left-wing bomb thrower because of my populist background. And I was there when Wright needed me."

works spending that stimulated his district's economy and pleased labor and the military suppliers. Besides dams, canals, and highway projects, Wright led the fight for production of the hotly debated F-111 fighter jet and the B-58 bomber—both made by General Dynamics, which has a large plant in his district.

In public Wright reveals a studied eloquence and mellifluence. He is a powerful, perhaps the most powerful, orator on the House floor. (Of President Reagan's refusal to accept a $5 billion jobs bill in 1982, Wright said to his House colleagues, "I can't believe that the President, who just got $231 billion for defense, will strain at a gnat while swallowing a camel.") And given O'Neill's reluctance to appear on TV interview programs, Wright frequently appears as a forceful spokesman for national Democrats. Yet in person Wright is warm and folksy, a veritable caricature of the soothing, arm-around-the-shoulder style of "let's reason together" Texas politics. He is even more relaxed behind his mammoth oaken desk. The majority leader's inner office is a spacious, airy room with fifteen-foot ceilings and tall windows (built before air-conditioning to help let a breeze in and avoid stuffiness and smoke-filled rooms, he says). There is an elaborate fireplace crowned with a gilded eight-foot mirror. A picture of every House leader's hero, Mr. Sam Rayburn of Texas, graces the wall on the leader's right. The crystal chandeliers, Wright explains with a wink, were sent over from the White House because Teddy Roosevelt said the breeze-blown tinkling made him nervous but might keep the congressional leaders awake.

Ronald Reagan has kept Wright awake plenty beginning in 1981. In a remarkably candid and self-critical interview with David Broder in December 1981, Wright told how betrayed he felt when Boll Weevils (Gramm, Hance) appointed to important committees at his urging voted against the Democratic leadership on key votes and when he had to run hard for reelection because local conservatives were not very loyal. "There have been rewards, of course, but they've come so seldom this year," he told Broder. "I have been singularly unsuccessful in providing the kind of leadership this post would seem to require. At least I haven't been able to produce a majority on the three big critical votes [on budget and tax matters]. . . . It makes me ask myself if I had what it takes to be a leader.''

But he and O'Neill recovered well by 1983, as the recession and Democratic wins in 1982 brought the President of the other party down to human scale. His doggedness won him points and friends. ''Of the 269 Democrats in the House, Jim Wright has probably been in the districts of 200,'' said Representative Udall. ''When he comes asking for your vote, what the hell are you gonna say to a guy who's been in your district singing your praises?'' Most significantly, Wright personally began to breathe easier after Speaker O'Neill announced in March of 1983 that he would run for reelection in 1984 *and* would support Wright for speaker when his time came, ''as Carl Albert supported me when I was majority leader.''

• *Howard Baker*—For such an amiable and unassuming man, Howard Baker's tenure as majority leader has been fraught with surprises—from successfully holding together his majority with such finesse that he was widely dubbed ''the best majority leader since Lyndon Johnson,'' to announcing his retirement from the Senate early in 1983.

Baker was born fifty-seven years ago to a very prosperous and political family in a small town in eastern Tennessee. ''The place is built around the Bakers,'' a neighbor said once to a profiler. ''It's like a feudal setting, and Howard was raised very much like the lord of the manor.'' After service during World War II he went on to join his father's Knoxville law firm and marry Illinois Senator Everett McKinley Dirksen's daughter Joy. When his father died near the end of Baker's seventh term in the U.S. House in 1964, he ignored his family's advice and ran for the Senate seat vacated by Estes Kefauver. Though he lost, Baker garnered more votes than any other Republican in the state's history. He became the first Republican senator ever elected from Tennessee in 1966, and has been running for higher office ever since.

The courtly Baker first gained national attention alongside former

Senator Sam Ervin during the televised Senate Watergate Committee hearings in 1973. Displaying his flair as a country trial lawyer, vice-chairman Baker twirled his eyeglasses before 70 million viewers and dramatically asked, "What did the President know and when did he know it?" Yet Baker was a party man to the last. Watergate majority counsel Samuel Dash accused Baker in 1976 of having been a White House double agent, trying to scuttle the investigation—a charge Baker vehemently denies. "I think he was working hand-in-glove with the Nixon White House at the time," one senior senator told *The Washington Post* in 1978.

Whatever Baker's role during Watergate, he played it with just enough of the virtuoso not only to escape going down with the Republican ship, but to float to the top as the photogenic do-gooder his tarnished party so badly needed.

In 1969 and in 1971, Baker had tried unsuccessfully to succeed his father-in-law as Senate minority leader. He also failed twice to capture the vice-presidential nomination under Nixon and Ford. Tiring of embarrassing defeats, Baker made an untypically low-key bid to deprive lackluster Whip Robert Griffin of the leadership in 1977. Griffin was the heavy favorite after serving seven years of drudgery as former minority leader Hugh Scott's whip and picking up the tacit endorsement of his fellow Michiganer, Gerald Ford. Griffin believed he had solid commitments from at least twenty or twenty-one of the party's thirty-eight senators and his staff had even chilled a stock of champagne for his victory party. It was never held. Baker unexpectedly won 19–18, with one abstention.

As minority leader, Baker used his cohesive Republican voting block to exploit differences between liberal and conservative Democrats. But the wily Tennessean cast himself in a far more important role than spoiler. President Carter owed both his main foreign-policy victories in his first two years in office to Baker. In return for his crucial, eleventh-hour support of Carter's Panama Canal treaty and Mideast plane sale package, the President had to swallow two "Baker amendments": one allowed U.S. military intervention in Panama in future emergencies; the other secured twenty additional fighter planes for Israel and a Saudi assurance that American-made planes would not be flown against Israel. When Baker and his Republicans stood up against a Carter foreign-policy initiative—as they did on the SALT II treaty—there was little Carter could do to win over the support of needed conservative Democrats.

Baker had sought the minority leadership less because he has any particular ideology to espouse than because, as leader of the "outs," he would have a national forum from which to criticize the President and run for his job. In 1980 Baker unsuccessfully sought the Republican presidential nomination, but his campaign and its theme—that Baker was a "professional politician"—never caught on. In part Baker's attentiveness to his leadership job in the Senate prevented him from devoting enough time to the shopping centers of New Hampshire. But voters also rejected the very cordiality and lack of philosophical commitment that was Baker's Washington trademark.

When the voters shocked even Baker by giving his party a majority of the Senate in 1980 his first instinct was to look over his shoulder. Republican ranks were swollen with a large number of extremely conservative freshmen, many of whom distrusted Baker for his support of the Panama Canal treaty. He feared that he would be challenged for his job by Paul Laxalt (R.-Nev.), the President-elect's best friend in Congress. So Baker called Laxalt at 7:00 A.M. the day after the election and asked for his support; he got it.

Baker's task as majority leader has been to maintain unity among the often petty and strong-willed senators of his party (ranging in temperament from easygoing Alan Simpson to doctrinaire John East) and to explain the facts of congressional life to President Reagan. Baker's performance has won him frequent press accolades, including being voted the "best" senator in one press poll. But, as journalist Helen Dewar wrote, "If Johnson won by twisting arms, Baker wins by stroking egos." Or as Senator William Roth (R.-Del.) once remarked, Baker "is like a political neutron bomb. He destroys his opponents and leaves their egos standing." One oft-repeated example of Baker's carrot-and-carrot approach was his offer to let Democratic minority leader Robert Byrd keep his grand majority leader's office, an offer Byrd accepted. His solicitousness has allowed him to gain major concessions from senators like Jesse Helms, whom Baker persuaded not to raise any of the contentious "social issues" (busing, abortion, prayer in the schools) until after President Reagan's economic program was enacted.

Baker's success at forging a majority bloc nearly as coherent as a minority was one key reason for Ronald Reagan's first-year victories. Consider, for example, the vote to approve the sale of AWACS planes to Saudi Arabia. When debate began, a resolution for disapproving the sale had fifty cosponsors, only one less than needed to pass. Baker coordinated the barrage of persuasion and pressure emanating from the Oval Office, telling the President's lobbyists which senators were wavering and how to change their minds—even to the extent of deciding which senators rode together on trips to the White House. Later, when the Senate began rejecting presidential initiatives with equal vigor, Baker would meet several times a week with the President to urge compromise. In the end, then, his success as leader of the Senate fluctuated in direct proportion to President Reagan's popularity in Congress. This is particularly true of Baker, who sees himself as an ally and "point man" for the President rather than an institutional foe.

The senator's reputation as a moderate rests more on his temperate personality than on his politics. A conservative Republican, he is an outspoken advocate of big business and massive defense spending, with none of the populist tintings of Finance Committee chairman Robert Dole. Although Baker called the President's economic program a "riverboat gamble," it was a gamble he willingly took. He has supported cuts in food stamps and other social programs, and supported the MX.

At the same time he promotes the budget-cutting agenda of the Reagan administration, Baker has demonstrated an undiminished appetite for pork-barrel projects. A leading example is the Clinch River Breeder Reactor, which the General Accounting Office estimated will cost $8.5 billion if it is built. Opposed by President Carter and at first by President Reagan, the unpopular project has survived solely because of Baker's clout. William Greider's famous *Atlantic Monthly* article quoted Budget Director David Stockman as saying, "It just wasn't worth fighting. This [economic] package will go nowhere without Baker, and Clinch River is just life or death to Baker."

The 1982 lame-duck session where Clinch River almost met its maker was a particularly grueling time for Baker. As the leading congressional Republican, he served as a natural go-between for Reagan and the Democratic House on contentious issues like the gas tax and a jobs program. Equally grueling was Baker's role as leader of a rapidly fragmenting GOP majority—with fellow Republicans like Jesse Helms and Lowell Weicker, Jesse Helms and Alan Simpson at loggerheads. Earlier Republican cohesion had in large part resulted from habits learned while the party was in the Senate minority. As memory of the long exile receded, so, too, did the philosophical and fraternal solidarity of that era. This process was only bound to continue. For in January 1983, Baker announced he would not run for reelection in 1984, and probably *would* run for President when Ronald Reagan retired.

• *Robert C. Byrd* of West Virginia has always been an irrepressible climber, a disciplined organization man, and, in his own words, a "workhorse," not a "showhorse." He is also the minority leader of the United States Senate, or as he prefers to be called, the Democratic leader of the Senate.

Bryd's up-by-the-bootstraps rise to preeminence resonates of Horatio Alger. The future majority leader was born in 1917 and abandoned by his father ten months later, after his mother's death. Raised by poor relatives in the hills of West Virginia, he didn't learn his real name until he was sixteen. He began college at Georgetown University sixteen years after finishing high school; ten years of night school later he received his law degree, in 1963. After laboring for years as a butcher, welder, and grocer, the musical Byrd literally fiddled his way into the state legislature at age twenty-nine. He still saws out country music on hectic one-day swings back home and has even released an album. He's a home-state hero who has never had a close reelection challenge, even though he hasn't actually lived in West Virginia for over twenty-five years. After three terms in the House, he advanced to the upper chamber in 1958.

He was now a senator, but Byrd still hadn't "made it" in his own mind. The fastidious legislator began driving himself day and night to meet the personal needs of individual senators. A willingness, even eagerness to take care of the detail work disdained by most of his colleagues enabled Byrd to build up a large ledger of political IOUs. He advanced inch by inch, and in 1967 he was chosen secretary to the Democratic conference, until then a largely meaningless position. By 1970, Byrd was the indispensable insider responsible for scheduling votes, lining up supporters, and undertaking small favors. Since he did most of the work, Byrd reasoned, why not get the credit? In a coup that surprised nearly everyone but himself, Byrd called in his IOUs and defeated Ted Kennedy 31–24 for the position of majority whip, in 1971.

When benign majority leader Mike Mansfield let Byrd assume the day-to-day drudgery of legislative leadership—such as scheduling and negotiating unanimous consent agreements with the often hostile minority—Byrd came to the aid of his colleagues in ways large and small. (When the wife and daughter of freshman Senator-elect Joseph R. Biden [D.-Del.] were killed in a car accident just days after his election in 1972, Bob Byrd drove two and a half hours at night in the rain to attend the memorial service. He was the only senator to show up.)

Thus, when Mansfield retired in 1977, Senate Democrats gave Byrd by acclamation the leadership role he had already filled. Some of his colleagues worried about his political past and views. Byrd spent many years living down his youthful apprenticeship in the Ku Klux Klan ("a mistake," he now admits) and his fervent opposition to civil rights legislation. He kept the Senate in session all night when he filibustered the 1964 Civil Rights Act by reciting police cases against black men who attacked white women. He opposed

149

Thurgood Marshall's appointment to the Supreme Court, but fought to save Nixon nominees Haynsworth and Carswell.

After 1970 he took several measured strides leftward into the Democratic mainstream. This moderation of his natural Southern conservatism helped make him palatable to enough northerners to dump Kennedy for the leadership. He voted for some antiwar amendments; he led unsuccessful battles to block the nomination of Richard Kleindienst as Nixon's attorney general, in 1972; he mercilessly grilled Nelson Rockefeller about his wealth; his relentless cross-examination of acting FBI Director L. Patrick Gray in 1973 helped flush out some early facts about the Watergate cover-up. Although he still vigorously opposes busing, Byrd voted to extend the Voting Rights Act in 1975—a measure he had opposed twice before. He also supported committee reform, public financing of congressional campaigns, and a stronger ethics code for senators. By 1978 even Senator Edward Kennedy, commenting on Byrd's scheduling of progressive legislation on the Senate floor, said that his original doubts about him as majority leader are "no longer justified."

As the Senate's ambassador to the White House under President Carter, Byrd insisted that the Senate "is not meant to be a rubber stamp and it isn't going to be a rubber stamp." Only five days after President Carter's inauguration he blasted the new President for not consulting the Congress enough. Later he advised the President to fire his best friend, Bert Lance, who was in trouble about financial dealings. His relations with the White House remained cordial, even if distant, throughout Carter's presidency. Later, in his memoirs, Carter would coolly comment on Byrd's "pride."

For a man with obvious pride it was not easy when Robert Byrd had to make the transition from majority to minority leader after November 4, 1980. "Byrd is not the sort of person that you want on TV representing your party's position," one northern liberal senator told journalist Martin Schram. "Byrd's self-identity was as the majority leader . . . and losing the Senate had a far greater impact on him than on anyone else here." A southern Democratic senator agreed: Byrd is "having a very difficult time adjusting to his new role. . . . He feels a loss of power. And when you lose the aura of power, you lose everything here. It can damage one's psyche."

Unlike O'Neill in the other chamber, Byrd was not a very vocal critic of President Reagan. Indeed, he voted *for* Reagan's original budget cuts (which passed the Senate 88–10), offering the following explanation: "The people want the President to be given a chance with his budget. So I'll vote for it, even though, based on the assumptions they're making, I don't believe they're going to achieve a balanced budget by 1984." As with a fortune cookie, anyone can read anything into this statement, which mirrors Byrd's innate caution on all matters. This trait served him well running the Senate for the majority party in 1977–1981, but has reduced his effectiveness as a national Democratic voice. Yet despite some dissatisfaction among his colleagues, "you couldn't get three votes" against him if he were challenged, according to a southern Democratic senator and Byrd critic.

3. IDEOLOGICAL LEADERSHIP. Some "rulers" of Congress have great influence neither because of party nor committee position. Their sway owes more to the power of personality, belief, and presence—to the leadership of a cause more than a caucus. The two most prominent follow:

• *Jesse Helmes*—Courtly, owlish Jesse Helms (R,-N.C.) does not wield his power through his committee chairmanship, for he is only head of the Agriculture Committee, nor does he wield it through legislative skill, for his crusades and filibusters have won him more enemies than friends among his colleagues. Rather, Helms is the most important ultraconservative lawmaker because he has invented what has been called "a new form of politics" through his ideological pugnaciousness and his far-flung network of aides, lobbies, and fund-raising groups.

Helms irritates his colleagues and electrifies his followers. Democrat William Proxmire asserts that "in a sense Jesse is like [Senator Joseph] McCarthy. He is a force unto himself." In a bitter exchange

151

during the lame-duck session in 1982, while Helms was engaged in a prolonged filibuster of a five-cent-a-gallon tax on gasoline supported by the overwhelming majority of his colleagues, Republican Alan Simpson asserted that ''seldom have I seen a more obdurate, more obnoxious performance.'' But NCPAC czar Terry Dolan gushes, ''I think he ought to be President.''

The Helms Difference is not that his politics are so conservative but that he appears to view the Republican party (he once contemplated starting a third party) and the Senate itself as mere pulpits for his crusade. His organizational flagship is a political action committee called the Congressional Club, which in 1980 raised $8.3 million. It spends lavishly enabling Helms to outspend his 1978 opponent by thirty to one; in 1980 it spent $4.5 million to help fellow conservative Ronald Reagan become President. That same year it also helped congressional candidates, especially former POW Jeremiah Denton in Alabama and Helms protégé John East in North Carolina.

This mega-PAC is merely the most public face of Helms's labyrinthine network: there is also the Congressional Club Foundation, which lobbies Congress; a marketing firm; an accounting firm; a group called the Coalition for Freedom; the Institute of American Relations; the American Family Institute; the Center for a Free Society; and the Institute on Money and Inflation. These groups publish newsletters, help candidates, generate blizzards of mail on issues ranging from the gold standard to aid to Nicaragua, and even pay for fact-finding trips—in 1980 Senator Orrin Hatch, for example, was sponsored on a trip to meet fugitive financier Robert Vesco.

The young aides who run this disparate assortment of organizations have become powers in their own ''Right.'' Considerably flashier than their staid employer (Rick Carbaugh, a top assistant until 1982, owns three red convertibles), these assistants wield Helms's power and title as a blunt club for their causes. In 1979 Carbaugh and another aide flew to London, where sensitive negotiations were taking place that would eventually lead to the transfer of power from Rhodesia's white minority to its black majority. The aides showed up at Rhodesian Prime Minister Ian Smith's hotel room to offer encouragement and support for his position.

Supporting all these efforts is a pulsing wave of computerized letters emanating from Durham, North Carolina. The fund appeals made by these letters stem, in turn, from the hundreds of controversial amendments Helms has introduced since entering the Senate in 1973. Often attached to important legislation, these amendments force lawmakers to vote on issues they would otherwise prefer to avoid—issues like busing, sex education, abortion, and school prayer. Framed so simply that voting against them is difficult for lawmakers to explain, they prompted one senator to lament, "I voted against one of Jesse's amendments on sex education and my mother called me up to complain." Before 1981, Helms's kamikaze amendments usually lost by lopsided margins. But each defeat was fodder for another cannon shot of fund-raising letters.

This legislative style has its roots in his pre-Senate career, when Helms was a television and radio commentator. In his more than 2,700 daily editorials he attacked the civil rights movement (whose leaders had "proven records of communism, socialism, and sex perversion"), Walter Cronkite ("a hysterical crybaby"), and even Richard Nixon (guilty of "appeasing Red China"). Elected to the Senate with the slogan "Jesse Helms: He's one of us," he still carries the emotional baggage of the segregationist South. Helms refers to blacks as "Freds," and he has none on his staff. "You find me a conservative, competent black," he explained.

His role as conservative tribune has given him great influence over the executive branch—more than he has in the Senate. Early in Ronald Reagan's term Helms delayed the Senate confirmation of several State Department officials he considered insufficiently conservative. After four months an exasperated Senator Charles Percy (R.-Ill.)—not the most assertive of Foreign Relations Committee chairmen—pushed the nominations through.

But his bully tactics have been far less effective in the Senate itself. His star has declined, ironically, since the Republicans took control, and by the end of the 97th Congress he had become easily the most unpopular member of the Senate. In large measure this was because Helms was infinitely better suited to agitation in a minority than governing in a majority. For example, the chief responsibility of any senator from North Carolina is the preservation of the tobacco subsidy. (Ever mindful, Helms thanks anyone he sees smoking.) The main task of the chairman of the Agriculture Committee, however, is to hold together the coalition of competing farm interests and gingerly shepherd the farm bill to passage. The two duties should be a perfect match, but in his first farm bill Helms attempted to cut subsidies for other crops while surreptitiously boosting tobacco. His legislative ineptness was so severe that Senator Robert Dole had to take over the floor managment of the bill to guarantee its passage. Another example was his filibuster against the gas tax. When the Senate finally broke the logjam, Helms strolled over to the desk of Alan Simpson (R.-Wyo.), stuck out his hand, and said, "Let's be friends." Simpson, a courteous man who was disgusted with Helms's obstructionism, stared straight at Helms and said nothing. Finally Helms retreated.

Home-state newspapers have fretted that the Senate chill may extend to tobacco as well, and it is widely believed that Helms is vulnerable to a challenge from popular Democratic governor James Hunt. And in 1982 the voters of North Carolina delivered an ominous portent: six candidates backed by the Congressional Club went down to defeat.

• *Edward M. Kennedy*—At first he was merely a dynast, the legatee of a famous name. His 1962 senatorial opponent said he would never even have been in the race were his last name not Kennedy—and surely this was true. But the people of Massachusetts apparently didn't mind, and gave him brother Jack's old seat when he was thirty years old, the constitutional minimum.

In return, he has proved to be more than a nostalgic name. Franklin D. Roosevelt, Jr., after all, probably had a more illustrious birth certificate, yet never managed to parlay it into more than a few undistinguished terms in the House. Beginning his third decade in the

Senate in 1983, Kennedy was already the most influential progressive U.S. senator of the past quarter century.

Several interacting ingredients enabled him to achieve this stature. First, his personal mix of shrewdness, toughness, plodding hard work, and Irish charm bring to mind Justice Oliver Wendell Holmes, Jr.'s comment that the two Roosevelt Presidents succeeded less because of their brilliance than their temperament. Second, Kennedy's eloquence in public address gives him wide coverage and exposure. In private conversation he talks earnestly in fits and spurts, yet his prepared major addresses, as at the 1980 Democratic convention, usually leave an enduring imprint on audiences, even non-Kennedy supporters. Third, a solid political base in Massachusetts frees him—as Lousiana freed Long—to say what he thinks and do what he says. He can favor compulsory school busing for racial reasons and a woman's right to abortion, without fear of being driven from office.

Finally there is his "inevitability"—the unavoidable sense that this senator may be a future President, a sentiment which survives both his painful performance in 1980 and his graceful withdrawal in 1984. Such perceptions can become self-fulfilling, as former colleague Edmund Muskie explains: "He knows that power is constantly enhanced when people perceive that you could be President someday; it gives you the clout to get the things done you really want done in the Senate."

This notoriety creates a predictable amount of envy and resentment in an institution of ample egos. As one former Senate staff aide put it, "What is amazing is how much he does even though most of them up there hate him." What Kennedy does is to to take the lead on an unusually broad range of issues. In the past few years he has been a leading sponsor of national health insurance, airline and trucking deregulation, tax reform, "public participation" funding, congressional representation for the District of Columbia, antimerger legislation, a new federal criminial code, new FBI and CIA charters, a drug reform act, infant formula safety, and pension rights of women—not to mention legislation on small claims courts, consumer class actions, and hospital cost containment.

For the two years of 1978 to 1980, the chairmanship of the Senate Judiciary Committee provided Kennedy with a new bully pulpit from which to advocate his already lengthy national agenda—and with more staff. But Reagan's rise did not lead to Kennedy's demise. Indeed, after a slight readjustment period, he became a leading voice of the "loyal opposition." His was the first voice criticizing the growing U.S. involvement in El Salvador. Appreciating the importance of the surging nuclear freeze movement, he cosponsored with Senator Mark Hatfield the resolution that framed the national debate. And when the Reagan team erred, it was Kennedy who forcefully shot arrows into their Achilles' heels. For example: after Attorney General William French Smith grossly exploited a dubious tax shelter, the Massachusetts senator blisteringly said "I am tired of hearing about waste in programs to help people from a President who just this week defended a tax loophole which permits his attorney general to take $66,000 worth of tax deductions on a $16,000 investment. Before the President talks about welfare fraud again, perhaps he should add a new anecdote to his arsenal—about his millionaire attorney general who has exploited an illegal tax shelter that is nothing more than welfare for the rich." Attorney General Smith dropped his tax shelter. As joblessness and poverty worsened in 1981 and 1982, Kennedy remarked that "since Ronald Reagan got his job, three million Americans have lost theirs" and "Ronald Reagan must love poor people, since he's made so many of them."

And within the Senate itself it is barely perceptible that Kennedy is no longer a majority party chairman. For he has invented a new congressional mode—"policy forums" where he presides, much as a chairman would. Indeed, in everything but name, these are congressional hearings where Kennedy performs in his best role—as a figure who can dramatize and draw attention to his themes. In early 1983, for instance, he held a policy forum to discuss President Reagan's proposed $1.7 billion cut in Medicare for 1984. One witness testified from a wheelchair and talked about the budget cut in moving, human terms. Said another, an often-hospitalized widow, "I would like the President to know he's wasting his time trying to squeeze the old folks."

Though neither a chairman nor in the minority leadership, Ted Kennedy is a "ruler" of congressional liberals. As a result of a confluence of skill, persistence, pedigree, and luck, this senator has become, in conservative columnist George Will's phrase, the Democrats' "heavy hitter"—despite the weight of Chappaquiddick and the fact of Reagan. And his withdrawal from the 1984 race frees him to present his ideas without the kind of press skepticism that greets all presidential prospects, especially him.

After a decade of unprecedented reforms the rules of Congress have changed, for the better. It is now easier to end an obstructive filibuster; seniority usually determines committee and subcommittee chairmanships, but not always; chairmen are more equal than others, but no longer arrogant autocrats; much authority has devolved to younger subcommittee chairs, breaking the lockhold that a few major chairmen had on Congress; the Rules chairman rarely if ever can thwart the will of Congress or Presidents; the House Ways and Means Committee no longer makes freshman Democratic committee assignments; secret markups and conference committees are the exception, not the rule; and there are recorded votes on floor amendments.*

Rulers, as well as rules, have changed, for three reasons. First, since the South is no longer a one-party region, there are more competitive races and fewer members who serve two, three, and four decades. Second, more generous pensions have lured many members into voluntary retirement. Last, the economic stagnation of the late seventies and early eighties had a volatile political effect,

---

*There are still congressional rules that sap efficiency. "Nongermane" amendments—e.g., a repeal of tax withholding on savings accounts stuck onto a jobs bill—are allowed in the Senate, though not in the House.

helping usher in many new Republicans in 1978 and 1980, and many new Democrats in 1982. For example, fourteen incumbent senators lost in 1978 and 1980, so that by 1983 *most* senators were in their first term. "I remember Senator Javits telling me," said Javits's successor Alfonse D'Amato in 1981, "that in all his twenty-four years in the Senate and eight years in the House, he was a subcommittee chairman only once. And here I am walking right into two chairmanships!" Over in the House eight freshmen elected in 1980 were under thirty years old. And such Pentagon critics as Les Aspin and Ron Dellums, due to their seniority and rapid turnover, became chairmen of two House Armed Services Committee subcommittees. "I love to think of those southerners going in for a piece of pork and having to talk to Ron Dellums," said a bemused Pat Schroeder (D.-Colo.) of Dellums' military construction panel. "I don't think anyone has ever said no to those good ole boys before."

Some critics blame these changes of rules and rulers for Congress's recent inability to legislate either efficiently or imaginatively. It's true that rapid turnover, especially in the Senate, has caused a large loss of institutional memory there. And in terms of sheer skill, Al D'Amato is no Jacob Javits and Charles Grassley no John Culver. And it's also true that what used to take a couple of calls from a Rayburn, LBJ or corporate president to a committee baron now requires the persuasion of several subcommittee chairs and two Houses of Congress.

But whatever the result in individual cases, electoral turnover is merely the democratic process engaging in perennial self-renewal. And rules changes were designed to promote not efficiency but accountability. "That committee chairmen can't ram their priorities through committees makes it harder to legislate, but is that a bad thing?" asked former Representative Jonathan Bingham in 1982, adding, "The old concentration of power was a bad thing." Richard Conlon of the Democratic Study Group agreed. "The old days were marked by most members being shut out of meaningful participation in the legislative process. We have created a more open, fairer and better legislative process." If indeed Congress often seems divided and confused, it is probably because so are the American people. Capitol Hill mirrors the public schizophrenia—being for lower taxes and more federal spending, cleaner air and less regulation, arms control and getting tough with the Soviets.

No, if Congress doesn't work, it's not because the Congress is more open and younger, but rather because members of Congress are obsessively worried about time and money. All the good of the past decade has been blunted by the paralyzing problems of committee- and PAC-proliferation, both of which have been previously discussed. Consider the representative example of Representative Peter Kostmayer, a hardworking Democrat from Pennsylvania. He spent $58,000 to win his seat in 1976, lost in 1980, and then spent $600,000 to win again in 1982—a 1,000 percent increase. The evening before a March 16, 1983, morning interview, Kostmayer had attended six receptions; that afternoon he had five different subcommittee sessions scheduled. As the workload grows and year-round fund-raising continues, our elected leaders are losing the ability to deliberate and legislate. Indeed the democratizing reforms worsen in one way the role of money, in Representative David Obey's view: "Because we have such a decentralized system, any little special interest can worm their way into the process by finding some subcommittee chairman to give them a hearing." The final irony is that as chairmen and the leadership become less tyrannical, the House becomes more vulnerable to the outside "permanent government"—those "special interests" of Woodrow Wilson's opening quotation to Chapter 2, who still guide the Congress and exploit its procedures and players.

So who rules Congress? A century ago it was "King Caucus," then King Speaker, then imperial Presidents, then autocratic chairmen—and now King Cash. Members are run by the special interests who enable them to run for office. The answer, then, to this book's opening three questions—Who owns Congress?

Who influences Congress? and Who rules Congress?—is the same. Until that changes, the Golden Rule of Politics will prevail in the parliament of the world's greatest democracy—he who has the gold, rules.

4

Congress versus the Executive:
The Constitutional Ebb and Flow

Oh, if I could only be President and Congress too
for just ten minutes.
                                        —Theodore Roosevelt

Throughout the history of the United States there have periodically
been shifting power alignments between the executive and the legislative branches of government. Varying with the era and the character
of the President, sometimes the Congress predominated, more often
the executive. This continuing constitutional tug-of-war is the result
of the Founders' design of a unitary executive which can respond
quickly in the event of an emergency, balanced by a large, slow-
moving deliberative body, the Congress.

More than a hundred years ago, in the decades leading to the Civil
War, those who remained in Congress—men like Daniel Webster,
Henry Clay, John C. Calhoun—had more to do with directing the
nation's policies than did presidents like Millard Fillmore or Franklin Pierce. John Quincy Adams ran for a seat in the House after
retiring from the presidency in 1829; one could hardly imagine
Jimmy Carter or Ronald Reagan doing the same thing in the modern
era.

Until the Civil War, Presidents swore off "executive interference"
in the legislative process, in the phrase of President William H.
Harrison. This Whig concept of a limited presidency was endorsed

161

as a matter of course by Representative Abraham Lincoln during his one term in the House (1847–1849): "Were I President, I should desire the legislation of the country to rest with Congress, uninfluenced by the executive in its origin or progress, and undisturbed by the veto unless in very special and clear cases."

The change in the President's relation to Congress—the transformation of the presidency into the preeminent branch of government—began, of course, when Representative Lincoln became President Lincoln in circumstances that did not permit a passive chief executive. President Lincoln responded to the exigencies of the first few months of the Civil War by declaring martial law, calling up 75,000 troops, suspending habeas corpus, and spending $2 million in Treasury funds without the consent of Congress. When Congress convened several months into the war, Lincoln dutifully asked it to approve of his actions, explaining that he had not had the time to wait for it to gather. Presented with such faits accomplis, Congress agreed.

Democrat Andrew Johnson succeeded Lincoln to face a hostile Republican Congress. In part because of policy differences over Reconstruction, but largely for personal and political reasons, Johnson was impeached and tried, but not convicted—an episode that began a shift in power toward the Congress that stretched from Johnson to McKinley. According to one leading scholar, Lawrence H. Chamberlain in his 1946 book, *The President, Congress, and Legislation*, of thirteen major pieces of enacted legislation between 1873 and 1897, the President took the lead in one (the Silver Purchase Repeal Act), pressure groups in two, and Congress in ten (e.g., the Sherman Antitrust Act). "The most eminent senators," wrote Senator George F. Hoar (R.-Mass.) of this period, "would have received as a personal affront a private message from the White House expressing a desire that they should adopt any course in the discharge of their legislative duties that they did not approve. If they visited the White House, it was to give, not receive, advice."

This era of what scholar Woodrow Wilson aptly called "congressional government" ended with the presidency of Theodore Roosevelt. His vigorous personality and use of the White House as a "bully pulpit" swung public opinion over to the view that a President should lead, not follow. The power and influence of the President has risen gradually since that time—except for dips during the laissez-faire administrations of Coolidge, Hoover, and, to an extent, Eisenhower. Franklin Roosevelt, in his attempts to deal first with the Great Depression and then with the war, expanded the executive powers vastly, and perhaps more lastingly than any other President. FDR expanded presidential power not merely due to external crises but also because he was a political genius who could dominate Congress by using his personality to command public support. As a result, said one commentator, Congress didn't so much debate the bills it passed during the "First Hundred Days," as it saluted them as they sailed past.

Presidents Lyndon Johnson and Richard Nixon contributed measurably to making Congress a "broken branch" of government. Johnson's ability to manipulate Congress, his prosecution of the war, and his secrecy about its costs accorded little more than lip-service to congressional prerogatives. And when the 93rd Congress convened in January 1973, so great was Richard Nixon's contempt for Congress as a coequal branch of government that he did not even deign to deliver his State of the Union address in person, choosing merely to send it to the Capitol by messenger. The "imperial presidency" was in its heyday.

But Johnson's Vietnam War and Nixon's Watergate exposed how presidential power could be abused. The result of these two presidentially inspired catastrophes was a public and congressional backlash that led to a significant realignment of congressional and presidential power. In the early and mid-seventies Congress enacted major legislation increasing congressional control over warmaking and over spending (the War Powers Act and the Budget and Impoundment Control Act), restricting the CIA and FBI, providing for a special prosecutor to weigh charges against executive-branch officials, instituting a system of the public financing of presidential campaigns— and it forced a President from office. Between the extremes of congressional government and presidential government, subsequent

Presidents have had to operate with greater restraints than either LBJ or Nixon endured. And as will be seen, their success or failure turned more on their political and personal skills than on mere institutional hegemony.

This brief chronology notwithstanding, it is misleading to discuss the legislative and executive branches so as to suggest that an equal struggle is on between two sides, and that whichever side is stronger on an issue will prevail. A battle does go on—and Congress has indeed recently won several important skirmishes—but the field of play exists far from the executive goal line. No matter how hard the Congress may struggle on one issue, it is frequently overwhelmed by the vastly greater forces and focus of the presidency.

Perhaps the clearest example of lost legislative initiative is in the proposing of new laws—among the most basic of Congress's jobs. In the years before 1900 the great majority of laws passed each year originated with Congress; senators or representatives drafted them, pushed them, saw them passed. During this century, however, the source of legislative initiation has shifted. The greatest change came at the beginning of the New Deal, when the President was so firmly in control of lawmaking that the speaker of the house could address freshman representatives like a pack of Marine recruits and say, "We *will* put over Mr. Roosevelt's program." Since then, according to political scientist James Robinson, Congress has "yielded to virtually exclusive initiation by the executive." As President John Kennedy told his friend Benjamin Bradlee, "They're [Congress] impossible. Ever since Roosevelt's day all the laws have been pretty much written downtown [in the agencies]."

In large part Congress's loss of initiative is the result of a lack of expertise to deal with the myraid issues that confront it. While Congress has substantial committee and personal staff to help it conduct its business, this is no match for the executive, which has the enormous resources of the bureaucracy to draw upon. The result has been that in the last three decades perhaps 80 percent of the major laws passed have started in the executive branch, including nearly all foreign policy bills. This is not to say that whatever proposals a President sends Congress will become law. But most of the laws that *do* pass will be proposed by the executive—a fact true even of Jimmy Carter, the first President since Eisenhower who came to this office lacking a congressional background. Despite legislative rebuffs, succcessful domestic bills such as civil service reform and a windfall profits tax were his creations. And the major tax and budget cuts of 1981–82 clearly came from Ronald Reagan's White House.

Logrolling and Arm-Twisting

To persuade Congress to pass the laws he sends them, the President can use the time-honored technique of logrolling. This is a game of trading favors, in which the President gives congressmen bonbons and pastries to make them give away steak and potatoes.

Willing to make innocuous appearances or concessions to obtain a vote for a bill, the President can obtain it at little cost by showing up alongside a representative at a local school dedication, or giving him a pen used at the ceremonial signing of a bill announcing mammoth outlays for his district. It is more than vanity which lets legislators succumb to these blandishments. For many congressmen, especially those who have moldered away in the House for years, a presidential pat on the back can be a big boost. Even if the congressman is from the other party, the impact is to let the voters know that their man circulates with the prominent man in Washington. If his daily schedule prevents traveling to the state or district, the President can give a congressman the feeling of power even more easily. The President or one of his top associates (Nixon used Henry Kissinger, Carter often turned to Walter Mondale, Reagan uses James Baker and David Stockman) will telephone the congressman or take him aside and whisper a few words in his ear. The congressman, obscure and ill-informed only seconds before, suddenly becomes an insider. He now understands the President's burdens—which his carping colleagues cannot fathom.

The most common type of presidential patronage is the distribution (or alternatively, the withholding) of government favors. Consider the case of former representative Chet Holifield (D.-Calif.), a sixty-nine-year-old member in 1971. He represented the city of Whittier, an area dear to President Nixon, but he was more important to the White House as chairman of the House Government Operations Committee. In 1971, Nixon revealed a proposal for reforming the government: an executive reorganization plan, announced in a special address, which would have lumped seven existing departments into four giant agencies. To no one's surprise Congress hated the proposal; since each congressional committee takes as much interest in the executive department it oversees as an Italian prince did in the security of his small domains, Congress naturally resists any change. Holifield leapt to the front of the opposition, denouncing "the whole grandiose plan" as "political grandstanding for the purpose of putting Congress on the defensive for the political use of the President in the 1972 campaign." His opposition mattered, because his committee would consider the plan.

But Holifield had other interests besides the minutiae of executive organization: main among these was nuclear power plants. Like other early boosters of nuclear energy, Holifield hoped that the final stages of the system—breeder-reactors—would be finished before he was. By coincidence, many of Holifield's constituents also worked for one of the main contractors, North American Rockwell.

Inconveniently, the Nixon administration did not share Holifield's passion for breeder-reactors. Not, that is, until March 26, 1971, when Nixon invited Holifield to take a ride on the presidential jet *Air Force One*. There is no way to know what was said on the flight, but afterward Nixon pushed the breeder-reactors, and Holifield found new virtues in the reorganization plan. Never a great bargainer, Holifield made another flight five months later in the plane, with similar results; Nixon again pushed breeder-reactors and Holifield supported an administration version of a consumer-protection law.

Since the many offices on the President's side of government determine when and where much money will be spent, the President can offer other favors. For John Stennis of Mississippi and former senator Margaret Chase Smith of Maine, the President's Defense

Department had arranged contracts for local shipyards. Even if the decisions are already made, the President can use them as bargaining tools by making them appear to be the product of a diligent congressman. And so, when President Nixon was fighting for Senate confirmation of his Supreme Court nominee G. Clement Haynsworth, he channeled an announcement of a $3 million urban renewal grant through the office of West Virginia Senator Jennings Randolph (instead of the usual route, through Representative Ken Hechler, who represented the district). *You scratch my back:* Randolph looked to the voters as if he'd fought for extra money. *I'll scratch yours:* Haynsworth got Randolph's vote.

When dealing with congressmen from the opposite party, the President may also give the political blessing of "benign neglect." On the night of October 15, 1978, President Carter was searching for the votes to sustain his veto of the $10.2 billion public works bill, which he had criticized as being inflationary. He placed a call to a conservative Ohio Republican, Representative Sam Devine. Reporter Martin Tolchin described the late-night call:

> "Sam, I need your help on this public-works veto that I'm sending up," the President said. "The Democratic leadership is against the veto, and I have to call on my Republican friends."
>
> "Mr. President," Mr. Devine replied, "it's pretty ironic your calling on me, when you're doing everything possible to knock me out of the Congress."

It seemed that the President and Rosalynn had both made trips to his district to help his opponent, and Miss Lillian had also been scheduled to speak there. The following day, he voted with the President, however, and the veto was easily sustained.

Representative Devine was one of 53 House members, many of them Republicans, who received telephone calls from the President on that issue. Some say the President told them, "Go along with me on this vote, and I'll see what I can do for you," and promised that it was a vote he would not forget.

167

Similarly, when a group of southern Democrats from swing conservative districts were being wooed by President Reagan on his tax and budget cuts, one complained about going along and still having to face a Republican opponent supported by the popular President. Replied Reagan, "I couldn't look in the mirror in the morning if I did that." An audible sigh was heard throughout the room.

His "citizen politician" aura notwithstanding, Ronald Reagan's White House has proven among the best at presidential logrolling. Representative Norman Lent (R.-N.Y.) was promised that the A-10 Thunderbolt II attack plane, made in his district, would not be phased out if he voted for Reagan's $99 billion tax hike of 1982; he did. When Representative Tom Hartnett (R.-S.C.) visited President Reagan on the same measure, he complained that John Lehman, Secretary of the Navy, had canceled a visit to a naval base in his district. "Oh, don't worry," said the President; as soon as Hartnett got back to his office, Lehman was telephoning from Japan to say he'd be there. To get the vote of Edwin F. Forsythe (R.-N.J.) on a supplemental appropriations fight, the White House agreed to approve controversial regulations barring Japanese tuna fishermen from certain U.S. coastal waters, such as those off Forsythe's New Jersey district. And when the vote of Louisiana Democrat John Breaux was needed for the 1981 budget cut, President Reagan promised he would no longer oppose a new price-support system that would put the federal government back in the business of buying and storing sugar. (Was he bought? a reporter later asked Breaux. "No, I was rented," he answered.) Yet when David Stockman, the director of the Office of Management and Budget, was asked if deals were made to win votes, he airily said there were only "adjustments and considerations." But he added, "You think they have suddenly turned into pure public-minded spirits up there, who vote strictly on the merits?"

Reagan's administration has pioneered in two related "arm-twisting" devices that greatly aided its early successes. First, President Reagan is a strong supporter of big business—and they are strong supporters of him. Unlike, say, Jimmy Carter, Ronald Reagan can command the fleets of business lobbyists on behalf of his causes. So when Bob Traxler, a Michigan Democrat, told Reagan he couldn't support his tax bill, Reagan's White House didn't give up. In short order he got calls from top executives of GM, Ford, Chrysler, and Dow Chemical. When the American Jewish Congress asked a high official at Halliburton why he was calling senators on behalf of the AWACS sale, since Halliburton had no interests in the Middle East, the executive said, "The White House asked, and I like to try to do what they ask." On a wavering senator or representative the combined lobbying of the White House *and* the Business Roundtable, the U.S. Chamber of Commerce, the National Federation of Independent Business, and dozens of individual firms can have a decisive influence. Second, add to that the corporate PAC-RNC (Republican National Committee) availability of money and you have a near hammerlock on rationally self-interested members. Lee Atwater of the RNC explained to Elizabeth Drew how the system works:

The big story of the campaign is that this is the first time the White House has really been involved with the political-action committees since their birth. Carter didn't really do anything with them. We have a full-time PAC operation at the Republican National Committee, under Rick Shelby. A lot of PAC money will be dumped in the targeted races toward the end—between seventy-five and two hundred and fifty thousand dollars. You add that to the nearly fifty thousand dollars the Republican National Committee and the congressional committee combined can give to a House candidate, plus the thirty thousand dollars that can be raised by a Cabinet officer's visit, and you get a total of three hundred and thirty thousand dollars. This is money outside the district that we're making sure they get. We're making sure that everyone gets from a hundred and fifty to four hundred grand extra, and that's a big wallop out there in a congressional district. Much of the PAC money will have already gone in, but there will be an extra spring there at the end.

If the carrot doesn't work, there is always the stick. Richard Bond of the Republican National Committee was quoted in *The Wall Street Journal* as saying he had persuaded two Republicans to vote for the President's 1981 budget cuts by telling them, "Look—what if I guarantee we'll max out on you?"—which meant a $25,000 contribution. They agreed. What if they had said no? "I would have nailed them to the wall," said Bond. After Senator Charles Percy (R.-Ill.), chairman of the Foreign Relations Committee, led the opposition to Ernest Lefever's nomination as the assistant secretary of state for human rights, his nominee for a U.S. attorney position was held up by Reagan's political aide Lyn Nofziger. Said Nofziger, Percy should "understand that it is a two-way street" and that a U.S. attorney "should receive the same kind of consideration as the appointment of an assistant secretary of state." Fifteen minutes after Senator Rudy Boschwitz (R.-Minn.) became the only Republican member of the Foreign Relations Committee to vote against the proposed sale of five AWACS planes to Saudi Arabia in 1981, the Minnesota congressional delegation was notified that an Air Force facility in Duluth, Minnesota would be closed. And after Senator Robert Packwood (R.-Ore.) led the Senate opposition to the AWACs sale, the White House retaliated by quietly helping Senator Richard Lugar (R.-Ind.) when he challenged Packwood for the chair of the Republican Senate Campaign Committee. (Lugar won.)

Thought Control

The President's grip on recalcitrant Congressmen tightens an extra bit when he takes advantage of his enormous propaganda power. As Max Ways wrote in *Fortune* magazine, "The President—any President—is easier to write about than any congressional situation. Journalists minimize the importance of Congress because they are reluctant to explain that 'can of worms.' This neglect, in turn, leads to an actual reduction of the power of Congress, because public expectation clusters around the more readily communicable person of the President. In this society, which is perhaps more democratic than is usually supposed, power tends to go where the people think it is. . . . Journalists who will risk life and limb to find out what the President had for breakfast wouldn't walk around the corner to hear a Congressman deliver a reasoned explanation of his vote.''

Studies corroborate the apparent. Presidents' share of column inches on the front page of *The New York Times* grew from 58 percent in 1958 to 73 percent from 1970–1974. Yet even more than print, it is television that contributes to presidential control of the public debate in America. This phenomenon began in 1960 with the first telegenic candidate and president, John F. Kennedy, who said to an aide, nodding to a TV set, ''We wouldn't have had a prayer without that gadget.'' A Harris survey showed that support for the Vietnam War at times increased 30 percent after LBJ made a nationally televised appeal. Later, as antiwar sentiment spread, President Nixon made his ''silent majority'' speech to 72 million viewers on November 3, 1969. ''North Vietnam cannot defeat or humiliate the United States,'' he said. ''Only Americans can do that''—and this jingoistic approach helped slow the antiwar movement.

Congressmen come to resent the slavish attention which television and newspapers give the slightest utterance from the executive oracle. Compared with the difficulty a representative has getting his proposals into any printed page besides the *Congressional Record*, the President has not only free advertising for himself and his program, but also a guaranteed pulpit from which to blast his enemies. When faint-hearts had been making trouble about the way the Vietnamization policy was going, presidential aide H. R. Haldeman appeared on the *Today* show to suggest they were traitors. In the same vein Henry Kissinger told a group of prisoner-of-war families that the people delaying their sons' and husbands' releases were the doves of Congress. But the networks *refused* an offer by a group of antiwar senators to buy time to explain their position. ''I could buy time to sell soap or woman's underwear,'' complained Senator Harold Hughes, ''but not to speak as a U.S. senator on issues of war and peace.'' As Majority Leader Byrd said in support of an experiment to televise Senate floor debate:

Where a struggle exists over spending authority, the President can use television to veto a bill in full view of the American population—he can take what could conceivably be a private act and make it public. The subsequent Senate vote to override or sustain the veto, however, cannot be seen by the general public, only by the 426 parties accommodated by the public gallery.

Of course, the leading presidential utilizer of TV, probably ever, is Ronald Reagan. He is to television what FDR was to radio. Since his professional training is to project sincerity electronically and since he made his national public debut with a widely heralded TV speech on election eve for Barry Goldwater's 1964 presidential bid, it is hardly surprising that President Reagan frequently and adroitly gives presidential speeches on TV. His talks before the 1981 budget and tax votes generated a record-setting volume of mail and calls to Capitol Hill, which helped pull waverers over to his position.

Like the private interests which prefer to avoid the bother of lobbying by getting the "right kind of men" elected in the first place, the executive would just as soon pass up all the arm-twisting and electronic propagandizing. The way to do this is to make sure the congressmen never get to know anything that would put wrong ideas in their head. The formal name for this is "congressional liaison," but the best metaphor for it is an Oriental court in which the emperor, sealed off from the world by high walls, knows only what his courtiers and mandarins whisper in his ear. In time he becomes their tool, since his world is bounded by what they choose to tell him.

To a surprising degree Congress knows little more than what the executive branch tells it. When it gets ready to pass a new law for missiles or highways, it turns to the Defense Department and the Federal Highway Administration. While a stray outside witness— from a public interest group, or perhaps a refugee from academia— may turn up at congressional hearings, the bulk of what congressmen find out about new laws comes from the President's departments.

172

Congress itself is largely to blame, since committees can choose their own witness lists.

A major practical explanation for this dependency is its staff capacity vis-à-vis the executive branch. Another important reason is that Congress has not fully figured out that "Information Is Power." Executive departments started to get the message shortly after World War II, and jumped into action. Led by the ever-vigilant Defense Department, they set up the congressional liaison system—which means congressional lobbying by the executive. Starting with one lone assistant secretary of defense for congressional liaison, the network has grown to include at least 531 agents from twelve departments. They have charmed their way into not only the congressional heart but its buildings as well; the alleged space shortage on Capitol Hill does not keep the Army from spreading its offices over a huge suite in the Rayburn Office Building.

The point of stashing these agents within the halls of Congress is to make sure Congress knows the right facts about each department. In theory the liaison agents are not supposed to "influence" the congressman, especially by appealing to the public to put pressure on Congress. A 1913 law, the Executive Antilobbying Act, says that "no funds may be used . . . to influence in any manner a member of Congress to favor or oppose, by vote or otherwise, any legislation or appropriation by Congress." The only exception is that executive agents may "communicate with Members of Congress on request, through proper channels"—a clause that has been opened up to let the whole liaison troop roll through. Ready to answer any congressional request with an illustrated brochure about, say, New Steps in Defense or Advances in Securities Regulation, ready even to anticipate requests and shove possibly interesting documents into open hands, the liaison offices assume that politicians, like mountains, can be worn away by light but steady pressure.

Many congressmen are unhappy about the hazards of relying on the executive, but their moans are often muffled as they sink deeper and deeper into the executive lap. One of the most heavily dependent committees has been the House Armed Services Committee.

Representative Ron Dellums, (D.-Calif.), reported *The Washington Post*, once "took excerpts of the committee section [of an authorization measure] on aid to South Vietnam and compared it to the testimony of the Pentagon witness, a major general. The Committee had copied the general's statement nearly word for word."

What's wrong with this cooperation? Not just the danger that the departments will deceive—as a former liaison for the Equal Employment Opportunity Commission said, "We don't lie to them. We just tell them what will be the most persuasive, and don't volunteer all the facts." The real issue is that Congress might as well not even bother studying or approving the executive's plans when all it has to go on is the executive's information. As an exasperated Senator Muskie remarked in February 1973, to Roy Ash, then the director of the Office of Management and Budget, the administration policy was to spoon-feed Congress "the information you decide we ought to have in the way you decide we ought to have it and at the time you decide we ought to have it."

The final problem is that Congress often can't even get the information it specifically requests. More and more the real policy decisions are made not by various department heads but by the President's personal staff. These men don't have to talk unless they want to. One week before the Cambodian invasion of 1970, Secretary of State William Rogers calmly told a congressional committee that nothing big was about to happen. Henry Kissinger, as Nixon's personal foreign policy adviser, rarely appeared before Congress. Senator William Fulbright considered it a great coup when Kissinger deigned to eat lunch with him in lieu of showing up before the Foreign Relations Committee.

As the presidential staff grows strong from sustenance gained at the expense of its satellite departments, Congress might well contemplate two further threats to its power. One is the President's blunt intrusion into the mechanics of legislating. Despite laws forbidding the Oval Office to formally lobby, in August 1972, the Senate was voting on the President's arms-limitation agreement with the Russians. As reported in the *Congressional Record:*

Sen. Church: Some could be misled as a result of what is going on right now out in the Vice President's office. I was taken in there a few minutes ago and shown two models. One model is of the [Russian] SS-9. It stands . . . fully two feet off the table. It is a very menacing looking weapon. One is especially struck by the size of the scale model of the SS-9 when it is compared with the model, also to scale, of the [U.S.] Minuteman missile which sits next to it . . .

Sen. Fulbright: May I ask the senator, since I have not been invited into the Vice President's room, whether the Vice President is now a substation of the National Security Council? Is it used for the purpose of influencing the votes of the senators? . . . I thought it was a ceremonial hall for the Vice President. However, it is now an exhibit hall for the National Security Council. Is that what it is now?

Sen. Church: Apparently so.

Sen. Fulbright: Mr. President, this is rather peculiar in view of the fact that officials of the National Security Council, including Mr. Kissinger, refuse to come to the Hill for committee hearings. Now instead of coming to the Hill to testify, they have the exhibits here and ask senators into the Vice President's room so they can see these models.

Unlikely as it sounds, the other danger of increased presidential power is the *even greater* amount of pandering to private interests it encourages. After a brief look at Congress's many cozy ties to private lobbies, it may be hard to imagine that any other part of the government could be as thoroughly influenced. Recent Presidents, however, have not just responded to the secret desires of private industries, but have actually spurred them on.

As mentioned previously in "Logrolling," President Reagan's White House has perfected the art of choreographed deployment of outside lobbyists and PACs on behalf of their cause. Journalist Hedrick Smith described the process before the first battle of the budget in April 1981:

175

[Lyn] Nofziger ran a political blitz in 51 swing Congressional districts, 45 of them in the South. His operation tapped wealthy organized groups like the Republican National Committee, the National Conservative Political Action Committee, the Moral Majority, business political-action committees linked with the national Chamber of Commerce, National Association of Manufacturers, the American Medical Association, local civic clubs and scores of other groups interested in cutting Federal spending and taxes. They were spearheaded by Administration and Congressional speakers and by a team of workers using direct mail and manning phone banks.

"The premise of the operation is that political reforms and the impact of media have made it so that a Congressman's behavior on legislation can be affected more by pressure from within his own district than by lobbying here in Washington," [Lee] Atwater explained.

This view of the President as promotion man is hardly reassuring to those who dream of a separation of Business and State. But it cannot come as a surprise when so many administration officials are on brief sabbatical from corporate work. It is useful to recall Eisenhower's cabinet of, as *The New Republic*'s TRB dubbed it, "eight businessmen and a plumber." Lyndon Johnson's former aides Clark Clifford and Myer Feldman now work as lawyer-lobbyists in Washington law firms. Nixon's former congressional liaison Bryce Harlow had to leave his job as congressional liaison for Procter and Gamble to come to the White House. When he left the administration, he returned to P&G where he teamed up with Mike Manatos— former special assistant to Lyndon Johnson. Peter Flanigan and John Connally both toiled for business interests in Washington after serving Richard Nixon's interests. The Nixon and Ford administrations' energy advisers, from William Simon to John Sawhill to Frank Zarb, all came from the Wall Street financial community. In the Reagan administration, Washington looked like a suburb of Wall Street. For example, here are the affiliations of the initial six staff appointments that the Reagan administration made at the Environmental Protection Agency: counsel to Johns Manville, counsel for Adolph Coors Company, attorney for the Business Roundtable, Exxon attorney, lobbyist for Crown Zellerbach, and communications director for Aerojet Liquid Rocket Company, which was charged by California with illegally dumping 20,000 gallons a day of toxic wastes. Little wonder that Washington wags began calling it the "Environmental Pollution Agency."

Power of the Purse

In an undertaking the size of the federal government, where percentage-point changes in spending for a single program can mean billions of dollars, control of the flow of funds is doubly important. On paper Congress has always had the power to appropriate money—to rein in the President by choosing where to spend allocated funds, to cut budget requests from executive agencies, to spend more than the President wants on social or military programs (often in collusion with the affected agencies themselves). But until recent reforms the struggle over power of the purse was decidedly one-sided, with Congress not even putting up much of a fight.

Fifty years ago economists led by John Maynard Keynes figured out that if countries wanted to avoid the boom-and-bust cycles which had led to the Great Depression, then *someone* had to keep track of how much money was coming into the government (through taxes) compared with the amount flowing out. The Budget and Accounting Act of 1921 gave the President the power to draw up a "national budget" for the whole federal government. Congress might have tried to share the power—and, for a few brave years in the forties, it did prepare a "legislative budget"—but then it gave up.

So from the time of Franklin D. Roosevelt to the time of Richard Nixon, Congress operated at a marked disadvantage when it came to drawing up the budget, partly through its own abdication. It did its budget work in the dark, with no independent source of information on executive requests and their overall economic impact. (Once during this period, when Senator William Proxmire pressed budget director Robert Mayo about items in the Defense request, Mayo loftily replied that "the President's flexibility is better served by not getting into a debate on what is and what is not in the Defense budget.") And it was hampered by the short amount of time it had, compared to the year of secret haggling within the executive branch leading up to the final budget requests. Most important, Congress's budget-making system was so scattered and haphazard that no over-all planning was possible. There are parts of the legislative process in which that didn't matter: those who authorize agricultural subsidies didn't need to know a thing about new weapons systems. But when dividing a set amount of money among many competing needs, there must be one giant funnel through which all the decisions pass. The White House and the Office of Management and Budget provided that. And Congress was also fettered by the two-tiered way it spent money, with first an authorizing committee (say, the Senate Armed Services Committee) authorizing the spending of money, and then the Appropriations Committee actually determining the amount spent.

The ultimate way that the President controlled the flow of funds was one that, when abused, finally forced Congress to seize the federal purse-strings. Before 1974 a President was de facto allowed to impound money allocated by Congress—that is, he could simply decide not to spend it. Chief executives before Richard Nixon had used the device sparingly, but on this as on so many other matters Nixon acted excessively and provoked Congress to pass the Budget and Impoundment Act of 1974. With regard to impoundments, Congress's victory was virtually complete: they were outlawed, with the exception of allowing Presidents to delay spending of money if Congress approves.

But two of the Budget Act's other provisions were even more important. First, the act finally created an independent source of information and economic projections, the Congressional Budget Office (CBO). The office's staff (currently 200) was headed from its inception until 1983 by one person, former Brookings Institution economist Alice M. Rivlin. As budget activities heated up each year, Rivlin testified two to three times a week before committees and subcommittees. In 1981 alone CBO used 31,000 pages of computer printouts a day. Rivlin was first appointed during a time when the Democrats controlled both houses, but members of both parties acknowledge that CBO's numbers have been the most accurate (and most pessimistic) of any during recent budget battles. In tandem with this new source of analysis, the President would now have to present his economic assumptions to Congress along with his budget message.

The Budget Act's other important effect was the creation of budget committees in each house and the initiation of a budget process itself. The budget committees were charged with considering each year's budget as a whole, recommending specific levels of spending, revenues, and public debt, fixing target budgetary surpluses or deficits, and dividing up the total among broad categories of spending such as defense or education. The appropriations committees continued to act on individual spending bills, but did so within the committee's budgetary guidelines. According to the original plan, Congress would vote on the committees' target figures in May before taking up the individual appropriations, and again in September, in order to reconcile its budgetary goals with its actual spending outlays.

The scheme was designed to increase congressional power, but from the beginning appropriations chairmen and subcommittee leaders and authorizing committee chairmen were wary of creating a "super-committee" that would absorb the entire legislative process into its purview. To avoid this the act specified that budget committee membership be rotated and that other committees be represented on it. And its powers were very tentative. The process did not fully come "on line" until fiscal year 1976; each subsequent year budget committee chairmen in both houses gingerly challenged bills that they thought would balloon into uncontrolled spending. For example, Representative Robert Giamo (D.-Conn.) opposed fuel assistance on budgetary grounds, even though it would benefit many of his constituents.

Such a committee has attracted a different breed of representative from most powerful committees, especially in the House. The members tend to be younger and more highly educated. Budget committee members of both parties have also tended to be more conservative than the congressional norm, with the Democrats on the House committee making up the core of the so-called "balanced budget Democrats" or "neo-liberals." These younger members' congressional education has taken a different path from most, for they are forced to balance the aggregate demands of competing interests rather than press the case of a special constituency. Explained one Ways and Means Committee aide, "Rather than being stuck in one committee—Education and Labor, Agriculture—and having to work for their interests, they have worked above it and have had to make trade-offs, early in their careers."

At the beginning of the 97th Congress Representative David Obey (D.-Wis.) and Representative Paul Simon (D.-Ill.) were defeated for the chairmanship of the House Budget Committee by a lawmaker far more typical of the panel—Jim Jones (D.-Okla.). The low-key Jones (who proudly asserts he is not "a flashy back-of-the-wagon pitchman with elixers") was a fiscal conservative very willing to go with the Reaganite flow in 1981, when budget battles made him, in *Newsweek*'s words, "the most influential budget-maker on Capitol Hill." Jones's conservatism and the priority he placed on drafting a budget that would win the support of the right wing of his party led him into frequent conflict with the more liberal speaker (who also had a different strategy for fighting Reagan). O'Neill's mistrust of Jones led him to appoint archrival Richard Bolling, who in 1981 called Jones a "Judas goat," to coordinate the Democrats' response to Reagan's second year budget proposals in 1982.

Even given its political culture of fiscal frugality, the Budget Committee would not have its considerable impact were it not for one tool placed in its hands by the Budget Act—reconciliation. This is the legislative device that brings aggregate spending goals into line with the money voted by Congress for various purposes (or, as used by Ronald Reagan, vice versa). Reconciliation was first used in 1980, but its scope was necessarily limited: it was used only at the end of the process, when the most important decisions had already been made, and it was used only on new programs, not previously authorized spending or entitlement payments.

Still, Congress had by the beginning of the 1980s gained an unprecedented amount of budget control. The process was streamlined, and increasingly powerful budget committees—now committed to using reconciliation to bring spending into line—were accruing influence and setting priorities. But centralized power in an institution, while it can strengthen the institution, can also be a source of weakness—if the central command point is captured by the enemy. In 1981, Ronald Reagan and his clever strategist, David Stockman, did precisely that, using reconciliation to force cuts in existing law and passing their entire program by presenting it as one budget resolution. The 1981 "Reagan Revolution" is a case study of how a President, using fully the power of his office, can still dominate the budget-making process.

This institutional turnaround would not have been possible without Ronald Reagan's political skill and the momentum generated by his decisive electoral victory—a combination described by a flattened Speaker O'Neill as a "velvet steamroller." Reagan was helped by the Republican majority in the Senate, which meant that in his first year nearly all his lobbying could be focused on the House, and by the newly feisty caucus of conservative southern Democrats, known in the House as "Boll Weevils," who desired even deeper spending cuts than the President.

But Reagan also used the institutional advantages of his office. Although the executive no longer has a monopoly on budget information, it can still release the data with enough drama thoroughly to command the public and congressional stage. OMB director Stockman's "Black Book" listing $40 billion in desired cuts was selectively leaked and then flung at official Washington; Reagan aides dominated the evening news and Sunday morning talk shows;

the President himself enthusiastically lobbied wavering Boll Weevils with trips to Camp David and gifts of presidential cuff-links; 450 supporters met at the White House to plan a grass-roots lobbying campaign. And following the assassination attempt, Reagan dramatically addressed a joint session of Congress to lobby for his budget. When he declared, "The old and comfortable way is to shave a little here and add a little there. Well, that's not acceptable anymore. I think this great and historic Congress knows that way is no longer acceptable," supporters leapt to their feet—and Reagan aides in the gallery, feverishly counting the number of Democrats who joined in, realized they had a majority.

The public reaction to the speech guaranteed the magnitude of that victory. On May 4 the House postmaster received an unprecedented flood of correspondence, overwhelmingly favorable to the President: 1,250,000 letters; 800,000 postcards; 600,000 mailgrams. There were, however, 800,000 pie plates reading "Save School Lunch" (which were forwarded to the Department of Health and Human Services—presumably with no postage due). The Gramm-Latta budget resolution (named after then-Democrat Phil Gramm of Texas and ranking budget committee Republican Del Latta of Ohio) passed the House on May 7 by 253–176, with 69 Democrats joining every Republican to vote yes.

The first budget resolution appeared to set merely a goal. (Reagan told lawmakers like Representative Matt Rinaldo [R.-N.J.], who chafed at the cuts, "You have to recognize that all I'm asking for is a vote on a broad parameter, the spending target.") But in fact the first budget resolution contained a revolutionary element, devised by Stockman: reconciliation instructions that ordered committees to make cuts before the appropriations process even began. And all the cuts would be voted on in a massive reconciliation package one month from the first budget vote. Staff members and committee leaders worked in a frenzy to make the necessary reductions; minority staff and White House operatives blanketed each other with paper, numbers, computer printouts, and vote counts. Changes in hundreds of laws, programs, and formulas were proposed with no hearings and scant deliberation. Some committees resorted to the "Washington Monument ploy" (threatening a cut unacceptable to everyone), like the House panel that proposed shuttering 10,000 local post offices. But by late June 1981 both the House and the Senate had made approximately $40 billion in cuts, in line with the budget resolution.

Even though the House committees made the required cuts, the White House wanted another win in the House, to maintain its dominance of the budget process. But its budget was still being drafted and rewritten in the basement "Rec (reconciliation) Room" as the vote approached. Events moved fast. At 8:12 P.M. on June 24, the Rules committee approved a rule supported by O'Neill but opposed by Jones allowing the Republicans to offer a substitute bill, but dividing the substitute into six parts. Therefore Republican lawmakers would be forced to actually vote to cut entitlements, raise defense spending, slash urban aid—rather than merely "voting for the President's plan." The Republicans, in turn, wanted a single up or down vote on "Gramm-Latta II."

The crucial vote would therefore be on the rule. House leaders rushed the bill onto the floor on June 25, 1981, when Reagan was in California. Dozens of Republican members stalled for time, making virtually identical speeches decrying the "gag rule" and clamoring for (in Jack Kemp's words) a "chance to work with the President to restore prosperity to America." While they spoke, President Reagan worked the phones from California, pulling members off the floor to cut bargains and offer favors. "They're making deals like crazy in the cloakroom," Jones observed as the day wore on. "It's like a tobacco auction in there." The debate, when it came, was angry. Minority Leader Michel shouted at the Democrats, "These are no longer our amendments. They are bastards of the worst order!" Bushy eyebrows dancing, Majority Leader Wright thundered that "No President, no President in the history of the United States—not Franklin Roosevelt, not Lyndon Johnson, not George Washington or Thomas Jefferson—ever demanded of Congress that we lie down submissively and give him every last detail just as his minions order it." Wright's fervor was no match for Reagan's persuasion. The rule was defeated, 210–217—and the next day the Reagan proposal would be voted on as a whole.

One problem remained: The plan was still not drafted. Not until the next day's five-hour debate did the 860-page document even reach members' desks. A photocopied mélange of old legislation, pencil-scrawled changes, dashed-off budget numbers and marginalia, it was impossible to absorb and contained internal inconsistencies and mistakes. (For example, it accidentally eliminated the Head Start program; the Community Economic Development program was denied funds in one part of the bill, authorized "such sums as may be necessary" in a second part, and totally repealed in a third part, according to the Democratic Study Group.) It even included the handwritten telephone number of a CBO assistant to be reached for information. Passed with much of it subjected to no hearings and no floor debate, affecting not only future law but also previously passed entitlements like Medicare and Social Security, and making multiyear cuts stretching three years into the future, it was perhaps the single most sweeping piece of legislation ever passed by Congress. Muttered Tip O'Neill after the vote, "Stockman did this. They turned the whole process over to him. Hell of a way to legislate."

The final component of the President's plan was his proposal for a three-year tax cut, which many members believed had less chance to pass than the budget cuts. Previous sections describe how Reagan won the "bidding war" with the Democrats for business support— and how adept he was at logrolling techniques. But Reagan's trump in the tax fight, again, was his ability to appeal directly to the public. On July 27, Reagan took to the airwaves with a speech so partisan that the television networks nearly refused to air it. Several times he called on citizens to "light up the switchboards" by contacting their representatives to urge support for the Republican tax bill. As with his budget speech, the outpouring was one of the largest deluges of communication the House had ever received. Two days later the House passed the Reagan tax bill, 238–195.

Reagan had persuaded Congress to swallow whole virtually every item on his 1981 agenda. But as soon as the tax bill passed and Reagan's political luster began to fade, budget matters quickly reverted to normal, with Congress regaining much of its hegemony. In the fall of 1981 even conservative lawmakers balked at passing further spending cuts in social programs. Also in September the President attempted to resurrect the device of impoundment, suggesting that he be allowed to impound funds for specific programs. Republican leaders were sympathetic, but the plan died when the House Appropriations Committee voted unanimously against it. Complained senior Republican Barber Conable, "We're not eunuchs yet, but we've lost a lot." Reagan eventually vetoed a spending bill, shutting the government down for a day, to force Congress to make further cuts. In February 1982 the Senate Budget Committee unanimously rejected Reagan's budget plan that called for more spending cuts and defense increases.

Budget making was again a shared responsibility. But the congressional budget process was not working well. In 1982 the House defeated seven budgets (the House Budget Committee budget, twice; the Black Caucus budget; a liberal budget introduced by Representative Dave Obey; a centrist budget supported by moderate Democrats and Republicans, labeled by one wag the "preppy" budget; and a balanced budget introduced by Representative John Rousselot [R.-Calif.]) before finally approving the conservative Republican budget. Some members voted for more than one budget; one election-conscious representative voted for all of them. The House found it virtually impossible actually to pass any appropriations bills. More and more agencies and at times the entire government were funded under a stopgap measure known as a "continuing resolution" which simply continues spending at current levels—a failure of congressional procedures better described as continuing *ir*resolution.

Even apart from its increasingly frequent breakdowns, the process has come under heavy criticism. President Reagan called it "the most irresponsible, Mickey Mouse arrangement that any governmental body has ever produced." Chairmen of authorizing committees were angered at their loss of power over programs and spending within their jurisdiction. And the amount of time taken up by the budget process in the 97th Congress gave credence to Morris Udall's complaint that "we don't have time to do legislation."

There are two more fundamental flaws. Representative Obey worries that the budget process is "irrelevant. It's nice, it's theoretical, it's irrelevant." The system as now constituted elevates "essentially a phony budget" and treats it as fact, since only unrealistically palatable numbers can pass; this whole process is divorced from and leaves little time for the appropriations process ("the real work").

The other fundamental flaw involves what political scientist Allen Schick calls the "fiscalization" of Congress—that is, an obsession with aggregate numbers at the expense of policy-making and dealing with actual programs and issues. *Time* magazine's description of a 1981 Senate Budget Committee meeting to decide the budget gives a flavor of what fiscalization means: "The 21 men and one woman seated around tables pushed together to form a hollow square called out numbers in what seemed a mystifying code. Aides chalked the figures on blackboards, erased them almost instantly, then chalked new ones." One intended effect of the budget process has been to lessen the importance of committees only interested in expanding programs for their favorite constituencies or favorite district. But the process now ignores a source of long-standing congressional expertise: committee and subcommittee chairmen who in dealing with technical issues (like health care programs or transportation subsidies) can learn which programs actually work.

There have been several proposed reforms of the current process. Obey, Representative Richard Gephardt (D.-Mo.), and four other lawmakers have introduced a "Truth in Budgeting" resolution that would bring the budget resolution and an omnibus appropriation bill representing all thirteen spending categories to the floor at once. Obey asserted, "There would be one whale of a fight on the floor for the whole month of June, but when it was over we would have a budget that would really be a budget. You would have winners and you would have losers. You would have decisions that are final and,

186

most of all, the process would be real." This reform has a fair chance of becoming reality, since it enhances the power of the Appropriations Committee and maintains most of the power of the Budget Committee.

Another frequently heard proposal would increase the length of the budget cycle from one to two years, thereby giving Congress sufficient time to debate and pass a full budget. But the periodic adjustments and calibrations necessary in a changing economy might take up almost as much time as the current process.

The chairmen and staffs of authorizing committees long desired to do away with the enforcement arm of the budget process—reconciliation. In 1982 and 1983 semisecret meetings dotted the Capitol as aides tried to figure out how to regain their power over policy. (A committee staffer told a journalist after one such meeting, "This wasn't a palace coup—unfortunately.") Indeed, many of these committees' early fears about loss of power to a super committee have been borne out. But if Congress is to retain its newly won control over the budget and the priorities of government activity, there must be a mechanism for enforcing compliance. If Congress does not have the discipline to police itself, the President will gladly appropriate the role.

Congress and the Courts

Congress has usually concerned itself most with the behavior and power of the executive branch. In the late 1970s and early 1980s, however, some members of Congress expressed special dissatisfaction with the active role taken by the third branch of government— the judiciary. These conservative legislators have gone beyond mere grumbling and have tried to stop the courts from deciding even constitutional questions. Their proposals, labeled "court stripping" by opponents of the measures and "withdrawal of jurisdiction" by supporters, would limit the ability of courts to order busing to achieve racial desegregation, limit school prayer, and allow abortions, to name a few topics. If passed, these proposals would signal a radical reorientation of our constitutional structure.

The issues are not new. But while the ability of the federal courts—and particularly the Supreme Court—to pass on the constitutionality of laws has been a hotly contested issue in American history, the conflict has usually been between the executive and the courts, with Congress taking the courts' side. When Franklin Roosevelt attempted to impose his will on a recalcitrant Supreme Court in 1937 by adding five new members, the Senate Judiciary Committee issued an oft-quoted rebuff that stopped the plan:

> Let us now set a salutary precedent that will never be violated. Let us, of the 75th Congress, in words that will never be disregarded by any succeeding Congress, declare that we would rather have an independent court, a fearless court, a court that will dare to announce its honest opinions in what it believes to be the defense of liberties of the people, than a Court that, out of fear or sense of obligation to the appointing power or fractional passion, approves any measure we may enact. We are not the judges of the judges. We are not above the Constitution.

The court packers of the 1920s (when progressive senators like Robert La Follette chafed at decisions striking down child labor laws) and the 1930s were liberals angry at a slow-moving court resistant to change. The judicial activism of the past three decades has angered a different breed. Beginning with the Supreme Court decision outlawing school segregation in *Brown* v. *Board of Education*, judges made constitutional decisions guaranteeing civil rights in areas where legislators often feared to tread. It was the courts that banned mandatory school prayer, declared a woman's right to have an abortion, ordered busing as a desegregation measure of last resort. The conservative upsurge of the 1970s that produced lawmakers like North Carolina's senators Jesse Helms and John East and Jeremiah Denton (R.-Ala.) largely aimed its rhetorical fire at the "secular humanism" that they believed was being implemented by unelected judges.

The constitutional arguments of those advocating "withdrawal of jurisdiction" rest on Article III of the Constitution, which gives power to "regulate" jurisdiction of lower and upper courts. (But not, argue opponents, all courts—just disputes between lower and upper tiers of the judiciary.) Senator East, writing in the book *Judicial Reform*, asserts that legislation channeling abortion and civil rights lawsuits to state courts do not violate a citizen's rights. "As a practical matter, disputes not resolved in the federal courts will usually be resolved in the state courts. . . . State judges take the same oath as federal judges to uphold the Constitution of the United States." Opponents of "court stripping" warn of the danger of essentially repealing a constitutional right (like the right under the fourteenth Amendment to attend an integrated school) by a majority vote of Congress.

When the 97th Congress opened, Helms and other court strippers had reason for optimism: the previous session Congress had passed an amendment to a bill that forbade federal courts from ordering busing to combat segregation. Since busing (as opposed to school prayer or abortion) was the issue where conservatives had the most support from other lawmakers, Helms and Senator Bennett Johnston (D.-La.) introduced a similar bill early in 1981. It passed the Senate in March, but in the House—where Democratic leaders were strongly opposed—it immediately ran up against several procedural roadblocks. The bill was "held at the desk" (meaning not assigned to a committee); supporters had to file a time-consuming "discharge motion" to get it assigned; it was held in committee and not assigned to a subcommittee; another discharge petition was needed. But House Judiciary Committee chairman Peter Rodino (D.-N.J.) had no intention of letting the legislation be voted on by the full House. His committee never reported the bill, and a discharge petition fell nine signatures short of forcing it to the floor.

Other bills introduced by Helms on abortion and school prayer were delayed by agreement with Majority Leader Baker, who wanted a clean calendar for budget issues in 1981. The delay worked to the advantage of opponents of court stripping, who waged an educational campaign to shift the focus of debate. Notes Irene Emsellem, chief lobbyist for the American Bar Association (which strongly opposes court stripping), "The press finally woke up and started writing about the court-stripping aspect of it. It wasn't 'Abortion Amendment Defeated,' it became the phrase 'Court Stripping.' "

Once that transformation in public attitudes occurred, Helms had an increasingly difficult task. Senator Lowell Weicker (R.-Conn.) filibustered throughout late summer and early autumn 1982, and Helms was unable to get the necessary 60 votes for cloture (cutting off a filibuster). The Senate did not enjoy the process. "I was determined from the outset to make it as disagreeable an experience as I possibly could, for everybody," recalls Weicker, "so they would think twice before doing this stuff." The coup de grace came when Senators Barry Goldwater (R.-Ariz.) and S.I. Hayakawa (R.-Calif.) offered motions to send Helms's bills back to committee, motions that passed.

Opponents of court stripping have probably won the intellectual contest for public opinion, and it may be impossible, given the different mood of the 98th Congress, for such legislation to be passed. But it should be remembered that while East et. al. did not have enough votes to achieve cloture, he *did* on several occasions have a majority for the substance of his bills.

The Invisible Czars

When Congress fails in its oversight responsibilities, two outcomes are possible: the agencies and departments may roll along unsupervised, or someone else may pick up the reins Congress has dropped. The second has happened, with the presidential staff in the driver's seat.

To see how the White House has succeeded, we need only review why Congress has failed. To do a good job of oversight, Congress would need, first, a larger staff of investigators. It would need some system for regular review of the agencies, instead of relying on haphazard coverage. It would need to know when policies or performance changed. Most of all it would need to know whether what the administrators told it was true.

Rolled together and placed on the White House staff, these reasons described the Office of Management and Budget. As part of the reorganization which changed its name from the Bureau of the Budget, the OMB was given greater responsibility for reviewing the impact and worth of programs, as well as their budgets. This, of course, is another way of phrasing "oversight." "I've been watching this process for ten years," said David Stockman on his appointment as director of OMB, "seeing the difficulty of injecting new ideas into the political structure. I've become convinced the OMB is absolutely the best forum possible to carry out that kind of agenda. Everything flows through here."

Because of its privileged position within the executive, the OMB can exercise both before- and after-the-fact review. Before any programs get under way, OMB analysts have screened budget requests and program proposals. While the projects are running, the OMB parcels out the money, or withholds it. And when agencies propose new rules or decisions, the OMB can often screen them before Congress has its chance.

This has led to a situation in which an appointed agency, entirely shielded from public scrutiny, has more impact on administrative policy than any elected congressman, or group of them. A few illustrations show the danger. While the President should have the right to coordinate the policies of the Labor Department or HHS, he has no place setting the policy or priorities of the independent agencies, which are not part of the executive branch. But in February 1972, the chairman of the Federal Power Commission, John P. Nassikas, came to Congress to complain that the President was doing just that. Nassikas told a Senate subcommittee that his agency was disappearing into the White House. Because he had to send his budget requests through the OMB—not directly to Congress—his agency was subject to the same policy coordination as the executive departments. This OMB screening, Nassikas said, "results in some control of the policies, programs, and priorities of the independent regulatory agencies." Drawing on Nassikas's testimony, Senator Lee Metcalf proposed a bill which would let the independent agencies send their budgets directly to Congress, avoiding the OMB filter. It did not pass—and "independent" agencies are still not that independent.

While exercising tight supervision over executive departments and "independent" agencies, OMB can interfere with whatever attempts Congress may make to assert its own supervisory power. The most important technique for doing so is OMB's screening of testimony administration witnesses plan to give Congress. Combined with the witnesses's usual ellipses, this means that congressmen are often frustrated when they try to oversee the executive. Consider, for example, Frank Spinney, an obscure thirty-seven-year-old Pentagon analyst whose internal study of the costs of weapon procurement indicated why the military budget had ballooned out of control. But when senators sought a briefing by Spinney, OMB and Defense Secretary Caspar Weinberger refused. "His work is purely historical," said Weinberger, which didn't satisfy Senator Charles Grassley (R.-Iowa), who threatened to subpoena Spinney to appear unless his superiors relented. They did, and he told the Congress how many of their cherished assumptions about the cost of weapons systems were misplaced.

Finally, the OMB can without fanfare function as a Cerberus at the gate of all executive branch regulation. Within a month of taking office, President Reagan created an unprecedented OMB oversight program. Executive Order 12291 required not merely that agencies *calculate* the costs and benefits of major rules, but also that they *prove* "potential benefits . . . outweigh potential costs" and that they send drafted rules twice to OMB for approval, before being proposed and then before adoption. Reviewing the OMB review is the Vice President's Task Force on Regulatory Relief, which comprises half the cabinet. Periodically it announces a hit list of regulations it wants reviewed—and then either eliminated or weakened.

The executive order appeared to have its intended effect. The White House pointed with pride to a slowdown in regulatory activity. "The number of final regulations issued by the Reagan administration is about 22 percent less than during the final year of the Carter administration," the task force announced in August 1982. The Federal Register had been reduced by a third; of 4309 rules reviewed by OMB, 13 percent were sent back because they didn't meet the standards of Executive Order 12291. As a result, said Christopher DeMuth, the executive director of the task force, agencies have to "think twice" before sending up a rule.

For example, the OMB repeatedly delayed infant formula regulations proposed by FDA; it instructed EPA to weaken regulations on lead in gasoline and hazardous waste in landfills. But what if the agency doesn't want to go along with such suggestions? One EPA official said of the lead standard, "We told OMB, 'You guys don't understand. Lead isn't good for people. We're not going to put our head on the political guillotine.' " But EPA did. In the words of James Miller III, in 1981, when he headed up the regulatory review staff of the task force, "You know, if you're the toughest kid on the block, most kids won't pick a fight with you."

War Powers & "Executive Agreements"

From Abraham Lincoln to Franklin Roosevelt, warmaking power has increasingly lodged in the President, the commander-in-chief. The most recent demonstration of this tendency was, of course, the conduct of the Indochina War by Presidents Johnson and Nixon. Whenever Congress attempted to reduce our involvement—by repealing the 1964 Gulf of Tonkin resolution, by voting a series of end-the-war amendments in the seventies—it found either that (as Nicholas Katzenbach told a hearing in 1967) the President didn't need the Tonkin resolution in the first place, or that (as Nixon said after an antiwar resolution was passed in 1971) the President could simply ignore antiwar clauses. In 1973, Congress finally managed to cut off Nixon's bombing of Cambodia that year, but only after failing to override his veto of efforts to end the bombing immediately. When Nixon said he would only accept a cutoff if given six more weeks in which to bomb, Congress acquiesced.

But angry over its diminished authority—after all, Article I, Section 8 of the Constitution says that "the Congress shall have power . . . To declare war"—Congress did pass the War Powers Act in 1973, over President Nixon's veto. The act requires greater prior consultation by the President with Congress before committing troops and allows Congress to direct the President to disengage troops if committed without a declaration of war or specific statutory authority. In a way, though, the law takes full advantage of Congress's traditional reluctance to act. Its key provision states that a President must stop hostilities after sixty days unless Congress votes its approval of his actions. But in the end, as Senator Thomas Eagleton has argued in *War and Presidential Power*, Congress may have simply conspired in its own undoing by passing a law which recognizes presidential powers that many feel did not exist under the Constitution in the first place.

A similar evolution has affected what are called "executive agreements." Although these secret arrangements, signed by the President and a foreign country, have the force of treaties, Congress knows little about them. Some 4,000 of the agreements were in effect in the mid-1970s. In fact, Presidents have increasingly used such agreements for some of their most important decisions with other countries, while treaties have been employed for less important matters. "Every day we vote on treaties that have to do with trivial matters," former Senator Frank Church complained in an interview in *Harper's* magazine. "In fact, the more trivial the matter the more inclined the executive is to submit it to the Senate for ratification as a treaty." In 1972, Congress passed a law requiring such agreements to be reported to Congress within sixty days, but did not require that they receive Senate approval.

Congress's "Oversight"

Congress is, or ought to be, the watchdog of the public purse. Even if it no longer initiates legislation, even if the President can play a shell game with the funds Congress has appropriated, Congress should vigorously and constantly yap at the executive's heels to make sure that funds are not squandered, that incompetent administrators don't fritter taxpayers' dollars away on worthless or marginal projects, that the executive is obeying the laws and enforcing the laws. Congress is the only representative of the people—whose money, after all, is being spent—that has the power to see that the executive is doing its work.

With felicity rare for congressional jargon, this area is called "legislative *oversight*." The double meaning is a perfect guide to the topic. For just as Congress tries to oversee its laws once they are passed, much of its weakness here is due to oversights. The reason for oversight—or "review"—is that laws don't always live up to their ambitions. Everyday experience provides examples of legislation that has not accomplished its purpose. In 1967, for example, after a series of nauseating articles about packinghouses, Congress passed the Wholesome Meat Act. By 1969 all state slaughterhouses were supposed to meet federal standards or be taken over by the U.S. (except for a special one-year grace period in some cases). The deadline came and went, and federal inspectors moved into only one state. The others were approved—not, in most cases, because they had improved their standards, but because the federal standards had dipped to meet them.

In addition Congress is responsible for the "quasi-legislative" agencies. These regulatory bodies, such as the Interstate Commerce Commission and the Federal Trade Commission, officially function with powers delegated by Congress. Because Congress cannot deal with each railroad rate claim or advertiser's complaint, it passes the powers to regulatory agencies. Congress is still responsible to see that the powers it has delegated to the agencies are used well.

The procedures for congressional oversight range from special hearings, or investigations of an agency, to informal queries, or questions at appropriations time. The important fact about all of them is that they have proved inadequate. As Jerry Cohen and Morton Mintz wrote in *America, Inc.*:

> In theory the deficiencies of the independent regulatory agencies and of units of the executive branch with regulatory powers would be alleviated and on occasion maybe even corrected if Congress reliably and seriously exercised its responsibility to oversee their performance. The unhappy truth is that reliable, serious, and sustained oversight is the exception rather than the rule on Capitol Hill. Not even in remote degree have the oversight mechanisms of Congress kept pace with the enormous growth of the executive.

Or as one member once complained "you wait two hours so you can get a shot at the secretary of defense, and then it lasts only five minutes. The only thing you know is that you're getting bullshit from him, and there's nothing you can do about it." And more common yet are no oversight hearings at all by the responsible committees.

Why? To an extent, bills sponsored and projects obtained can be used in the constant quest for reelection, but oversight usually wins little public attention. More importantly, congressional staff—whose mission it is to undertake executive oversight—simply lack the numbers and information to perform adequately. Congress's other potential ally is the General Accounting Office, the legislature's staff of investigators. The GAO is a relatively bright spot in Congress's general prospect, and any reassertion of congressional investigative power will probably begin there.

The GAO is an arm of Congress; its job is to help congressmen study the government. Before 1950 it spent most of its time doing purely accounting work. After the Korean War, however, Comptroller General Joseph Campbell led GAO into more adventuresome areas. Campbell began a series of studies of war industries and produced, during the fifties, reports on profiteering and wasteful construction. Campbell, who had been treasurer of Columbia University before coming to the GAO in 1954, favored a candid style rare in government reports. His audits were studded with such phrases as "excessive cost" and "congressional intent as to cost limitations circumvented," shockers in a society accustomed to squishy government prose.

Campbell soon ran afoul of the Defense Department and the defense contractors; by 1965 they had conveyed their unhappiness to Representative Chet Holifield. In his response to the Pentagon complaints, Holifield illustrated one of the most potent executive tactics for controlling the legislature: by setting up one congressman with favors and patronage, the executive can count on him to beat down other critics. The Committee on Government Operations held hearings on the GAO in 1965, which then chairman Holifield began by mentioning "the great concern that has been shown in industry circles, and, recently, in the Department of Defense over the difficult and sometimes awkward situations created by the GAO audit reports." By the end of the hearings, the GAO had been tamed. It agreed to a list of conditions, including an agreement to stop using company names in the reports and an effort to be more "constructive."

With that behind it the GAO walks a fine line between toadyism and giving offense, but it still is the most important investigative tool Congress has. It showed its split personality well in a recent study of, once again, defense contractors. While the audit itself was factual and critical—revealing that seventy-seven weapons systems would cost $28.7 billion more than estimated and that the average profit rate was a fantastic 56 percent—the GAO sent the report to the industry before publishing it, and then incorporated many industry alibis into the text and toned down its own charges.

Despite its occasional disappointments, the GAO offers congressmen their main defense against the analysts of the White House and the OMB. Whenever members ask, the GAO will make studies of specific problems. Representative Elizabeth Holtzman (D.-N.Y.), for example, was dissatisfied in 1976 with the Department of Labor's answers to her questions about its CETA jobs program. She requested a GAO study which uncovered many abuses in the program. Unfortunately, few members of Congress take advantage of the service. In 1981, for example, only 464 reports were made to members of Congress and congressional committees. In fact, only 25 percent of GAO's studies are done at the request of representatives and senators—the remainder are the result of the GAO's own initiative.

If, indeed, information is the key to the executive's power, Congress will have to do more than ask for an occasional GAO study. What is needed is a major overhaul of Congress's information sources so that it can better monitor the executive. As Joseph Califano, former special assistant to President Johnson and HEW secretary, once wrote between his stints in government:

> The Congress is presently the separate but unequal branch of the federal government. . . . The basic reason for the decline in congressional effectiveness and status, however, lies not with the executive branch or some federal bureaucrats. . . . Responsibility for its separate but unequal status rests largely with the Congress itself.
>
> The Congress is dependent upon the executive branch for most of its information, with an occasional and too often superficial assist from outside experts.
>
> Congress has ignored the revolution in analytical technology. . . . The Congress has only three or four computers, and those computers operate in large measure on payrolls and housekeeping matters. Contrast the executive branch, which now has some 4,000 computers working almost entirely on substantive policy issues.
>
> The stark fact is that neither Congress nor any of its committees has the consistent capability—without almost total reliance on the informational and analytical resources of the executive branch—of developing coherent, large-scale federal programs.

Belatedly, press revelations have shaken Congress awake to the need for effective oversight and information about executive branch activity. After Seymour Hersh reported in *The New York Times* that the Central Intelligence Agency, contrary to its charter, had conducted domestic spying operations, and after *The Washington Post* disclosed that the FBI had been collecting derogatory information on the members themselves, Congress erupted with expressions of indignation and outrage. As members and committees began vying to investigate the charges, the Senate and House each gravely announced the creation of special select committees, similar to the Watergate committee, to investigate not only the FBI and the CIA, but the intelligence units of the Army, Navy, and Air Force, the Secret Service, and the Justice and State departments, not to mention a host of less well-known agencies pocketed throughout the bureaucracy.

The alacrity with which Congress responded to these disclosures hardly spoke well of the oversight that had apparently not previously existed. Neither the FBI nor the CIA had been subjected to anything but the most cursory examinations in the past, even though the CIA was the specific responsibility of no fewer than four subcommittees in the House and Senate. Before these subcommittees finally came in from the cold, however, their collective failure was probably best summed up in an exchange between Alan Cranston of California and former senator Allen Ellender—then the chairman of one of the subcommittees—in a 1971 debate on CIA operations in Laos:

> *Cranston:* The Chairman stated that he never would have thought of even asking about CIA funds being used to conduct the war in Laos. I would like to ask the Senator if, since then, he has inquired and now knows whether that is being done?
>
> *Ellender:* I have not inquired.
>
> *Cranston:* You do not know, in fact?
>
> *Ellender:* No.
>
> *Cranston:* As you are one of the five men privy to this information, in fact you are the number one man of the five

men who would know, then who would know what happened this money? The fact is, not even the five men know the fac in this situation.

Ellender: Probably not.

Even after Watergate had unearthed a substantial amount of ev dence of questionable CIA activity, the subcommittees took n action. Fully a year before *The New York Times* disclosures, CL Director William Colby had briefed the chairmen about the domesti spying operations, yet they still could not bring themselves to take an kind of action. In 1974 one of the committees managed to meet si times, another met five times, one met twice, and one had n records of any meetings. It took the promise of national publicity the forced resignation of several CIA officials, and the beginning c a presidential investigation to force Congress to face an issue.

The reasons behind the failures of oversight are displayed clearl in the few *successful* instances of oversight. Representative Joh Moss (D.-Calif.) retired from Congress in 1978 after thirteen terms but not before he had earned a reputation as "the father of oversight." As chairman of the House Oversight and Investigations subcommittee in the 95th Congress alone, he tackled and issued major reports o HEW birth control policy, unnecessary surgery, the cost of drugs pesticide regulations, Firestone tires, and the world uranium cartel among others. He threatened to hold HEW Secretary Joseph Califan in contempt for failure to turn over documents pursuant to subpoena— until Califano finally complied.

In recent years there have been occasional other instances o effective congressional oversight. Senator Proxmire's solo scrutin of the Defense budget has often embarrassed the Pentagon int response. Former chairman William Fulbright of the Foreign Rela tions Committee went so far as to have that committee hire its ow investigators to make on-the-spot studies in Laos, Greece, an elsewhere. Also, the past chairman of the Administrative Practice and Procedures subcommittee, Senator Edward Kennedy, creatively sent out "protective subpoenas" to FDA medical officials—whic enabled them to testify publicly, without fear of agency reprisal, about the way the FDA harassed staff who raised too many safety questions about pending drugs. And it was a desirable reform when Senator Sam Nunn (D.-Ga.) got an amendment enacted in 1981 requiring the Pentagon to notify Congress whenever there was a cost overrun of 15 percent or more on a major weapons system.

The arrival of the Reagan Administration showed the Janus-like quality of congressional oversight. Especially given the troubles many of his top appointees would get themselves into (Donovan, Watt, Burford), President Reagan's selections sailed through their confirmation hearings as was the case with FDR's program during the First Hundred Days. One glaring example of the inability or unwillingness of Congress actually to give its "advice and consent" was the Senate's confirmation of William P. Clark as Deputy Secretary of State. Clark was so uniformly uninformed about foreign affairs before the Foreign Relations Committee (for example, he didn't know the name of the Prime Minister of Zimbabwe) that Senator John Glenn (D.-Ohio) remarked, "I have never seen anything like such ignorance of foreign affairs and lack of preparation for a confirmation hearing in my years here in the Senate." Yet he was approved 10–4, with the majority saying things like the President was entitled to his own team and a person he could trust. If so, why bother with Senate confirmation at all?

But as the Reagan "honeymoon" with Congress and the public subsided, the Senate and House began increasingly to scrutinize a President who overreached in many ways. The same Senate Foreign Relations Committee that lost its critical judgment with Judge Clark became vigorous interrogators of Ernest Lefever and Kenneth Adelman— Lefever being a person who didn't believe in a human rights policy abroad yet who was selected to be the assistant secretary of state for human rights, and Adelman being similarly hostile to his mission of arms control as the nominated head of the Arms Control and Disarmament Agency.

According to the widely shared view of columnist Anthony Lewis, "Mr. Lefever was an extraordinarily evasive witness, unresponsive, disingenuous: so much so that he annoyed senators of both parties." For only one example, when Lefever denied ever calling the opposition to his nomination "Communist-inspired," Chairman Charles Percy shot back, "You did. I heard you." Adelman, too had a desultory appearance before the panel. Opposition in the Republican-run Senate was so substantial that Lefever was forced to withdraw and the White House had to lobby strenuously to pass Adelman's nomination.

Over in the House the situation of a chamber of one party facing an administration of another began to resuscitate the lost art of congressional oversight. Among the leading overseers were John Dingell, head of the Energy and Commerce Committee, and Albert Gore, Jr. (D.-Tenn.), chairman of the Oversight and Investigations Subcommittee of the Science and Technology Committee. Dingell initiated the contempt citation of Anne (Gorsuch) Burford when she refused to turn over subpoenaed Superfund documents. She said the President claimed executive privilege (though no one in the White House had read the documents in question) because the documents related to sensitive law-enforcement matters. Dingell charged a possible cover-up of illegality—and the House agreed by voting out a contempt citation 259–105, making Burford the highest ranking executive branch official ever to be so held. Inspired, fully six subcommittees began separate investigations of EPA, uncovering a governmental dump site of politics, mismanagement, and sweetheart settlements. Though the subcommittees should have coordinated their investigations better, a consequence of this congressional vigilance was the firing or resignation of thirteen top EPA officials, Burford included.

Gore, a thirty-four-year-old former journalist and law student with an eye on Howard Baker's Senate seat, understands the three things needed for successful congressional oversight: he and his dogged staff pour in long hours on an investigation; they know how to dramatize it with a sympathetic victim and a culpable official; and Gore can telegenically and analytically make witnesses squirm under his withering questions. In 1982, for example, he held hearings on infant formula because "it is the sole source of nutrition for little human beings" and because the very same company that had marketed a bad batch in the 1950s had done it again in 1982. By the time of the March 11, 1982, hearing, American Home Products Corporation still hadn't recalled three million cans manufactured without an essential vitamin. Gore showed a film of an adult woman who was severely retarded because she had consumed the firm's defective formula of twenty-five years before. When asked why American Home Products didn't immediately recall the 3 million cans, Charles Hagan, a company witness, explained that while some were defective, others were not. "Would you ask us to recall those?" At this Gore exploded. "Yes, yes," he shouted, the film of the retarded woman still in his mind, "if that is the only way to get to them, of course, you ought to recall them." Shortly after the hearing the entire batch was recalled.

From Impotence to Overkill—Legislative Veto and Sunset

The framers of the Constitution devised the presidential veto as a principal means of check and balance between the executive and legislative branches—though they never intended it to be employed as frequently as it is today. Like the congressional power to impeach, the framers envisioned the veto as an emergency safeguard to be used to correct outrageous and temporary legislative whims.

But after FDR became a master at using the veto to protect his New Deal programs, his successors continued using the veto as a political tool. Former President Ford vetoed 17 bills in just one year (1975). President Carter occasionally vetoed legislation passed by a majority of his own party—perhaps to prove that even a Democratic Congress couldn't push him around and get away with it. And President Reagan throughout his term has frequently threatened to veto spending bills that "bust the budget." Yet if Madison and Hamilton could not envision the routine use of presidential veto power to thwart the will of the people's representatives, they could hardly have foreseen the congressional counterassault and overreaction known as the "legislative veto," which was finally found unconstitutional by the Supreme Court in 1983.

When made part of a bill, a legislative veto provision gave one or both houses of Congress, and in some cases a congressional committee, the authority to overrule specific agency regulations within a specified number of days, usually sixty. Until the decision legislative veto provisions covered such matters as the commitment of American troops abroad, large international arms sales, Federal Election Commission regulations, some Department of Transportation rules, Office of Education rule-making, most executive reorganizations, and, most recently, Federal Trade Commission rules.

While the legislative veto was not new, its popularity accelerated recently, following Richard Nixon's abuses. Between 1932 and 1968, Congress included them in an average of only three bills a year. Yet twenty-four legislative vetoes were passed by the 93rd Congress alone. The Congressional Research Service found that by 1978, 295 legislative veto provisions had been scattered among 196 pieces of legislation.

The impulse behind the legislative veto movement was understandable, and its rhetoric fetching. Its boosters, led by Representative Elliott H. Levitas (D.-Ga.), argue that as Presidents appropriated more and more power from acquiescent Congresses, and as bureaucrats increasingly allocated billions in benefits and costs, the bureaucracy became a fourth branch of government. As Levitas testified before the House Rules Committee:

> We have seen our legislative efforts frustrated and distorted when the implementing rules and regulations are published. . . . The ratio between bureaucratic rules and regulations and acts of Congress runs about 18 to 1. . . . Are we going to continue to let unelected bureaucrats continue to pass laws without effective Congressional controls? . . . Who makes the laws in this country—the elected representatives of the people or the unelected bureaucrats?

Understandable and fetching—but also, as the Court ultimately ruled, unconstitutional and unworkable. The constitutional objections are substantial. Article I states that to become law a bill must pass both houses of Congress and be signed by the President—or be vetoed by the President and then overridden by two thirds of each chamber. The legislative veto simply erases the President from this process. It turns the Constitution on its head to have the President write the laws and Congress veto them. Furthermore, the Constitution vests legislative authority in the House and Senate acting together. But one-house veto plans would let either house unmake the laws alone. Thus, whenever the House and Senate disagreed, they could veto each other when the regulations were published. These constitutional problems persuaded President Reagan, like all his predecessors in the past forty years, to oppose the legislative veto and protect presidential prerogative (even though as a candidate he *favored* the idea as a way of combating "big government").

Beyond its constitutional Achilles' heel, the frequent passage of legislative veto provisions only worsened the frenzy and institutional paralysis besetting Congress. Some lawmakers made a "burden of review" argument, pointing out that the huge volume of agency regulations would, in the name of countering bureaucracy, convert Congress into a super-bureaucracy itself. And by forcing votes on specific regulations affecting specific industries, the mechanism heightened the intensity of outside pressure on Congress. The subjection of FTC rules to the legislative veto saw repeated drives by narrow interests—funeral directors, used-car salesmen—to overturn fair-trade restrictions; the consuming (or grieving) public could never match the industries' regiments of lobbyists and PAC-men.

It was the mechanism's constitutional infirmity, not its institutional flaws, that led to its demise. On June 23, 1983, the U.S. Supreme Court overturned a law that had allowed a representative to deny a waiver of immigration rules to a Kenyan student, Jagdish Rai Chadha. But the Court's ruling in *Immigration and Naturalization Service* v. *Chadha* went beyond the case at hand, firmly repudiating the principle of the legislative veto. Chief Justice Warren Burger's majority opinion was unequivocal: "With all the obvious flaws of delay, untidiness, and potential for abuse, we have not yet found a better way to preserve freedom than by making the exercise of power subject to the carefully crafted restraints spelled out by the Constitution." By the reckoning of Justice Byron White, who dissented from the Court's opinion, the decision "sounds the death knell for nearly 200 other statutory provisions . . ." Others predicted that the War Powers Act, the sections of the Budget and Impoundment Act prohibiting impoundments, and the statutes allowing vetoes of arms deals (like the sale of AWACS to Saudi Arabia) would all be struck down. In fact, the ruling's impact on specific laws is in doubt—the War Powers Act may well be secure, for instance, since the Constitution gives only Congress the power to declare war.

And the decision may force Congress to finally grasp the reins of its responsibility and legislate concrete policy. Under the legislative veto, explains Harvard Law School professor Laurence Tribe, "Instead of going through the cumbersome and politically painful process of standing up and being counted, Congress [said], 'Why don't we just give a blank check to the executive agencies, and if we don't like the results, we'll say so.' " Congress can no longer loudly pass something beneficent, like a health and safety regulation, and then quietly balk at its impact on a favored constituency.

Like the legislative veto, the idea of "sunset" legislation shows how an insecure Congress can overreact to its historic weakness vis-à-vis the executive. The idea behind sunset is simple. Because Congress inadequately oversees the executive branch, an action-forcing mechanism is needed to terminate periodically all federal programs unless a program can justify its continued existence to Congress.

Undoubtedly, the task of reapproval is massive, but no one knows just how massive. The number of programs to be reviewed depends on who is defining the term "program." While a Governmental

Affairs Committee "table of federal programs" lists 1,250 units, the Senate Rules Committee estimated there could be 50,000 programs. Even taking the lower figure, Congress would have to review more than 200 programs per year under the proposed S. 2, or better than one program each day that Congress is in session. Colorado's sunset process, involving just thirteen regulatory agencies a year, is one thing; one program per day is quite another. As Senator Thomas F. Eagleton (D.-Mo.) observed, "I hear my colleagues mutter about how we senators are becoming captive creatures of our burgeoning office and committee staffs; with sunset, 'burgeoning' may well become 'bloated.' "

The workload problem cannot be easily dismissed, especially for a proposal that would guillotine agencies if Congress did *not* act. Given this burden and the fact that the Congress, like many college students, does most of its work at the end of the term, the likely result would be a perfunctory thumbs-up or thumbs-down on many programs. Yet such a cursory review is the very evil to which sunset is addressed.

Worse is sunset's inherent bias against "people" programs—those protecting consumer health and safety, safeguarding civil rights, aiding the needy. While it is not difficult to tally up the costs to business of health and safety legislation, such as the Auto Safety Act or the Occupational Safety and Health Act (OSHA), it is difficult and at times impossible to quantify the benefits to society. How do you put a price tag on the avoidance of cancer in future generations because the government prevented an employer from using a toxic substance? Or the benefit of a six-year-old not being disfigured by flammable pajamas?

Human welfare programs usually have diffuse and unorganized constituents: welfare mothers, consumers who may buy a dangerous car or drug, workers who may lose an eye. Corporate welfare programs usually have politically powerful constituents, such as major contractors for weapons systems or the merchant marine for the Maritime Administration. In the struggle to keep Congress from failing to renew their programs, the latter are far better equipped to play power politics. For example, the most prominent federal agency terminated has been the Office of Economic Opportunity (a benefit program for poor people), not the Department of Commerce (a benefit program for big corporations). Congress abolished the Renegotiation Board, an agency which benefited taxpayers generally but was strongly opposed by military contractors seeking the highest benefits possible.

Due to powerful corporate opposition, health/safety programs often require a catastrophe to come into existence. Tough food and drug laws were passed in the wake of the 1938 and 1962 drug scandals; a report on 30,000 annual deaths from product hazards led to the creation of the Consumer Product Safety Commission. Their extinction should not depend on a successful filibuster or a presidential veto. Opponents of these social programs—needing only 145 House votes or 34 Senate votes to sustain the veto of a hostile President—would have undue leverage over the content of fundamental programs. As Sierra Club official Carl Pope has written, "By the end of Gerald Ford's unelected term in office, under some sunset proposals, we would have lost the Clean Air Act, the Clean Water Act, OSHA, and possibly NEPA (National Environmental Policy Act). Each of these would have been up for review, and none would have been signed by the President in an effective form."

To say that the sunset solution is defective is not to say that the problems of inadequate congressional oversight and executive agency misregulation are not real. Yes, Congress must exercise ultimate control over federal programs. But as journalist Al Hunt of *The Wall Street Journal* has pointed out, "There is nothing to prevent Congress from passing a law overturning what is seen as an unfair rule. That is exactly what the lawmakers did in 1977 when the Food and Drug Administration banned saccharin." Or why not require instead congressional committees (i.e., an "action forcing" mechanism) to undertake periodically a complete review of the cost, performance, need for, and alternatives to all federal programs and tax expenditures? A program or authorization would then be eliminated only if Congress affirmatively passed legislation, which was then signed by the President, but not if it did nothing.

This shift in burden would help protect against extinguishing agencies, in the words of a Senate Finance staff report, "through scheduling inadvertencies or from being held hostage by a President or by a determined minority interest against the will of the majority of Congress." For Congress to insist that elimination result from nonaction betrays a lack of confidence in its own ability to act where necessary, and, like the legislative veto, may be a cure worse than the disease.

Watergate and Impeachment

The most spectacular recent example of congressional oversight was also the most significant confrontation of the past century between the President and Congress—Watergate, that "third-rate burglary" that grew into a constellation of crimes that eventually toppled a President. Looking back, it appears an obvious morality play—Richard Nixon's arrogance and excesses versus the decency and righteousness of John Sirica, Peter Rodino, and Sam Ervin. Congress slays the dragon. Yet if it were not for a vigilant, contentious press and the President's own self-wounding ways, Nixon might never have had to take a helicopter off the White House lawn on August 9, 1974. "Nixon essentially impeached himself," said Representative John Conyers (D.-Mich.), a member of the House Judiciary Committee. "Most of the members had a clear distaste for impeachment. Where the evidence was so overwhelming as to be unavoidable, they had no choice—Nixon had done everything possible to show them how guilty he was. We were just lucky, that's all." And far from an easy-flowing stream of revelations, the proceedings hesitated and tripped along the way toward their conclusion. Or as an aide to one Judiciary Committee member noted:

It's important to understand that the process wasn't as inevitable as it's beginning to look now that it's all over. Congress wanted a way out of this decision and an appearance of irresponsibility on the part of the committee would have given them the excuse they needed. It could easily have gone the other way if too many false steps had been made in the beginning.

The congressional beginning was of course the Senate Watergate hearings, a major spectacle unfolding amid the chandeliers and high marble pillars of room 318 of the Old Senate Office Building. People whose TV fare encompassed only daytime soap operas now turned to the Watergate hearings like junkies to a fix. They learned more about their President and their Congress than they had ever known before, or perhaps wanted to know. But lavish media attention, while heightening the committee's impact and importance, did not obscure its weaknesses. Follow-up questions on important points often went unasked, while witnesses who showed the proper signs of contrition were sometimes dismissed with an oratorical slap on the wrist.

Once the process shifted to the House Judiciary Committee, Chairman Peter Rodino, a sixty-four-year-old representative from Newark, New Jersey, became the focus of attention. An undistinguished and obscure back-bencher who had been chairman less than a year, with a scratchy voice more "Joisey" than Churchillian, Rodino was an unlikely individual to weld the bipartisan majority essential to preserving the credibility of the inquiry. But Rodino's meticulous efforts to mold the committee into at least a semblance of nonpartisan unity and sober judgment went far to make the idea of impeachment less frightening to Congress and the public. It also helped to undermine the White House tactic of dismissing the committee as a "partisan lynch mob" intent on harassing a beleaguered President.

On one side of the inquiry were seven insistent impeachment advocates, ranging from Father Robert F. Drinan (D.-Mass.) to wily Texas millionaire Jack Brooks. The Texas Democrat found it achingly difficult to act in the impartial, judicial manner that he thought was expected, as he showed in an interview with James Naughton of *The New York Times:* "It's gonna be a fun year, I'm gonna watch all those Republicans and Southern Democrats sit down to a bullet breakfast . . . In a matter of dealing with Nixon, whom I opposed in '52, whom I've never been close to, who doesn't represent my point of view—we're just not compatible, that mother——.'' Rodino had to struggle to prevent these members from alienating the unconvinced.

On the other side were nine conservative Republicans who made it clear from the start that they would go down the line for the President's defense. They ranged from Charles Wiggins (Calif.), whose lawyerly bearing cloaked partisanship with objectivity, to Michigan's Edward Hutchinson, ranking minority member of the committee, who stated at the beginning of the inquiry that Nixon should not be removed from office "for every little impeachable offense." The chairman sought to give the undecided members— such as Flowers, Thorton, Railsback, Mann, McClory, Cohen, Butler, Froehlich, Hogan, and Fish—room to move and time to decide. Most of them had to wrestle with their consciences—and with their constituencies as well. Each of them would face reelection in just over a year, and it was clear that this was the issue on which they would be judged.

Rodino recognized that history was looking over his shoulder and would want to know not only what the committee concluded about Nixon, but also whether it had acted fairly. The members were not only judging Richard Nixon, but were establishing standards by which to judge all future Presidents. Part of this legacy for the future was a report entitled "Constitutional Grounds for Presidential Impeachment," which rejected the Nixon White House notion that a President could only be impeached for committing an indictable crime. The report pointed out that "some of the most grievous offenses against our constitutional form of government may not entail violation of the criminal law," and that "it would be anomalous if the founders, having barred criminal sanctions from the impeachment remedy . . . intended to restrict the grounds for impeachment to conduct that was criminal."

This report was supplemented by the staff's presentation, in closed session, of the evidence against President Nixon. The members received thirty-six looseleaf notebooks which contained over 7,200 pages of evidence and 650 findings of fact. Most of the material focused on the Watergate break-in and cover-up, allegations of bribery in the ITT and milk price support cases, domestic surveillance, abuse of the IRS, and the activities of the special prosecutor. Several of the original subjects of the inquiry, such as the secret bombing of Cambodia and the impoundment of funds appropriated by Congress, were given less attention, or ignored altogether. "Ironically, the allegations that received the least attention from the staff, and, ultimately, from the Committee," recalled one staff member, "were the ones most directly related to the relative roles of Congress and the executive branch and the balance of power between the two."

The staff report and presentation, however, was quickly rejected by the conservative Republicans, who looked instead for absolute proof that Nixon had committed an impeachable offense. The search for a "smoking gun" was enhanced by the White House's self-destructive ability to shock Congress and the nation at frequent intervals. The catch phrases for the building body of evidence against the President—Saturday Night Massacre, 18½-minute gap—were constantly on the lips of the committee members and the nation.

Finally, in July 1974, committee counsel John Doar began to summarize the case against Richard Nixon, telling the members that "reasonable men acting reasonably would find the President guilty." Doar's presentation was of great importance to many of the undecided members. "It's one thing to have four great big volumes of evidence that tell you the facts about Watergate," said Thomas Railsback (R.-Ill.). "It's another thing to have an advocate's brief that boils down the relevant facts and gives you legal theories. You get a much better picture of the case."

Armed with Doar's summation, and the knowledge that a decision could not be put off much longer, the members of the so-called swing group gradually made up their individual and collective minds to vote to impeach the President of the United States. Walter Flowers (D.-Ala.) described the agony of how he made his decision:

The more I thought about it, and tried to think about doing something else, I realized I couldn't. Then the undecided people got together and we started talking among ourselves. Most of us probably started out looking for a way to support the President. My whole background and upbringing would make me that way. Who I am and where I come from. But when you got all of the evidence before us so-called "persuadables" and we all came down on the same side that really struck us. . . . I tried to look at it from the side of what happens if we fail to impeach. It's worse.

Beginning on July 24, before a national television audience, the articles of impeachment were considered. Three were passed. One, which passed 27–11, charged the President with pursuing "a course of conduct or plan" to cover up the Watergate break-in. The other two involved his failures to "faithfully execute" his office and to respond to congressional subpoenas for 147 taped conversations. Three more articles charging misuse of government moneys, tax fraud, and the secret bombings of Cambodia failed to pass.

A week after the committee filed its charges, the White House bowed to a unanimous Supreme Court and released the transcript of a tape of three conversations between Nixon and Haldeman that proved Nixon had ordered the beginning of the cover-up six days after the Watergate break-in. The tape proved to be the so-called "smoking gun" neither the President nor Congress could ignore. Within hours of the transcripts' release, the remaining eleven Republican members of the Judiciary Committee had announced their support for the first article of impeachment.

What did the committee's proceedings on impeachment have to say to future Presidents? Probably that impeachment may be easier to contemplate and more difficult to pursue. Representative Elizabeth Holtzman (D.-N.Y.) commented that "when the subject of impeachment was first brought up everyone was saying that the country wouldn't tolerate it, that people wouldn't understand the constitutional and political questions involved. We've shown that they can and we've also made it clear that in future questions of impeachment, a President will be held responsible directly and through his aides.''

To John Conyers, however, author of the aborted Cambodia resolution, there was a slightly different lesson. ''I think the advice we've left for the next President interested in subverting the Constitution is quite simple—don't tape yourself. I think we've set impossibly high standards for any future impeachment inquiry . . . In the areas where there were no tapes and smoking guns, the issues that involved interference with the Congress, we either acted in a very confused manner or we didn't act at all.''

Congress v. Carter and Reagan—A New Balance?

For decades Congress was a broken branch of government. When confronted with national problems or overreaching Presidents, it receded and acquiesced. Its ability to initiate legislation, shape the budget, participate in war or foreign policy, and oversee the executive bureaucracy went slack and atrophied. ''The Congress does not like to take responsibility,'' wrote Elizabeth Drew in 1974. ''It would prefer not to have to end a war, delay development of a weapon, raise taxes, or take on a President—except when it appears safe to do so. And after it has taken an important action, it usually wants to take a rest.''

Finally, in the mid-1970s, members of Congress responded to their institutional erosion because, as Governor Adlai Stevenson once said in another context, they could ''see the handwriting on the wall only when their backs [were] to it.'' Nixon and Watergate put their backs to the wall. The passage over Nixon's veto of the War Powers Act was the first shot in the power realignment. It was followed by the congressional refusal to approve a supplemental appropriation to ''wind down'' the Indochina War and the near-unanimous passage of the Budget and Impoundment Control Act of 1974. Finally, the Watergate and impeachment hearings dramatically demonstrated the ultimate power of Congress over the President when executive abuses reach a critical mass.

By the time Jimmy Carter came to the White House, Congress had been in a fighting mood for several years. According to Representative Morris Udall (D.-Ariz.), "Anybody who took the oath on that January day in 1977 was going to face this giant, which had awakened after slumbering for many years . . . You could have resurrected Lincoln, Washington, and Franklin Roosevelt, had a synthesis of them all, and I'm sure [President Carter] would still have trouble." The adversarial habit, provoked and unleashed by Nixon, now seemed hard to stop, which upset Representative John Anderson. "There is a confluence of historical forces that have brought an erosion in executive power. It was necessary for a while but there has been an overreaction that has caused the pendulum to swing too far." To Senator Alan Cranston, however, the recent congressional assertiveness is not something to fret over. "Congress has reawakened to its Constitutional role," he said in an interview. "Executive-legislative relations were *too* perfect under Johnson. . . . There are supposed to be tensions and differences between the two branches." And Carter, being the first "non-congressional" President since Eisenhower, seemed to pay for his lack of prior allies in the Congress. President Kennedy, for example, won 83 percent of his congressional votes; President Johnson, 90 percent; and President Nixon, with the opposite party controlling Congress, 76 percent. President Carter won 77 percent during his first two years in office. When he was then asked by Bill Moyers what had been the most unpleasant surprises of his presidency, he answered that "one was the inertia of Congress, the length of time it takes to get a complicated piece of legislation through Congress."

Carter, certainly, won some significant legislative victories in his one term in office—from enactment of the Panama Canal treaty to passage of a civil service reform bill. But his is widely remembered as a presidency that failed, because he failed to exercise adequate leadership with Congress. Carter critics blame his underwhelming "congressional liaison" office, his lack of coherent philosophy and unwillingness to horse-trade with legislators. (During a flight to Boston in the 1980 general election campaign, President Carter told a startled speaker Tip O'Neill and Senator Edward Kennedy, "I never did like politics.") Carter allies observe that no President could look good when OPEC tripled energy prices and Khomeini held fifty-two Americans hostage. Whatever the reason, by the time voters rejected him in 1980, many commentators were agreeing with former President Gerald Ford when he said, "We have not an imperial presidency but an imperiled presidency." Two thoughtful books—*All Things to All Men* by Godfrey Hodgson and *None of the Above* by Robert Shogan—worried that the inability of Presidents to fulfill high public expectations was leading to a string of failed presidencies. Joseph Califano, former high aide to both Johnson and Carter, described in his own book *Governing America* how nearly impossible it was for a President to get Congress to enact significant change.

Yet in apparent sharp contrast came Ronald Reagan, who successfully got his major economic program of tax and budget cuts through a Congress that (at least nominally) was half Democratically controlled. The kudos, at least in the first half of his term, were deafening. "The chief executive is well on the way," said *U.S. News and World Report* of Reagan's hundredth day, "to reshaping American government more radically than any occupant of the Oval Office since Franklin D. Roosevelt." In the view of political correspondent David Broder, Reagan's first year "proved that a President and his party, using nothing more than the existing tools of politics and persuasion, were all that were needed." James L. Sundquist, author of *The Decline and Resurgence of Congress*, wrote that only four times in this century had a President done so well with Congress as Reagan had in his first year: after Wilson's first election, after FDR's first election, and LBJ in 1965–66. "The system works well at only one time—right after a landslide election," added Sundquist. "This is one of those brief periods in our history when a President comes riding a great tide of personal popularity."

Since Reagan's first-year success and difficulties thereafter roughly reflect the ups and downs of the modern President, it would be useful to summarize why he was considered so initially successful.

Rather than overload the congressional circuitry, he insisted that Congress focus only on his self-defined mandate—to cut spending and taxes. His history in movies and as a corporate spokesman had perfected his ability to go over the heads of Congress and telegenically appeal for public support via television; members couldn't help but notice the tons of mail and calls generated by his trained sincerity on TV. The combination of his personal charm in private meetings (UN Ambassador Jeanne Kirkpatrick referred to his "implacable affability") *and* the willingness of his staff to logroll won over many wavering officials. The White House's ability to mobilize the money and contacts of supporting corporate PACs and business lobbies was unprecedented—and gave Reagan a decisive edge over Carter in working a Congress very attentive to well-endowed business constitutents. Reagan's lobbying office was widely regarded as more experienced, professional, and responsive than Carter's. Tom Korologos, a predecessor, said admiringly of Max Friedersdorf, the head of congressional liaison at the Reagan White House, "He knows the hill, what makes them tick—and he knows what kind of cigars Tip O'Neill smokes. That's what's important. The big things, like welfare reform, the MX missile, SALT, take care of themselves. What's really important is knowing what door to send the car to when you're picking up a senator."

Perhaps. But for Reagan what was ultimately important was Republican congressional unity. Much press focused on Reagan's wooing of four dozen southern Democratic "Boll Weevils" in the House. But it's traditional for many southern conservative Democrats to vote with a conservative Republican President. What was unusual was how many northern Republican moderates did so. On the two major budget votes and tax cut of 1981, *all* Republican senators voted in favor each time and *all* of the 192 House Republicans did so except two (Claudine Schneider of Rhode Island and James Jeffords of Vermont). An envious Tony Coelho (D.-Calif.) saw it as akin to the "parliamentary discipline" that characterizes Western European

217

governments, not ours. Especially after the assassination attempt, Republican legislators—glued together by ideology, a popular President, and often Republican National Committee money—were in no mood to buck Ronald Reagan. Their unity plus the usual number of defecting "Boll Weevils" (a.k.a. "Dixiecrats") gave the President de facto control of the Congress.

But as was the case with Wilson and Johnson, this window of opportunity closed fast. Reagan's economic program got enacted, but it didn't work as advertised. His popularity fell, Democrats picked up 26 House seats, and he lost control of Congress. The first telltale sign was the House rejection of his MX missile plans in the lame-duck session in late 1982; this was quickly followed by a jobs bill initiated by House Democrats (and signed by Reagan) and the passage of the House Democratic budget in March 1983 by a comfortable 33 vote margin. Nor did Reagan help his cause by shrill ideological attacks on congressional Democrats (e.g., claims that the other party's budget, because it increased military spending "only" $70 billion over four years, would "bring joy to the Kremlin"). Nineteen eighty-three, then, began a period of consensus government, in which neither branch dominated since both had the wherewithal to veto the other.

The decade from 1973 to 1983, then, saw a Congress lurching to and fro between what Arthur Schlesinger, Jr., called "the imperial presidency" and what Daniel Patrick Moynihan called "the imperial Congress"—or what authors Hodgson, Shogan, and Califano worried was the incapacity of Presidents to fulfill their electoral mandates. This swing was simply a more compressed version of a historical and constitutional ebb and flow between these two branches of government. Occasionally Congress seems strong—largely due to weak and/or inexperienced Presidents. But according even to former Senator Edmund Muskie, himself a candidate for the presidency and architect of the Budget Act, "No matter how assertive [Congress] is, or how creative and qualified for leadership individual members are, maybe the institution is not really equipped to act as a strong leader."

There is no such doubt about the powers of the President overall. With few exceptions the executive branch remains ascendant, due to its sway over national media, the budget process, appointments, foreign policy, projects and contracts, the intelligence and law enforcement apparatus, and the expertise of the bureaucracy. Presidents will predictably complain about their institutional inadequacies—as the chapter's epigraph by Theodore Roosevelt reveals—but they still sit in the cockpit of power in Washington.

5

Lawmakers as Lawbreakers

*It could probably be shown by facts and figures that there
is no distinctly American criminal class except Congress.*
—Mark Twain

When national leaders cried out for "law and order" in the late
sixties and early seventies, no one thought to apply their words to
themselves. Now we know better. If nothing else, Watergate—which
has become as much a cliché as a lesson—should have instructed us
that it is folly to assume that people of prominence and power will
invariably be law-abiding. A good place to apply this wisdom is the
American Congress. The most obvious reason is symbolic: if chosen
people have the power to make the law, then they should respect the
law. If they do not, they can scarcely expect that others will.

Corruption involving criminal conduct has shaken Congress at
least since 1873, when the House censured two members for their
roles in the Crédit Mobilier stock scandal. While Congress and the
country have passed through fundamental metamorphoses since then,
one constant theme has been the public's suspicion of the people it
sends to Washington. This was not the constitutional mistrust that
had plagued the Founding Fathers—the gnawing fear that people in
power would become tyrants. Instead, it was the suspicion of personal venality, that those in government were somehow turning a
profit.

In 1965, Gallup pollsters found that four times as many people thought that "political favoritism and corruption in Washington" were rising as thought them falling. Two years later, as Congress washed its hands of Adam Clayton Powell, Gallup asked whether the revelations about Powell had surprised the public. Sixty percent thought that Powell's offenses—which the questionnaire called "misuse of government funds"—were fairly common. (Twenty-one percent disagreed.) Powell had protested, in victimized anguish, that he was only one public scapegoat among many quiet offenders. "There is no one here," he said to his accusers, "who does not have a skeleton in his closet."

The skeletons vary in size. The smallest are the personal peccadilloes—which are the stuff of public amusement, scorn, and regular exposure by Washington columnists. Outweighing these in importance are the systematic violations of Congress's own rules and laws, offenses which are not quite crimes, but which are the next biggest skeletons in congressional closets. Finally, there is the *summum malum* of congressional crime, instances of bribery, perjury, and influence-peddling. Taken together the pervasiveness of lawbreaking amounts to a grim commentary on those who govern us.

Not Quite a Crime: Peccadilloes, Rules, and Laws

Congressmen are people, and subject to the same temptations and flaws as other people. At times their visibility makes them suffer more for their failings than they otherwise would. An omission or mistake which would pass unnoticed in a plumber may become big news when attached to a politically important name. This does not excuse congressional misconduct. Just as the public expects higher standards of personal morality from those who instruct its children than from those who fix its pipes, so it expects high standards from those who make its laws.

In order to assure them freedom to exercise their duties free from harassment, congressmen are granted immunity from arrest for statements made, or actions taken, in Congress or while coming from or going to Congress. This desirable privilege, however, has frequently been abused by congressmen caught in unsavory escapades. In his prepresidential days, for example, Senator Warren Harding was surprised by two New York policemen while visiting friend Nan Britton in a hotel room. As the police prepared to arrest him on charges of fornication, carnal knowledge, and drunken driving, Harding successfully argued that as a senator he could not be arrested. It was hardly what the Constitution intended for congressional immunity, but it worked well in that situation.

Several years ago Texas Representative Joe Pool rammed his car into the back of another car stopped at a red light. Pool refused to accept a traffic ticket from a policeman and, later, from his sergeant. Instead he repeated over and over, "I am a congressman and I cannot be arrested." Unimpressed, the police held him for six hours before releasing him. "He kept saying he was a congressman," said the policeman, "but he didn't look like one or sound like one." Later Pool confided to a friend, "I thought they couldn't arrest a congressman unless he'd committed a felony. But it turns out they *can* unless he's en route to or returning from a session of Congress."

They *can*, but they *don't*. On the way to a party in the summer of 1972, Mississippi Representative Jamie Whitten—who normally conducts himself with decorum—ran a stop sign in Georgetown and struck a car, an iron fence, two trees, a brick wall, and another car on the other side of the wall. Whitten said his accelerator stuck, but an investigating officer said at the scene, "The guy's been drinking; there's alcohol on his breath. I don't think he's drunk. But he's shook up." No arrest was made and no charges were filed. "The first thing [Whitten] did," said the owner of the wall, "was to get out of the car and begin shaking everyone's hand."

In fact, there are numerous instances of congressmen driving amok. In October 1982, Representative Joel Deckard (R.-Ind.) ran his car into a tree while drunk (and lost his reelection bid the next month). The year before, Representative Larry Winn, Jr. (R.-Kans.) pleaded guilty to a charge of driving while intoxicated. Back in August 1972, House Speaker Carl Albert drove his car into two cars shortly before midnight, and several witnesses reported that he "was obviously drunk"—a characterization Albert denied. In addition he reportedly told a police officer on the scene, "You can't arrest me, I got you your raise." Of course, there was also the "Tidal Basin incident"—wherein, among other bizarre happenings, Wilbur Mills's car was speeding with its lights off. These last two incidents have two things in common: a congressman was involved and his name never appeared on a police blotter.

Annoying as these cases might be, they are small potatoes. They involve single, unplanned romps, not deliberate self-enrichment or serious affairs of state. If this were the extent of congressional lawlessness, we could require a special driver's education course as a condition of entering Congress or the Oval Office and all sleep a little easier at night.

But it's not. Worse is the hypocrisy of congressmen abusing their own rules. Consider, for example, junketing.

Congressmen who legislate about foreign affairs or military bases may do a better job if they've seen some of the areas for themselves. That's the theory, and it's valid for some. In practice, however, many trips are personal vacations with family rather than public fact-finding. In 1971, then Senator William Saxbe had a dismal 45 percent roll-call record because of his many excursions. "I took every free trip I could get," admitted the candid Saxbe. "I like to travel." In the same year, 51 percent of Congress—53 senators and 221 representatives—took foreign trips at public expense; the total cost to taxpayers was $1,114,386. Hong Kong and the Caribbean turned out to be favorite destinations for those supposedly seeking self-education. By 1977, 255 representatives or senators (47 percent) took a total of 415 trips costing $1,532,326. "Scratch hard in December," one congressman has joked, "and you'll come up with a quorum in Hong Kong." There may even be motives beyond the chance of a vacation. "Those who do get away," Jerry Landauer wrote in *The Wall Street Journal*, "will enjoy little-known opportunities [double-billings, for example] for lining their own pockets—opportunities that some have exploited in the past."

In August of 1981 so many members left Washington to go abroad that Congress looked like the UN at the end of a session. For example: seven members went on an eighteen-day trip to New Zealand, Australia, and Southeast Asia; five left for a week to Bermuda and Panama; eight flew off for eighteen days to four African countries; two went to visit four European capitals for three weeks; several were destined for China and Japan. Beyond such full-scale trips is the frequent use of expensive military aircraft as a kind of personal shuttle service which congressional rules say is to be used only "when travel is in the national interest and commercial travel is not available." *U.S. News & World Report* says that more than a quarter of the Congress used the Air Forces's 89th Wing for such travel—costing taxpayers $2 million in 1982—travel, the magazine said that occurred even though commercial flights were often available. Senator Goldwater, for example, flew on a Navy A3 from D.C. to Las Vegas and back to attend a meeting of Navy pilots; although the commercial round-trip fare was $690, the special flight cost taxpayers $13,000. When Armed Services chairman John Tower was to be a guest speaker at West Point, the 89th flew him and his wife round-trip for $5,555.*

A second hoary example of bending the rules for private benefit is abuse of the franking privilege—the congressman's right to free postage. Every time you receive mail with his signature where the stamp usually goes, you are receiving franked mail. In theory the frank can only be used for official business and never for political mail. The line is fine, and the effort it would take to inspect the hundreds of bins full of mail which roll down congressional office corridors every day would hardly be worthwhile.

The cost of abuse can still be serious. In 1968, Senator Everett Dirksen was found to have given some of his franked envelopes to an overtly political organization—a Republican voter registration group. There was no estimate of the cost involved, but there was in

---

*Both chambers do prohibit lame ducks from traveling abroad after election day and before their retirement.

an earlier case involving Senator Robert Griffin. After looking through some of the newsletters Griffin had sent out during the 1966 campaign, the Post Office decided that some were political campaign material. In a typical, doomed display of strength, the Post Office demanded $25,000 from Griffin to pay for the postage. Griffin, astonished, said that his mail was no more political than anyone else's. This gives scant consolation to the Post Office or the taxpayers, but it removed the heat from Griffin. The Post Office conceded the struggle with the droll statement that use of the frank is "a matter strictly between the member of Congress and his conscience."

Large-scale juggling of committee rules (as discussed in Chapter 3) and committee staff is also widespread. It is almost impossible, for example, to separate people who work for chairman Dan Rostenkowski from those who are supposed to serve the House Ways and Means Committee. This sort of thing springs less from any special avarice in chairmen's souls than from the committee and seniority systems. The fond references that a chairman will make to "my" committee show how deep the confusion runs. When a chairman lifts a researcher from "his" committee and puts him to work on some other task, more than the committee suffers. The system of fortresslike power bases, built around the mighty chairmen, grows stronger as well. Before his downfall, Senator Tom Dodd reportedly had thirteen of the twenty-one staff members of the Juvenile Delinquency subcommittee working for Dodd's office. Occasionally voices rise in complaint. In early 1975 a seven-part series in *The Washington Post* documented the exploitation of committee staff and field hearings in painstaking detail—naming names for those who cared.

Congressmen suffer equally mild twinges of conscience about using their own staff members for political campaigns. The element of abuse is clear: staff people are paid by the government, not by the senator or representative; they are paid to serve the office, not to help the man who happens to be in office to stay there. In 1968 the two senators Kennedy admitted that twenty of their staffers were working on Robert Kennedy's presidential campaign.

But it *is* illegal: Public Law 89–90 says an assistant can't be paid "if such does not perform the services for which he receives such compensation, in the offices of such Member . . ." Because the law is so widely violated, violation becomes custom, and custom replaces law. There are many instances of this phenomenon. Nearly all congressmen violated the archaic 1925 Federal Corrupt Practices Act (replaced in 1972), which aimed to limit campaign funding and to require some disclosure of campaign finances; yet no one has ever been prosecuted for it. An 1872 law directs House and Senate officials to deduct from a member's salary a day's pay for each day's absence, except for illness; in the last hundred years this has been done exactly twice, although there are unjustified absentees daily.

Nor is Congress always attentive even to international or constitutional law. Former Representative John Rooney, for example, for years managed to obstruct American funding of the International Labor Organization because he disliked its allegedly leftist leanings. In so doing, he violated our UN obligation to help support the ILO. And an enterprising *Fort Worth Star-Telegram* reporter in 1974 discovered that at least twenty senators and representatives had odd requirements for staff positions, like "only a white girl, prefer Floridians" (Representative James Haley, D.-Fla.), "white only" (Senator William Scott, D.-Va.), "attractive, smart, young, and no Catholics . . ." (Representative Albert Johnson, R.-Pa.). Indeed, that August the Congressional Office of Placement and Office Management had to delete discriminatory job requirements from some 80 percent of the job orders from 140 congressional offices. Senator John Glenn (D.-Ohio) calls Capitol Hill "the last plantation."

Violation of equal opportunity standards is only one of several laws members of Congress might violate—*if* they permitted the law to apply to them. But since they are the lawmakers, they have decided that they are above the following laws that private employers and citizens have to observe:

• Equal Pay Act. This law guarantees women the same pay that men receive everywhere, except on Capitol Hill.

• Age Discrimination in Employment Act. Workers between the ages of forty and sixty-five are protected from discrimination by this law, except in Congress.

• The National Labor Relations Act. Congress is exempt from this law, which requires employers to recognize unions, and protects employees from unfair labor practices.

• Fair Labor Standards Act. This law, which set minimum wage, overtime pay, and child labor standards, affects all institutions except Congress.

• The Civil Rights Act of 1964. It forbids discrimination on the basis of race, color, religion, sex or national origin—but does not apply to Congress.

• Freedom of Information Act. Congress ordered the executive branch to open its files to the public, under this law, but decided to keep its own records closed to the people who pay the congressmen's salaries.

• Conflicts of interest. Federal law prohibits executive branch employees from participating in federal transactions involving companies in which they have a financial interest. Members of Congress have no such restriction.

• State and municipal taxes. Members are exempt from paying local income taxes in Maryland, Virginia, and Washington, D.C.

• Privacy Act. Congress ordered the executive branch to tightly guard the personal records of individual citizens, but exempted itself from the law.

• Occupational Safety and Health Act. This law requires all employers, except in Congress, to maintain federal health and safety standards in the workplace.

In feudal societies man and job were identical. The king and the shepherd lived their roles every hour of the day. When 5:30 P.M. rolled around, they did not put down their work and retire to identical houses in the suburbs. The king had his courtiers and courtesans to remind him of his rank; the shepherd slept with his sheep. Though things have changed since Louis XIV said, *"L'état, c'est moi,"* the pull of old ways is strong—especially to those on top. Like their feudal predecessors, the men who make our laws begin to see themselves as part of the law itself. They are only temporary potentates, brief occupiers of office—but in their few moments of power they feel themselves as durable and as permanent as law. They know that they will decide the rules that the rest of us must live by. If they can shape and manipulate the laws that are to come, can they not manipulate the laws which already exist?

"Men tinged with sovereignty," Senator Paul Douglas once said, "can easily feel that the king can do no wrong." The privileges of the office—the staff, the prestige—inevitably start to seem like natural rights. In most cases congressmen do not think they are doing wrong. For such small stakes—avoiding a traffic ticket, junketing to Hong Kong—few would consciously hazard the glories of office. If money were their only goal, they could follow George Smathers' route from the Senate to the wealthier fields of Washington lobbying. The lawlessness we see is simply the result of guidelines gone rotten from neglect.

Conflicts of Interest

Congress correctly demands a high standard of impartiality from those it confirms for executive and judicial appointments. In 1969, when President Nixon tried and failed to get Judge Clement Haynsworth onto the Supreme Court, the most compelling reason against the nomination was that Haynsworth had tried cases involving businesses in which he held small bits of stock. When industrialist David Packard was nominated as assistant secretary of defense, Congress required that he put $300 million of his personal fortune in a "blind trust," one which manages the money entirely out of Packard's sight. The rationale behind these requirements is biblical and clear: since no man can serve two masters, Congress insists that federal officials put their private interests aside before assuming public duties.

Unfortunately this diligence stops when it comes to the congressmen themselves. No one insists that members sell sensitive shares of stock. The only group with the power to screen the members—their voting constituency—is usually too ill-informed to make any serious judgment.

229

And such conflicts are not considered a crime. In many states they violate the law, but not in Congress, simply because Congress, which writes the laws, chooses not to call what it does illegal.

With so few barriers against it, potential conflict of interest becomes commonplace in Congress. "If everyone abstained on grounds of personal interest," former senator Robert Kerr claimed, "I doubt if you could get a quorum in the United States Senate on any subject." Kerr's own position neatly illustrated the problem. As a multimillionaire oilman from Oklahoma, Kerr stood to lose or gain huge sums, depending on the government's tax rules for oil. As a powerful member of the Senate Finance Committee, Kerr was one of the men who decided what the tax laws would be. It does not take long to see the conflict. "Hell," Kerr bragged, "I'm in everything."

This pattern extends to other business holdings. From evidence turned up in 1976 financial disclosure forms, *Congressional Quarterly* reported that 44 representatives had holdings in one of the top 100 defense contractors, 48 had real-estate interests, 41 held oil or gas stock, and 20 were in pharmaceuticals. That year 12 representatives and 9 senators had direct or family interests in commercial radio or television stations and 81 House members reported an ownership interest in or income from banks, savings and loan associations, or bank holding companies—including two on the Banking Committee and eight on Ways and Means.

In the late 1960s, Clarence Brown of Ohio, for example, held the majority stock in a broadcasting station—and sat on the House subcommittee regulating broadcasting. Brown might have been wise enough to keep his personal affairs out of public decisions. But whenever he took a stand—such as his opposition to public television—his financial stake in the outcome gave at least the appearance of impropriety. (In rebuttal Brown claims that technical FCC rules prohibited him from selling his stock for three years. Accepting this, why then continue to sit on a broadcasting subcommittee?) Former Representative Robert Sikes (D.-Fla.) sat on the House Appropriations Committee that approved the Pentagon budget; at the same time he was a director and shareholder in an insurance firm that sold more than $300 million of life insurance to servicemen on and around military bases—despite the fact that, according to investigator Philip Stern, 145 companies offered cheaper rates.

One of the few congressmen who have bothered to defend such self-serving behavior openly is multimillionaire Senator Russell Long of Louisiana. Like Kerr, Long is an oilman. In the five years before 1969, for example, his income from oil was $1,196,915. Of that, $329,151 was tax-free, thanks to the curious oil depletion allowance. Long was for years chairman, and is now the ranking minority member, of the Senate Finance Committee, which recommends tax plans, including oil depletion clauses, to the Senate. A conflict of interest? Not to Long. "If you have financial interests completely parallel to [those of] your state," he explained, "then you have no problem." What Long is saying is that each senator is the sufficient judge of his own propriety. Once he convinces himself that his companies are really in the best interest of his folks back home, "then you have no problem." It must ease Long's conscience to know that he is helping others when he helps himself.

Occasionally there are men for whom even these lush fringe benefits of political office are not enough. They count the moments wasted which they must spend on the tedium of bills and votes. Such a man was George Smathers. Even while serving as a Florida senator, Smathers was melancholy. "A person with my background can make more money in thirty days [as a lobbyist]," he said, "than he can in fifteen years as a senator."

In preparation for the easy days ahead Smathers spent the closing days of his Senate career collecting IOUs from private interests. According to *Newsday,* Smathers led a posse of Florida congressmen in a secret attempt to salvage a floundering Florida company, Aerodex. Because of what the Air Force called "poor quality work which was endangering the Air Force pilots and aircraft," the Defense Department wanted to cancel a several-million-dollar contract with Aerodex. After Smathers's effort the contract stood.

In 1969, when Smathers retired, he claimed some benefits. He became a director of Aerodex and got an attractive deal on stock:

$435,000 worth of it for $20,000. The company also put Smathers's Washington law firm on a $25,000-a-year retainer. Smathers is now comfortably installed as a lobbyist, fulfilling his earlier exuberant prediction that "I'm going to be a Clark Clifford. That's the life for me."

A second routine conflict involves personal use of campaign funds, what *The New Republic* referred to in a seminal 1982 article as "an outright abuse of the system [that] is neither isolated nor inconsequential." "Although House rules prohibit personal use of campaign funds," said Lisa Myers in an NBC report, "they are conveniently silent on where the campaign ends and where living high on the hog begins." She went on to point out the example of Representative Robert Badham (R.-Calif.), who out of his 1982 campaign funds spent $4,758 to take his wife to Germany, Bermuda, and Panama and $1,467 for three designer dresses. He explained, "I have a pretty wife who is my first campaign asset. Anything, therefore, that puts her in a good exposure light with me . . . *is* beneficial to the campaign." Some members simply pocket surplus campaign money when they retire. The House in December 1979 prohibited future representatives from such conduct but permitted it for themselves. So when John Dent retired in 1978, he kept $44,033 to buy a Florida condominium; Mendel Davis and John Wydler in 1980 diverted $45,047 and $38,510, respectively, to personal use when they decided not to seek reelection. This self-dealing bothers Representative Andy Jacobs, who has introduced legislation to stop the practice. "Campaign contributions involve a trust they will be spent for the purpose for which they were given," he says.

A third important type of conflict of interest comes from congressmen who maintain legal practices. The moral problem here is subtler than that of the oilmen or bankers. A lawyer's business, like a doctor's or writer's, is built on reputation and skill. But when a lawyer also holds government office, his clients might conclude that he can do more for them than another person of similar talent. A widely circulated, widely respected study by the New York City Bar Association strongly condemns the lawyering congressmen. They are the fiduciaries of the public—administrators of public functions, the 1969 bar study says. Accordingly, they must administer this public trust for the public's benefit, not their own. Instead, "law practices have played a disproportionate role in the history of congressional scandals."

More than a century ago New Hampshire's Daniel Webster kept in practice for his Senate orations by appearing as a private lawyer for the Bank of the United States. He argued the private bank's case some forty-one times before the Supreme Court. There was no Committee on Ethics then, and Webster did not have to conceal the relation. When, in his senatorial role, he was considering legislation to extend the bank's charter, he wrote his clients to remind them that "my retainer has not been received and refreshed as usual." While the standards change, certain practices do not. The irrepressible Thomas Dodd, writing to his Hartford law firm for more money, stated the problem candidly: "I'm sure you know that there's a considerable amount of business that goes into the office because of me. Many men in public life receive a steady income from their law practices because of the value of their association [and] my name and association is a realistic fact which definitely has value."

An 1863 statute forbids congressmen-lawyers from representing clients who have claims before the federal government. To avoid embarrassing problems while keeping the business thriving, congressmen used to have an ingenious "two-door" system. On the front door of the law firm was the congressman's name; through this door came the many clients who valued his help. Another door was just the same, except the congressman's name was missing. Here entered those proscribed clients with claims before the government. The ruse was within the letter of the law, but it still irritated purists. Journalist Robert Sherrill, for example, wrote that former representative Emanuel Celler's double doors were "one of the longest-standing and most notorious embarrassments to Congress." To this, Celler had a standard reply: "Your constituents are the final arbiter of any conflicts, and I'm always reelected."

In 1972, after fifty years in the House, Emanuel Celler lost in his Democratic primary to Elizabeth Holtzman.

In 1976 there were still 66 members who reported at least $1,000 in income from outside law practice. During the debate over the ethics bill in 1977 some member-lawyers warned about the impact outside earnings limits would have on their practices. "There are four guys here who have admitted to me they earn more than $130,000 from outside law practice," said Representative David Obey (D.-Wis.), head of a major House inquiry into its ethical practices, in an interview. "One of them told me, 'I don't spend any time practicing law. As my seniority and committee influence increases, these groups keep throwing more business to my firm and I get my cut.' "

As a result of this cashing in of public trust for private gain, the House in 1982 limited outside legal income to 30 percent of congressional pay, or $20,000. There is no limit, however, in the Senate. The tradition of the "two-door" congressmen survives.

Crime and Punishment

It takes no special knowledge of franking laws or staff rules to understand the overt crimes, the calculated offenses against law and morality, committed by congressmen. Motives are easy to find when the potential payoff is millions of dollars, risks for some people become worthwhile. Between 1941 and 1971, according to journalist William Grieder, there were fifteen criminal prosecutions against members, or one every two years. Between 1972 and 1982 there were 29 prosecutions, or three per year—a fivefold increase. Overall in the 1970s twenty-nine members of Congress and nine staff were either convicted of crimes, under indictment by 1979 or being investigated for serious charges by an Ethics committee: "The arrest rate for members of the 95th Congress," wrote journalist Jack Newfield, challenging two stereotypes simultaneously, "was higher than the arrest rate among unemployed black males in Detroit."

What follows is a "Roll Call of Congressional Illegality" of the past twelve years, and ten profiles of some of the most members of recent times who lost their legal comp

ROLL CALL OF CONGRESSIONAL ILLEGALITY

NAME	CHARGE	DISPOSITION (JUNE 1, 1983)
Representative George V. Hansen (R.-Idaho)	Filing false financial disclosure statements (including failure to report a loan from Nelson B. Hunt).	Indicted April 1983.
Representative Frederick W. Richmond (D.-N.Y.)	Tax evasion, possession of marijuana, participation in kickback scheme.	Plea-bargained in August 1982; in exchange, not prosecuted on charges of assisting an escaped convict, or other lesser charges. Agreed to pay SEC $400,000; sentenced to one year and a day prison sentence. Began serving in January 1983.
Senator Harrison Williams (D.-N.J.)	Bribery, conspiracy, accepting outside compensation for performing official duties and racketeering (Abscam)	Convicted May 1981. Senate Ethics Committee voted unanimously for expulsion in August 1981; resigned March 1982 to avoid certain expulsion. Sentenced to three years, $50,000 fine.
Representative Raymond Lederer (D.-Pa.)	Bribery, conspiracy, acceptance of illegal gratuity, aide to racketeering (Abscam)	Reelected in 1980. Convicted January 1981. Resigned May 1981, the day after Standards Committee urged expulsion. Sentenced to three years, $20,000 fine.
Representative Richard Kelly (R.-Fla.)	Bribery and conspiracy (Abscam)	Convicted January 1981. Lost 1980 primary. Conviction overturned by judge who held that the FBI's tactics were "outrageous." Conviction restored by higher court, May 1983.

NAME	CHARGE	DISPOSITION (JUNE 1, 1983)
Representative John Murphy (D.-N.Y.)	Bribery, conspiracy, acceptance of illegal gratuity (Abscam)	Defeated for reelection, 1980. Convicted December 1980. Conflict of interest charge overturned on appeal; others upheld. Sentenced to three years, $20,000 fine (lowered to $10,000).
Senator Herman Talmadge (D.-Ga.)	Incomplete and inaccurate campaign expense reports; using campaign gifts for personal activities	"Censured" by Senate in 1979. Defeated for reelection, 1980.
Representative Frank Thompson (D.-N.J.)	Conspiracy, acceptance of unlawful gratuity (Abscam)	Convicted December 1980. Defeated for reelection, 1980. Sentencing postponed due to ill health; appeal pending.
Representative John Jenrette, Jr. (D.-S.C.)	Bribery and conspiracy (Abscam)	Convicted October 1980. Defeated for reelection, 1980. Resigned from House in December 1980 just before Ethics Committee was to vote for expulsion. Not yet sentenced.
Representative Michael Meyers (D.-Pa.)	Bribery, conspiracy and interstate travel to aid racketeering (Abscam)	Convicted August 1980. Expelled from House October 1980. Sentenced to three years, $20,000 fine.
Representative Daniel Flood (D.-Pa.)	Bribery, conspiracy, and perjury	Indicted, 1978. Hung jury, 1979. Reelected to 96th Congress but lost Appropriations subcommittee chair. Resigned from Congress, 1980. Pleaded guilty to conspiracy charge one month later, and placed on one year probation.

Name	Charge	Outcome
Senator Edward Brooke (R.-Mass.)	Failure to disclose finances accurately to Senate	Senate Ethics Committee in 1979 concluded that he gave "false testimony under oath" and that "violations within the jurisdiction of the committee had occurred"; since violations were "minor," no sanctions were recommended. Previously defeated for reelection 1978.
Representative J. Herbert Burke (R.-Fla.)	Disorderly intoxication, resisting an officer—in connection with incident in bar	Pleaded guilty. Fined $150 and sentenced to three months probation. Lost reelection bid, 1978.
Representative Charles Diggs, Jr. (D.-Mich.)	Federal mail fraud and salary kickbacks	Convicted on 29 counts, 1978. Sentenced to three years. Reelected (overwhelmingly after) his conviction. Censured by House. Served seven months in prison, 1980.
Representative Joshua Eilberg (D.-Pa.)	Conflict of interest	Pleaded guilty February 1979, to illegally accepting money for aiding the procurement of a federal grant. Sentenced to five years probation, $10,000 fine. Defeated for reelection, 1978.
Representative John McFall (D.-Calif.)	Violation of ethics rules for failing to report campaign contribution of South Korean businessman Tongsun Park	Reprimanded by House, 1978. Defeated for reelection, 1978.
Representative Edward Roybal (D.-Calif.)	Same as Representative McFall	Reprimanded by House, 1978.
Representative Charles H. Wilson (D.-Calif.)	Lying to the House Ethics Committee about money he took from Tongsun Park	Reprimanded by House, 1978.
Representative Henry Helstoski (D.-N.J.) (1965–77)	Bribery	Indicted, 1976. Case still pending.

NAME	CHARGE	DISPOSITION (JUNE 1, 1983)
Representative Andrew Hinshaw (R.-Calif.) (1973–77)	Bribery	Indicted, 1975. Convicted, 1976, and sentenced to 1–14 years. Served seven months.
Representative Richard Tonry (D.-La.) (1977)	Violation of federal election laws	Pleaded guilty, July 1977. Served six months in prison.
Representative James Hastings (R.-N.Y.) (1969–76)	Mail fraud, salary kickbacks	Indicted, 1976. Convicted on 28 counts, 1977. Sentenced to twenty months–five years. Paroled, 1978; after serving fourteen months.
Representative Wayne Hays (D.-Ohio) (1949–76)	Misuse of office account	Resigned from Congress 1976, after disclosure that he kept mistress on congressional payroll in return for sexual favors.
Representative James Jones (D.-Okla.)	Campaign financing violation	Pleaded guilty, January 1976, to a misdemeanor charge of failing to report receipt of a cash contribution from the Gulf Oil Corp., in 1972. Fined $200.
Representative Frank Brasco (D.-N.Y.) (1967–75)	Conspiring to accept bribes	Indicted, October 1973. Convicted and sentenced to three months in jail and fined $10,000.
Representative George Hansen (R.-Idaho)	Campaign financing violation	Pleaded guilty in federal court, February 1975, to charges of failing to file one campaign financing report and lying in another. Sentenced to two months in jail, reduced to $2,000 fine.

Representative	Charge	Outcome
Representative Bertram Podell (D.-N.Y.) (1968–75)	Bribery, conspiracy, conflict of interest	Pleaded guilty to conspiracy and conflict of interest, 1974. Sentenced to six months in prison, fined $5,000.
Representative Wendell Wyatt (R.-Ore.) (1964–75)	Failure to report expenditures of campaign funds	Fined $750, 1975.
Representative Frank Clark (D.-Pa.) (1955–74)	Mail fraud, perjury, income tax evasion	Indicted, 1978. Pleaded guilty to one count of mail fraud, one count of income tax evasion in February 1979.
Representative Richard Hanna (D.-Calif.) (1963–74)	Conspiracy to defraud government	Pleaded guilty. Sentenced to six to thirty months in prison.
Representative John Dowdy (D.-Tex.) (1953–73)	Perjury	Indicted, March 1971. Convicted and sentenced to 6 months and fined $3,000.
Representative Nick Galifianakis (D.-N.C.) (1967–73)	Lied to House about taking $10,000 from Tongsun Park	Indicted, May 1979.
Representative Cornelius Gallagher (D.-N.J.) (1959–73)	Income tax evasion	Indicted, 1972. Convicted and served six months and fined $10,000.
Representative J. Irving Whalley (R.-Pa.) (1960–73)	Mail fraud, obstruction of justice	Indicted and convicted, 1973; three years probation, fined $11,000.
Representative Martin McKneally (R.-N.Y.) (1969–71)	Failure to file income tax report	Indicted, 1970. Pleaded guilty, 1971; placed on probation, fined $5,000.

NAME	CHARGE	DISPOSITION (JUNE 1, 1983)
Recent Congressional Staff		
Robert T. Carson (Senator Fong)	Perjury, conspiracy to accept and offer bribes	Indicted, 1971. Convicted and sentenced to eighteen months in prison and fined $5,000.
Albert De Falco (Representative Helstoski)	Extortion	Indicted, 1975. Convicted and sentenced to six years.
Stephen B. Elko (Representative Flood)	Bribery	Indicted, 1977. Sentenced to three years in prison. Received immunity for testimony against Representative Flood.
Pauline Girvin (Speaker Albert)	Mail fraud	Pleaded guilty, 1975, to misdemeanor extortion charge. Sentenced to one year in jail. Reduced to sixty days plus two years probation.
George A. Haag (Representative Collins)	Mail fraud, obstruction of justice	Convicted, 1972. Sentenced to six months–three years.
Michael McPherson (Representative Clay)	Mail fraud	Pleaded guilty, 1976. Sentenced to six months in prison, eventually served three and one half months.
Alfred Porro (Representative Helstoski)	Obstruction of justice	Indicted, 1976. Case still pending.
Martin Sweig (Speaker McCormack)	Perjury	Convicted, 1970. Sentenced to thirty months and fined $2,000.
Vincent Verdiramo (Representative Helstoski)	Conspiracy to obstruct justice	Indicted, 1976. Convicted September 21, 1977. Sentenced to two months in jail and paid $2,500 fine.

* * *

BOBBY BAKER. In 1942, with sixty dollars in his back pocket, fourteen-year-old Bobby Baker left Pickens, South Carolina, and never looked back. Like a lamprey searching for a host, he made his way to Washington, found the Senate, and attached himself for a twenty-year-ride. First as page, then as clerk, he moved up the ladder. His break came when he made a friend, Lyndon Johnson. His friend became majority leader of the Senate and did not forget the small people he had met along the way. From 1955 until 1963, even after Johnson had left the post, Baker was secretary to the majority leader. "You're like a son to me," Johnson said as he helped Bobby up. To Baker, Johnson was, if not a father, at least "my best friend around the capital." By 1960, Baker was being introduced to freshman page boys as "a powerful demonstrator of just how far intelligence combined with a gracious personality can take a man."

The tragedy of 1963 was a bad omen for Bobby. His old friend had become President—but had risen too high to keep in touch with Bobby. Critics began to grow suspicious about Baker's wealth. From a net worth of $11,000 in 1955, he had become a multimillionaire—an annual rate of increase of $200,000–$300,000—all while earning a salary of $19,600 per year. One explanation for the gap came when a civil lawsuit claimed that Baker had used his influence to help a firm win a government contract. With that the Senate Rules and Administration Committee took a closer look at him. By 1965 the Democratic majority had issued a report citing "many gross improprieties" in his behavior—but no legal violations. To many senators, both Republicans and Democrats, this looked like a crude whitewash. Over the next few months Senator John Williams of Delaware earned himself the title "conscience of the Senate" by hounding Baker and his apologists.

The legal ax fell in 1966, when Baker was finally indicted for fraud, larceny, and tax evasion. The major charge was that he had collected $100,000 from a group of California savings and loans executives for campaign contributions, and then kept $80,000 of it himself. Even as he protested his innocence, Baker realized that his exposure was straining some of his former cronies. "My friends in Congress," he said with slight bitterness, "have had no choice but to think of me as a bad dream or something." No one had less choice about the matter than Baker's best friend, the President of the United States. He retained public composure, even indifference, over the matter—which did not entirely surprise Baker, who had seen friendships bloom and die in the seasons of convenience. He knew that "the American people would have destroyed and defeated President Johnson had he attempted in any way to do anything on my behalf."

Baker went to trial, was convicted, and was sentenced to one to three years. By 1971, when he was released, the bad memories may have lingered, but the punishment was over and he was still rich. And unremorseful. His 1978 best-seller, appropriately titled *Wheeling and Dealing*, tried to excuse Baker's crimes by portraying him as a "child of the Senate":

> Like my bosses and sponsors in the Senate, I was ambitious and eager to feather my personal nest. . . . As they presumed their high station to entitle them to accept gratuities or hospitalities from patrons who had an axe to grind, so did I. As they took advantage of privileged information to get in on the ground floor of attractive investments, so did I. As they used their powerful positions to gain loans or credit that otherwise might not have been granted, so did I.

ADAM CLAYTON POWELL. It was not his romances that drove the white folks mad—his colleagues had tolerated that in others—nor was it his laziness, nor his endless vacation trips. It was not even the way he turned every power of his office toward his boundless hedonism. Congress had seen it all before, and had forgiven. Adam Clayton Powell's sin was flagrance—his refusal to hide what he was doing. Others might filch dollars from the cash box at night: Powell skimmed off his profit in full public view. While Congress was in session and the committee he chaired slogged away at its work, Powell posed for photographers with Miss Ohio at his island haven in the Caribbean.

For a while Powell tapped a special mood of the times. The same panache which enraged other congressmen made Powell a hero to his Harlem constituents: he was winning at the white man's game. In the two decades of his prime—at the time when he was being ridiculed in the House cloakroom as "the congressman from Bimini" or "the Harlem Globetrotter"—Powell sailed through elections as if anointed. He won his first term in 1944. By 1961 enough other congressmen had died or lost so that Powell became chairman of the Education and Labor Committee—the second black chairman in congressional history.

Toward the mid-1960s, after an earlier vigor and productivity, Powell began to spend large chunks of the terms vacationing— sometimes using false names, usually with lady friends, always at government expense. He kept up his family ties by putting his wife on his office payroll at $20,000 per year, a gracious gesture to a woman then living in Puerto Rico. A first brush with the law left Powell unscarred: in 1958 he was indicted for income tax evasion, but escaped the charge after paying $28,000 in back taxes and penalties. If he had stopped then, curbing the excesses and cutting down on the publicity, Powell might have spent another ten terms as pleasantly as the first ten.

He could not, or did not, stop, and in the late sixties Congress caught up with him. Already he had become an exile in his own district. After being convicted of libel—for calling a woman the "bag lady" for a graft operation—Powell could not return to the district he represented for fear of being arrested. In 1966 the disgruntled members of his committee began to hack away at his powers. Other congressmen sharpened their knives, too.

Their grievance was that Powell was bringing them all down. When one congressman is a clown, how seriously could the rest take themselves? Their own self-respect was only part of it. The constituents were also angry. "Nobody blames me for Howard

Smith or H. R. Gross," one congressman said, mentioning two of the chamber's troglodytes, "but whites all over America blame their congressman for Adam." Morris Udall produced a letter from a constituent, addressed "in care of Adam Clayton Powell's Playboy Club (formerly U.S. House of Representatives), Stinksville Station (formerly House Post Office), Washington, D.C."

In 1967 the Democratic Caucus voted to remove him as chairman. By a thumping 365–65 vote the full House then voted to deny him his seat pending further investigations. Soon afterward the Justice Department compiled a fifty-page draft indictment telling of falsified expense vouchers worth $20,000 and of Powell's secret destruction of incriminating papers from his committee; but the department never sought an indictment. Finally, the House declared his seat vacant and ordered a special election for April.

Powell won the election, and then won a more important victory when the Supreme Court ruled that his exclusion had been unconstitutional. The only formal losses were his seniority and a $20,000 fine for penance. Powell had survived, but in the process something had gone sour between him and his district. In 1970 he lost in the primary to Charles Rangel. Two years later, unrepentant, he died, at age sixty-three.

THOMAS DODD. "I believe in God and Senator Dodd and keepin' ol' Castro down," Phil Ochs sang. And Dodd fit the billing. When the young Tom Dodd faced one of life's forking paths, he grappled with the question of whether he should become a priest. Instead he plowed his energies into politics. If he was not combating sin in the individual soul, he could attack its manifestations in the national spirit; perversion, pornography, communism—all must be defeated.

Although Dodd's targets were the classic ones, his attacks in the Senate won him few friends. In a body which is almost as tradition-conscious as the Church, the Connecticut senator stepped roughly on others' dignity. He overlooked the minor niceties; he called names; he impugned motives.

Thomas Dodd would not be a household word today if impoliteness had been his only error. Dodd's talent was invested in another cause, his financial frauds. His staff were the first to notice. They had gathered evidence of a stunning range of dishonesty. Dodd had pocketed, for private use, at least $160,083 raised at campaign dinners, supposedly for campaign expenses; he had double-billed the government and other groups for other expenses, keeping the surplus; he had taken repeated private vacations and charged the government; he had used his office to promote the career of a retired major general who was a propagandist for German right-wingers; he had taken money from private firms, and then pressured government agencies for special treatment.

Doubts and difficulties afflicted the staffers. "To whom do you go to get a U.S. senator investigated?" asked James Boyd, Dodd's closest aide for the previous twelve years. The Senate Ethics Committee was likely to forgive an erring brother; the Justice Department was part of Johnson's administration, and Johnson was one of Dodd's friends; even the FBI was suspect, since Dodd had once been an agent. Their minds set, Boyd and Dodd's secretary Marjorie Carpenter eventually took seven thousand documents from Dodd's files and gave them to the trustees of frustrated exposés, Drew Pearson and Jack Anderson.

Pearson and Anderson unloaded the charges in twenty-three columns, but for a while Dodd felt safe in ignoring them. Senators closed ranks against their threatened fellow; Birch Bayh wrote, "We're all with you on this yellow attack by Pearson," while Russell Long said, "I'll support you all the way on this, Tom, even if you're guilty." Dodd had his own explanation for the trouble: "The Communists have always regarded me as a prime enemy."

But Dodd made a crucial mistake. He demanded a Senate inquiry. It was a dramatic ploy, but one which proved his undoing. "Never ask for an investigation," one of his cohorts had said. "You might get one." The Senate Ethics Committee thus began its first investigation. Its report was less than Boyd might have hoped, but did unanimously recommend that Dodd be censured on two counts: for diverting the campaign money, and for the double-billing. On June

23, 1967, Dodd was officially censured by the Senate for the first count. His defense was an inspired peroration on the Senate floor, which concluded, "I am telling you the truth and I am concealing nothing. May the vengeance of God strike me if I am doing otherwise!" The plea moved many but convinced very few. By a vote of 92–5 (Dodd, Ribicoff, Tower, Thurmond, and Long against), the Senate censured Dodd for his personal use of the campaign funds. Having done this much, the Senate pulled back and refused, by a 51–45 vote, to censure Dodd for double-billing.

Dodd's formal punishment was light. He served three more years in the Senate, then gamely but unsuccessfully ran as an independent for reelection in 1970. But the scandal left Dodd broken. He died of a heart attack in 1971, a bundle of contradictions. Exhorting law and order, he placed himself above the law; demanding staff loyalty, he was loyal to none but himself. In the mid-sixties, after Bobby Baker's fall but before his own, Dodd had angled to get the great glass chandelier that hung in Baker's office. He never got it, and shared with Baker only his acquisitive ways.

WAYNE HAYS. Sometimes a congressman abuses his public position with such skill and arrogance that only an incidental scandal can finally force his colleagues to investigate his conduct. A classic case is former Representative Wayne Hays (D.-Ohio), a behind-the-scenes House potentate who manipulated three committee chairmanships to control everything from the price of haircuts in the Capitol barbershops to staff salaries and the dispersal of Democratic campaign contributions. "I got where I am because people feared me," he once told reporter Myra McPherson.

One person who did not seem to fear Hays was his tattletale ex-mistress, Elizabeth Ray. In 1974, Hays made Ray a clerk in, appropriately enough, his Oversight Committee and paid her $14,000 a year in public funds. "I can't type, I can't file, I can't even answer the phone," Ray admitted, adding that her main responsibility was to pander to the personal needs of Chairman Hays. Following a press and public uproar, the House leadership pressured Hays to resign from Congress.

Hays's power to intimidate derived from his ability to control single-handedly the flow of perquisites representatives have grown dependent upon. As chairman of the House Administration Committee, Hays had the power to increase, without a House vote, the size and salaries of House staff and allowances available to members. As chief housekeeper, Hays treated service employees like personal staff and appeared to relish his tyrannical control over them. Following an altercation with two elevator boys under the jurisdiction of the House Judiciary Committee, Hays threatened to hold up appropriations for the then pending Nixon impeachment inquiry; the elevator boys, after meeting with an anxious Chairman Peter Rodino, quickly apologized. As chairman of the Democratic Congressional Campaign Committee, Hays decided which candidates got how much money and when. From his International Relations subcommittee chair he pulled the strings on precious foreign travel junkets and was himself dubbed "Marco Polo" for spending $6,589 of tax money overseas in just one year.

All this may mean no more than a few bucks to Peoria, but it put high in the House saddle one of the most hostile and acerbic of congressmen. "Getting into a debate with him is like wrestling with a skunk," said a representative. "The skunk doesn't care; he likes the smell." But whether he obtained his status despite his arbitrariness or because of it, he had, as *The Washington Post* noted, "carved out a position of power in the daily operation of the House unmatched by any member except [then] Speaker Carl Albert."

Hays's power base, though, was being challenged well before the sex scandal gave Democratic leaders an excuse to purge him. Democrats uncomfortable under Hays's arbitrary bureaucratic discretion to dispense patronage and services tried to dethrone him as Administration Committee chairman in 1975. Hays not only survived, but he retaliated by creating new bureaucratic structures to reinforce his influence. He created new subcommittees on packing and paper conservation, as well as ad hoc committees to manage House restaurant operations and the computer system. Finally, he created the infamous Oversight Committee—to keep an accurate check on what all the other committees and subcommittees were doing.

However influential, his style of intimidation foredoomed his dreams of becoming majority leader. And before the scandal broke, one Hill observer prophesied his demise to author Marshall Frady: "One of these days ole Wayne's going to violate one amenity too many and find he's run out of grace all of a sudden. Then they'll converge on him, and when they're done, all he'll have left of his empire is the stub of his gavel."

CHARLES C. DIGGS. Stylish and apparently wealthy, the first black congressman elected from the state of Michigan, the son of the first black state senator elected in Michigan, Charlie Diggs was for years a relatively popular and powerful spokesman for black interests in the House. His Detroit constituents liked the idea that their representative was the most senior black in Congress and was called "Mr. Africa" due to his self-made expertise on that continent. His people believed in him so completely that they overwhelmingly reelected him to a thirteenth term in November 1978—despite his October 1978, conviction on twenty-nine counts of federal mail fraud and taking salary kickbacks from his congressional staff.

Diggs entered politics while still studying law, in 1951. He replaced his father in the Michigan state senate after the elder Diggs was refused his seat because he had been sent to prison for taking graft from a lobbyist. In 1971 he helped found and became the first chairman of the congressional Black Caucus, a group originally established as a "shadow cabinet" to monitor federal enforcement of civil rights laws. Two years later he became chairman of the House District Committee and he soon pushed through a compromise home rule bill giving the predominantly black district government more autonomy and power. He also served until 1979 as chairman of the House Foreign Affairs subcommittee on Africa, a post he used to make frequent and controversial tours of Africa.

Diggs's corruption and fall from power began about twenty years ago when, reluctant to live less elegantly than his better situated peers, he began borrowing and refusing to repay. On top of this overextension were his family obligations. Married three times, divorced twice, with six children and his mother to support, Diggs faced alimony payments and private tuition bills in addition to gambling losses and extravagant tastes in clothes and furnishings. When the family funeral business went bankrupt, Diggs saw approaching financial and political doom as creditors closed in and began taking him to court.

By 1973 his personal predicament was so taxing he decided to solve it the only way he saw available—by appropriating a slice of the public funds he was trusted to manage. His indictment alleged that between 1973 and 1977, Diggs "did devise and intend to devise a scheme and artifice to defraud the United States of America [of more than $101,000] in the form of salary kickbacks from certain House of Representatives employees and payments to others on the House of Representatives payroll who performed no work for the House. . . ." Diggs supplemented his income by giving three of his aides big salary increases, then pressuring them to kick back as much as two thirds of their salary to pay his personal debts. He also paid the family lawyer, accountant, and a funeral home employee with federal funds, though they did not work for the government. Diggs was convicted and sentenced to three years in prison in October just before the 1978 elections and he agreed to stay away during the remaining three days of the 95th Congress. The next month he was easily reelected.

But the issue of his role in Congress remained. Realizing how demeaning it is to the rest of Congress for a convicted lawbreaker to remain a full participant in the drafting, passage, and execution of our laws, the Democratic majority in the new Congress had to face the issue of what powers Diggs should exercise while his appeals were pending. Republicans and several young Democrats called for Diggs to resign his committee chairmanship, refrain from voting, and consider resigning from Congress.

Intense pressure by the Democratic leadership did force Diggs reluctantly to resign his two committee posts, but he insisted he had the right to remain a voting member of Congress. Diggs's defenders argued that to deprive him of his right to work in committees or vote on legislation would mean unconstitutionally disenfranchising his district. His lawyers also charged that since taking public funds for personal use was "relatively common" in the House, Diggs should not be singled out for punishment.

Majority Leader Jim Wright argued that the caucus can withhold chairmanships, since establishing committees at all is an administrative prerogative of the members; but preventing an elected member from serving his constituents is a different matter. "I don't think he should be expelled from the House," Wright said. "Membership in the House is not ours to bestow. We can't give that to anybody. The constituents are entitled to have the representatives of their choice." Wright argued that expulsion is such an extreme sanction that only three members have ever gotten the boot—all in 1861, for supporting the Confederacy in the Civil War. He also noted that the House did not expel Andrew J. Hinshaw (R.-Calif.) who was convicted of bribery in 1976, or J. Parnell Thomas (D.-N.J.), who was convicted in the late 1940s for offenses similar to Diggs's.

The oust-Diggs group, led by the Republican leadership and Representative Peter Kostmayer (D.-Pa.), argued that Wright and the keep-Diggs contingent were trying to obscure the difference between expelling and excluding a member. When the 90th Congress tried to exclude former representative Adam Clayton Powell, the Supreme Court held that in deciding whether a member is fit to be seated, "Congress is limited to judging members in terms of the qualifications [age, citizenship, and residency] prescribed by the Constitution." However, Justice Douglas's concurring opinion in that case noted that the Congress does have the constitutional prerogative to expel any of its members, once sworn in, by a vote of two thirds or more. The Constitution reads: "Each house may . . . punish its members for disorderly behavior, and, with the concurrence of two thirds, expel a member." To many congressmen it is inconceivable that systematically embezzling tax money, an offense for which a President could be impeached, does not qualify as conduct unbecoming a congressman.

Finally, on the recommendation of the House Ethics Committee, the House voted 414–0 to censure Diggs, the first such reprimand in fifty-eight years. After the Supreme Court upheld his conviction, he entered prison at Maxwell Air Force Base in Alabama in June 1980, serving seven months of a three-year term. And when he got out, he went back to the funeral business where he had originated.

DANIEL FLOOD. During his more than thirty years representing the impoverished anthracite coal region of northeastern Pennsylvania, Representative Daniel J. Flood (D.-Pa.) had been a hero to his blue-collar constituents back home in Wilkes-Barre—and it was not merely due to the waxed moustache, cape, and cane he acquired during his youthful days as a Shakespearean actor.

Because Flood had been a member of the "College of Cardinals"— the nickname given Congress's thirteen powerful Appropriations subcommittee chairmen—he was able to go far beyond the usual individualized constituent services his colleagues thrive on. As chairman of the Appropriations subcommittee for Labor and Health, Education, and Welfare, Flood had a virtual stranglehold on many agency budgets within those departments. Thus, aggressive pork-barreling and federal largess have made it possible for Flood's constituents to be born at the Daniel J. Flood Rural Health Center, educated at the Daniel J. Flood Elementary School, employed in the Daniel J. Flood Industrial Park, and retired to the Daniel J. Flood Elderly Center.

He was also a ranking member of the Defense Appropriations subcommittee, a position he used in 1960 to persuade the Army to convert its 8,000 coke-burning barrracks furnaces in West Germany to use Pennsylvania anthracite. Army efforts to reconvert the furnaces to oil, which would save more than $20 million annually, all died in the House Appropriations subcommittee. "Hell, yes, I stopped it," he said with typical flair. "I did it by twisting arms and hammering heads." And when Hurricane Agnes and the raging

Susquehanna River devastated most of his district in 1972, Flood obtained needed supplies and equipment from the Pentagon and rushed home aboard Secretary of Defense Melvin Laird's personal helicopter, declaring, "This is going to be one Flood against another."

Despite his renown as an effective and hardworking ambassador from Wilkes-Barre, Flood developed a tendency over the years to use his legislative skills to feather his personal nest as well as his district. Most of the charges against Flood originated with his administrative assistant Stephen Elko, who was sentenced to three years in prison after admitting, in 1977, that he took $25,000 in bribes from former Washington lobbyist Deryl Fleming. In exchange for immunity from further prosecution and a reduced sentence, Elko told how his former boss received some $100,000 in cash and bank stock from various organizations in return for legislative favors. Or as Flood reportedly told him, "Get all you can while you can get it."

Among the subsequent tangle of other illicit deals for which Flood was prosecuted or investigated:

• While sitting amidst the wreckage of Hurricane Agnes in his relief "command post," Flood took $5,000 in a cash bribe from a businessman trying to sell disaster relief housing to the federal government, according to testimony by the businessman at Flood's trial in January 1979.

• In 1972 a chain of California trade schools were about to lose their accreditation, and millions of federal aid dollars as a result. But after Elko and Flood each allegedly received a series of payoffs—a total of $50,000 by company accounts—former education commissioner Sidney P. Marland, Jr., bowed to persistent pressure from the Appropriations chairman who oversaw his agency and gave the unqualified school temporary accreditation.

• In return for Flood's drafting helpful legislation and pressuring the Labor Department to grant millions of dollars in federal subsidies to a small religious school in Brooklyn, Rabbi Lieb Pinter testified that he gave Flood at least five $1,000 bribes. The money was covered up as an honorarium for Flood's appearance at a 1975 dinner in New York. Although the school used some of the subsidies to provide a free lunch program and training for Jewish immigrants from the Soviet Union, the judge gave Pinter a two-year jail sentence because the people had a right to believe that there was not "a price tag on their representatives."

• A Pennsylvania home-builder testified that he personally handed $2,000 in cash to Flood in return for his help in obtaining federal financing for a housing project.

• Banker Joel Harpel testified that his bank transferred $4,000 worth of bank stock to Flood's account in return for his influencing the Treasury Department to approve the merger of two banks.

• Elko also described how he served between 1971 and 1973 as the delivery boy for regular cash payments from the Arlie Foundation to both Flood and former Representative Otto E. Passman (D.-La.). The foundation president, Dr. Murdock Head, was later convicted of passing as much as $49,000 to the two representatives in return for their help in increasing AID's family planning funds in 1972. Elko also testified that Head was so anxious about election surveillance and fingerprints that he would only meet Elko in places like Arlie's soundproof screening room, would write with marker on a flip-chart instead of speaking, and would only handle the cash-stuffed envelopes with facial tissue.

To a man with enough nerve to wear red, white, and blue sneakers to a formal dinner at the White House, however, defeat does not come easily. Despite the federal prosecution of Flood on eleven counts of bribery, perjury, and conspiracy to defraud the U.S. government, his home town named him Man of the Year in 1978 and his home district reelected him in November. But all floods recede, and so did this one. On January 31, 1980, Representative Flood resigned from Congress "for health reasons." The next month he pleaded guilty in U.S. District Court to conspiracy to solicit illegal campaign contributions and was immediately placed on one year probation. In exchange for this guilty plea to a misdemeanor charge, the government dismissed more serious conspiracy, bribery, and perjury charges.

*   *   *

HERMAN TALMADGE. The son of late Georgia Governor Eugene Talmadge (who responded once to charges of thievery by telling supporters "Sure I stole, but I stole for you"), Herman Talmadge also served as governor (1948–1956). He entered the Senate in 1956 by defeating twenty-five-year veteran Walter George—then chairman of the Foreign Relations Committee. Reelected the next three times with little opposition, Talmadge rose steadily to the chairmanship of the Agriculture Committee, until overtaken by events in the 1970s.

The unraveling began in the course of a property settlement following an acrimonious divorce in 1977 when a *Washington Star* reporter discovered a curious item. From 1970 to 1976 the millionaire senator had written only one check to "cash." At first Talmadge said that he did not know where he got his spending money. But the Senate Ethics Committee began to examine his finances after *Star* reporter Edward Pound disclosed—and Talmadge acknowledged—receipts of "small gifts of cash . . . to cover his expenses" from the Georgian's friends and supporters. "They come up and say they know I have a lot of expenses back in Washington and they want to help me," Talmadge said. The help came in the form of cash, free meals, lodging, and clothing as well as special "birthday dinners" sponsored at $25 a plate—none of it reported as income (for tax purposes) or as campaign receipts.

By December 1978, the Ethics Committee completed a preliminary investigation and listed five areas of possible violations. The most serious was the charge that Talmadge maintained a secret bank account in which he deposited illegal campaign contributions. The committee's special counsel said: "Although [Talmadge] has continuously claimed that his source of cash was small gifts made by friends and supporters, the evidence will disclose that he had cash on hand in fairly substantial amounts, and that it came in whole or in part from [a secret campaign account] . . . or from other campaign contributions."

Talmadge denied all wrongdoing and called his former top aide and

254

chief accuser, Daniel Minchew, "a proven liar, cheat, and embezzler." Minchew testified that he had opened the account at a local Washington bank in Talmadge's name and on his orders. The *Star* reported: "Nearly $39,000 in mostly unreported campaign contributions and illegally claimed senate reimbursements were funneled through the account and converted to cash." (Talmadge finally repaid $37,000 for the expense account overpayments, claiming they were due to oversights by members of his staff.) The ethics panel also charged that Talmadge had received about $24,000 in payments from the Senate for vouchers submitted by the senator for "official expenses" which he had not incurred. Another $11,000 was for items actually spent but not considered legitimate official expenditures by the Senate.

Herman Talmadge has been a powerful senator, a member of "the club," but that did him little good in the face of these public charges. In 1979 the Senate voted 81–15 to "denounce" ("censure" was considered too historically harsh) him for his "reprehensible" conduct of his official finances. And although he won reelection in 1974 with 72 percent of the vote and outspent his 1980 challenger four to one, Talmadge lost his seat by two percent to a little-known Republican.

KOREAGATE. Far broader than any individual wrongdoing was the episode tagged Koreagate, which seemed crafted after an espionage thriller, with secret foreign agents, code words, black market deals, squealing defectors, and handsome political payoffs delivered in plain, unmarked envelopes. *The Washington Post* called the charges in late 1976 "the most sweeping allegations of congressional corruption ever investigated by the federal government." Others dismissed it as "third-rate bribery," an ironic example of reciprocal foreign aid. However broad and deep the corruption, it is clear that Koreagate cost Congress a great deal of time and integrity, and proved how difficult it is for a legislature to investigate itself.

The plot began in 1968 when former representative Richard T. Hanna (D.-Calif.) and Tongsun Park met in Seoul with then Korean

CIA Director Kim Hyung Wook and agreed to have Park appointed the Korean government's exclusive agent for purchasing rice in the U.S. In return, according to the KCIA chief's testimony, Hanna and Park agreed to use a portion of the $9 million they received in rice commissions between 1970 and 1976 to organize a campaign to influence the American Congress on Korea's behalf. Hanna, for example, initiated "goodwill trips," to Korea for congressional officials, who were showered with expensive gifts (brought back duty-free), honorary degrees, and envelopes full of "expense" cash to cover the cost of bringing their wives.

From the Korean perspective, Park's "Operation Ice Mountain" seemed quite reasonable. Park Chung Hee's prosperous little regime lived in constant fear of its communist half-brother to the north. With Seoul's skyline nearly within artillery range of a hostile border, the South Koreans felt justified in using almost any means to keep getting plenty of U.S. military and economic aid. And, after all, they were using methods learned from their trainers, the American CIA. Korea wanted to buy off what they considered to be "leftist" and "procommunist" forces in the U.S. Congress—including legislators, like Speaker Tip O'Neill, Majority Whip John Brademas, and former whip John J. McFall.

One important suspect in the whole scheme was Korean ambassador Kim Dong Jo. His official spokesman at the embassy testified before the House Ethics Committee that he saw the diplomat stuffing two dozen unmarked envelopes full of $100 bills. When asked where he was taking the bulging briefcase of money, Kim looked at his aide as though the question was naive and replied, "To the Capitol." A secretary to Representative Larry Winn, Jr. (R.-Kans.) testified at the same hearings that Kim gave her boss an unmarked envelope that Winn returned when it was found to contain what she described as "more money than I'd ever seen in my life."

If Leon Jaworski, recruited by Speaker O'Neill to take over the stalled investigation in late 1977, could have acquired the testimony of Ambassador Kim, many congressmen might have found themselves behind bars. Jaworski himself said he had "not the slightest doubt that he [Tongsun Park] was serving as a foreign agent,'' but he couldn't prove it. While congressmen who took cash from Park could always say (and they did) that they were unaware he represented the KCIA, no congressman accepting an envelope from an ambassador could claim he did not know he was violating Article II of the U.S. Constitution, which forbids accepting remuneration of any kind from a foreign government. But Korea kept Kim under close wraps.

"This whole thing was run right out of the Korean embassy," Jaworski said, and he accused Congress and the State Department of impeding his efforts to force Kim's testimony despite Korean claims of diplomatic immunity. He finally quit the investigation like his predecessor Phillip A. Lacovara, bitter at Ethics chairman John J. Flynt, Jr. (D.-Ga.) who Republican leaders accused of "foot-dragging" to protect Democratic members.

By 1979, when the inquiry ended, evidence indicated that Korea rice dealer Tongsun Park had handed out more than $850,000 in "gifts" to thirty-one House members between 1970 and 1976—and that at least ninety current and former members of Congress had accepted gifts and favors from the South Korean government and its agents. While fifteen members were mentioned in the Justice Department's 1977 indictment as recipients of cash, it took the House Committee on Official Standards of Conduct (more commonly known as the Ethics Committee) eighteen months to finally release a report that wrist-slapped four current members, and cleared nine others with a suggestion that they be more careful about whom they take money from.

The four accused of breaking rules were former majority whip John J. McFall, who admitted back in 1976 that he did not report $4,000 in cash received from Park in 1972 and 1976, but instead placed it in a secret office account; and Edward Roybal, Charles Wilson, and Edward J. Patten, all California Democrats, who failed to report and then lied to the committee about $1,000 contributions they received in cash from Park between 1974 and 1976. The committee referred perjury charges against former representatives

John R. Rarick (D.-La.) and Nick Galifianakis (D.-N.C.) for lying in sworn depositions about cash they took from Park in 1974 and 1972, respectively. The Democratic Caucus showed how seriously they take the Ethics Committee by blocking, just months after disciplinary action was urged against the four, an attempt to deprive Roybal and Wilson of their subcommittee chairmanships. (Meanwhile the Senate Ethics Committee concluded that three senators may have violated senate rules or public law: two deceased senators, Hubert Humphrey [D.-Minn.] and John McClellan [D.-Ark.] allegedly received campaign contributions from Park and failed to report them; it also said that Birch Bayh accepted a contribution from Park in the Capitol—it is a crime to receive a political contribution in a federal building—though Bayh denies the charge.)

When he discussed the House's handling of the Koreagate probe before the American Bar Association convention in late 1978, Jaworski said the investigation was hampered by public skepticism about the ability of Congress to investigate itself, by the rules of the House, by "camaraderie" among the members who seem determined to protect each other, and by the inability of committee members to sit and listen to witnesses, ask hard questions, and devote the time necessary for a proper investigation. Jaworski argued forcefully that any future investigations of wrongdoing by members of Congress or the executive branch must be handled by an outside commission appointed by the President.

In one sense, that's just what happened with the next great congressional scandal, which in scale dwarfed all prior incidents. And the outside "commission" was the FBI.

ABSCAM. The FBI "sting" known as Abscam was Congress's first multimedia scandal, with its bribery and conspiracies preserved for prosecution and posterity on black-and-white videotape. Seven congressmen (six of them Democrats) were convicted of accepting cash or stock in exchange for help for a supposed Arab sheik. The FBI's methods have been questioned, but what stands out most clearly is the high percentage of the lawmakers offered the money who eagerly took it.*

What was ultimately to involve 100 FBI agents began obscurely in 1978 with an FBI sting operation to nab dealers in stolen artwork. To do the conning, agents hired a champion con-man, diamond pinkie rings and all—convicted swindler Mel Weinberg. (Asked at a later trial whether he had, for instance, swindled his uncle out of $50,000, Weinberg nonchalantly denied the charge. "It was a cousin.") The agents created a fictional Arab sheik, Kambir Abdul Rahman, prepared to dole out cash for stolen goods, and rented a house in Georgetown that they specially equipped with cameras and tape recorders. The reason for the frills was that Weinberg began to bring in political figures, starting with Camden, N.J., mayor Angelo Errichetti. The mayor said he would help the sheik invest in Camden, for a fee of $400,000. As word began to spread among politicians and their cronies that lucre was flowing, the sheik began receiving some surprising supplicants. The biggest fish was also one of the first:

Harrison Williams, senator from New Jersey for twenty-one years, journeyed with Errichetti to Abscam's yacht in Delray Beach, Florida. FBI videotape cameras recorded the sheik (played by an agent who communicated in nonsense Arabic and grunted English) telling Williams that he wanted to invest in a titanium mine, and captured Williams's response: "You tell the sheik I'll do all I can. You tell him I'll deliver my end." In seven meetings with Kambir and other sessions in Virginia and New York, Williams accepted secret part ownership of the mine in exchange for help in getting the government to buy its titanium.

The deal was complex, and Williams never took cash—so there was debate among the prosecutors whether to attempt to try the case at all. But Williams was indicted in 1980 and stood trial in April

---

* "Abscam" is derived from "Abdul Enterprises," the dummy corporation set up by the FBI, and "scam," its function.

1981 while still in the Senate. On the witness stand he asserted that his promises of help had merely been "baloney" to "impress the sheik" so he would invest in the mine, which was owned by friends of the bushy-browed senator. The jury was not convinced, convicting Williams on May 1, 1981. Outside the courtroom he vowed not to resign.

This left the Senate in a bind. Only twice before had it voted to expel a member for criminal activity other than treason. Williams did not make the decision any easier: he sent letters lambasting the FBI; he argued he was merely following "a script"; he enlisted the help of fringe presidential candidate Lyndon LaRouche; he made his case in a rambling six-hour speech before the Senate. But when it became clear that he would be expelled, he resigned in August 1981.

Mayor Errichetti also introduced the oil-rich potentate to Philadelphia lawyer Michael Criden, who in turn introduced four northeastern Democratic congressmen: *Frank Thompson* of New Jersey, *John Murphy* of New York City, and *Michael "Ozzie" Meyers* and *Raymond Lederer* of Philadelphia. The most surprising of these felons was Thompson, the highly respected chairman of the House Administration Committee. He at first appeared reluctant to accept cash—saying he was "not looking for any money"—but ultimately Criden, with Thompson watching, told an FBI agent that "Frank understands the situation" and picked up the valise containing the money. Thompson's $50,000 was in exchange for helping the sheik "immigrate" to the U.S. Indicted in 1980, Thompson was defeated by Republican Chris Smith before his trial began.

Thompson was responsible for bringing his friend, Merchant Marine and Fisheries chairman Murphy, into the scheme. Murphy also received $50,000 for help on the immigration matter, although he, too, directed Criden to physically take the money. (Observers were less surprised about Murphy's involvement; his financial dealings with the Shah of Iran and Nicaraguan strongman Anastasio Somoza had been frequently probed.) Murphy, too, lost his 1980 reelection race. On December 3, 1980, Murphy and Thompson were convicted of conspiracy and acceptance of an unlawful gratuity; Thompson was also convicted of bribery.

"Ozzie" Meyers, a gruff former dockworker from Philadelphia's South Side, seemed to relish his role as bribe recipient. Boasting to undercover agent "Tony DeVito" that he could help ease the sheik's immigration problems and use his Mafia contacts to aid on other projects, Meyers added, "I'm gonna tell you something real simple and short. Money talks in this business, and bullshit walks." (He also groused about having to split his $50,000 with friends, but noted, "Who am I going to complain to? My congressman?") At his trial Meyers insisted he was not being bribed—because he never actually intended to *do* any of the things he had promised. Convicted on August 30, 1980, he was expelled on October 2 of that year, the first representative to be kicked out of the House since the Civil War.

Raymond Lederer was another Philadelphia congressman, but one with particularly loyal constituents—he was reelected in 1980 after being indicted. Convicted in January 1981, he resigned from the House in May, a day after the House Ethics Committee unanimously urged his expulsion. While waiting for his appeal decision he returned to his precongressional job as an ironworker. "I go where the union tells me and just do my job," he told a journalist.

The two snared southern congressmen were also the two most creative defendants. *John Jenrette* (D.-S.C.) blamed it all on drink. For instance, when jurors saw and heard him say, "I've got larceny in my blood—I'll take it in a goddamn minute," Jenrette testified that he had *really* said he had "alcohol in my blood. I'll do anything to get out of here." Convicted in 1980 of accepting the by-now-standard $50,000, Jenrette lost to a Republican in that year's election. His wife Rita gained notoriety for herself when she posed nude in *Playboy* and announced that she had found $25,000 in a shoebox in her husband's closet (money that turned out to have nothing to do with Abscam). The Jenrettes have since divorced.

Richard Kelly of Florida, the lone Republican snared in the Abscam net, was equally resourceful. He was captured on videotape patting down the cash in his suit and asking FBI agents, "Does it show?" But he claimed there was a reason he took the money: he was conducting his own investigation of "shady characters." Kelly was unable to explain why he did not report his suspicions to a law enforcement agency or why he spent some of the money, and he, too, was convicted.

Many in Congress, especially senators like Alan Cranston, were furious at the FBI's tactics. Williams and the representatives were entrapped, they asserted, and cajoled into committing crimes by an overreaching Weinberg. Columnist William Safire condemned Abscam as an "honesty test" that rubbed lawmakers' noses in temptation and dared them to resist it. More to the point, widespread press leaks on the case led to heavy coverage before a grand jury had even been convened. (NBC News staked out Senator Williams's house for days and were able to show his look of shock when he was informed of the investigation by U.S. marshals.)

How did this greatest show of congressional illegality end? All seven members indicted were convicted; their appeals will be exhausted by the end of 1983. And after Senator Larry Pressler (R.-S.D.) gained inadvertent notoriety as the only congressman who refused the bribe, FBI Director William Webster called him to say he acted "beautifully."

FRED RICHMOND. The respected leader of the Congressional Arts Caucus, investigator of agribusiness and the coffee cartel on the House Agriculture Committee, defender of the food stamp program, dapper millionaire Fred Richmond was a parlor favorite in Washington. But his suave front was not enough to obscure the tangled skein of corruption that led to his resignation from Congress and sentencing to a year and a day in jail in 1982.

Richmond (D.-N.Y.) represented a mixed area of Brooklyn, populated by blacks, Hispanics, orthodox Jews, and affluent white professionals. He himself lived on Sutton Place in Manhattan, in an apartment decorated with paintings by Picasso and Chagall. After making an estimated $32 million as a businessman, Richmond decided to enter politics. Rather than working his way up the ladder of the Brooklyn Democratic machine, he created the Frederick W. Richmond Foundation which gave grants and gifts to community groups and institutions. Representative Charles Rangel (D.-N.Y.) later wryly noted, "They say there are more organs in the Baptist churches in his district than in any other part of the country."

The district he had chosen was represented by a venerable incumbent, John W. Rooney; in 1968, Richmond challenged him in a primary and lost, despite spending $200,000 of the foundation's money for local causes. Although after the election Richmond said of Rooney, "He's a sick and vindictive old man," two years later he managed the incumbent's campaign for reelection. And when Rooney retired in 1974, Richmond was his anointed successor.

His tenure in Congress was successful and uneventful for most of the time he served. He developed an expertise on food issues and was viewed with respect by his colleagues, who were later baffled by his erratic private life. "He was remarkably generous and friendly," said Representative Tom Downey (D.-N.Y.). "He was a very dedicated progressive. It's a great tragedy that his personal life was, to say the least, chaotic." Richmond's decline began in 1978, when he was arrested and charged with soliciting sexual favors from a sixteen-year-old boy. (Columnist Les Whitten, who broke the story, recalls Richmond blurting out, "Oh, my God, I'll never get to be senator now.") Richmond survived the incident by immediately admitting the charges, apologizing to his constituents, and spending lavishly in order to win reelection. The Brooklyn Democratic machine reluctantly backed him, although party leader Meade Esposito characterized him as "sick."

But federal investigators and the Securities and Exchange Commission began to close in on another unsavory aspect of Richmond's behavior. He had made his fortunes as president of a company called Walco, which specialized in buying up shares of other companies—scaring them into thinking a takeover bid was imminent—and then selling the stock back at inflated prices. When the House passed the ethics code in 1977, Richmond "retired" from the company and was given a $1 million "pension" paid in annual installments of $100,000. But he continued to run Walco's daily affairs; and company funds paid for campaign workers, some congressional staff, his apartment, car and chauffeur, and Richmond Foundation grants (so he would get the credit for donations). All this was either illegal or against the House code of ethics, and none of it was declared as income to the IRS.

As judges issued findings and Richmond stood defiant, another part of his wall of unreality crumbled. On March 25, 1981, police arrested a young man who had propositioned an undercover officer for money. The car he was driving sported U.S. Congress license plates, and the key chain in the ignition was emblazoned FWR. The man was Earl Randolph, an escaped convict (he was in prison for attempted murder) who, with Richmond's assistance, had gotten a job at the House Doorkeeper's office. Now Richmond faced possible felony charges for harboring an escapee. And the grand jury looking into his affairs was hearing reports that he had ordered his staff to buy cocaine and marijuana for his use. The grand jury was also told that Richmond had paid the college tuition of the daughter of a naval employee—who then awarded a Navy contract to a Richmond campaign contributor. All the while he was unrepentant, telling *The New York Times*, "I'm not ashamed of anything I've done. I've done nothing wrong."

In the face of what columnist Sidney Schanberg aptly called a "one-man crime wave," the House Ethics Committee responded with a blinding flurry of . . . inactivity. The panel did not even begin to investigate Richmond until the allegations had been public for several months. By the time he resigned, the committee had not reached the stage of offering any comment on the year-old controversy.

Fred Richmond's congressional career finally ended when even the loyal Brooklyn Democratic machine told him it would oppose him if he continued to run for reelection. On August 25, 1982, Richmond pleaded guilty to tax evasion (for not reporting his Walco salary), marijuana possession, and participating in the tuition-payment scheme—and he resigned from Congress. Richmond began serving his prison term early in 1983.

These cases portray some of the way Capitol Hillers can run afoul of the law. And they illuminate how they are caught, how they explain their behavior, and how they are sanctioned.

Most congressional corruption is discovered and publicized either by staff whistle blowers or by outside muckrakers, like Jack Anderson. Tom Dodd's staff ultimately decided their highest loyalty was to the public, not their employer. James Boyd then went to Pearson and Anderson, whose revelations have discomfited many officials. One can be quite certain that many politicians in Washington immediately scan the Anderson column in *The Washington Post* to check whether that bribe/lady-from-Duluth/slush-fund has been publicly exposed. When they are—as James Boyd describes the scene—

> The Senator's strength drains out in a puddle. He slumps in a flaccid heap and stares glassily at the accusing phone; the knowing place in the pit of the stomach sinks into infinity. . . . It is the moment of maximum hazard to a political career; a too-defiant denial, a telltale dodge, an injudicious admission can . . . undo 30 years of patient conniving. The Senator's glazed eyes conjure up newspaper headlines, the dock, the recall of Congressional credit cards, the cell door clanking shut.

This moment of "maximum hazard" can be met in various ways whether the accused is culpable or not (false but spectacular charges are an occupational risk for politicians). Some of the following categories were developed in *The Washington Monthly* by Boyd himself, not unfamiliar with what he calls "the ritual of wiggle."

• Ignore it—Some disconnect their phones, leave for a trip, or simply say "no comment." The idea is that the thing will blow over. It can work if the accused or the event is inconsequential enough (a condition Abe Fortas did not appreciate) or if the reply is sufficiently disparaging (e.g., Dirksen said he could not "make heads or tails" of charges over abuse of his congressional frank, and the issue disappeared).

• Blame invisible enemies—This is especially handy for crusaders, who can always blame their problems on their historic targets. Of course, such targets may never have been prosecutors or accusers, but when one seeks scapegoats this does not matter. Thus we had Dodd's "communists" and Diggs's "racists" (though he was convicted by an all-black jury).

• Deny the obvious—If repeated often and honestly enough, it can sometimes work. After Representative Seymour Halpern, already in debt, got his $100,000 in unsecured loans while ruminating over banking legislation on the Banking Committee, he announced that there wasn't any conflict of interest. He suffered some bad publicity but was easily reelected. Robert Carson, former aide to Senator Hiram Fong, claimed that his $100,000 offer to Richard Kleindienst to help out an indicted friend was just a campaign contribution. The jury, however, called it a bribe and gave him eighteen months in jail.

• Say you'd do it for anyone—In 1971 lobbyist Nathan Voloshen and Martin Sweig, a close associate and aide, respectively, of Speaker McCormack, were convicted of influence-peddling and perjury; specifically, they defrauded government agencies by using the speaker's office and prestige on behalf of private clients. At their trial, Representative Robert Leggett testified that it was not odd to give a lobbyist the run of one's office. He considered the whole country as his constituency and would certainly be willing to allow anyone to use his office for commercial clients. This performance led one juror to say that "after hearing him, it is my opinion they should investigate *all* the members of Congress."

• Announce for reelection—This because the best defense is a good offense. Dodd declared for his third term the day he was censured. McCormack did so on the day he held a press conference to deny participation in Voloshen's and Sweig's schemes.

• Plead for mercy on national television—The Nixon-Checkers

and Kennedy-Chappaquiddick speeches are too well known to belabor, but their successes have not been forgotten.

• Say you'll give it back—In the early sixties Representative John Byrnes, then a ranking member of the House Ways and Means Committee, helped get a favorable tax ruling for the Mortgage Guaranty Insurance Corporation from the IRS. He then purchased $2,300 of their stock on terms not generally available, and within two years it was worth $25,000. In an emotional, lachrymose floor speech denying any wrongdoing, Byrnes announced that he would give any profits made to a scholarship fund for needy youth. His colleagues cheered. Seymour Halpern, when his bank loans were questioned, said he would pay them back, if necessary, by selling off his prize collection of famous signatures, which he had spent a lifetime collecting. It was, to many, a touching and convincing gesture.

• Threaten suit—This hardly ever works, but it makes good copy. The difficulty is that it is nearly impossible to prove libel under existing law when the person at issue is a "public figure." Dodd actually filed a $5 million libel suit against Pearson and Anderson, losing every count.

• Get a senatorial okay—Although all that may be involved is some classic backscratching, it is helpful to get exonerated by An Important Person. Former Senator George Murphy began to worry shortly before his 1970 race about his arrangement with Pat Frawley of Technicolor. Frawley gave the senator $20,000 annually, gave him free use of a credit card, and paid half of his $520 monthly rent. Murphy first asked Everett Dirksen if the arrangement was unseemly, and Dirksen gave his blessing—as he had given it to himself many times. Then John Stennis, chairman of the Senate Ethics Committee, performed the laying on of hands. Senator Edward Long also got Senator Stennis to whitewash Long's "referral fees" from Teamster lawyer M. A. Shenker, with hardly a glance at what really went on. But the voters sent both Murphy and Long looking for a new line of work.

• Claim immunity—Failing other ploys, many take refuge in procedural defenses. Congressional immunity is one way to finesse a tense situation, at least temporarily. Former Representative Thomas Johnson was convicted in 1963 of pocketing $17,500 in exchange for helping a savings and loan office escape federal prosecution. But the Supreme Court reversed the conviction because part of his offense involved a floor speech for which, the Court said, he was immune. (He was reconvicted in 1968 and went to jail for six months in 1970.)

What, finally, were the sanctions meted out to the Roll Call of Congressional Illegality? In the past twelve years 29 members of Congress have been indicted; 14 have been convicted, 11 have pleaded guilty, and 14 have been sentenced to prison. And of seventeen incumbents involved in or charged with illegal conduct who ran for reelection, nine were defeated and eight reelected. It is obvious that scandal does not always override a district's habit of returning an incumbent to the office he has been guilty of abusing. The attitude often seems to be "he may be a thief, but he is *our* thief." Indeed, Jim Curley in the forties, Tom Lane in the fifties, and Adam Clayton Powell in the sixties all initially won reelection despite the fact that the first two were actually in jail and the last had been forbidden to participate in House activities.

"The problem is that we used to rely on the people's sense of smell to police this place," Representative Barber Conable, Jr. (R.-N.Y.), has said. "In other words, we put our faith in democracy. But that only works when the choice is viable. Now the people's sense isn't enough. The power of incumbency is so great that a Wilbur Mills can get reelected after the Tidal Basin incident, a Wayne Hays can get renominated after the Elizabeth Ray affair, and Bob Leggett can get reelected after he's admitted he's living with his secretary and forged his wife's name on a deed and had an affair with Suzi Park Thomson." So it is well to realize that Congress at times resembles Gambetta's description of the French Chamber of Deputies—"a broken mirror in which the nation cannot recognize its own image."

The Congressional Response

Timeless customs, inherited from the night-long vigils of tribal societies, bind members of a group together. The doctors' unwritten code discourages one from testifying against another. Opposing lawyers are forbidden to criticize each other in court. Congress, too, watches out for its own. For nearly two centuries after its founding, Congress traditionally adopted a laissez-faire policy on ethics, assuming that each individual member wanted to police his own conduct. Congress, for example, has never attempted to define for its members and the public what constitutes a "conflict of interest." Senate rules have never barred a member from voting when he or she has a personal stake; across the rotunda, House rules vaguely advise representatives not to vote when they have "a direct or pecuniary interest." Only the increasing numbers of indicted legislators and the Watergate, Koreagate, and Abscam scandals provided the necessary shove for each chamber to take more formal steps toward self-regulation. In both houses the immediate response was a two-part system: the establishment of ethics committees and the requirement of financial disclosure.

If the name "Ethics Committee" is encouraging, its creation was not. The Senate Select Committee on Ethics had an almost accidental conception. Its parent was the special Senate investigating committee which dug into Bobby Baker's past. The committee's chairman, Senator Everett Jordan, made it clear to his colleagues that the group might be questioning senators' employees, but was "not investigating senators." That satisfying setup might have lasted indefinitely, save for the Senate's absentmindedness. At a routine session in 1964 a motion came up to establish a committee to investigate senators themselves. An aide to Clifford Case recalls what happened:

> John Sherman Cooper offered the motion to set up the select committee and, to his and everybody else's amazement, it passed. I remember because I was on the floor talking with Senator Case. . . . As he talked with me he was listening to the

tally and suddenly he broke off and said, "It's going to pass," and he went over to congratulate Cooper, and Cooper was looking stunned. Mansfield, who was nonplussed and didn't know what to do next, said "We'll have to consult the lawyers," and they recessed. It was one of the funniest things I've ever seen.

The Senate took to its new offspring with all the glee of a father who has found an illegitimate child dumped on his doorstep. For two years no senators were assigned to seats on the committee. Few were eager to judge their peers. Even reformer Paul Douglas (D.-Ill.) turned down an offer, his aide said, because "he didn't have the stomach for it." John Stennis of Mississippi finally stood where others had faltered; with Stennis as its first chairman the Ethics Committee was ready for action in 1966. Its nominal powers were impressive: it was to take complaints, investigate alleged misconduct, and recommend disciplinary action.

Tom Dodd's case was the first to come before the committee, which, to the surprise of many, took the difficult step of recommending that Dodd be censured. Even while doing so, however, the committee shied away from some of the most serious complaints against Dodd. "How will Americans ever learn about patterns of privilege and conflict of interest," complained one of those who had exposed Dodd, "if only 10 percent of his unethical activities—and those the least important—are made public?"

Fears that the Ethics Committee might act aggressively as a partisan tool of the majority proved groundless, not because the Republicans and Democrats each were given six seats, but because the committee did relatively little. By 1975 the Senate committee had only two staff employees and a paltry budget of $54,000—almost all going to the staff.

The House Ethics Committee (officially called the Committee on Standards of Official Conduct) was established in 1967 after a 400–0 vote ("Who can vote against ethics?" a California representative asked). In its first three years of operation it conducted just two preliminary investigations—one of Representative Cornelius Gallagher and another of "ghost voting" (the trick by which members have their votes recorded at times when they are actually away from the Capitol). "If my acknowledging only two preliminary investigations makes it sound like we don't do any work," said a member of the committee's staff at that time, "then it will just have to sound that way." Indeed, in its first nine years of operation, the committee never *formally* investigated a representative. It didn't until Common Cause literally shamed it into investigating Representative Sikes's conflicts of interest.

The first major investigation the House Ethics Committee felt worth its time and money was a futile attempt to discover who leaked a secret committee report on the CIA to CBS correspondent Daniel Schorr. When it came to scandals involving possibly illegal conduct by legislators, however, the two ethics committees seemed less eager. Congress's institutional reluctance to investigate itself appeared hypocritical, coming so soon after investigations by two congressional committees forced a President to resign from office. The same Congress that investigated conflicts of interest among Nixon's staff still allowed its banking committee members to own bank stock. John Gardner, then chairman of Common Cause, called the ethics committee in the House "the worst kind of sham, giving the appearance of serving as policeman while extending a marvelous protective shield over members of Congress."

Instead, the House and Senate committees have been turned into supermarkets for ethical dispensations. Senator Adlai E. Stevenson III (D.-Ill.), chairman of the Senate Ethics Committee from 1977 to 1979, said that his staff has been overwhelmed by inquiries from members about what conduct does or does not satisfy the new ethics code. Some offices check the acceptance of nearly every gift and contribution with the ethics panel as an insurance policy against future reprisals. "Members frequently ask us about their activities," said John Flynt, Jr. (D.-Ga.), outgoing chairman of the House panel in 1978. "We research federal laws, our own House rules, and our House precedents to find the answer for them. They aren't looking for what you'd call 'blue cover'—trying to justify what already was done. They are seeking guidance.''

It is not hard to understand the political and personal reasons why elected officials would prefer to give guidance than to investigate wrongdoing. ''It's not much fun sitting in judgment on your colleagues,'' said Richardson Preyer, former head of the House Ethics Committee. At the start of the 96th Congress not one Democrat volunteered to serve on either of the two ethics committees. And it was perhaps predictable that ethics committees would only respond to public pressure rather than initiate inquiries. The Senate investigated Dodd after the press thoroughly did; and the House began probes into Diggs, Flood, and Richmond months after their misdeeds had been publicly documented. ''A member should be in flagrant abuse of his office for the House to act,'' Representative Flynt said. ''This committee of ours never was set up to be our brother's keeper.''

But then no one ever forced a citizen to be paid $69,800 a year to serve the public in Congress. It should not be impossible to expect that the Senate and House would both avoid conducting witch-hunts *and* avoid drawing their wagons in circles around accused colleagues. An impulse toward the latter clearly predominates. At the start of the 96th Congress the House Democratic Caucus in secret session voted against two reform proposals: one would have barred any member convicted or indicted of a felony from serving as chairman of a committee or subcommittee; the other would have required the House to vote on the question of expelling any member convicted of a felony. One irate citizen subsequently wrote the *Washington Star* that ''an important principle was at issue in the Democratic Caucus. In a civilized country, are certified felons to be allowed to make the laws? A congressional group will probably never be confronted with a simpler, more clear-cut ethical question, and its members did not have the ethical sense to see it, or the political courage to act on it.''

While the ethics committees gave guidance and little else, the public became increasingly outraged by what seemed to be a continuing stream of revelations about congressional corruption. A Harris poll conducted in 1977 for the House Ethics Committee indicated that of eleven institutions, the public ranked Congress ninth in integrity, slightly better than large corporations and labor unions. As a result, the House established a special Commission on Administrative Review to look into possible ethics, committee, and administrative reforms. The commission, chaired by Representative David R. Obey (D.-Wis.), proposed a new more stringent code of ethics for the House, highlighted by broad financial disclosure rules, an end to office slush funds, an $8,625 ceiling on annual outside earned income by members, and limitations on the franking privilege and foreign travel.

The reform proposals seemed to excite greater passions in the House than any military or civil rights legislation which would affect only the lives of innocent millions. At stake, after all, were formulas for congressional salaries and criminal liabilities. Passions also ran high because Speaker O'Neill strongly supported ethics reform, both to improve public confidence in his besmirched institution and to justify the $13,000 annual pay increase members sought.

The cornerstone of these recommendations is the sweeping requirement of disclosure. The financial disclosure provisions for the House, and a similar version for the Senate, require that congressmen report the source and amount of all income and gifts over $100; any gifts of transportation, food, entertainment, or reimbursement totaling more than $250; the approximate value of any financial holding having a fair market value of at least $1,000; and the identity of any debt of more than $2,500, unless it is a mortgage. Most controversial by far, though, was the proposed limitation on outside earned income to 15 percent of salary. Earned income includes money generated by work that requires a substantial investment of time and effort (law practice, speechmaking), but does not include dividends, capital gains, and family business income. This standard presumes that members of Congress should be full-time public officials.

In the 96th and 97th Congresses, Abscam has had one strongly positive result: the de facto adoption of a "felony rule" by Congress. Every congressman convicted of a felony in Abscam was expelled, forced to resign, or retired by the voters. This is a good precedent, but it is still too informal. Congress should codify what it now appears to (and should) believe: that a felon should not sit in Congress. This aside, the trends have not been hopeful.

As memories of Watergate began to fade and the so-called Koreagate scandal began to bore even the guilty, the push for ethics and reform on Capitol Hill rapidly lost momentum in the 95th Congress. Its members were already taking for granted a pay raise nearly equal to the medium family income in America and was regretting all the outside income they had sacrificed to what many saw as a temporary hysteria for ethics.

A backlash spread. Suddenly, by 1978, "ethics" and "reform" became dirty words in the halls of Congress. A package of reforms developed by the Obey Commission, to improve administration of the House and establish a grievance procedure for Capitol employees, was defeated. The House voted against the public financing of congressional elections. Congress did pass an ethics bill dealing largely with the executive and judicial branches—only after House leaders quelled an attempt to repeal the 15 percent limitation on outside earned income.

Even Representative Obey, author of several frustrated reforms, observed that Congress "just got so damn fed up seeing the House broadbrushed by every damn demagogue in the country and nobody back home is being told how much we've reformed. . . . If you've got a bum the people to blame are the people who elected him, not the people who have to work with him." According to Illinois Democrat Morgan Murphy, "The whole atmosphere here—with all these investigations—is that a majority of the members of Congress are crooks or have something to hide. There's a suspicion every time you call someone in the bureaucracy on behalf of a constituent that you're doing someone a favor because you owe him something. The pendulum has swung too far since Watergate."

Obey and Murphy each have a piece of the truth. The House has adopted several important reforms; and most members of Congress aren't crooks. Indeed, many are models of probity, independent of the existence or extent of any ethics code. Former senators Wayne Morse and Paul Douglas began publicly disclosing their financial holdings years ago. Senator Charles Percy put his $6 million fortune in the hands of a blind trust in the 1960s. His predecessor, Paul Douglas, also refused all contributions for personal expenses or from people with a financial interest in matters before the Senate. Former Representative Ken Hechler (D.-W.Va.) gave up his commission as an Army reserve colonel—one year short of a guaranteed $220-per-month pension—when the House considered a military pay bill which would have boosted his pension about 10 percent.

But such exemplars are measures of how far their colleagues have to go. It is difficult to ignore that the 1970s saw the greatest documentation of congressional corruption in this century. True, the people of a district may elect a "bum," but this individual influences policies that affect 434 other districts and 49 other states. If the scandals of the past decade were not enough to motivate Congress to prohibit convicted members from serving as chairmen, prohibit members with substantial commercial interests from chairing committees with jurisdiction over such interests, require the public funding of campaigns, insist that its ethics committees investigate charges of corruption and censure rather than wrist-slap those guilty of corruption, then one wonders what will be necessary to spur Congress to complete its cleanup.

Few, if any, people run for public office with the secret intent of profit by illegal means. Rather, there is something in the congressional environment which raises this temptation and then lowers resistance—a something that may well inhere in the legislative process itself. Laws can seriously affect important people; politicians need money to stay in office; important people can give money to politicians in order to influence them. Thus there are two sides to the coin of the congressional power: there is the potential to improve the lot of all Americans and there is the potential of corruption.

It would be polite to end a discussion of congressional lawlessness by intoning that, while there are a few rotten apples, the overwhelming majority of congressmen are honest. This appears true, but how would we know? Existing public financial disclosures do not tell us enough, nor are the ethics committees vigilant enough to make us sanguine. By failing to police itself adequately, Congress—especially given the cynicism inspired by Watergate and other scandals—has failed to elevate itself above suspicion. A critical observer can hardly take heart at the number of congressmen and staff who have been caught. There are no cops regularly patrolling Capitol Hill corridors, and law enforcement agencies usually do not devote resources to congressional crime. The luckless few are exposed more by fluke than by investigation, which predictably leads friends and cynics alike to wonder not so much what congressmen do as how many of them get away with it.

The consequent cost in loss of public trust in our public lawmakers— indeed in our democracy—is great. William Fulbright, speaking as the newly invested dean at the University of Arkansas in 1939, described the price we paid for official corruption.

"I used to advise my best law students to go into politics," he said, "and some of them were horrified that I should want them to engage in such a corrupt business. You might have thought I had advised them to be bootleggers. This attitude has kept many of our best minds from politics, and this attitude has been largely created by their parents and teachers. Too many of our older citizens have adopted the attitude that nothing can be done about politics. This defeatist view is, in my opinion, the greatest single threat to the preservation of our democratic form of government."

6

Games Congressmen Play:
The Capitol Culture

This damn place is a plenary of Rotarians. The House acts, thinks, and reacts in terms of some stodgy old Philadelphia club.

—A representative

Every small town has its Elks Club or Kiwanis. But only Washington has a club which runs the country. Compared to any Masonic lodge, Congress is not unusually quaint; compared to the hierarchies of the film industry, or backdoor intrigue at the Vatican, its rituals of power are not particularly occult. In most of its ways Congress is, as one senator put it, "just like living in a small town." Just as their executive relations and the committee system say something about the way they govern the country, so do the congressmen's customs and folkways.

The Politics of Deference

When the Constitutional Convention was hammering out new provisions in 1787 its members did not have to worry that their comments would be flashed back to local voters on the evening news. With a candor that modern publicity makes hardly possible, Pennsylvania's Gouverneur Morris said at the convention that he hoped the Senate "will show us the might of aristocracy." Poorly as this seems to fit normal ideas of representation and democracy, it comes closer to catching the Senate's spirit than many other definitions. Spectators watching from the Senate galleries understand Morris's meaning; while members of the House scurry in and out like harried businessmen or tired farmers, the senators emerge from the cloak-room doors and glide onto the floor with the weighty tread of men who know they are being recognized. House members make fun of the Senate for this difference; but both houses pay extraordinary attention to rituals designed to boost prestige.

On first glance the most noticeable feature of congressional pro-ceedings is the antique language and minuettish courtesies which encase them. Before beginning an attack on another congressman's proposal, a member will hang garlands of "my distinguished friend" around his or her neck. Former House speaker John McCormack, for example, warmed up for an attack on a Gerald Ford position by noting that "we are all very happy in the justified and deserved recognition that our distinguished friend, the gentleman from Michi-gan [Ford], received yesterday . . . when the city of Grand Rapids set aside a special day in recognition of such an outstanding legisla-tor and in recognition of such a great American." To make sure that no one missed the point, McCormack's colleague, then majority leader Carl Albert, chimed in, "I wish to join our distinguished and beloved speaker in the tribute paid to our distinguished minority leader." Then, like boxers who had completed the ritual glove touching, they dug in.

After sitting through one too many of these syrupy prefaces several years ago, Massachusetts Senator Edward Brooke suggested that if the word "distinguished" were eliminated from the proceedings, the legislators could save 10 percent of their time. To which Major-ity Leader Mike Mansfield replied, "I appreciate the remarks of the distinguished senator from Massachusetts for his views."

The model for this behavior is, of course, the world of diplomacy— what presidential candidate Adlai Stevenson once called, in words also evocative of Congress, a place of "protocol, alcohol, and Geritol." There, each delegate represents a nation, and a little ceremony is in order. Congressmen emulate other parts of the diplomatic procedure as well. While the pope or the English queen might get away with saying "We" instead of "I," congressmen prefer third-person references to themselves. When he was majority leader, Lyndon Johnson couched one opinion in the following cumbersome prose: "The senator from Texas does not have any objection and the senator from Texas wishes the senator from California to know that the senator from Texas knew the senator from California did not criticize him." In the haste of quick-moving debate, congressmen may even forget "the senator" and refer to themselves as states.

To keep the rituals up, congressmen have developed a number of unwritten social rules. One, according to Majority Leader Jim Wright, is "that old 11th Commandment that was drilled into each of us as we entered in the 1950s and 1960s. 'Thou shalt not demagogue with thy colleagues.' Some members wear out their welcome here by trying to appear universal authorities on all subjects or making speeches aimed at their home constituencies." Another is "Thou shalt not attack thy brethren." In private, congressmen may call each other (as they did in some of our interviews) "screaming idiots" or "jackasses." In public this would provoke outrage. There are strains involved—"It's hard not to call a man a liar when you know that he is one," said one senator—but most keep themselves under control. If their resolve slips, they can remember the case of Representative John Hunter—who in 1867 was formally censured by the House for saying of a colleague's comment, "So far as I am concerned, it is a base lie."*

At times the elaborate courtesy and deference that mark Senate proceedings surrenders to playful jibes. During the hectic last day of the 95th Congress, Senator James Abourezk, conducting a one-man

---

* An extension of floor deference is the informal rule that senators don't go into another state to campaign *against* a colleague. Ruffling feathers in 1982 was Senator Slade Gorton (R.-Wash.), however, who campaigned in Wisconsin against Senator Proxmire. Proxmire, who himself has been known to ignore some senatorial traditions, said "It's a mistake. . . . Somebody will be your opponent one day, and your ally the next. It weakens a senator's effectiveness because it tends to make a permanent enemy."

filibuster on an energy bill, noticed that the chamber's clerk looked tired. "Mr. President, may the clerk be seated while he is reading?" he asked. "I object," snapped a weary Russell Long. "May the clerk remain standing?" Abourezk shot back. "I object," Long said again. Senator Wendell Ford, the presiding officer, then announced that "the clerk will stand on his head and read." Later that day, when Senator Proxmire wanted to continue the filibuster by demanding a quorum call, he was ruled out of order because there was no pending business. Okay, he said, announcing that "I ask unanimous consent that the Republican party be abolished." "I object," Senator Robert Dole (R.-Kans.) quick-wittedly replied, fortunately for the party of Lincoln.

Yet verbal banter or lack of political etiquette can go further—into the realm of physical violence. Just as a prim Victorian England encouraged a very racy pornographic subculture, so the constant constraint of deference can at times lead to its opposite. During heated debate over the Compromise of 1850, Senator Henry S. ("Hangman") Foote brandished a pistol at Thomas Hart Benton; before Foote could fire, other senators subdued him. Six years later, during the Kansas debates, a South Carolina representative bludgeoned Senator Charles Sumner so severely that he could not return to the Senate for three years.

Today's violence is not nearly so serious, but it still occurs at times. Ex-members Bert Podell and James Delaney of New York City got into a shoving match at a luncheon in the early 1970s after Delaney dressed Podell down for defeating him for a seat on their party's steering committee. And Senator Strom Thurmond, a physical culturist, engaged in a lengthy wrestling match in the Senate Office Building with former Senator Ralph Yarborough when Yarborough tried to dragoon Thurmond into attending a committee hearing.

Since freshman congressmen are inexperienced in proper political deference when they arrive, careful instruction is necessary. In the first few weeks freshmen from both parties put aside political differences to attend briefings. There they learn, according to a *New*

Yorker profile of the late Allard Lowenstein, "the special political etiquette of favors that members expect from each other and should be prepared to repay." In addition, they learn the wisdom of Sam Rayburn's famous maxim, "To get along, you've got to go along."

Historically, freshman learned their special role in this hierarchy of deference. The more florid levels of posturing were reserved for their seniors. When they did make a sound—in their maiden speeches—they were urged to be concise, modest, and well prepared. In this they followed the advice George Washington gave in 1787 to a nephew who was about to enter the Virginia house of delegates: "Should the new legislator wish to be heard, the way to command the attention of the House is to speak seldom, but to important subjects . . . make yourself perfectly master of the subject. Never exceed a decent warmth, and submit your sentiments with diffidence."

Slow learners got reminders. In the 1950s a freshman senator found himself sitting next to Walter George, who as longest surviving senator had earned the title of "Dean." Wishing perhaps to show George that he was eager to learn, the youngster leaned over and asked how the Senate had changed during George's countless years as a member. George paused, then icily responded, "Freshmen didn't used to talk so much." And the late Carl Hayden used to recall his first speech in the House in 1913. He had kept quiet for many months until a matter unimportant to the House but very important to his native Arizona came up. Hayden spoke to the chamber for only a minute, and returned to his seat next to a more senior member, who turned to him and angrily said, "Just had to talk, didn't you?"

This system is tolerated only because its victims know that someday they will be on the other end of the sneer. It is perpetuated with a powerful system of informal sanctions. "They can give you the silent treatment," said one representative, "and the real whip is delayed action. You may think you are not going to be punished for your failure to stay in line because there is no immediate penalty. Months later, however, something happens which makes you realize they were just waiting for the proper moment to strike. There is no doubt about it," he ruefully concluded, "if you are going to be independent around here, you are going to pay a steep price for it."

Contrary to form was the 1974 class of feisty freshmen, who voted several senior chairmen out of their positions and spoke out on numerous issues. One of its leaders was Andrew Maguire (D.-N.J.), who said two terms later that "if you trim your sails, if you genuflect to the leadership, if you bow to the committee chairmen, you don't make a difference." Younger members, contrary to tradition, are now far more likely to give passionate floor speeches or introduce major amendments on the House floor, as representatives Elliott Levitas (D.-Ga.) and Dan Glickman (D.-Kans.) have done. After only two terms, representatives Henry Waxman (D.-Calif.) and Michael Barnes (D.-Md.) became chairmen of two very important subcommittees—respectively, the Health Subcommittee of the Energy and Commerce Committee and the Inter-American Subcommittee of Foreign Affairs. But though such members are far more independent of the leadership than their seniors were, personal civility is still the norm, especially for freshmen. As one of the most independent and outspoken of young congressmen, Toby Moffett (D.-Conn.) concluded toward the end of his second term, "All the pressures are to be a member of the club."

Freshmen and sophomore members join with their more senior colleagues in not crossing a line both chambers struggle to toe—charges that impugn another member or group of members by name. It was frowned on, for example, when during a budget debate in 1982, Senator Jake Garn (R.-Utah) blurted out, "I am angry at Congress—and I do not care which party, Republicans or Democrats—because there are weak-kneed, gutless politicians on both sides who won't face up to the issues." Going further, Senator Daniel Patrick Moynihan (D.-N.Y.), who has been known to use words as hammers, once called an amendment by Senator Malcolm Wallop (R.-Wyo.) "inane, devoid of intellectual competence or even rhetorical merit . . . Are we to reduce the United States Senate to a playground, a playpen of juvenilia, to the fantasies of prepubescent youth?" The next day he apologized.

In 1974, then House majority leader Tip O'Neill called a parliamentary maneuver by freshman Republican Representative Robert Bauman (Md.) "a cheap, sneaky, sly way to operate." Bauman quickly protested to Speaker Carl Albert that this characterization violated the House rule that one member may not impugn the motives of another. And Speaker Albert upheld Bauman over the majority leader, striking the offending words from the record. Perhaps unfazed, O'Neill, as Speaker, a few years later attacked freshman Representative Bruce Caputo (R.-N.Y.) in an interview because "from what I've been told he has two employees on his payroll who check the sex life of his colleagues . . . It's a rare occasion when a man the type of Caputo comes to the Congress of the United States, and I don't think he's good for Congress." Again, O'Neill had to apologize, this time on the House floor in an unusual one-minute speech. "I guess what it comes down to is this," he concluded, "that as Speaker, a constitutional officer of this House, I must be more charitable and responsible toward my colleagues than they sometimes are toward me."

Indiscretions like these of course occasionally occur, but if they should become chronic, or if they are not followed by repentance, they eventually push their authors into a special class within the congressional society. The newspaper-reading public may think of these congressmen as colorful or frank; but within Congress they are pariahs. If they please their constituents enough to stay in office and gain seniority, they may eventually get some power in Congress. But such exiles can forget about the many stepping stones open to those who follow the rules.

REPRESENTATIVE RONALD DELLUMS (D.-Calif.) who as a black "radical" was already suspect in the eyes of many colleagues, earned the opprobrium of the House when he told a reporter that most senators and representatives "are mediocre prima donnas who pass legislation that has nothing to do with the reality of misery in this country. The level of mediocrity of the leaders in the country scares the hell out of me.'' For this comment, Dellums was challenged by Representative Wayne Hays on the floor:

> *Hays:* Did the gentleman make that statement?
> *Dellums:* Yes. Do you want me to explain it?
> *Hays:* No, I do not need you to explain it. I just wonder if you then want a bunch of mediocre prima donnas to pay more serious attention to your amendment?
> *Dellums:* If I don't, then my statement has double merit. I would simply say that [congressmen] go around strutting from their offices to the floor of the Congress and do not deal with the human misery in this country.
> *Hays:* You may strut around from *your* office to the floor and to God knows where . . . but do not measure, as my father used to say, everybody's corn in your own half-bushel.

But Dellums was apparently unperturbed by criticism from people like Wayne Hays. A person accustomed to saying what he thinks, he denounced the ''white, male, chauvinist, racist press'' during a House debate on ethics in 1978.

FORMER REPRESENTATIVE JOHN LeBOUTILLIER (R.-N.Y.), who served only one term before being summarily retired by the voters, described himself in one interview as a ''noisemaker.'' At twenty-seven, the youngest member of the House when he was elected in 1980, LeBoutillier lost no time in spraying his colleagues with gobs of vitriol. Most of his victims were Democrats like Senator Daniel Patrick Moynihan (''a drunken bum''), Jimmy Carter (a ''complete birdbrain''), and George McGovern (''scum''). He also lashed out at fellow Republicans like Senator Charles Percy, at whom he hurled a veritable buffet of abuse (''a turkey,'' ''a shrimp,'' and ''a weak fish''). Washington, D.C., he opined, is ''a tumor on America,'' and both the State Department and liberals should be ''eliminated.''

But the young conservative's main target was Speaker O'Neill, whom he branded ''big, fat, and out of control—just like the federal government.'' LeBoutillier launched a campaign to ''Repeal O'Neill'' and even went to the Speaker's district to campaign against him. (O'Neill's supporters were ready, bearing placards that read, ''Keep the Tipper; Boot the Gipper.'') O'Neill's droll response was that he ''wouldn't know [LeBoutillier] from a cord of wood''—to which the freshman responded with a press conference designed to show how inflation has boosted the price of wood.

As such antics might indicate, constructive legislation did not seem to be near the top of LeBoutillier's priority list. His most widely discussed bill, introduced as the centerpiece of his reelection bid, was the ''Arctic Penitentiary Act of 1982,'' which would have sent hardened criminals to a ''polar prison'' in Alaska.

He seemed far more interested in fulfilling his stated goal of appearing on television, and observed, accurately, that his outrageous remarks were what got him on *Good Morning America*, not his legislative brilliance. They were also why his district rejected him in his reelection bid. And voters may have also wondered why they should send him back to serve in an institution he had derided as ''a joke.'' No matter—LeBoutillier, unrepentant, has indicated he will seek to regain his congressional seat.

FORMER SENATOR JAMES ABOUREZK (D.-S.D.), who served from 1973 to 1979, had ''a marvelous unwashed style and a howitzer laugh that he used constantly to shoot down Senatorial pomposities,'' wrote Robert Sherrill. His candor was refreshing in an institution that leans toward obfuscation. In late 1973, Abourezk wrote Senator Jackson, supposedly tough on the oil industry, urging that his committee subpoena industry records to see what its oil reserves were; the South Dakotan never received an answer. Once Abourezk complained long and hard on the chamber floor that the Senate was backing away from requiring President Nixon to end the bombing of Cambodia by August 15, 1973. Liberal colleagues urged him to compromise. ''How the hell do you compromise when you're bombing people,'' said the freshman senator. ''I was going to talk all night until I found there wouldn't be enough guys to help me.'' His tenacity forced Minority Leader Hugh Scott, well-schooled in Senate etiquette, to remonstrate, "The Junior Senator from South Dakota hasn't been here long enough to know the ways of operating in the Senate."

Five years later he still hadn't. Believing that the deregulation of natural gas rates was a fundamental bilk of consumers, he began a two-week postcloture filibuster that had his colleagues bitter and frazzled. "Flaky," "quixotic," he was called. He called them things in return: "Politicians up here are encouraged to run forever because of the seniority system and the benefits. So they will avoid anything that will defeat them. They figure controversy is what will prevent their reelection." Intensely controversial, he chose not to run for reelection, and left with the same bluntness that characterized his term there. "I can't wait to get out of this chicken-shit outfit," he said at the close of the 1978 session.

For those who can adapt to the folkways of the congressional society, there is a reward far different from the exile endured by LeBoutillier. This is membership in the "club"—the informal roster of those who meet the Senate's and House's standards. Though the faces may occasionally change and despite a reallocation of power to younger members, the Senate's dignity and pomp—some would say pomposity—endures. To columnist Meg Greenfield, "Even in their stocking feet, senators in the chamber are always 'on,' always looking as if they were aware of their importance, always engaged among themselves in a kind of forced touchy-feely bonhomie—a back pat here, a handclasp there, a playful minishove, an earnest clutch of the other fellow's lapel. . . . The Club: it lives. Senators of every style, age and political persuasion love to tell you about how various forces and individuals outside the Senate make a terrible mistake by offending that august body or inconveniencing it in some fashion."

To enter The Club's portals, some degree of personal submission is required. Ambitious John and Robert Kennedy never learned this lesson, and were never popular among senators. Other traits can offend as well: Wayne Morse was too belligerent and blunt, Eugene McCarthy too detached and cerebral, Jacob Javits too . . . well, too New York. Those who best qualify have power (Lyndon Johnson and Howard Baker), dignity (Richard Russell and Paul Douglas), amiability (Alan Simpson) or seniority (those remaining southern patriarchs).

Although club perquisites come more naturally to older members and to conservatives than to young liberals, there is no ironclad age or ideological test for those who seek entrance. No clearer proof can be given than the case of Allard Lowenstein, one-term representative from New York. Before his election in 1968 his career as a political organizer and architect on the "Dump Johnson" movement placed him well to the left of most congressional liberals. But on his arrival Lowenstein managed to play by House rules. Other congressmen "found that he is not the wild-eyed maverick most people thought him to be," said one colleague. "He's quietly doing his homework, and as a result he's gaining much respect in the House." When first introduced to Mendel Rivers—grand promoter of the defense industries Lowenstein fought—Lowenstein said, "Mr. Chairman, I have relatives who are constituents of yours"—adding that their name was Rivers. "Well," rumbled Rivers, "there's been a lot of intermarriage down there." After that, the two would call each other "cousin." He also managed to charm Carl Albert, who told Lowenstein, "You're not a long-hair-and-beard type at all." After he had served a few weeks in the House, Lowenstein won the unusual privilege for a freshman of presiding over the floor for a few minutes in Albert's absence.

Another freshman who managed to win over the clubmen's hearts was Republican Senator Charles Mathias of Maryland. In his first term, in 1969, Mathias established himself to such an extent that one colleague said, "On those quickie votes on amendments, you waltz on the floor and the first things you ask are 'What is it?' and 'Whose is it?' If it is Mathias, that's worth about ten votes."

Called Mac (a boyhood name) by all factions, Mathias has struck the right mixture of dignity and affability. "He's always got that cherubic smile and sort of twinkle in his eye," says one senator. Another adds, "He doesn't take himself so serious as to be ponderous." Mathias deftly displayed a due courtesy toward the Senate's demigods in response to questions about his future goals. He replied that the ideal senator was someone like Robert Taft, Sr., of Ohio, "whose word and position were respected in the areas in which he was a leader."

Congressional Cliques

Richard Nixon had Bebe Rebozo, Harvard has the Porcellian Club, Yale has Skull and Bones—and the American Congress has, among others, the Chowder and Marching Society, the Prayer Breakfast Group, the Sundowners, the Monday Morning Meeting, the Tuesday Morning Breakfast Club, the Wednesday Group, the Blue-Collar Caucus, the Suburban Caucus, the Arts Caucus, and the Congressional Environmental and Energy Study Conference, perhaps the largest with 361 participating members.

As in any tradition-ridden society, these clubs play a crucial part in the social structure of Congress. Any implication of frivolity or lightness is usually deserved. Like basketball players on the court, or collegians coming home after heavy dates, congressmen "don't just speak to one another," then Representative Donald Riegle once wrote. "They punch each other on the arm, slap each other on the knee, grab each other's jackets and—occasionally—give each other the goose." The main difference between the congressional club system and university fraternities, both of whose members give allegiance to the rules and habits of the group, is that in Congress the fraternity atmosphere makes a difference in the way the rest of us live. In trying to understand some of the inexplicable outcomes of our legislative process, it is important to note the roles of three kinds of social clubs.

The first category is made of the purely good-times groups. Congressmen, like the rest of us, want to relax when the day is over. For some the best way to do this is with their colleagues. Current social clubs include the Doormen's Society, which meets each year for a "Knight's Night." In 1971, Representative Gerald Ford was finally made a member; not really joking, he said, "It took me sixteen years to become minority leader, but it's taken me twenty-three and one half years to become a Doorman, which I take as a measure of its prestige." Older members meet in the Sundowners Club, while former members make up the Former Members of Congress. This is one of the largest groups—its ranks boosted after each election—and has some four hundred members.

When these recreational activities are loaded with political overtones, they lead to the second category of congressional clubs. In these, business is pleasure; votes are traded over card games and glasses of gin; good joke-telling or expert arm-wrestling may make the difference between success and failure for an education or defense bill. They descend from the nineteenth-century School of Philosophy Club, where it was hard to separate the poker from the politics. An equally misnamed group, Sam Rayburn's "Board of Education," used to meet in the late afternoons in Mr. Sam's hideaway office in the Capitol to sip whiskey and play politics. Today the Chowder and Marching Society (founded in 1949 by, among others, Richard Nixon) gives its fifteen members the chance to talk intimately with a Treasury or Defense secretary. On his admission to the club former Representative Thomas Railsback said, "It was the best thing that has happened to me from a political standpoint." Another Republican group, SOS (allegedly for "Save Our Souls"), includes all the upper stories of the GOP power structure. "The groups do groom people for leadership," says a Chowder man, "perhaps not by a conscious effort but as a result of the close relationships the members form."

A variant of this type of group is the Prayer Breakfast Club. About thirty to forty-five representatives meet weekly for prayer and fellowship, creating bonds which appear later in legislative cooperation. Since 1955 a room has been set aside in the Capitol for their prayer and meditation. "Normally used sparingly at the beginning of a session," writes Charles Clapp in *The Congressman: His Work as He Sees It*, "the room is much frequented when critical complex issues are before the House." Over on the Senate side, a quarter of that chamber meets weekly and hears one of them "address in total openness a subject of importance that has a spiritual dimension."

The third type of group fits more closely the textbook model of what congressmen do with their spare time. These clubs—like the Democratic Study Group or the Black Caucus—are purely political alliances, the structural manifestations of congressional allegiances and blocs. The first one began in 1959, when eighty House liberals settled on the bland title of "Democratic Study Group" (DSG) in order to discourage the press from referring to them as insurgents. In its early days the group remained intentionally loose and informal; to do more, Representative Eugene McCarthy said then, "might be construed as a direct challenge to [House Speaker] Rayburn's leadership." In the last decade-and-a-half the DSG has become more active, providing much-needed information on bills to members, and lining up votes with its own "whip" system. It also produces fact books for the public, such as ones on the defense budget and tax reform, and it has spearheaded the reform drive in the House for making committee chairmen more accountable (partly successful) and for implementing the public financing of congressional elections (not yet successful). Its 1983 membership of 230 is slightly smaller than its 1978 high of 245, and its budget is $700,000.

Another ideological group is the Black Caucus. The 21 congresspeople who make up the caucus use the group as an organizing center for congressional action on issues of importance to black Americans. Members of the Black Caucus pay $2,000 dues a year, much more than members of most other caucuses; also, a rule change prohibiting caucuses from taking private money forced it to cut its staff from ten to three people and give many of its functions to a private foundation. The members make the extra effort because of its special purpose. By holding unofficial hearings, issuing press releases, developing legislation, and keeping black constituents of other congressmen informed of their votes, the group puts pressure on resistant and vulnerable points in Congress. Since the inauguration of President Reagan, who has met with the group only once, it has expanded its scope to deal with a broader range of liberal issues. In 1982 the Black Caucus developed a budget with the lowest deficit of any Democratic proposal before the House, but it received only eighty-six votes, and only two congressmen who opposed the plan even made the effort to speak against it. Resentful caucus members felt certain that had the budget been introduced by whites, it would have gotten a different reception. "The bottom line," says caucus chairman Walter Fauntroy, "is that people aren't prepared to accept black legislators in a leadership role, the quality of their work notwithstanding."

A Little Bit of Pomp

Buckingham Palace would probably run without its guards; the United States Supreme Court would probably not suffer if it had no clerks to yell, "Oyez, oyez, oyez . . . God save the United States of America and this honorable court." Congress, too, would survive, shabbier but no less efficient, if its quaint customs and rituals were streamlined away. But Congress would be poorer for the loss—as would forests without their beautiful hummingbirds or envelopes without colored stamps.

Congress has a Capitol architect, who has only rarely been an architect; it declares a national emergency after each summer vacation to comply with a moldy statute permitting autumn meetings only at time of crisis. The most obvious tradition in daily performance is the emphasis on parliamentary decorum. There are tales from prewar Germany of Jewish families who dined in controlled calm as storm troopers burst through the front door. Congress too, gives that impression of order in the face of adversity. In 1932 a department store clerk leaned from the House galleries waving a gun and demanding a chance to speak. Panic broke out below, and representatives fled for cover. But as Representative Thomas S. McMillan, then in the presiding officer's chair, decided that his life, too, was worth saving, House parliamentarian Lewis Deschler told him solemnly, "You can't leave. You're presiding." Deschler, who recently retired as the parliamentarian, was proud of the resolve displayed several years later by Representative Joe Martin. As four Puerto Rican nationalists began to rain shots down at representatives from the gallery, Martin managed to blurt, "The House stands recessed," before running for his life.

Beneath this crust of decorum, some customs have a more important effect on how well Congress gets its work done. One ritual is the quorum call, a parliamentary device of making sure there are enough members on the floor to conduct business. In practice it is a stalling technique. When congressmen want to check the arrangements for an upcoming bill, look over the draft of a speech they're making, filibuster, or head off an upcoming vote, they say, "Mr. Chairman, I suggest the absence of a quorum." Then the whole machinery of government grinds to a halt, and buzzers ring throughout the Capitol buildings. Members drop what they are doing—holding committee hearings, listening to constituents—not because there's anything important on the floor, but because they want to have a good attendance record. Most members know precisely how long it takes from the ring of the first buzzer until their name is called, and they time their arrival so they can stride onto the floor, register their presence with an electronic device, and head back without breaking stride. "Two minutes after its conclusion," says writer Larry King, "one couldn't find a quorum with bloodhounds."

Few of these charades would be possible or worthwhile without the help of the *Congressional Record*—which is, in its way, the greatest charade of them all. In purely technical terms, the *Record* is an impressive operation: each day, within thirteen hours of the close of debate, the congressional presses have turned out 400,000 copies of another thick edition of the *Record*. The cost is $6.3 million a year, with 42 workers toiling over 42 Linotype machines and three video consoles. As congressmen arrive for their morning's work, they find tall stacks of the *Record*, still glistening with printer's ink, waiting outside their door by 7:00 A.M.

But while the production of the *Record* may be impressive, its content often is not. The *Record* is a subsidiary service for congressmen, producing by the thousands whatever item they choose, coming to rival the Sears, Roebuck catalog or the *People's Almanac* for arcana. Although it costs $479 a page to produce, the back section of the *Record*—often half or two thirds of its bulk—is made of various insertions: articles from *Reader's Digest*, speeches boosting some favored constituent, clever items from the hometown paper which have caught the member's eye. One day shrewd doctors and dentists will learn to stock their waiting rooms with copies of the *Record*, knowing that their anxious patients may relax with items like Representative Jack Kemp's kudos to the Moog synthesizer. It is an electronic device manufactured near Buffalo, which Kemp noted in the 1982 *Record* was "easily the most popular" item in a traveling exhibit of small businesses' "12 most innovative inventions of the past 200 years." Or consider this:

> *Representative Thomas Ashley:* Mr. Speaker, it is with great pride that I take this opportunity to congratulate the Whitmer High School debate team of Toledo, Ohio, for winning its second consecutive national debate championship in the National Forensic League tournament held at Wake Forest University in Winston-Salem, N.C., from June 19 to June 22.

The *Record* cannot be accused of sensationalism, either. When Puerto Rican nationalists shot five representatives from the galleries on March 1, 1954, the *Record* for that day dryly notes that "at approximately 2 o'clock and 30 minutes P.M. a demonstration and the discharge of firearms from the southwest House Gallery (No. 11) interrupted the counting of the vote; the Speaker, pursuant to the inherent power lodged in the Presiding Officer in the case of grave emergency, after ascertaining that certain Members had been wounded and to facilitate their care, at 2 o'clock and 32 minutes P.M. declared the House in recess, subject to call of the Chair."

To put the appropriate close on these congressional customs, we should note the tradition of prayer. Strict rules govern the prayer which begins each morning's session: the House chaplain emphasizes the bipartisan tone of his calling by sitting first on the Democratic side, then with the Republicans, after his speech; he cannot favor any denomination over another; he can give no spiritual guidance on upcoming votes. The Senate chaplain, sixty-six-year-old Richard Helverson, had previously been a pastor in Hollywood, California; working with people there in entertainment "has helped me in this job where political recognition is so important."

At times visiting ministers are permitted to deliver the prayer. The member who represents the minister's district invariably rises afterward to congratulate the guest speaker, which naturally pleases him and, the member hopes, his flock. One visiting prayer became a classic when the minister decided to incorporate parliamentary jargon into his talk:

> O Supreme Legislator . . . Make seniority in Your love ever germane to their conduct. Make them consistently vote yea in the cloakroom of conscience that at the expiration of life's term they may feel no need to revise and extend. . . .
>
> When the Congress of life is adjourned and they answer the final quorum call, may the eternal committee report out a clean bill on their lives.

Perquisites: Nice Work If You Can Get It

Congress has rarely had a problem recruiting members to fill its seats. But—as part of the sad irony that loads most benefits on jobs that would be satisfying anyway and gives least reward to tasks of dull drudgery—the side benefits (called "perquisites") of being a congressman have steadily risen. Some are small but meaningful: cheap, tax-free meals in House and Senate restaurants; inexpensive haircuts ($3.50 for representatives and $4.00 for senators); free plants from the botanical garden; free photography service; free ice; thirty-three free trips home per year; free travel abroad if an official reason can be found; cut-rate weekends provided by the National Park Service at retreats such as Camp Hoover in Virginia; even a gravesite at the congressional cemetery, a small forgotten burial area a mile from the Capitol.

Other privileges are invisible on the record books, but can take the breath away when seen at first hand. Policemen spread their arms to part the traffic on nearby streets when congressmen pass. Special elevators marked SENATORS ONLY whisk their occupants away while the masses stand waiting for the unrestricted cars. Congressmen park their automobiles (with their prestigious license plates) at special parking lots when they go to the National Airport, and clerks there will delay planes when they are late. "Certainly I'll be reluctant to leave," said departing Senator Nicholas Brady (R.-N.J.) in 1982. "I'm like everyone else. I like having ten people call you Senator and open doors as you walk down the hall."

Then there is the pay—$69,800 for representatives and $60,662 for senators (who earn less in salary because they earn more in special interest honoraria, as discussed in Chapter One).

Legislative pay has been a controversial issue throughout history. In ancient Greece members of the assembly received no pay because the honor of serving Athens was considered reward enough. When Congress voted in 1816 to raise its salary to $1,500 per year, there was a voter backlash which defeated many members. The newly elected Congress promptly repealed the increase. A century and a half later, shortly before voting for a salary hike, a member admitted, "My lips say no, no, but my heart says yes! yes!"

In 1977 Congress said yes to a jump from $44,600 to $57,500—or an *increase* which alone was twice the average annual income for a family of four at the poverty level. In return both chambers agreed to limit outside income to 15 percent of salary. In 1979 Congress voted for a hike to $60,662, with a loosening of the outside income restriction.

From the moment they voted the increase and outside income limit, many members of Congress itched for a way to raise their salaries further—but without actually voting for the boost. First they tried going through the back door. One quiet route was the easing and then, for the Senate, the lifting of limits on outside income.

Another was the granting of a hefty tax break for congressmen in December 1981. Grafted onto a bill dealing with black lung benefits for coal miners, the tax break was a complex layer cake of deductions. Most important, in place of a long-standing $3,000 automatic deduction, members got a $75-a-day deduction for living costs in Washington. (Even this would not do, reasoned many members, since Congress often meets only three days a week and the deduction was just for days spent in Washington. So they devised a new calendar based on "congressional days" that included within the deduction four-day weekends spent in the district.) A lawmaker taking a blanket deduction could lop $19,875 off his taxes—and more if he itemized his deductions. Just to make sure that the coal miners got the point, the deduction was made retroactive to January 1, 1981.

The public, to paraphrase Queen Victoria, was not amused. Its displeasure resulted in an outpouring of letters-to-the-editor that many newspapers called unprecedented. Ten thousand taxpayers sent complaints to the IRS. The tax break even inspired a song, recorded by a Turtle Creek, Pennsylvania schoolteacher to the tune of the Battle Hymn of the Republic, with lyrics like these: *Remember all the tax breaks / That you took so greedily / The junkets and the freebies / Seem so contradictory / Increasing your expense accounts / With this economy / We'll remember in November / When we vote.* Panicked at the thought of thousands of constituents humming their way to the voting booths, the Senate in June, 1982 overwhelmingly voted to return the deduction to $3,000. The House went along, but demanded that the Senate also cap honoraria. Growled Representative Silvio Conte (R.-Mass.), "You got a bunch of fat cats up there raking in the big bucks. They can be big statesmen because they can collect those big honoraria." Eventually the two squabbling houses agreed to the $3,000 limit.

The spat was but a precursor of the fracas that would come over pay during the 1982 lame-duck session. If the automatic pay raise were allowed to take place, members would have gotten a politically disastrous 27 percent increase. The House voted instead to take a mere 15 percent hike—to its current salary of $69,800. The Senate, knowing a bargain when it saw one, refused the pay hike but also refused to accept limits on honoraria. Jealous House members balked; "The Senate is actually getting much more of an increase than the House," complained Representative Jamie Whitten. Senator Ted Stevens (R.-Alaska), always in favor of a pay raise whatever its form, crafted a "compromise"—the House got the raise, the Senate kept the honoraria. Six months later, when the Senate accepted a delayed cap on honoraria, its salary was raised to match the House level.

Some of the arguments for 1982's pay increase were strong. The cost of keeping two homes, one of them in expensive Washington, is quite high, and a few members of Congress have said they retired as a result. On the other hand, most people in the country can give perfectly good reasons why *they* should get a raise, too. Then there are those who believe Congress should set an example for the rest of the country. During the Depression, Congress took a pay *cut* in the interest of frugality. In 1981, however, Congress exhibited not frugality but hypocrisy: the tax break was voted on two days before Congress voted to cut Medicare, food stamps, and welfare. Even so, a regularized pay increase would be far better than the current two-track wage scale in which senators are paid partly—sometimes mostly—by private interests. Members of Congress should set an acceptable salary level for both houses and peg it to some reasonable economic indicator to maintain but not increase the already ample ratio of their pay to that of an average worker. That way they would be spared the agony of debating their pay every session, and we would be spared the agony of watching it.

For both taxpayers and the congressmen the most financially important congressional resource, of course, is the office and staff allowance. The congressman has free allowances at the government stationery store; there is an adequate budget for office equipment. Senators are allowed between $846,225 and $1.5 million, depending on the size of their states, to hire secretaries and professional staff; representatives get $366,648.

Beyond even the perquisites, salary, and expenses are the pensions.

For example, an eleven-term member can retire and draw $30,840 a year for life, not counting regular cost-of-living adjustments. "The pensions are generous because Congress itself determines the level of benefits for departing lawmakers, usually without much debate," wrote Jerry Landauer in *The Wall Street Journal*. "As a result, men and women leaving Capitol Hill get substantially more money than if they had served in the Executive Branch, and they can retire at an earlier age." In addition about three dozen members receive yearly pensions of up to $12,000 due to former military service—from Senator John Glenn, who says he earned it and should keep it, to Representative Charles Bennett, who returns his monthly VA check for $1,109 because "I'm drawing such a big income from the government that I don't want to be greedy."

For the first time ever, members made general net worth statements in early 1978. The Senate had at least nineteen millionaires, led by two freshman Republicans worth $7–$17 million each, John Danforth of Missouri and John Heinz of Pennsylvania. The average senator had a net worth of $444,000, and the average chairman a net worth of over $1 million—which suggests that over time all the perquisites and salaries can add up.

Members and their staffs work out of official offices, which themselves become a next level of perquisites; or, as it is said, where a man stands depends on where he sits. Like so much else, allocation of office suites depends on seniority. In order to get a three-room suite in the spacious Rayburn Office Building, one has to be at least a five-term representative. (You can also get three rooms in the older Longworth Building, but "the third room may be down the hall or upstairs," said ex-House building superintendent A. E. Ridgell.) As suites open up, the most senior members get first pick. Former governors like Dale Bumpers and Mark Hatfield, accustomed to a state mansion, chauffeured car, and #1 license plate, have the most difficult time adjusting to their lowly freshman status.

Only the most senior can get a crack at one of the seventy-five secret hideaways within the Capitol Building itself. These high-ceilinged and chandeliered rooms provide quiet retreats from the bustle outside, and have been used for pastimes ranging from office dictation to parties to Sam Rayburn's "Board of Education." Lyndon Johnson, before moving to 1600 Pennsylvania Avenue, had seven of these rooms, together known as "LBJ Ranch East." To distribute the other rooms, Johnson "put together rooms like a subdivided building or tract," said a senator's aide. "When you wound up in one of those windowless basements where the walls sweated all day, you got a pretty good idea of where you stood with LBJ."

Today the fifty-five most senior senators have such second offices, though the allocation is kept secret by the Senate Rules and Administration Committee. "Everyone is scared because every senator is on the take" from the Committee, says one Senate aide, "and desperately needs what he gets from the committee and does not want to rock the boat." The dispensations can cause tensions. In 1981, Labor and Human Resources chairman Orrin Hatch discovered to his horror that two senators he was meeting with, Kennedy and Domenici, both had hideaways and he did not. Ever the gentleman, Domenici sent for his secretary and said, "Here, Orrin, here's the key to *my* Capitol hideaway. It's now *your* Capitol hideaway." Looking a gift perk in the mouth, Hatch replied, "Can I take a look at it first?"

To house these offices, stately and lowly, and to give a final perquisite, Congress has sponsored a building boom inspired by the judgment and tasteful restraint of Albert Speer and Ramses II. As recently as 1900, congressmen had no formal "offices." If they couldn't do their work at their desk on the floor, they took it back to their boardinghouse room. As business expanded, and as the committee system added a new bureaucratic order to congressional operations, both houses decided in the early years of the century to outfit themselves with adequate offices. In 1903 the first House building was completed, and a year later the Senate moved into its office building, now called the Russell Building.

The need for working space was certainly acute, but there is reason to doubt that the enormous piles of marble on Capitol Hill are the appropriate remedy. The recent buildings include the Dirksen Building (1958), the extension of the east front of the Capitol

(1960), the Rayburn Office Building (1965), and the Hart Senate Office Building (1983).

If the Hart Building knew the terrible things being said about it before it was even completed, it would probably have crawled back into the hole in the ground whence it came. At various points during the battles over funding the Hart Building's frills (like a proposed penthouse restaurant), it was called the "senators' pleasure dome" by Senator John Danforth (R.-Mo.) and a "palatial monstrosity" by Senator John Chafee (R.-R.I.). Senator Proxmire, who gave it one of his Golden Fleece awards, opined it "would make a Persian prince green with envy." When the building was started in 1972, its estimated cost was $47.9 million; by 1978 it had climbed to $135 million. In 1979 the Senate came within two votes of actually halting construction on the two-thirds completed building.

In 1982 the Senate voted to eliminate the proposed restaurant, a $300,000 Alexander Calder sculpture, and yet a third senatorial gym, this one with a full basketball court. But as construction neared completion Capitol architects "found" $4 million left over and decided to build the gym at a bargain cost of only $736,000. Calling the expenditure "especially ridiculous," Proxmire successfully embarrassed the Senate into blocking the expenditure.

Ironically named—Philip Hart was one of the least ostentatious of Senators—the recently opened building is still luxurious. Senators enter the building through automatically opened doors and work in blindingly white two-story suites arrayed around a cavernous atrium. Each lawmaker's individual office has a private washroom and a sixteen-foot ceiling ("to inspire them to the dignity of the office," according to the architect). Even the pillars in the basement loading docks are cased in gleaming stainless steel. Palatial or not, the building has serious design flaws: No longer do senators have hidden doors allowing them to avoid staff and constituents when running to a vote; also, in order to walk from office to office on the top floors, one must traverse vertigo-inspiring walkways.

Despite (or perhaps because of) the luxury, the Hart Building was politically an anathema to senators when it opened. Preferring the familiar to the new and expensive, members battled to stay *out* of the edifice. Eventually the offices were occupied by party leaders (hoping to set an example) and junior members (who had no choice).

For precedent, critics of the Hart Building need only have glanced across the Capitol lawns to the even larger edifice known as the Rayburn Office Building. As the construction costs rose from the early estimates of $40–$65 million to the eventual record-setting $122 million, so did the grandiose dreams of its designers. In a design that has been called "Mussolini Modern" and "Texas Penitentiary," its 720 feet of frontage and 450-foot depth contains 50 acres of office space, 25 elevators, 23 escalators, garage space for 1,600 cars, a swimming pool, a gymnasium, and several overnight rooms. In sum, in the words of architectural critic Ada Louise Huxtable, it is "a national disaster. Its defects range from profligate mishandling of 50 acres of space to elephantine aesthetic brutality at record costs. . . . It is quite possible that this is the worst building for the most money in the history of the construction art. It stuns by sheer mass and boring bulk."

This desultory recent history is proving no bar to further construction. There is currently a long-range plan to develop six more House and Senate office buildings to handle projected staff increases in the next several decades.

Perhaps all these buildings make congressmen feel important, the way pyramids made pharaohs feel godlike. When the buildings and the offices and the staffs combine with the less ostensible emoluments of citizen deference to the member's station, what one observer has called the "elevator phenomenon" sets in. A new congressman may arrive with humility intact, but when he gets instant elevator service while others are kept waiting, he begins to realize that he is, well, different. For the perquisites and their general status can create a gigantic congressional ego, a state of self-reflection which has a serious influence on how the members relate among themselves and to outsiders. "On the hustings they are all good Joes," said a Senate staffer, "but when they are here [in Washington] a good many of them try to play God." Representative

Otis Pike (R.-N.Y.), upon announcing his retirement in 1978, said that "congressmen are treated, in Washington at least, like little tin Jesuses. Seven employees are there to fetch me a cup of coffee, get me a hamburger, look things up, take dictation, pamper me, flatter me . . . and generally ease my way through life."

Love and Marriage

In an oft-quoted observation Mrs. Oliver Wendell Holmes once told Teddy Roosevelt that Washington is "a place full of famous men and the women they married when they were young." One result, especially recently, has been the breakups of politicians' marriages. Nearly all congressmen arrive married. But the tensions of political life apply strains that some marriages cannot endure. Mrs. William Proxmire, who separated temporarily from her husband and then rejoined him, bemoaned the difficulties of "living in a fishbowl and the long separations." "Everyone else has first claim on the senator," says Mrs. George Aiken (who should know, since she was Aiken's staff aide for years). Consequently marriage and family life often take a second seat to the fulfillment of the spouse's political career. When Mrs. Albert Quie called her husband to say that her baby was about to arrive, Representative Quie replied, "Well, I've got to make a speech against Secretary Freeman first." He did, and was still in time to get to the hospital.

Another burden on marriages is the sexual temptations public officeholders face. Using power as a love potion, mixing with the glamorous, some congressmen put aside marital loyalties as carelessly as they shed other duties. There is not much discussion of this in print, since it is unfair to single out a congressman or congressmen as a group for something not unique to Washington. But at the same time it would be naïve to assume that only fidelity flourishes on Capitol Hill. Recall how congressional powers such as Wilbur Mills and Wayne Hayes were brought down by their affairs with, respectively, stripper Fanne Fox and nontypist Elizabeth Ray. Then occasional lobbyist Paula Parkinson admitted she had affairs with

302

several House Republicans. "The advantage of being a pretty woman lobbyist is that you have a slightly better chance of getting into a congressman's office," she said, as she posed in only a scarf, garter belt, and briefcase in *Playboy*. Finally, there was the disclosure of mid-1983 that Representative Daniel Crane (R.-Ill.) and Gerry Studds (D.-Mass.) had engaged in sexual relations with seventeen-year-old pages—lapses that led to the House censuring both.

Washington Post reporter Sally Quinn describes how "one senator offered me a ride home from a party and it was raining and so I accepted. On the way he mentioned his wife was out of town, and put his hand on my head, then on my neck, and pulled me close. I pulled away from him. 'I thought you were offering me a ride home,' I said. He looked at me and said, 'What do you think I'm running, a taxi service?' "

Or there can be something seamier. Arthur Marshall, state's attorney for a county near Washington, D.C., has said there have not been many prosecutions for prostitution in his area since they arrested a call girl "who had a substantial index file containing the names of many important men, including members of Congress." Agreeing with this view was veteran reporter Eileen Shanahan, who described on CBS's *60 Minutes* "the situation—which I believe to exist—where lobbyists procure call girls for members of Congress and their staffs."

There is at the same time a priggish streak in Congress, which is every bit as exaggerated as the more publicized salacious side. Representative Chalmers Wylie (R.-Ohio), to take one example, wanted to delete from the federal budget the $100,000 it cost to reproduce a braille edition of *Playboy* for the blind. Although this edition contained only words, not pictures, and although it was the seventh most popular magazine in braille, Wylie attacked it as "a disgusting way to spend taxpayers' money." He added, "I don't read the magazine myself." Said blind radio archivist Ron Stanley of Wylie's crusade, "He calls it budgeting, but I call it censorship."

Beyond the extremes of call girls and *Playboy* in braille, there are the very real strains of the job that affect all congressional spouses. In reaction many simply "fulfill" themselves through their famous husbands. Others contribute directly to their mates' work: Eleanor McGovern and the late Marvella Bayh were political confidantes as well as spouses. A few chart their own lives: Jane Hart, wife of the late Philip Hart, had been a peace activist, with several proud arrests on her record. Senator Bill Bradley's wife, Ernestine Schlant, is a teacher and author. When Roger Jepsen first told his wife he wanted to run for the Senate in 1978, she cried. And then she decided that if he won, she'd join his staff full time without pay so they could work as a "team," which is what happened.

But some marriages cannot withstand the tension of wives tending the households, alone, while their husbands politik. In the last few years Edward Kennedy, Robert Dole, and Donald Riegle have gotten divorced. Alfonse D'Amato has separated from his wife. Edward Brooke and Herman Talmadge have gone through anguishing divorce proceedings that splashed embarrassing financial secrets onto front pages everywhere. Indeed, formal divorces—as opposed to dead but unburied marriages, of which there are many—have become more frequent in recent years, as national taboos have relaxed and as politicians like Nelson Rockefeller have shown that a broken marriage need not end a political career.

Relatively few congressmen seem to have considered one other alternative: sacrificing their political hopes. When Representative Gary Myers announced he would not seek reelection in 1978, choosing instead to return to his old job as foreman in a Butler, Pennsylvania, steel plant, he offered this explanation: "The amount of time it takes to do this job is just not compatible with how much time I want to spend with my family. . . . I just wanted to know my kids before it was too late." Four years later forty-year-old Representative William Brodhead, a popular three-term congressman who had chaired the Democratic Study Group, also hung up his spikes. "I have a strong desire for more time with my family and more quiet goals in my life," he said, explaining his decision to take his wife and two children back to Detroit to practice private law. "I had no friends, no energy. I had nothing except my job."

At Play

Mike Mansfield would relax in his garden, Representative James Symington thought karate "a great conditioner," and seventy-seven-year-old Senator Strom Thurmond jogs, lifts weights, and performs calisthenics. William Cohen pens verse and Howard Baker is an amateur photographer. All is not intrigue in cloakrooms or debate over issues of national moment. Congressmen, too, know how to relax.

Even before Richard Nixon became de facto coach for the Washington Redskins, sports were popular on Capitol Hill. Senators Metzenbaum and Percy are avid tennis players, rising at daybreak to get in a few swings before starting work. Senator Alan Cranston, sixty-eight, is a serious sprinter, the former holder of the world record for fifty-five-year-olds in the hundred-yard dash (12.6 seconds). An admitted "track nut," Cranston wakes up at six o'clock most mornings to work out. And nearly every year since 1961, Republican and Democratic House members have squared off in the congressional baseball game. Speaker Joe Cannon had banned the games near the turn of the century because he considered them beneath the dignity of the House. Speaker Sam Rayburn at one time banned them as too dangerous. But they endure because the members simply enjoy them too much. (When the Republicans won 4–3 in 1978 for their thirteenth win in seventeen outings, Representative Mendel Davis [D.-S.C.] had had enough. "I tell you, they're always pulling something shady," he said with a smile. "No wonder Nixon got kicked out of office.")

Many members of the House work out in the Rayburn pool and gym, two places forbidden to visitors. Members of Congress regularly swim in the twenty-by-sixty-foot pool. Perhaps the most popular Capitol Hill sport is paddleball, a cross between squash and tennis. It is rumored that some members will ask for quorum calls so they can sneak down to get a choice court when the paddleball players scatter for the floor. Representative Guy Vander Jagt (R.-Mich.) was a recent president of the paddleball players and winner of the annual Bullshot of the Year award. While nominally awarded to the Congressman who cheats and argues most during the game, it is actually a reflection of peer esteem. (The only responsibility it carries is to preside over the gym's annual dinner, which invariably ends with congressmen dipping their napkins into water pitchers and hurling wetballs at each other in athletic romp.)

At times business and pleasure can combine, athletically speaking. During the 1981 baseball strike, 14 representatives, most representing cities with major league franchises, wrote baseball commissioner Bowie Kuhn urging that he use his "extraordinary powers" to end the strike by submitting the key issue of free-agent compensation to binding arbitration. The letter originated with Representative Wyche Fowler (D.-Ga.). "I'm a baseball fan, pure and simple," said Fowler, who is an Atlanta Braves supporter. "I could have gotten 150 signatures on that letter." Indeed, when club owners forced Kuhn out in 1982, among those publicly mentioned as a replacement was . . . Wyche Fowler.

A different "sport" practiced by some congressmen is drinking. Given that there are 10 million alcoholics in America, and many millions more who drink heavily, it is understandable in as pressured and fast-paced a world as Washington that not all members are teetotalers. The extent of real alcoholism on Capitol Hill is hard to measure, though Washington correspondent Martin Arnold has written that "there's hardly a reporter in Washington who could not reel off a long list of alcoholic and philandering Representatives [and] Senators . . ." But in a custom of ancient origin, what is known is little discussed—at least not until recent years. Recently, however, Wilbur Mills and Senators Long, Williams, and Talmadge have all acknowledged they were, though no longer are, alcoholics.

There is a rule that liquor cannot be brought onto the floor of either chamber. This was reportedly established in March 1865, after Vice President Andrew Johnson reeled into the Senate to take his oath of office and triggered a scandal. Nevertheless, many members' offices contain well-stocked liquor cabinets which swing open at the end of a long day. "There has never been one night session of the Senate in all my experience," complained the late Wayne Morse of this practice, "that hasn't witnessed at least one senator making a fool of himself and disgracing the Senate." As for the impact of all this imbibing, Representative Richard Bolling revealed in an interview that, as part of the strategy for passing the 1971 plan to expand the House Rules Committee, it was necessary to get one key representative drunk before the voting.

A more open way that congressmen play is to party. Washington has come a long way since a French envoy said upon his arrival there in 1803, "My God! What have I done to be condemned to reside in this city?" If anything, there is a surfeit of partying. There are some hundred embassies which each throw two parties a year. Lobbying groups almost nightly throw lavish get-togethers for interested members in House and Senate meeting rooms. There are many hundreds of national associations, 50 state delegations, and of course 535 senators and representatives, many of whom also throw bashes, which combine play and work. Journalist Lynn Rosellini described how "in just twenty minutes a skilled congressman can arrive, seek out a few key individuals, pump their hands, and then depart, perhaps even grabbing a snack on the way out."

Night life does, at least, enable you to know colleagues and their spouses in a way the House and Senate do not facilitate. When Birch and Marvella Bayh first came to Washington from the Midwest in the early 1960s, they were invited to a typical party. "I wondered how I'd fit in," Mrs. Bayh admitted. "But everybody was so nice and so helpful and I realized that almost everybody in Washington had the same experience. . . . I remember one night sitting next to Senator Estes Kefauver of Tennessee and he turned and asked me if he could finish my dinner if I wasn't going to eat it and I thought then how these are just people like us."

7
Work Congressmen Do

*My father served in Congress from 1909 to 1919 from the
state of Texas. . . . A representative got about fifteen letters a week. Only at rare intervals would a constituent
come to see him. He had no pressure groups to contend
with. Because Congress enacted only a few bills each
session, legislation got the deliberative attention it deserved.
. . . A good debater had no trouble getting a large audience in the chamber. Most of the member's time was spent
on legislation. There was little else for him to do.*
  —Representative Martin Dies, 1954

As the new congressman heads off in glory to Washington, he
knows that power, duty, and a role in the nation's future lie ahead.
But he may be puzzled by the same question that John Kennedy
asked himself as he settled behind the Oval Office desk after his
inauguration: Just what am I supposed to *do* all day?

In the early years of the Republic the answer would have been
"Not much." A member of the First Congress, Senator William
Maclay, recorded the events of April 3, 1790, in his diary: "We
went to the Hall. The Minutes were read. A message was received
from the President of the United States. A report was handed to the
chair. We looked and laughed at each other today for half an hour,
then adjourned."

Today it's a different story. Joseph L. Fisher, elected in November 1974, said he had perhaps "a day off" before being swamped
with "about a hundred letters a day" from lobbyists, special interest
groups, and local clubs and well-wishers. After a congressman has
been in office a few weeks, the pace picks up. Starting early and
sometimes working into the night, a member of Congress goes to
committee meetings and listens to hearings; answers mail and woos

constituents; fields phone calls and courts government agencies; gives speeches and prepares legislation; seeks out campaign monies and rushes to roll calls; returns to the district and speaks wherever two or more are gathered. ''Eighty percent of us are mentally and physically exhausted,'' says the hard-driving Mike Synar, a thirty-two-year-old representative from Oklahoma. ''Our concentration span is down while demands on us are up.'' Fourteen-hour days are common, and things get worse at the end of a session. Senator Carl Levin (D.-Mich.) calculated that in one three-and-a-half-day period during the 97th Congress's lame-duck session, he got a total of ten hours of sleep. Congress used to convene on March 4 and adjourn by July 4. Now it convenes the first week in January and doesn't go home until sometime in the late fall, if not December.

Although most congressmen work long and hard, it is still impossible for them to accomplish more than a small fraction of what is expected of them. Which is why every member has a staff. As used in Washington, ''the staff'' refers to one of the great cryptic institutions of government, the secretaries, administrative assistants, and legislative aides who make up a congressman's alter ego. Ranging in number from 18 to 66 per member (depending on whether one is a representative or a senator, from a small or large state), staff assistants can be as important as the members they work for. As Nicholas I once lamented, ''Not I, but ten thousand clerks rule Russia.''

The staff person's duties are identical to the textbook listing of a congressman's duties. In each stage of the legislative process—from opening the mail to drafting a bill—the staff does most of the legwork. This is a curious institution—in which talented people pour their efforts anonymously into another person's performance and prestige. But it has also become a necessary one as Congress's workload has grown. Someone must answer the eight thousand letters Senator Daniel Patrick Moynihan receives each week. And someone must assist Senator Lowell Weicker, since he serves on four committees (chairing one of them) and thirteen subcommittees (chairing three) and since he may be scheduled for half a dozen hearings in any one morning. Because the number of senators has not expanded to keep pace with the Senate's volume of business ("Our most precious commodity," a staff man has generously said, "is senators"), Moynihan could not hope to keep up with the work without the help of his staff, which numbers about fifty in Washington. (During one week in 1977, Congress's 54 committees and 269 subcommittees held 249 hearings. A House study that year showed that 38 percent of the time members are supposed to be in two committee hearings at the same time.)

Less grandly, congressional assistants must gauge what to feed their employer, and when. Too much information is as bad as too little. One aide to the late Senator Philip Hart said, "You can walk down the hall with Hart or [the late] Senator Hubert Humphrey and say, 'These are the six things you have to remember—tick, tick, tick, tick, tick, tick.' And they'll remember every detail. But it wouldn't have done a damn bit of good to give them information a week ahead." And they must do what their boss would rather avoid. "You need them for protection," said former Senator Eugene McCarthy, "to go to lunch for you."

The ideal staff must be like the ideal hairpiece: effective but unobtrusive. One person runs their show, and at no time should they entertain loyalties to anyone besides "the senator" or "the representative." What lures them to perform this uncelebrated work? Partly it is money; a good senior administrative assistant can earn nearly $60,000 after a few years in Washington. A prominent staff position can provide a platform for a try at elective office itself. Some staff become representatives (like Washington's Norman Dicks) or even senators (like Kansas's Nancy Landon Kassenbaum). In the mid seventies, thirty-eight serving members had once been staff.

But for most the goal is not in public prominence. "To be a politician you have to go out and shake a lot of hands," says Ken McLean, minority staff director of Senate Banking, Housing, and Urban Affairs. "It's a lot more fun to be a staffer." There is the sense of power that comes from intimacy with the mighty—the chance to put one's hand, however, lightly, on the nation's legislative tiller. Although the senator's name is attached to a speech or

311

bill, the staff man who wrote it can always think of it as his. But whatever the benefit to the staff assistant, the benefit to the representative or senator is obvious. "A good administrative assistant can make or break his boss," said one staff person. "If he's good he can make an ordinary guy look great. In all the years I worked there, the only times I ever heard of a congressman or senator getting into real trouble came from one of two reasons. His administrative assistant let him down, or there was hanky-panky in his office."

Staff overreaching is not unknown. In one blatant example an aide to a Senate appropriations subcommittee published in a committee hearing volume an entire dialogue between witnesses and senators—for a hearing that never took place. He made up plausible dialogue to show how busy the subcommittee was . . . and was fired.

With such obvious influence there is the danger, said an aide, that "you begin to think you're brighter than your boss. Some people start acting as if they're really the senator or congressman." Columnist James Reston worries that "in many cases these congressional staffs don't merely assist Senators but tend to replace them. They tell many of them what to say. They write their speeches and Op-Ed articles and sit by their side, suggesting what their questions and answers should be in Congressional committees . . . there is a danger that this professional bureaucracy could become an anonymous and unelected fifth estate of our democracy."

All important congressional staff assistants carefully and ritualistically minimize their prominence, crediting all to their legislative employers; so Richard J. Sullivan, sixty-one-year-old veteran chief counsel of the House Public Works Committee, dismisses as "nonsense" suggestions that he really runs that committee, saying that "the job of the staff is to be in the background and carry out what the committee decides." But as Representative Norman Dicks, who was a staff aide for eight years to Senator Warren Magnuson, says in jest, "People asked me how I felt being elected to Congress, and I told them I never thought I'd give up that much power voluntarily."

Consider, for example, how dozens of staff budget experts met in "subconference" in the summer of 1981 to try to resolve three hundred differences between the House and Senate versions of the budget. As Senator Kennedy and colleagues entered the crowded room, he glanced around and remarked teasingly, "Can we sit in while you make these decisions?"

Names like Peter Murphy, Ari Weiss, and John Carbaugh are not publicly known—except by those aware of how Congress really operates. Peter Murphy, with a House Appropriations subcommittee involved with military spending, was largely responsible for deleting millions in funding for the development of the E3A airborne warning system in 1978. His work demonstrates how staff can have an immense subterranean power on seemingly small parts of larger issues, here a $120 billion military budget.

Ari Weiss, who barely looks his twenty-nine years, is Speaker O'Neill's eyes and ears around the House. Due to his mentor he is often courted like some senior chairman, and he is reported to have been the author of the idea to have an ad hoc energy committee in 1977. More recently Weiss has played a crucial role in the budget battles between Congress and the White House. In the spring of 1982 a make-or-break summit was set up between O'Neill and Reagan. The speaker insisted that Weiss be brought into the meeting; Reagan countered with Stockman. Soon a White House conference table was crowded with aides in an escalating protocol war. John Carbaugh, top political aide to Senator Jesse Helms until 1982, deployed a wide variety of contacts in the bureaucracy and the press to push for conservative State Department appointments and block appointees he considered too liberal. During Carbaugh's tenure with Helms many members of Congress found it difficult to tell when he was acting on his employer's instructions and when he was acting on his own.

Even with such superstaff, as well as the others—there were fewer than 2,000 staff in 1955, and 6,900 by 1979—there are perennial complaints that staff support is inadequate. Former Senator Walter Mondale, for example, complained that a 1973 hearing was a case of "myself and one college kid versus the U.S. Navy and everybody

313

who wanted to build a carrier. . . . We foolishly handicap ourselves by failing to properly staff ourselves." This problem has been exacerbating over time. There were only four fewer senators fifty years ago, but the population was only half as large and the problems of society far less complex. Workload has recently been increasing: in just the area of legislation, while there were 7,845 measures introduced in the 78th Congress (1943–45), the current 98th Congress will probably process 30,000 proposed bills. Consequently congressmen and their staffs must carefully choose where to invest their time and energy.

Servicing Constituents

Greenhorn congressmen may imagine that they will spend all day innovating great ideas into laws, which is hardly the way it works. "I thought I was going to be Daniel Webster," said one disillusioned representative, "and I found that most of my work consisted of personalized work for constituents." Senator William Cohen (R.-Maine), who in 1982 coauthored with Ken Lasson *Getting the Most Out of Washington: Using Congress to Move the Federal Bureaucracy,* estimated that "as much as 40 percent of staff time is spent in case work." Representative Les Aspin, a six-term Democrat from Wisconsin, explains why: "In the old days you had the ward heeler who cemented himself in the community by taking care of everyone. But city machines died once Franklin D. Roosevelt brought in the federal government to take care of everybody. Now the congressman plays the role of the ward heeler—winding his way through bureaucracy, helping to cut through red tape and confusion."

The reason congressmen invest such effort in constituent services is evident; said one, "My experience is that people don't care how I vote on foreign aid, federal aid to education, and all those big issues, but they are very much interested in whether I answer their letters." The politics of personal favors is not new. King Solomon regularly assisted his subjects with their personal problems—as the story of the two women who quarreled over an infant shows—in a manner not unlike the way congressmen help their constituents understand Social Security laws or veterans' benefits.

There is, for example, Representative Geraldine Ferraro (D.-N.Y.), who has five caseworkers in her district office handling nothing but immigration, Medicaid, Social Security-type problems. "In my first two terms we handled thirteen thousand complaints. I'm talking about out-and-out cases. Not a one-phone-call thing," she says. "You're really helping people. That's what it's doing for them. What's it doing for you? It's dynamite. You help someone with a problem, and they walk away thrilled that you're there in Congress. Would I want someone else to do that for me? No way." One other representative, of whom B. F. Skinner would be proud, was even more specific. "A survey indicated I had three thousand farmers in my district who had to go over half a mile for mail, so I started a campaign [for mailbox extensions]. By the last election I had gotten thirteen hundred extensions. They think of me every time they go get that mail."

Answering mail is the mainstay of constituent services. Mail is delivered five times a day on Capitol Hill. Representatives and senators get from 5,000 to 500,000 letters a year for a total of 88 million letters in 1980, up 30 million from only four years before. Offices are at times swamped by waves of letters. The replies that go out are usually form letters which state the member's views on something and thank the writers for their opinions—a genre which, if done well enough, can make most people believe their member has penned a personal response himself.

In addition there are the eccentric requests by those who consider their congressman a glorified valet, and there are the crank letters. One woman requested help with replacing her broken china; another asked a representative in the early 1970s to get President Nixon to purchase a wooden spoon for her while he was in Europe; someone wanted a gold brick from Fort Knox; and one citizen asked that travel arrangements be made for his trip abroad with his wife. The crank letters aim more to irritate than inquire. In a classic response to one of this genre, Representative John Steven McGroarity of

California wrote in 1934, "One of the countless drawbacks of being in Congress is that I am compelled to receive impertinent letters from a jackass like you in which you say I promised to have the Sierre Madre mountains reforested and I have been in Congress two months and haven't done it. Will you please take two running jumps and go to hell." Former Senator Stephen Young was long envied by his more cautious colleagues for his biting ripostes to crackpot critics. When one correspondent requested that his horse be transported at public expense since the First Lady's horse had been, the irascible Young replied, "Dear Sir: Am wondering why you need a horse when there is already one jackass at your address."

While there are often complaints about the level of incoming mail, many members seem eager to increase outgoing mail. Most offices have staff who pore over local newspapers for notices of weddings, births, deaths, or for Girl-Scout-of-the-Month, Million-in-Sales winners, or college queen contestants. A note of congratulations is immediately shipped out. Even though the congressman himself may never participate in this process, it shows that he cares. It seeks good will in the short run and some votes in the long run. But it can occasionally backfire. One man in east Texas who shotgunned his wife to death and said he was glad he did it received a condolence card while in prison from then Representative John Dowdy. Due in part to such frivolous enterprises, the volume of franked mail sent by members of Congress has increased from 24 million pieces in 1938 to 65 million in 1958, 178 million pieces in 1968, and *321* million pieces in 1974. (By 1983, the Congress and Post Office had lost count.)

A more serious form of outgoing mail is the congressional newsletter. Ninety percent of the members send them, usually averaging four a year. They tell constituents about important current events, tell them what their congressman is doing, and tell them what a terrific guy he is. Though often merely a form of vanity press, they also include Representative Henry Waxman's useful tips on how to make the health bureaucracy work for you and Representative Morris Udall's literate and informative monthly newsletters (his staff swears he writes them himself). Some congressmen include questionnaires in their newsletters. These are supposed to take the pulse of local views while flattering the voter by showing that someone is interested in him. "Polling your people with question-naires is a greater gimmick than mailing out free flower seed," said one.

Mail is only one component of servicing constituents. Voters often visit Washington and "drop in on their congressmen." It has become a growing burden for many, as noted by an assistant to former Senator Eugene McCarthy. "In 1948, we got letters. In 1954 we started getting wires. By 1959 it was telephone calls. And around 1964 people started showing up. Now you get here in the morning and you find people waiting." To avoid wasting work time some members enter their office through special doors to avoid person-to-person encounters. But others see it as an important part of their job, even giving visitors a tour of the Capitol, complete with a picture taken on the spot.

While most representatives and senators realize the political divi-dends of constituent services, and act accordingly, most also dislike the menial tasks. "I came here to write laws and what do I do?" protested a congressman in Jim Wright's book *You and Your Congressman*. "I send out baby books to young mothers, listen to every maladjusted kid who wants out of the service . . . and give tours of the Capitol to visitors who are just as worn out as I am." When representatives Otis Pike and Michael Harrington announced their retirements in 1978, they cited, respectively, "wasting time on drivel" and the "errand boy" function of members.

There is some worry about the ethical questions raised. What if a local union, a local bank, and a local radio station all financially support a congressman's campaign, and then (1) the union wants pressure applied to the Tariff Commission for higher tariffs, (2) the bank wants a friendly word passed on to the comptroller about its pending merger, and (3) the station wants help at the FCC to enable it to stay on the air more hours? None of these are legislative matters; all are purely administrative problems. There is clearly the risk of preferential treatment if a congressman pressures a downtown agency or even if he inquires about the status of a matter. Of such constituent favors former Senator Joseph Clark noted, "There is a certain amount of wear and tear on the conscience involved in all of them."

The frequency of constituent complaints suggests that citizens should be protected against the pettiness and inefficiency of the federal bureaucracy. But is Congress—with its 535 separate agents, all concerned about individual cases—the best candidate for the job? Such servicing takes away from the legislative process, which is what the Constitutional Convention really had in mind when it formulated Congress in 1787. Congress neglects key legislation and conducts inadequate oversight over independent agencies, as Chapter 4 argued, in large part because so many resources are devoted to ministerial tasks for constituents.

This informal, case-by-case pleading by so many members can also hamper efficient administration in the agencies. Two congressmen have proposed different approaches. The recently retired Henry Reuss suggests the ombudsman, based on a system begun 165 years ago in Sweden. Teams of people trained in draining the administrative swamps would process the casework now bogging down Capitol Hill. Representative Les Aspin (D.-Wis.) would create an ombudsman for each local district. Trained by a federal center in Washington, the ombudsmen would have similar skills and parallel solutions to problems. Reuss and Aspin's ombudsmen could also call on the backup authority of congressional committees or members, if necessary, as a way of persuading obstructionist bureaucrats that their requests are to be treated seriously. Still, neither proposal has received a serious hearing. As Richard Bolling wrote in his book *Power in the House*, "Constituent service can help a member be reelected, and that is the main reason it will not be handed to someone else."

Morris Fiorina, a political scientist, appreciated the irony, if not hypocrisy, of congressional casework in his 1977 book *Congress: Keystone of the Washington Establishment*:

318

Congressmen earn electoral credits by establishing various Federal programs. The legislation is drafted in very general terms, so some agency must translate a vague policy mandate into a functioning program, a process that necessitates the general promulgation of rules and regulations and incidentally, the trampling of numerous toes. At the next stage hopeful constituents petition their congressmen to intervene in the complex process of the bureaucracy. The cycle closes when the congressman lends a sympathetic ear, piously denounces the evils of bureaucracy . . . and rides a grateful electorate to ever more impressive electoral showings. Congressmen take the credit coming and going.

Debating and Investigating

Of the five senators the Senate has selected as its most esteemed— Webster, Clay, Calhoun, La Follette, and Taft—the first three were famed as orators. Schoolchildren remember from their history books the Webster-Hayne debates, the 1830 struggle over states' rights versus constitutional sovereignty, which ended with Webster's injunction of "Liberty *and* Union, now and forever, one and imseparable!" Upon hearing Webster speak, a listener said, "I was never so excited by public speaking before in my life. Three or four times I thought my temple would burst with the rush of blood. . . . I was beside myself and I am still so."

Like home canning and minor-league baseball, such debate has been a casualty of modern times. Congressmen spend large chunks of time on the floor (26 percent of the average congressman's working time) and talk a lot there, but the amount of high-class debate is small. "The Senate—the so-called greatest deliberative body in the world—hasn't had even a third-class debate in years," said William Proxmire "and even if we had it no one would be on the floor to hear it, except the two or three senators doing the talking."

Not until March 1970 did the House get around to first debating a

319

proposal to end the Vietnam War—the Nedzi-Whalen amendment. Even then, most speakers were allowed only one minute to make their points. In another "debate" over the war, Richard Bolling refused to yield the floor to Representative Robert Drinan because, as he later told Drinan, he was afraid Drinan would ask him questions he couldn't answer. Instead of debate, the bulk of congressional proceedings consists of small inserts for the folks back home—items which only those from the district could not consider trivial.

Incisive debate is so rare that the late Senator Carter Glass of Virginia, after spending more than thirty years in both houses of Congress, said that he had never seen a single mind changed by congressional debate. Senator Patrick Leahy (D.-Vt.) told how the great Panama Canal debate "resembles the plot line of a television soap opera. You could listen to the debate for several days, leave for a week or two, and come back to it having missed very little. All the arguments are being forwarded again and again." The problem is not merely one of repetition or boredom, but of content as well. It is not surprising that members are not eager to engage in floor colloquy with someone like the hyperbolic Orrin Hatch, who said that the Panama Canal treaty "is the culmination of that pattern of surrender and appeasement that has cost us so much all over the world. . . . Is America really going the way of Rome?"

Not surprisingly, few congressmen take floor activity seriously. Writer Larry King, who spent ten years as a congressman's assistant, described the scene in the House: "Members lounge while signing mail, reading newspapers, or eyeing the visitors' galleries for familiar faces or pretty ones. Some sit with their knees propped against seats in front of them chatting or laughing; others lean on the rail at the rear of the chamber to smoke or swap jokes. Congressmen wander in and out aimlessly."

There are occasional breaks in this tranquil front. In 1954 the late William H. "Wild Bill" Langer, a frontier-type representative from North Dakota, broke the top of his desk by pounding on it during a debate on the Eisenhower farm program. In an unusually blunt 1968 speech Senator George McGovern rebuked his colleagues:

Every senator in this chamber is partly responsible for sending 50,000 young Americans to an early grave. *This chamber
reeks of blood*. Every senator here is partly responsible for that
human wreckage at Walter Reed and Bethesda Naval and all
across our land—young boys without legs, or arms, or genitals,
or faces, or hopes. . . . Don't talk to them about bugging out,
or national honor, or courage. It doesn't take any courage at all
for a congressman, or senator, or a President, to wrap himself in
the flag and say we're staying in Vietnam. Because it isn't our
blood that is being shed (emphasis added).

In 1982, when Senator Dale Bumpers (D.-Ark.) proposed a National Peace Day, things got testy. Senator Jeremiah Denton (R.-Ala.)
objected because Bumpers' wife was a sponsor of the day and
affiliated with a group called Peace Links. Said Denton, "Four
organizations on the Peace Links advisory board are either Soviet
controlled or openly sympathetic with, and advocates for, communist foreign policy objectives." An angry Senator Gary Hart (D.-Colo.)
stood up, turned to Denton, and dramatically pointed a finger at
him. "I intend consciously and on purpose to breach the protocol of
the United States Senate and address the Senator from Alabama
directly. I say to the Senator from Alabama, 'Shame on you.' "

But mostly it is considered bad form to get too strident or
argumentative—or long-winded, which is most obvious as House
floor activity drones on toward dinner. If a bill is pending, impatient
members begin to chant, "Vote, vote," and woe to the representative who then delays the proceedings.

The other faded glory of Congress is the congressional investigation.
In earlier days this was a sure route to headlines and reputation. The
1913 Pujo Commission investigated the concentration of wealth on
the "money trust." The Nye Commission, probing the munitions
industry in 1936, popularized the phrase "merchants of death," and
Gerald Nye was talked up as a potential Republican nominee for
President or Vice-President. Harry Truman won national prominence
as chairman of the World War II Committee to Investigate the

National Defense Program. Senator Estes Kefauver became a presidential contender (and vice-presidential nominee) after widely viewed televised hearings into organized crime. Throughout the fifties other committees investigated topics from the Communist Menace (the Hiss-Chambers and Army-McCarthy hearings) to corruption in business, labor unions, and government (rigged TV shows, disc jockey payola, teamster illegalities, and Bernard Goldfine's vicuña coat).

Some of those investigations may have contributed to the current decline. After watching Joe McCarthy and the House Un-American Activities Committee smear reputations, both Congress and the public appreciated the danger of hearings held for their own spectacle, and not for any legislative purpose. The few senators who have made names in recent investigations have run them less as witch-hunts than as seminars—for example, Philip Hart's antitrust subcommittee hearings on economic concentration; former Senator Fulbright's Foreign Relations Committee hearings on the war; or Senator Edward Kennedy's hearings on the Food and Drug Administration. The Senate Watergate hearings of 1973 and the Senate and House hearings on the CIA and FBI are spectacular exceptions to the recent lapse of congressional inquiries.

Legislating and Voting

Debating and investigation lay the foundation for the work most people associate with a member of congress—legislating and voting. Legislation occurs largely within the framework of the committee system. Although this was discussed in Chapter 3, it is important to stress again how small a role legislating plays in the life of an average congressman. Representatives farm out their serious legislative research to the Library of Congress; their serious bill drafting to the Office of Legislative Counsel, to the executive branch, or even to private lobbyists; and their serious thinking to committee chairmen and staff. For there is always the problem of the pressure of time. Given all they are expected to do, it is no wonder that their eyes dart around, their fingers drum, and their attention spans go

322

perhaps one minute. As a Louis Harris poll on the allocation of a representative's time concludes, "Rarely do Members have sufficient blocks of time when they are free from the frantic pace of the Washington 'treadmill' to think about the implications of various public policies."

Even for those who try extra hard, there are barriers. It is unusual for a representative or senator to have his or her piece of legislation considered unless he sits on the committee that would handle it. (Representative Jack Kemp's "Kemp-Roth" tax bill was a prominent exception, since Kemp does not sit on Ways and Means.) "Sometimes you get the idea that everything is managed at the top and that the decisions are none of your business," complained one member. When he retired in 1982, Representative Marc Marks (R.-Pa.) candidly admitted what many colleagues also think of themselves. "I've had a very undistinguished career in the six years I've been here. When I came, I expected I could change the world, and I found out pretty damn quickly I couldn't. As I look back, I don't think I left a fingerprint, let alone a thumbprint."

The final claim on the congressman's time is voting—the expression of the congressman's will and, theoretically, that of his constituents. With hundreds of bills to vote on, how does the member of Congress make his choice?

A standard reply is that he or she is merely a delegate of his constituents and should mirror their views. As Abraham Lincoln put it during his campaign for the Illinois legislature in 1836, "While acting as a representative, I shall be governed by [my constituents'] will on all subjects." This sounds nice in theory, but how does one know what his constituents want? There are general indicators, like election results, polls, the mail.* But as Senator John Kennedy

---

*Although it is important evidence of citizen sentiment, the mail is far from a perfect barometer. Often it reflects the view of *aroused* citizens, not all citizens. When FDR proposed repealing a provision of the Neutrality Act in 1939, tons of mail were sent to Congress which ran 5 to 1 against repeal. Yet a poll showed the public for repeal 56 to 44 percent; Congress approved it. In 1940, 90 percent of the Senate mail opposed a selective service system. At the same time, a poll showed the public 70 percent for it; Congress approved the draft.

admitted in his 1956 book *Profiles in Courage*, "In Washington I frequently find myself believing that forty or fifty letters, six visits from professional politicians and lobbyists, and three editorials in Massachusetts newspapers constitute public opinion on a given issue. Yet in truth I rarely know how the great majority of the voters feel, or even how much they know of the issues that seem so burning in Washington."

Such doubts led then Senator Kennedy to propound the trustee theory, that a member of Congress is a free agent who should follow his own convictions. Kennedy argued that "the voters selected us, in short, because they had confidence in our judgment and our ability to exercise that judgment from a position where we could determine what were their best interests, as a part of the nation's interests." Edmund Burke's 1774 speech to the English Parliament is considered a classic explanation of this viewpoint. "Your representative owes you not his industry, but his judgment," he said, "and he betrays, instead of serving you, if he sacrifices it to your opinion. . . . You choose a member indeed; but when you have chosen him, he is not a member of Bristol, but he is a member of Parliament." (Burke, incidentally, was not reelected.)

When members do contradict the perceived opinion of their constituents or of powerful interest groups, they became, according to Kennedy, "profiles in courage." This does not happen very often, but some members do take risks. Former representative Ken Hechler of West Virginia would fight his state's coal mining interests; Representative Morris Udall, from hawkish Arizona, was vigorously antiwar; when Representative Jim Corman (D.-Calif.) cast a vote in 1980 to allow busing to achieve integrated education, he turned to a colleague and said, "This vote will cost me my seat"—and it did; in 1981 Dale Bumpers (D.-Ark.), representing a state which the year before had voted out of office a governor moderate on race issues, was the only southern senator to vote against the court-stripping bill dealing with busing; Senator Paul Hatfield (D.-Mont.), in office just a few months following the death of Lee Metcalf, cast the deciding vote in favor of the Panama Canal Treaty, which 80 percent of his state opposed according to one poll. He lost his Democratic primary three to one two months later; and although Grumman saturates his Long Island district and has subcontracts for the B-1 bomber, freshman representative Robert Mrazek (D.-N.Y.) voted against further development of the B-1.

Some votes are decided back at the office, because of the merits of one position, or staff advocacy, or regional demands, or the exhortations of a major contributor that "we really need this one." Indeed, at times the presentation of compelling facts can sway votes, regardless of prevailing slogans or party entreaties. Representative Henry Hyde, a conservative Republican from Illinois, was "outraged" by the "preclearance" procedure of the Voting Rights Act, which required Justice Department prior approval before any election law changes could be made by states and areas with a history of racial discrimination. But after hearings showed how minorities were often denied the right to vote, he switched. "You're not being honest if you don't change your mind after hearing the facts. I was wrong, and now I want to be right."

But many members go to the floor not knowing how they are going to vote, nor exactly what they're voting on—which is perhaps predictable when there are 700 recorded votes a year in the House of Representatives.

The floor scene itself resembles a cross between a commodities future exchange and Portobello Road. Members are milling and chatting, haranguing and lounging—a great hubbub of noise out of which votes are cast and public policy made. At the most primitive political level, representatives of the Democratic and Republican leadership often stand at the doors of the House chamber with their thumbs up or down. There also are the major sponsors and opponents of the bill repeating code phrases about the measure—"oppose more federal spending," "vote for jobs." Hurried members, says Majority Leader Jim Wright, "react instinctively to one or the other of the slogans. It's dangerous. It does not provide the kind of deliberation the public is entitled to."

Simultaneously our hypothetically undecided representative may

325

seek out a bellwether-colleague he trusts in the area under consideration—perhaps Representative Fernand St Germain (D.-R.I.) on banking or Representative Leon Panetta (D.-Calif.) on the budget or Representative Richard Ottinger (D.-N.Y.) on the environment or Senator Henry Jackson (D.-Wash.) on defense. Or he may look to a colleague generally admired for his/her intelligence. "Tom Foley and Barber Conable are like E. F. Hutton," said Representative Dan Glickman (D.-Kan.). "When they talk, people listen." Or he may simply seek out a colleague he socializes with or works out at the gym with, or whose wife is friendly with his wife. One congressman told how many members come over from the gym with their tennis shoes on. "Someone won't really understand what the vote is on and will vote the wrong way. Everybody will then yell at him: Hey, Joe, what're you doing. You voted the wrong way. He'll then change his vote."*

Perhaps the member will go along with a colleague on an item of no great interest to him or his district, so that he can garner his colleague's vote when the situation is reversed—such horsetrading has long been decried but is as much a part of the ongoing legislative process as are quorum calls. Perhaps the member will realize that he recently voted against a major interest behind the bill—say labor or business—so he now feels he "owes them one," a balancing act that keeps members off political "enemies lists." If it's a major issue, Speaker O'Neill or Majority Leader Baker may be on the floor pleading for party loyalty, though less strenuously than in the days of Sam Rayburn and Lyndon Johnson.

Three final variables enter into consideration. "The largest factor in members' voting is momentum," said Representative Toby Moffett (D.-Conn.). Many representatives hold off voting early, watch the

---

*The problem of the frenzied last-second vote has only worsened with the advent in February 1973 of an electronic voting system in the House. Instead of the House clerk taking thirty-five minutes to read through the roster of 435 names, giving the tardy time to appear, representatives now have just fifteen minutes to tally their votes by inserting a plastic card in an electronic console.

drift of voting, and then courageously join the winning side. Then, of course, there is the ultimate electoral calculation—who will remember this vote on election day, who will forget it, who as a result will contribute or not contribute campaign money, and how much. Finally, there is Leon Panetta's test: "Eventually I ask—can I justify it to myself? If I can't, then I surely can't to my constituents."

All these swirling considerations affect the member, who filters them, weighs them, and then puts his plastic I.D. card in one console or the other.* It is not a neat process, but it is the way it works. Or as some wag once said, anyone who likes sausage or legislation should not watch how either is made.

For only one of thousands of examples of the results of this hectic process, consider the late Senator Lee Metcalf. He walked out of his office on the afternoon of August 2, 1971, fully determined to vote against the Lockhead bailout bill. No big-business slush funds, the Montana populist said to his staff and himself. But as he approached the floor he was cornered by his friend Alan Cranston of California, home of potentially unemployed Lockheed workers. Senator Cranston beseeched his Democratic colleague not to supposedly throw 30,000 people out of work. Metcalf, weakened, finally chose employment over ideology and voted for the Lockheed loan, which slipped by the Senate 49–48.

But every bill does not possess the drama of such a close vote on such an important issue. Of 30,000 bills introduced each Congress, perhaps 600 bills will become law some of which are very unearthshattering. In 1982, for example, 71 bills passed designating special "days" and "weeks," such as National Oldtime Fiddlers Week, Positive Mental Attitude Week, Queen Isabella Day, and National Elvis Presley Day.

---

*Even after a vote, members hover around to possibly reconsider their action. Representatives may switch their vote if it doesn't effect the final outcome and will help them back home, or if it *does* affect the final outcome and a leader or friend twists their arm. "Bills are won and lost in the well [of the chamber]," according to the late Representative Phillip Burton, who was wise in the political nuances of the House. "If you see a guy who has voted for you in the well, he is going to switch."

A Congressional Composite

Congressmen can easily become homogenized once they adapt to their institution's demands and folkways. But there are still enough differences among the 535 lawmakers to keep journalists busy. Nowhere is this clearer than in their working habits. From the range of potential activities—legislating, handshaking, debating, investigating—each congressman focuses on a few, since there is not enough time for all. As a result there is a rough division of labor among the members. Some, feeling the pull of national prominence, speak up on every major issue. Others, forever intent on the next election, think that the only major issues are those that affect their district. Some legislators seize the reins of power with confidence and talent; others remind one of Henry James's comment that a Senator is "like a begonia, showy but useless." When studying members of Congress past and present, certain categories of work styles emerge:

The Overachievers—To them Congress is not a sinecure but an opportunity—to produce reports, release exposés, let fly speeches, and in general stay in the news. "As if increase of appetite had grown by what it fed on," their hunger for work is never sated.

The kingfish overachiever has to be Senator William Proxmire. His high school classmates at Pottstown, Pennsylvania, voted him the class's "biggest grind," and he's been pushing himself ever since. Through Yale, the Harvard Business School, military counterintelligence, newspaper reporting, and three unsuccessful campaigns for governor of Wisconsin, he exercised spartan self-discipline and finally won a special election for the seat vacated by the death of Joseph McCarthy in 1957.

But success never spoiled Bill Proxmire. He jogs five miles to his Senate office every day, rain or shine, after doing one hundred pushups. One can almost see the adrenaline pumping through his taut, hyperactive body.

Proxmire used to be saddled with a different reputation, one that any overachiever risks: that of an aggressive maverick. Early in his career his overbearing ways irritated many of his colleagues. During his freshman term he rebuked Majority Leader Lyndon Johnson on the floor for efforts to "dominate" the Senate. Sixteen years later his outspokenness on a wide range of issues still could not be contained: when the head of the Joint Chiefs of Staff made some anti-Jewish remarks, within hours Proxmire publicly demanded he resign; when *The New York Times* exposed domestic surveillance by the CIA under Richard Helms, within hours Proxmire demanded that he resign as ambassador to Iran. Such quick-trigger judgments on subjects not covered by his committees make more traditional senators both marvel and mutter. Staff members of his committee told a profiler in 1977 that Proxmire's grandstanding, vanity, and unwillingness to compromise often destroy his effectiveness. Indeed, Senate Democrats at the start of the 98th Congress took the unusual step of slotting Senators Stennis and Byrd above him as the ranking minority members of the appropriations panel; said a colleague: "There was some dissatisfaction that we really couldn't rely on our own ranking member [of Appropriations]. He's just not much of a team player." And although his Golden Fleece awards generate enormous publicity over absurd spending—$97,000 for a study on "The Peruvian Brothel, A Sexual Dispensary and Social Arena"—many scholars regard his efforts as anti-intellectual demagoguery.

But, with a few successes and some seniority, Proxmire has more impact than the "maverick" label would imply. In his specialty, defense spending, he has made "cost overruns" common parlance. He led successful efforts to kill two of the biggest defense "cost overruns" in history—the SST program and the B-1 bomber. He also exposed C-5A overruns, causing Congress to roll back the number of planes produced from 120 to 81—saving some $2.5 billion. In less well-known efforts, Proxmire has pushed ethics reform, opposed the Capitol west front extension, put the Import-Export Bank back under the government budget, authored the Truth in Lending Act, defended. A. Ernie Fitzgerald's whistle-blowing activities, and vociferously fought red-lining in the inner cities.

329

In 1977, Proxmire welcomed Jimmy Carter to Washington with a barrage of opposition to the appointment of Carter's Georgia banking buddy Bert Lance as director of the Office of Management and Budget and to White House plans to bail out New York City with federal aid. Although he let New York survive in the end, he continued to oppose Lance's confirmation. He grilled him in committee, made a harsh speech opposing his confirmation on the Senate floor, and eventually cast a lone nay vote. "He was simply unqualified. He had no background at all in handling a government budget."

As if this frenetic pace on the issues weren't enough, Proxmire has not missed a Senate roll-call vote since 1966, casting his 8,000th straight vote in late 1982, and he returns home to Wisconsin nearly every weekend. The result: he spent all of $146 to win reelection with 64 percent of the vote in 1982.

The Underachievers—To say that they are not household words puts it mildly. Their seats, usually from safe districts, are a form of Social Security to them—steady income for little or no work. Others may do the legislating; these people are content to stay out of sight. There are more of them than of the overachievers.

Former representatives Philip Philbin and Robert Nix exemplified this species of congressman.

Philbin (D.-Mass.), who served fourteen terms ending in 1971, was uncontroversial, uninterested, and inactive in all House affairs. His indifference extended even to the Armed Services Committee, where he became vice-chairman through circumstances beyond his control (he had twenty-eight years' seniority). *The Wall Street Journal* wrote that "the 72-year-old Democrat regularly arrives on the House floor for the day's debate, affably greets his cronies, takes a seat up front near the speaker's rostrum—and then almost always falls asleep." But Philbin was a kind and friendly fellow who won affection from other representatives and his district despite his lethargy. He left office long after he had retired from it.

Nix, after sixteen years in Congress, was the second most senior black representative in the 95th Congress (1977–79), as well as the first black representative ever elected in Pennsylvania. Other men might have used this as a platform for legitimate publicity. Nix modestly remained an entire unknown, both in his district and in the Capitol. The Philadelphia political machine, rubbing salt in the wounds of democratic theory, ensured his reelection (until his defeat in 1978). But once in Congress Nix did little but take up space. In the 1970 campaign Nix's opponent kept referring to him as "the phantom congressman."

The local Philadelphia newspapers rarely covered him, for there was not much to cover. But in early 1971, a *Philadelphia Tribune* columnist managed to interview him at length one night. After the article had been written, the columnist discovered that Nix's exact words that evening on Martin Luther King, the UN, Israel, education, and income tax had come directly from his October 1970 newsletter (he sent out one a year). Nevertheless Nix got a fellow Philadelphia representative to insert the article in the *Congressional Report*. And in December 1971 an unabashed Nix reproduced copies of the *Record* pages containing the article and then sent them out as his 1971 newsletter.

Districters—These congressmen worry little about affairs of state. They see themselves as tribunes of the people, and their highest calling is to serve their constituents' immediate problems. And that usually means in person, not by mail.

The exemplar of the congressional tribune was William Barrett, a fourteen-term representative from southwest Philadelphia. He flew back to his district *every night* from Washington to hold office hours from 9:00 P.M. to 1:00 A.M. At the corner of 24th and Wharton Streets in south Philadelphia, in the shabby office of a building he owned, Barrett sometimes saw as many as 750 people a week, "on marital matters, child welfare, foreclosures, evictions—everything that affects the human person," he said. For this his constituents called him "the Reverend" and the night sessions "the confessional." Stephen Isaacs wrote in *The Washington Post*: "Folks line up to tell

Bill Barrett their problems. He sits behind his desk, listening, his fingertips poised—barely touching—in front of his chin. And, as he has been doing for forty years—the last twenty-six as a congressman—he does something about their problems. He gets them taken care of.'' He cared little about his legislative duties (although he was the second ranking Democrat on the House Banking and Currency Committee), to the extent that one Hill staffer observed that ''his knowledge of legislation only goes as far as how many patronage jobs it will produce for him in Philadelphia.''

The Orators—Following in the tradition of Cicero and Webster, a few congressmen try to make the chamber ring. Although a small band, they occasionally provide bright moments on the chamber floor.

Looking back on twenty-five years in the Senate, William Proxmire considers him the chamber's best orator. For at five feet four inches and 150 pounds, former Rhode Island senator John Pastore attracted attention by the discrepancy between the size of himself and the size of his voice. A snappy dresser with a trim moustache, he would jump, prance, jerk, and, with stentorian voice, boom his way through a speech or debate. One Senate worker claims he heard Pastore while sitting at his desk one story above the floor, across a corridor, and behind two closed doors. Pastore's golden moment of oratory was when 65 million Americans heard his typically energetic key-note speech to the 1964 Democratic Convention. ''Look, maybe this doesn't read too well,'' he said about the speech, ''but it sounds good. Maybe no one would give me the Pulitzer Prize for this, but I'm not lookin' for the Pulitzer Prize. I'm lookin' for the audience.''

Johnny-One-Notes—According to a Chinese proverb, ''He who hunts two deer, catches none,'' a lesson not lost on these legislators. Unlike their colleagues who school themselves in broad issue areas like health or defense, they focus on one narrow issue. They will press their point over and over and over again—and, on occasion, the rest of the orchestra will start picking up the tune.

Representative Jack Kemp (R.-N.Y.) has ridden one issue to a prominent role in the Republican party: supply-side tax cuts to stimulate business activity and productivity. His tax cut plan, introduced with Senator William Roth (R.-Del.), became the basis for much of Reaganomics. Kemp-Roth failed as a campaign issue in 1978 and in several votes before 1981. But Kemp never gave up hope; he finally sold it to presidential candidate Reagan in 1979. Keeping the faith even when his star pupil wavered, Kemp opposed the Reagan-backed tax increase in 1982. The forty-eight-year-old former Buffalo Bills quarterback preaches his economic gospel with an intense, true-believer fervor that mixes dry economics and heart-felt populist rhetoric. "My ambition has been to help lead a revolution," he says.

Another is Representative Elliott Levitas (D.-Ga.), who from his first term has been concerned with asserting legislative control over the "faceless, unelected bureaucrats" of the regulatory agencies. To this end Levitas introduced legislation patriotically numbered H.R. 1776 in the 97th and 98th Congresses that would have permitted Congress to wield legislative vetoes over nearly all regulatory agencies. He succeeded occasionally—Congress was able to veto Federal Trade Commission rules—though the whole approach was tossed out in 1983 as an unconstitutional violation of the separation of powers. Levitas also carried his crusade to the field of more traditional oversight, as when he persuaded the Reagan administration to give Congress documents during the controversy over the Environmental Protection Administration's management of the Superfund in 1983.

A Johnny-One-Note of a different sort is Senator Jeremiah Denton (D.-Ala.), for eight years a POW in Vietnam, who "has a habit of spooning his intellect into a funnel: all the force of his brainpower comes out in a narrow, constant series of obsessions," according to Eleanor Randolph in the *Washington Monthly*. Denton's chief worry is the "new threat" of terrorism, directed by Moscow and aimed at the United States. His subcommittee on Security and Terrorism was set up to investigate the danger. "If we continue to ignore the threat or define it away by academic gymnastics, the sand in which we bury our heads will eventually bury our nation,'' he thundered at the first hearing, where he also bared his chest to demonstrate that he was not wearing a bulletproof vest. (To be fair to Senator Denton, he also devotes considerable attention to another issue: teen-age chastity.)

Organization Men—Some men are born great, some have greatness thrust upon them—and others edge their way up the greasy pole, almost unnoticed. In big cities it's the ward heelers, who take care of details for their bosses. In the Congress it's the people who aid the leadership in their daily chores. It may not be the most glamorous way to power, but it's one way.

Robert Michel, the minority leader in the House of Representatives (he prefers the title Republican leader), holds his party members in line with the same technique that got him the job: patient attention to small details. Wandering the floor of the House, he huddles with members and takes note of their problems on a three-by-five card he pulls from his pocket.

He retains the manner and speech of his native Peoria, Illinois, fabled center of the heartland. (Reporters and other congressmen are not surprised to hear unpretentious utterances like "super-duper" and "hell's bells" from Michel's lips.) A congressional aide before he was elected to the House in 1956, he led a quiet life on the Appropriations Committee until he was elected Republican whip in 1974. In the job he spent long, tedious hours on the floor of the House, attending to the needs, problems, and idiosyncracies of the minority members. In both his committee work and as whip, he excelled at line-by-line negotiation of legislation rather than heated polemics.

This conciliatory style came in handy when he defeated a more ideologically charged opponent, Representative Guy Vander Jagt (R.-Mich.), for the minority leader position in 1981. Since then he has kept a low public profile even when playing a pivotal role in budget negotiations. Michel's ministrations were a big reason that so few Republicans defected on the crucial budget and tax votes of

1981. "By constantly making certain you're in the process, he creates a moral or political obligation to vote for the final product," Representative Thomas J. Tauke (R.-Iowa) told the *National Journal*. On more contentious issues—aid to the Nicaraguan *Contras*, the Burford contempt citation—the approach has not worked as well.

Michel has the second highest seniority among House Republicans, and his deputies—Whip Trent Lott (R.-Miss.), Policy Committee head Richard Cheney (R.-Wyo.), and Republican Conference chairman Jack Kemp—are younger firebrands. But even though he is the chief, Michel remains the organization man. He explains: "If you're not concerned over who gets the credit, you might be doggone surprised over how many things you can get accomplished."

Parliamentarians—If you're not keen on policy-making, you should learn the rules of procedure. If you are perennially in the minority, you must learn the rules of procedure. For you can often win procedurally what you could never achieve substantively on the merits. It is a lesson southern senators and representatives have memorized and taken to heart.

Senator James B. Allen of Alabama was the best recent example. Elected in 1968 at the age of fifty-six, Allen had served in the Alabama state legislature for eight years and as lieutenant governor for two terms. When he came to the Senate, he understood the importance and content of parliamentary politics better than most freshmen. Allen publicized the fact that he won the Senate Messengers Golden Gavel Award three times for spending the greatest number of hours presiding over the Senate. In a newsletter home he proudly described his role as "keeping watch in the Senate to see that our position is not prejudiced by adverse parliamentary maneuvers."

In August 1972 Allen showed the value of picayune rules when the Senate considered the House's antibusing bill. Usually bills are read twice and referred to committee. Allen drew on an obscure precedent to prevent the second reading and keep it from going to the liberal Labor and Public Welfare Committee. Instead it remained on the calendar of the full Senate, where senators intimidated by public opposition to busing were more likely to support Allen's cause.

But Allen's acknowledged forte was the filibuster, which he wielded, in his words, to check "the abuses of an unbridled majority." His filibustering defeated a major tax reform proposal of Senator Edward Kennedy in 1973, and delayed Senate passage of the eighteen-year-old vote change and campaign financing reform. In late 1974 Allen led a Senate filibuster against a proposed Consumer Protection Agency ("he was a one-man wrecking crew," said one observer of these events), a filibuster that a near record four cloture votes couldn't stop. His crowning performance in the 1975 battle to reform the filibuster has already been recounted. (After Allen died in June 1978, his wife was appointed to his unexpired term. When Senator William Hathaway of Maine, a prominent liberal, saw her reading the Senate rulebook at her desk, he raced over and pulled it from her hands, jokingly announcing, "My God, we can't let *you* read *that*.")

Absentees and Attenders—Some children play hooky, while others never miss a day of school. And some members of Congress avoid floor activity, while others relish the chance to attend everything.

Running to and from roll calls and sitting through floor proceedings can be a bore. "It would be a delightful thing," wrote George F. Hoar in 1897, "to attend Unitarian conventions if there were not Unitarians there; so too it would be a delightful thing to be a United States senator if you did not have to attend the sessions of the Senate." Perhaps anticipating this advice, only eight of twenty-two senators showed up at the opening of the first session of Congress on March 4, 1789.

Adam Clayton Powell was, of course, the prince of the absentees. In explanation he wrote in 1963, "I refuse to answer quorum calls. Most of them are instigated mischievously and very few of them serve any importance whatsoever. . . . To answer or not to answer a quorum call has nothing whatsoever to do with voting. It is, of course, very obvious that it is the vote which counts." By 1966

Powell wasn't even voting, but his distinction between answering quorum calls and voting calls has merit. Some, like Powell, fail to attend because they consider attendance on the floor unimportant, others are just lazy, while yet others have competing commitments. John Kennedy came only 39 percent of the time in 1960, Eugene McCarthy a paltry 5 percent in 1968, and George McGovern 51 percent in 1972. One representative in the early 1960s made only 17 percent of all roll calls; controlling his local party machinery and coming from a "safe" district, he felt no pressure to attend and impress the people back home.

The absentees make the attenders mad. Until her hip operation in 1968 ex-Senator Margaret Chase Smith had made 2,941 consecutive roll calls, then an all-time Senate record. (Even Lou Gehrig only played in 2,130 consecutive games.) On December 21, 1971, she attacked her colleagues who failed to show up for work. "The Senate is a club of prima donnas intensely self-oriented," she said, "ninety-nine kings and one queen dedicated to their own personal accommodation." Majority Leader Mike Mansfield, who had to attend regularly because of his job, became testy about the problem. On February 8, 1972, he lectured his colleagues that "none of us was drafted for this job. Every single member of this body sought this position, and with the position goes a duty . . . to attendance on the floor of the Senate. The record of this body over the past month is, to put it mildly, abominable." On September 9, 1974, it seemed that not much had improved. For on that day the Senate voted unanimously for a bill creating an agency to police the commodities exchanges—by a 5–0 vote.

Compelling attendance on the floor is a difficult, and perhaps unwise, task. During a debate over the Lower California River Project in 1927, a no-nonsense presiding officer issued "warrants of arrest" and legally dragged the necessary number of senators onto the floor. Senator Smith recommended expulsion of any member who missed more than 40 percent of roll calls. But these steps surely go too far. A member has many responsibilities, of which being on the floor is only one. A 100 percent or even 80 percent attendance record is no guarantee of congressional efficiency or productivity; a 50 percent attendance record may or may not be an indication of negligence. Short of the draconian solution of arrest or expulsion—and as long as the Senate ignores an 1872 statute that orders deduction of a day's pay for every unexcused absent day—the contest between the absentees and attenders will no doubt continue, with the only effective judge being the voters.

Lone Rangers—Some members feel so strongly about certain issues that they are willing to rub up against the grain of tradition, party loyalty, or congressional courtesy. What they gain in popular acclaim they may lose in the scorn of their colleagues.

One is Senator Howard Metzenbaum (D.-Ohio), who near the end of a term can be seen stalking the Senate floor and posing uncomfortable questions to his fellow legislators seeking to slip through a bill or two. "Who is it for?" he demands. "Is it fair?" "Who benefits?" Metzenbaum has made a specialty of filibustering and blocking last-minute special-interest bills beloved by other members. He calls them "rip-offs, bailouts, [and] sweetheart packages." For his aversion to tax code giveaways, Senator Robert Dole nicknamed Metzenbaum "the tax commissioner." During the lame-duck session after the 1982 election he single-handedly blocked or significantly altered 12 bills that he considered anticonsumer—among them bills that would have given antitrust immunity to the beer and shipping industries and the National Football League.

Such persistence can earn the enmity of other members. Senator Ernest Hollings (D.-S.C.) referred to Metzenbaum in one debate as the "Senator from B'nai B'rith." On another occasion Metzenbaum successfully blocked a bill introduced by Senator Ted Stevens (R.-Alaska) that would have turned over a federally owned railroad to the State of Alaska, gratis. Stevens called him a "pain in the ass" and angrily threatened to campaign in Ohio against Metzenbaum—who offered to buy him the necessary plane ticket.

But those scorned within the chamber are often lionized outside its walls, often for the same reasons. At the same time Metzenbaum was infuriating his colleagues, he was winning the plaudits of the press. In an article in *The Washington Post* headlined "Thank God for Metzenbaum!", Ward Sinclair exulted: "He drives his Senate colleagues bonkers, he give big business apoplexy and many cynics in the press view him with disdain, as a bit of an arrogant grandstander. But that aside, he's about the most important man on Capitol Hill these days. Nothing moves through the Senate without his say-so."

Another "lone ranger" was more of a pariah, Representative Phil Gramm (R.-Tex.), who so angered his Democratic colleagues that they stripped him of his seat on the House Budget Committee at the beginning of the 98th Congress. He resigned from Congress and again won election, this time as a Republican. Gramm had been a leader of the conservative southern Democrats known as "Boll Weevils." While sitting on the Budget Committee he lent his name to the "bipartisan" Reagan budget and secretly negotiated its details with David Stockman. Furious Democratic leaders agreed with Majority Leader Wright, who said, "If you wear the jersey and are privy to the huddle, you shouldn't be allowed to tell the plays to the other team." Gramm, in turn, replied that "everybody knew what team I was on." He derided "the idea that some liberal was going to come up and say to me, 'Psst. This is the secret.' "

To be a congressional lone ranger requires thick skin and a healthy sense of self. Gramm, for instance, is prone to trumpeting his integrity with salvos like: "Everybody's got to answer first to themselves and then to their constituents. I've made my decision. I'm a big boy." But as party discipline in both houses continues to break down, congressmen willing to brave the anger of their peers for what they believe in are on the increase.

While being a senator or representative looks glamorous from the outside, it has its drawbacks and disappointments. Congress devotes itself to what it was not essentially designed to do—running small favors for complaining constituents. What Congress *is* supposed to do—legislate—it does not do well. It is the executive that now initiates most legislation, and it is the Supreme Court that has made many of the important human-rights breakthroughs in the past twenty-five years—equal education for blacks, reapportionment, rights for criminal defendants, near abolition of the death penalty, the right to an abortion. To get major legislation passed often requires a major national trauma: the 1937 and 1962 drug amendments followed the Elixir and thalidomide scandals; President Kennedy's death gave impetus to his successor's civil rights and Medicare achievements.

Legislation-by-trauma, however, can fail for two reasons. First, the crisis still cannot overcome a determined vested interest (so, after a decade of assassinations by shooting, there was still no adequate gun-control law); and second, the structure of both houses ensures that a good piece of legislation can founder on one of many shoals, with only an occasional one sailing surprisingly out of the harbor. A new congressman once marveled at working conditions in the Capitol: "We work in a political environment, surrounded by lobbyists, constituents, the leadership, and jangling telephones and we virtually have no time alone to think and reflect upon the problems before us. The big miracle is that somehow all of this works. On paper, looking at the situation, you'd say it couldn't possibly work and yet the fact is that it does." So the miracle of Congress, as Sam Johnson said of a dog that could walk on his hind legs, may not be that it does its task well, but that it does it at all.

But how well it works is another question. Some, frustrated by the formal ways of the Senate and House, creatively plot out new approaches to solving problems: Senator Gaylord Nelson sponsored Earth Day, which helped initiate the entire environmental movement; former Representative (and now Senator) David Pryor worked secretly as an orderly in a nursing home and later set up a headquarters in a trailer near Capitol Hill to aid the elderly, all in an effort to focus attention on the problems of old age; Representative Henry Reuss rediscovered the unused 1899 Refuse Act, sent out a kit of instructions on its use, and thereby encouraged a process whereby water polluters could be hauled into court; after generations of members had genuflected to Pentagon budget estimates and expertise, Senator William Proxmire and Representative Les Aspin simply developed an expertise and expert staffs of their own to conduct the first congressional counteroffensive against military budget waste.

Such breakthroughs are the exception. Unless they are committee chairmen or chamber leaders, most members readily admit their powerlessness. They come to Washington in the flush of victory and with a sense of self-importance, but are then odds-on favorites to sink into oblivion. "Usually only scandal, longevity, or death distinguishes a member from the pack," writes columnist Mary McGrory. Representative Dante Fascell metaphorically complained that "being in the House is sometimes like trying to push a wheelbarrow up a hill with ropes as handles."

So why do they do it? Why make less money than they could in another field, and why go to all those weenie roasts in the district every weekend? Power and prestige. "It's a marvelous job," said Henry Reuss on retiring in 1982. "Where else do you have a daily opportunity to do good, and get paid for it?" For others fame can be more fun than money, and an ounce of history in Washington is worth a pound of success back home. So for most, simply *being there* is reward enough. It justifies (especially for the representatives, with their trying two-year terms) always running for office instead of performing in it, being content only to service specific constituents on personal problems rather than also to represent them on the larger issues.

8

Staying Elected

All members of Congress have a primary interest in being reelected. Some members have no other interest.
— Former Representative Frank E. Smith

It was early in the campaign, and the challenger, Bill McKay, was having trouble developing a strong attack against incumbent Crocker Jarmin in the California senate race. As he went to make a speech, news came that a forest fire had broken out in Malibu. Canceling his engagement, McKay raced to the scene to denounce the disregard for watersheds that led to such fires. As the television cameras and newspapermen crowded around the young candidate, however, a helicopter flew to the scene and Senator Crocker Jarmin jumped out. McKay stood helplessly by while the incumbent announced that he had received the President's personal assurance that federal disaster aid would be forthcoming; in addition he would introduce a bill on the Senate floor to protect watersheds and to insure the property for those whose property was damaged by mismanaged watersheds.

The Advantages of Incumbency

The scene is from the movie *The Candidate*, but the script is familiar. He who holds office also holds the powers of office and can use them to promote his own reelection. The only deviation from the script is that in *The Candidate* incumbent Jarmin eventually lost the election. It is not usually so. Since 1950, 92 percent of all representatives who ran for reelection won; in the Senate, 76 percent of these running for reelection prevailed.* This overall success rate contrasts sharply with public opinion polls showing that only 20 percent of the electorate give Congress high marks institutionally and only 39 percent approve of their representatives' performance.

According to *Congressional Quarterly's Guide to the Congress of the United States*, in the 1870s more than half the representatives sent to the House every two years were freshmen, and the mean length of service was just over two terms. By 1900 only 30 percent of each new crop of representatives arrived in Washington for the first time; in 1970 the figure was about 12 percent and in 1982, 18 percent.†

The reason is incumbency. By comparing a member of Congress's winning margin in his first successful race to his margin in his second, we can get a rough idea of how many votes incumbency is worth. Figures compiled by the writers show that a representative gets 5 percent more of the vote the second time around than he did on his first, a "sophomore surge" which can frequently prove decisive. In recent Senate contests incumbents gained three percentage points in the vote total over their first run for the roses. While

---

*There are several reasons for the lesser security for senators. A representative by diligent casework and campaigning can get to know or see personally most people in his district; a senator can't. Because there are many congressional races but only one Senate race in most media markets, Senate challengers are assured at least some minimal TV and radio coverage while House challengers are not—so far more House challengers languish in obscurity. Also, citizens are more likely to blame one of their two senators than one of a couple dozen representatives for some national problem (unemployment, illegal aliens). So in a year with a weak presidential nominee, like 1980 with Carter, more Senate incumbents from that party will likely lose (50 percent, 1980) than House incumbents (12 percent).

† A small portion of the increase in length of service must be attributed to longer life expectancies; as fewer senators and representatives die in office, more live to complete their full terms, and to be reelected, than they did a century ago.

the gain from incumbency is smaller in the Senate than in the House, it is equally significant, as senatorial elections tend to be closer fought than House elections.

According to Kenneth Harding, who previously headed the House Democratic Campaign Committee, "There's no reason a House member should ever lose, after a term or two, if he's using the tools of office properly." Or as Common Cause president Fred Wertheimer has put it, "For Congress today we have neither a Democratic nor a Republican party. Rather we have an incumbency party which operates a monopoly."

The origins of this invulnerability—and of why Congress is unpopular generally though its inhabitants routinely get sent back—are not difficult to find. One reason is simply that the best vote-getters tend to win, and because they are good vote-getters, to win again and again. But aside from the survival of the fittest, there are powerful special privileges available to incumbents that cannot be enjoyed by their challengers. The most familiar advantage is the one we saw in the scene from *The Candidate:* incumbents, unlike their opponents, are already in office and can service constituents, introduce bills, take credit for bills they have merely cosponsored and for federal spending in their district or state, or preempt their opponents' ideas by putting them into effect themselves.

Another key advantage that accrues to the incumbent is financial. Even before the November election the incumbent is much less likely to have to conduct an expensive, hard-fought primary campaign than his opponent. Many have no opposition at all. Challengers can expect a tougher battle, so even when they win a primary they take a divided party into a general election.

Of course, some incumbents do lose in the primaries, but surprisingly these casualties do not necessarily come from the fierce primaries in one-party districts. Instead the losers are almost invariably either old men beaten by younger, more vigorous challengers or incumbents redistricted into another incumbent's district. Thus the risk of a hard primary battle is not a threat to the vast majority of incumbents—those who have served a few terms—but only to congressional elders who have reaped the blessings of seniority (e.g., Paul Douglas, Clifford Case, Emanuel Celler) or to members unlucky or unpopular with their reapportioning state legislatures.

Despite these automatic advantages, most incumbent members of the House also outspend their rivals. Excluding spending for primaries, incumbents outspent challengers better than two to one.

If veterans can double the tenderfoot dollar for dollar, or better, it is because they have easier access to outside sources of campaign funds. Many of the sources of this money have been spelled out in Chapter 1, but it is worthwhile to mention several points here. The first financial advantage incumbents have is that they already have been assigned to committees. A corporation or labor union knows whether a given congressman is likely to serve on a committee with jurisdiction over subjects important to it. For example, if a representative has been assigned to the House Agriculture Committee, it is a good bet that he will continue to serve there if reelected—which means that a farm conglomerate will be more likely to give money to him than to his opponent, who might well be assigned to the Public Works Committee. Conversely, trucking executives will sooner support a Public Works committeeman than his opponent, who may end up on Agriculture. It is not impossible that a sly senator or representative might request a committee assignment precisely because a corporation or a union gave him a sizable campaign contribution, with promises of more.

A second financial advantage is that incumbents are "viable candidates." They have won at least once and, at least statistically, can be expected to win again. No reasonably self-interested campaign contributor wants to throw good money into a losing cause; he wants his man to win. The phenomenon applies to all aspects of campaigning from collecting endorsements from celebrities to getting press coverage to getting money. The presidential campaign of George McGovern was like a typical senatorial campaign in these respects. Before he won the Wisconsin primary, party notables were notable for their absence; the media was lackadaisical in its coverage; and the money was coming in in nickels and dimes from small contributors, not from the big ones. Within a week after the Wisconsin victory the coffers were brimming; as McGovern's momentum built up, the money built up, too. When, after the convention and *l'affaire* Eagleton, McGovern's campaign was in trouble again, the money again dried up, and McGovern went back to the nickel-and-dimers who had served him so well before.

A third asset in fund-raising is that incumbent members of Congress are worth more to contributors than freshmen, because they have stored up seniority and the power and influence that came with it. The advantages of seniority are recognized not only by the special private interests who give more to ranking members, but also by the House and Senate congressional campaign committees which distribute party money.

Seniority and committee assignments help incumbents at the polls as well as financially. Mendel Davis, who won a special election to fill the seat vacated by the death of his patron, Mendel Rivers, in late 1970, ran his 1972 campaign on the slogan "Building Seniority for You." In his successful 1974 reelection campaign one of Senator Jacob Javits's advertising themes against challenger Ramsey Clark was "Senior is better than Junior." (There can even be the advantages of ethnic seniority. One surrogate speaker for Javits would remind synagogue audiences: "Never has a Jew risen so high on the Senate Foreign Relations Committee; we can't afford to lose him.")

Most members are not quite so blatant, but they do trade on seniority as a reason for reelection. If they want to be more subtle, they may suggest to the voters that they cast their choice for the "most experienced" candidate. Of course, experience and seniority ought to make their positions on the substantive issues more responsible. It has been said of one representative, "He does terrible things. What makes him worse is that he does them *effectively!*" Most voters, apparently, don't catch on.

Committee assignments open the much-discussed pork barrel, and the scent of pork brings in votes. Members of Congress can be instrumental in getting a host of federal projects and grants for their constituents: post offices, dams, roads, airports, bridges, harbors, federal buildings, military installations, irrigation projects, shipyards, mass transit systems, sewage plants, veterans' hospitals, and grants for an infinite variety of medical, educational, social welfare, military, environmental, and other projects. These make such news back home as to turn tightfisted conservatives into unparalleled big-spenders. After President Reagan first proposed $40 billion in budget cuts in 1981, Republican Senator Orrin Hatch of Utah sent out two press releases: "Hatch Pleased With Budget Cuts" *and* "Budget Cuts Won't 'Slow-down' Completion of Central Utah Project, Hatch Says." Reaganite Representative Clay Shaw, first elected in 1980, said his Florida district needed more federal money for roads, airports, and harbors. "Every conservative becomes a liberal when he talks about his own district."

Attempts to oppose pet projects for reelection purposes meet with about as much success as Sisyphus had with his rock. In 1973, when the Senate Public Works Committee was drafting the Water Resources Development bill, Senator James Buckley of New York suggested that several projects proposed in the legislation be dropped "not because of their cost, but because they appeared to be special interest projects offering localized benefits without reference to any national policy," or "pork" as Buckley clarified his remarks. Not only did Buckley feel that special interests were in the back of the minds of his fellow senators, but he felt that those colleagues with more seniority were getting more projects. When Buckley carried his arguments to the Senate floor, Chairman Jennings Randolph of the Public Works Committee played dumb to the whole issue of pork: "If political pressures were the source of public works projects in the past, it is certainly not true today and has not been during my tenure in the Senate." One wonders which Senate Mr. Randolph has been a part of. Buckley's proposal, of course, failed.

The pressure to vote for pork projects can be heavy-handed and persuasive. Representative Les Aspin (D.-Wis.) cites the case of Rockwell International, a large aerospace firm and prime contractor of the B-1 bomber, which costs $70 million apiece though many experts believe it is unnecessary. When Rockwell representatives met with Aspin's staff to urge congressional support for the B-1, only brief mention was made of the merits of the plane. The nuts and bolts of the discussion were purely economic: contracts let, number of states involved, jobs created, beneficial effects on the national economy. For Representative John Seiberling (D.-Ohio), Rockwell even converted its statistics to illustrate the benefits to his Akron congressional district. As long as members of Congress know that elections are won and lost on the basis of pork in their districts, and Rockwell knows that the members know this, then Rockwell will continue to be welcomed on Capitol Hill.

How much is the pork barrel really worth in terms of votes? No one knows exactly, but it appears that it's worth relatively more to freshman congressmen than to veterans. Congress Project researchers took a sample of first-term representatives and grouped them according to the amount of federal spending that went to their districts. Those with the least federal spending added 4.6 percent to their original victory margins when they sought reelection. The next group, with more federal spending, received a 6 percent hike in the victory margin. The lucky ones who procured the most local public works added a whopping 8.9 percent to their share of the vote. After the first term in office, however, the increase in victory margin does not fluctuate with the amount of federal spending. This suggests that a first-termer who wants to be reelected should go all out to bring home the federal bacon, but that he or she can relax a bit thereafter.

Not all is cushy for incumbents, it should be noted, especially when being a part of "big government" has such an odious connotation. One representative thought he had done his people a big favor by voting for a dam in the district, only to discover that it would cause dozens of farms to be flooded out. The farmers helped send him into early retirement. Further, constituents may have unreal expectations of what their senator or representative can do, and may blame him for things beyond his control. Congressmen also complain that they are hampered precisely because they have a record; this, they say, allows challengers to attack or distort what they have done, without having to endure similar attacks. For example, a member who voted against a,major bill to fund the Vietnam War that also contained a small provision for aid to Israel could be labeled—as George McGovern discovered—"anti-Israel" by an opponent. Answering such charges is difficult, because issues can quickly become complicated beyond the attention span of an often uninterested electorate, especially when the charge and the defense are condensed by newspapers and broadcasters.

Despite these and a few other disadvantages, incumbents have far more strength than their opponents. One of the biggest advantages— though many representatives say it's their biggest headache as well—is that an incumbent representative is running all the time he is in office. His reelection campaign begins the moment he takes his oath of office, a fact that led one representative to say, "You should say 'perennial' election rather than 'biennial.' It is with us every day."

Members of the House have complained about the two-year term— the real cause of the perennial campaign—for decades. Since Congress first met, some 120 resolutions have been introduced to lengthen the term to three or four years. (The Constitutional Convention considered a three-year term, but quickly rejected it.) Only two of them ever got out of committee, and only one ever came to a vote—and lost. Even if it somehow managed to carry in the House, such a proposal would die a certain death in the Senate. One of the advantages an incumbent senator enjoys is that the two-year House term makes it impossible for a representative to challenge him without sacrificing his House seat, since no one may run for more than one office at a time. Yet the short tenure of representatives is clearly anachronistic. As Clem Long has written:

> It was instituted at a time when the average congressman represented only a few thousand, instead of hundreds of thousands of constituents; when Congress met a month or two instead of nearly all year; and when the federal government confined its activities to national defense, the excise tax, and a

few internal improvements, instead of pervading every aspect of personal and business life and spending a quarter to a third of all the income of the economy.

The many prerogatives of office—the staff allowances, the free trips home, the cut-rate stationery, the allowances for office equipment and for setting up a district office, and, of course, the franking privilege—all help in the perennial campaign. The cost of a member's salary, his or her staff's salaries, Washington and local district office space, furnishings, stationery, and telephone service are worth over $600,000, according to a 1980 study done by the Americans for Democratic Action—and this amount precedes the two-to-one fundraising advantage incumbents have demonstrated in general elections.

The servicing of constituent demands, described in the previous chapter, is an invaluable reelection tool. According to John White, past chairman of the Democratic National Committee, "What counts in the election of a congressman or senator is how the candidates have met constituents' demands for getting social security checks delivered faster, or helping smooth out a dispute between Washington and the local school district." And in a rare instance of concurrence, his then GOP counterpart, Bill Brock, said "I couldn't agree more." For example, at a seminar for newly elected Democrats immediately following the 1982 election, newcomers were told repeatedly by incumbents to "keep in close touch with your district and serve your constituents."

Members, especially renowned chairmen, forget this lesson at their peril. Al Ullman (D.-Ore.), as the chairman of the House Ways and Means Committee, was a much-attended-to Washington figure, but he had lost touch with his district. Shortly before his defeat in 1980 a local reporter presciently said, "Most people out here don't even know what the Ways and Means or Appropriations Committee is, and what the chairman does. That's three thousand miles away and peripheral to the concerns of people here." Or in Speaker O'Neill's famous words, "All politics is local."

Doing favors for the home folk and making use of his congressional allowances lets a congressman get a jump on his future competitor: he can campaign even before his competitor is chosen, and campaign before the voters think he is campaigning. As one representative said, "You can slip up on the blind side of people during an off-year and get in much more effective campaigning than you can when you are in the actual campaign." Some representatives find casework personally satisfying, especially during their early years in office, when, lacking seniority, they aren't able to contribute much to more exalted activities of the House. One such representative is Wisconsin's David Obey, who helped out a soldier who received orders that would have sent him to Vietnam two days before his long-scheduled wedding. Obey got his departure delayed a week. He feels good about it—and, as he told a *Wall Street Journal* reporter, he knows that the story of his good deed is being told over and over by the friends and families of the bride and groom.

Media Control

There is one more edge: domination of all the media of electioneering—the mails, the newspapers, radio, and television. Aside from the postage allowance, the basis of incumbent domination of the mails is, of course, the franking privilege.

One new representative was told by his father (a former representative), "Son, I have three pieces of advice for you if you want to stay in Congress. One, use the frank. Two, use the frank. Three, use the frank." Franked mail is marked with a bold, florid signature that supposedly says, "This mail is my official business," but that all too often means, "I want to be reelected." Consequently and unsurprisingly, outgoing congressional mail doubles in an election year. A recent law does forbid the use of the frank by an incumbent within sixty days of an election, a law which is at best mere gesture: no public record is kept of when franked mail is sent and no enforcement machinery exists to encourage compliance; and if an incumbent sends out of his office hundreds of thousands of free mailings two days before the cutoff, mail which arrives three weeks later because it sat around the House post office, a challenger can't do anything about it.

Although the frank is supposed to be used only for "official business," not to aid a member's reelection, it is a rule often observed in the breach. Senator Javits had his Small Business Committee hire a direct mail specialist for his political campaign, a specialist who, in his words, devised a "master plan" to use franked mail for "the kind of identification that can be translated into a vote at the polls. . . ." Shortly before his narrowly successful 1982 reelection bid, Representative Stan Parris (R.-Va.) sent a newsletter at government expense to 240,000 households listing "misstatements" about his record next to the "truth." Senator John Heinz (R.-Pa.), perhaps the wealthiest senator, sent 15 million pieces of mail at no cost to himself in his 1982 election year. The subsidized value of this mail exceeded all that his opponent was able to raise and spend.

Heinz went overboard, but all members of Congress ply their voters with newsletters, questionnaires, reprints of speeches on issues of interest, and the like. The newsletters, numbering over 148.5 million a year, help keep the public informed, and also assist the incumbent's reelection. First, they increase the representative's visibility. Second, the content of the newsletters, if not frankly political, often leans that way. In 1966, William C. Love analyzed the materials sent to constituents by congressmen. In the House, Love found that 38 percent of the representatives could be classified as "self-promoters," 22 percent as "persuaders," and 17 percent as combination promoter-persuaders; much smaller percentages were found to be "reticent" or "educators." The Senate was worse: 44 percent were promoters, 28 percent persuaders, and 10 percent a combination of the two. What is more significant is that freshman senators and representatives were much more likely to be self-promoters than the secure veterans, who tended toward the "reticent" end of the spectrum.

Challengers, forced to rely on stamps instead of signatures, cannot hope to compete. To send one mailing to each of the 150,000 households in a typical House district would, at 20 cents apiece, set a challenger back $30,000 just for postage—not counting the printing (which the member, but not the challenger, can obtain at cost.)

Common Cause thought this one-sidedness an unconstitutional denial of equal protection to challengers, and sued. In 1982 a federal district court ruled against them, saying the frank, while a great advantage, was a reasonable prerogative of office. "If one candidate can draw heavily on government funds to overwhelm his opponent," said Ken Guido, the Common Cause attorney on the case, "competition is no longer possible and the foundation of our political institutions is undermined."

Beyond franked mail is the exponentially growing use of targeted, computerized direct-mail solicitations by candidates. This political mode originated in 1952 with Eisenhower, who developed and built up a donor list with the assistance of DeWitt Wallace of *Reader's Digest*. Goldwater, Wallace, McGovern, and the Republican Party later used direct mail to raise huge funds from the aggregation of many small contributors. Now a half-billion pieces a year are mailed and 5.5 million citizens respond with contributions. Called "part science, part art, and part hokum" by journalist Dom Bonafede, political direct mail is very hyperbolic and negative; Democrats invariably want to promote pornography, say the Republicans—and Republicans secretly desire to abolish Social Security, say the Democrats. Such letters are carefully tailored to appeal to particular ethnic, religious, income, and regional groups, to the extent that a *Washington Post* editorial referred to them as "the MIRV of politics: it allows special messages to be independently targeted." The undisputed king of direct mail is ultraconservative Richard Viguerie, whose company has 5 million conservative names on computer tape and 300 employees who send out 80 million solicitations a year. All of which gives credence to the remark of Alan Baron of the *Baron Report* newsletter, that we live in a new era of machine politics, except the machine is a computer.

* * *

Domination of the press is another media advantage enjoyed and exploited by incumbent members of Congress. One study found that about a third of the members of the House said that newspapers in their districts printed their news releases verbatim, and another third wrote their own columns for the local press—a dependency probably due to the fact that three fourths of the 1,760 daily newspapers in the U.S. do not have their own, or a shared, correspondent in Washington. This press control traces to the glory and trappings of office, which shroud the congressman until he doffs his stateman's gown and reenters the political fray at election time. Typical congressmen pour out well over a hundred press releases each year; atypical congressmen, those from not-so-safe seats, pour out many more.

This formidable press barrage naturally does more good for congressmen from rural areas than those from big cities. The small-town editor, anxious to fill his columns, and having no Washington bureau to prepare stories for him, relies on the newsmaker more than, say, a reporter from *The New York Times.* In Representative David Obey's rural Wisconsin district, all the daily newspapers and half the weeklies publish his newspaper column, which appears every week. Obey and his peers are able to obtain reams of free publicity that are simply not available to anyone hoping to challenge them, and at the same time the columns act as the filter through which news reaches the constituents.

When Murray Watson challenged nineteen-term Representative W. R. Poage in an east Texas Democratic primary, local newspapers totally ignored Watson's candidacy. "Watson's name never appeared in the paper except in ads," said Roger Wilson, his aide. The papers refused to print Poage's votes on environmental and consumer issues. "We finally ended up running them as ads," said Wilson.

Domination of the broadcast media, radio and television follows a similar pattern. More than half of all representatives have their own regular radio or television broadcasts, which are eagerly aired by stations who must demonstrate their willingness to air public-

355

service programing if they wish to keep their FCC licenses. The shows are taped very inexpensively in the Senate and House recording studios, which have a mock congressional office, with an elegant desk and a window giving a glorious view of the Capitol dome in the background. The House and Senate recording studios charge members of Congress only the cost of materials when they use the studios. The Nader Congress Project found that an incumbent pays $2,500 to make a year's worth of weekly reports, though equivalent production costs for a challenger would cost about $60,000. The facilities are supposed to provide an inexpensive means for a member of Congress to inform his or her constituents about their congressman's professional duties and issues of interest.

That's the idea, but it's not always the case. The late Senator Everett Dirksen used the studios to record his smash-hit single, "Gallant Men," and thus got a leg up on other recording stars. The Capitol Hill News Service investigated whether the recording studios were producing campaign advertisements. "We don't concern ourselves with the content of the members' spots," said one House studio staff member initially. But when asked how frequently the recording studios were producing budget tapes and films for incumbents' campaign use, the reply was simply, "Oh, heavy." Since House floor speeches have been televised, members now can send tapes of their orations to local TV stations. Speaker O'Neill admitted that floor deliberations were being slowed up by members speaking to be taped for home consumption.

Another hotbed of incumbency advantage lies with the House majority and minority printers. They fill print orders from representatives for just about anything requested—including campaign literature, posters, and bumper stickers. Taking an attitude of "If-they-want-it-we-print-it," the printers (and some members) do not seem to consider that tax dollars are paying much of the cost of the printing operation, and therefore, using the facilities for campaign purposes may not be legal.

Many members also employ a press secretary as a staff assistant to help keep themselves in the news. It is estimated that senators spend

$2.5 million annually in tax dollars to pay their press secretaries. Though it is understandable that former newspaper and broadcast media people are often hired as press people for members of Congress, Representative Joseph McDade (R.-Pa.) has gone one step further—he hired a currently employed reporter for the *Scranton Tribune* to work part-time as his "public relations assistant." The managing editor of the *Tribune* saw no conflict of interest for the reporter.

All these self-benefiting rules, techniques, and minor exploitations, along with the fact of their official status, have the desired result: senators and representatives are media celebrities back home. They are sought out whenever the media wants them to comment on the news, which is often. In 1965 members of the House told researchers that they averaged four TV and eight radio appearances a month while Congress was in session. Members of the Senate, who are pursued by the networks for national coverage more often than House members, have it even better. And in an election year challengers are hard pressed to approach the media impact obtained by experienced and well-connected incumbents.

The result of all this attention in the mails and the press and on television and radio is a much higher degree of voter recognition for the incumbent than a challenger can hope to obtain except by extraordinarily high spending. Though only half the voters know the name of their congressman at any given time, far fewer have ever heard of his or her opponent.

What do they know about the incumbent, besides having heard of him? Voters asked this question will usually answer, "He's a good guy," or "He does a pretty good job." Only rarely do they know what he thinks or how he votes. One remarkable survey taken by the American Business Committee on National Priorities found that "in almost every instance, between 80 percent and 100 percent" of the voters were unaware of how their representatives had voted on key issues that had drawn national attention. The Business Committee in 1971 polled ten House districts represented by important legislators; in all of them, a majority of voters expressed opposition to continued funding of the SST. But eight out of ten representatives voted for the

SST, and apparently could get away with it, since 85 percent of the voters didn't know how they had voted and the 15 percent who thought they knew were wrong as often as they were right.

What this seems to mean is that voters are more likely to vote for the image of a person than for his/her legislative record, and are more likely to vote for the image of someone than for his/her party. Only this can explain some of the surprising representation sent to Congress. Michigan, for example, would regularly return Phillip Hart, a very liberal Democrat, and Robert Griffin, a very conservative Republican, to the Senate. Senators from Hawaii, North Dakota, Iowa, Idaho, and Utah similarly contrast—one liberal, the other conservative.

The need to "image-build" has created a cottage industry of "media consultants" who can make almost any candidate look good, at the price of $2,000 to $20,000 a month. Described best by Sidney Blumenthal in his book *The Permanent Campaign*, these advisors have become as common as bumper stickers in congressional races—writing the literature, designing TV and radio spots, even reshaping candidates' clothes and appearance to fit their campaign strategy. Here's how a political TV producer, Robert Goodman, describes his work with Malcolm Wallop, Republican of Wyoming. The campaign largely consisted of Wallop riding a horse over a soundtrack of TV-Western music; turning to the camera, he says, "Ride with me, Wyoming." "We dig up Wallop, he doesn't know where he's going. He was behind 72 to 18. He was nowhere. I invented that candidacy. . . . We took him, a man of the landed gentry, and created the most spectacular, invigorating Wyoming campaign they had ever seen. We won by 12 to 15 points."

With the power to supervise the laws governing his own reelection, with the ability to make news, with the power to cater to special interests, incumbents have enormous opportunities for corruption, for unfairness, for deceit and manipulation of the public. Members of Congress have from time to time indulged in these opportunities, and stories of votes bought and sold, smear campaigns, and malicious distortion of the facts crop up in every political campaign.

But there are far more important conclusions to be drawn from the advantages of incumbency than the predictable one that many congressmen and their challengers don't fight fairly. One of them is that every single member of Congress is a walking, talking embodiment of conflict of interest. On the one hand he has an interest in staying in office, in being reelected; on the other he has, or ought to have, an interest in serving his constituents and the nation honorably, conscientiously, and well. The congressman who lambastes the high amount of federal spending will nonetheless accept a public works project in his district, and it's difficult to see how even the most scrupulous member of Congress could refuse what may be a boon for his people, even if it's a boondoggle for the nation.

Clearly, too, the men who framed the Constitution expected that representatives would not get reelected as regularly as they now are; that is the whole argument behind the two-year term for members of the House of Representatives. The Senate would represent continuity, the House change. The Senate (before the Constitution was modified to provide for direct election of senators by the people) would represent the states, the House the people. Ironically, in a mass society, where each member of the House has about half a million constituents, the two-year term has come to accomplish exactly the opposite of its purpose. It was supposed to give the *people* a chance to hold their representatives accountable every two years. As George Washington wrote in a letter, in 1787, power ''is intrusted for certain defined purposes, and for a certain limited period . . . and, whenever, it is executed contrary to [the public's] interest, or not agreeable to their wishes, their servants can and undoubtedly will be recalled.''

Now, however, the two-year term has given *special interests* a chance to hold their representatives accountable every two years. It would seem to the uninitiated that the need to seek frequent reelection would make representatives listen more closely to the opinions of their constituents. Instead, because the costs of campaigning are so high, the perennial campaign makes representatives listen more closely to their campaign contributors. As the influence of political parties, House leadership, and presidential leadership wanes, the role of big givers in reelection campaigns becomes even more decisive. Unlike many of the voters, the contributors know the candidate's name and how he or she voted.

The representative or senator who must finance election campaigns is faced with a real and difficult ethical dilemma, which well can be illustrated by the case of former Illinois senator Paul Douglas, one of the most conscientious, honest, and distinguished members of the upper chamber. Douglas had no reservoir of personal wealth to dip into when he ran for reelection. Nor did he use his office to increase his wealth. He had no outside business interests that might have posed conflicts. Every year he made public his net worth and income. But he did have to run for reelection every six years, and he needed money to win in populous, volatile Illinois. He got a large portion of it from organized labor. And in the Senate he voted the labor line. While Douglas generally agreed with labor anyway, the fact remains that he could not, politically, afford to offend it.

If even the most scrupulous members face this temptation, it is no wonder that those of less conscience joyfully embrace it. As former Senator Albert Gore said, "Any person who is willing to sell his soul can have handsome financing for his campaigns." The congressional Dr. Faustus who sells his soul becomes accountable to the special-interest Mephistopheles who buys it, and who may be looking down upon him from the gallery.

The quest for reelection not only leads members of Congress into special-interest dependency, but into a perversion of priorities as well. Congressmen distort the criteria by which they are to be judged, trivializing the work of legislation—except for lists showing how many bills they have introduced—and emphasizing the work of constituent service. There's nothing inherently wrong with servicing constituents; it is useful that aggrieved citizens feel that there is somewhere they can turn. But dwelling on service to the significant exclusion of more substantive legislative work not only misleads voters but encourages congressmen, for instance, to pay less attention to whether more defense spending is needed than to whether the spending is going to their districts. It demeans both the issues presented to the voters and the work done by the members.

But one can't quarrel with the results: the number of "marginal seats" has dramatically declined. According to Professor Morris Fiorina of the California Institute of Technology, in the mid-nineteenth century 40 to 50 percent of congressional seats changed with each election. Today it's one third that amount. And change is due more to retirements than defeats: one fourth of current House members defeated incumbents, while three fourths won an "open seat." In 1948 four of ten congressional victors won with under 55 percent of the vote; today it is one in ten. This shift, wrote Michael Herwitz in the *Washington Monthly*, "has a direct bearing on the political accountability of congressional incumbents. If congressional seats only change parties because of retirements or sex scandals, the public's control over Congress is seriously endangered."

Such entrenchment can further discourage voter participation, which further weakens the public's control over Congress. "I really don't think there's much you can do about anything," Gladys Grand told *The New York Times* after the 1978 elections. "It's getting to be frustrating. I'm just a little person who doesn't have much pull. But that's the way of the world, I guess." Grand was among nearly 100 million Americans eighteen and over who did not vote. Since 1962 the percentage of eligible adults voting has been declining in off-year elections. In 1978 about 38 percent voted, the lowest since 1942; in 1982 it was 40 percent. (In Canada 75 percent vote, in West Germany 91 percent.) "Apathy is too mild a word," said Curtis Gans, director of the Committee for the Study of the American Electorate. "There are substantial numbers of Americans who are disenchanted with the political process, disgusted with their leaders and disillusioned by the failure of government and of both political parties to meet their needs."

To some extent citizens are to blame as much as their representatives. People do not make the effort to hold Congress accountable, do not check voting records and campaign financing information, allow themselves to be lulled into a lazy, hazy accept-ance of their congressman as he/she is, not as he/she ought to be.

But citizens can make a difference. They can lobby their congressmen. They can vote them out of office. They can hold them accountable. But until they do so, the proud lords of legislation can travel luxuriously on taxpayers' money, frolic in the gym, vote themselves pork-barrel legislation, accept the money of special interests, abuse the franking privilege, obstruct important legislation, and be reassured by the knowledge that it is extremely unlikely that these pleasures and powers will be taken away by the voters.

Epilogue
Taking on Congress: A Primer for Citizen Action

Liberty means responsibility. That is why most men dread it.
— George Bernard Shaw

Some citizens, peering into the chasm between congressional potential and congressional failure, may understandably shrug their shoulders in indifference. But mixed among all the cases of sloth, corruption, insensitivity to injustice, and massive lobbying are remarkable instances of citizen power. Congress has been moved by men and women with no special wealth or influence, little or no political experience, and no uncommon genius, but with the modest combination of commitment to a cause and the facts to make a case. Not often, but enough to show the way, citizen advocates have taken on industrial giants, bureaucratic inertia, public indifference, antipathy to "troublemakers"—and they have won, or at least made a difference.

One of them, Randall Forsberg, started out with something simple: an idea. Speaking in Louisville, Kentucky, in 1979, she proposed a blunt approach to the escalation of nuclear arms. The only way to "stop the arms race is to stop it," she declared. "Enough is enough." The audience reaction was so strong that the thirty-six-year-old weapons researcher returned to Boston and put her ideas on paper: "A Call for a Nuclear Freeze." She and Randy Kehler, a St. Louis schoolteacher, persuaded traditional peace groups (the Quakers,

SANE, Mobilization for Survival) to back the idea of a verifiable, bi-lateral nuclear freeze, which was placed on the ballot in several Massachusetts counties. The voters endorsed it—even while at the same time voting for Ronald Reagan—and the resulting enthusiasm began to radiate outward.

The nuclear freeze movement was the first time that citizens stood up and began to take an active role in the complex debate surrounding nuclear weapons. For twenty-five years the spiraling arms race had been the purview of a small group of experts in and out of government, and even the best-intentioned arms control approaches were so complex that a popular constituency in support was impossible to build. The freeze changed that. Explained Jeremy Stone, director of the Federation of American Scientists, ''What the freeze is asking is the severance of the nerves and sinews of the nuclear establishment.''

Rather than make their case at the outset in the halls of Congress, freeze advocates won the backing of the churches, town halls, and state capitols of America. As Ronald Reagan's rhetoric and the statements of his aides about winning nuclear wars and firing atomic ''warning shots'' fanned popular unease about the arms race, grass-roots pressure built. The Massachusetts and Oregon state legislatures passed Freeze resolutions in June 1981; a former National Security Council official named Roger Molander, alarmed by the failure of arms control, set up an educational organization, Ground Zero, which held seminars at 151 college campuses across the country in November 1981; the legislatures of five states, eight city councils, and fifty national and international organizations endorsed the freeze in January 1982; hundreds of New England town meetings—a symbol of participatory democracy—backed the concept shortly thereafter. By the beginning of 1982, 20,000 people were actively working for the freeze. And on June 12, 1982, 750,000 people streamed through the streets of New York into Central Park for the largest political demonstration in U.S. history.

In the spring of 1982 the arms control establishment, the national media, and members of Congress awoke to the depth of popular emotion and scrambled to catch up. Senators Edward Kennedy (D.-Mass.) and Mark Hatfield (R.-Ore.) announced their nuclear freeze resolution in an American University press conference evocative of President Kennedy's test ban speech made in the same auditorium. Even William Colby, former director of the CIA under Republican Presidents, signed on, insisting that a freeze accord would be verifiable. But as freeze cosponsor Representative Jim Leach (R.-Iowa) emphatically said, "No elected official led this movement."

But elected officials would have to pass a freeze resolution in Congress. So—earlier than they had wanted to—freeze leaders began to make the transition from being solely a grass-roots upheaval into a relatively polished Capitol Hill operation. Though the Washington office of the Campaign for a Nuclear Freeze (the national umbrella for the disparate freeze groups) did not even open until a month before the House of Representatives voted on the resolution, thirty lobbyists from liberal, church, disarmament, and labor groups implored members to back the freeze. It took a full court press by the Reagan administration—which had consistently opposed the concept as "simplistic" and the movement as "dupes"—to defeat it, 204–202. More needed to be done. The elections of November 1982 helped; freeze referenda passed in eight of nine states, 38 of 40 towns and cities, and the Democrats gained 26 seats in the House. By December a Gallup Poll found that 71 percent of those polled backed the concept.

But when the freeze passed the House by 287–149, on May 4, 1983, nine months after its first defeat, it was largely because of the newfound sophistication of the movement. This time organizers staged a citizen lobby week that brought 5,000 activists to the capital. The movement was helped when Common Cause, with its wide citizen network, made nuclear weapons its number one issue after an overwhelming vote by its members. And the movement was helped in the House by having an energetic young spokesman like Representative Edward Markey (D.-Mass.), a politician who understood the value of a citizen movement. But despite its recent professionalism the freeze remained a distinctly grass-roots phenomenon. Explained Reuben McCormack, chief lobbyist in Washington, "A hundred people working hard in a district will have much more impact than a hundred lobbyists going to see that member of Congress."

By the end of 1983 the Senate had not passed the freeze, and of course President Reagan is no supporter of the concept (although all the major Democratic presidential candidates are adherents). Still, the distance the movement has come since it started out as a Ph.D. candidate's brainstorm in 1979 shows that concerted citizen action can force congressional action, if not achieve complete victory.

Consider also Abe Bergman, a young pediatrician at Seattle's Children's Orthopedic Hospital. In his hospital Abe Bergman saw burned, scarred, and mutilated children—three a week, or even a day—victims of flammable fabrics, lawn mowers, and poisons alluringly packaged. Instead of shrugging off what he saw, he decided to do something about it. He learned how laws governing unsafe products are made—who makes them and what influences their decisions. He learned that one of his senators, Warren Magnuson, then chairman of the Commerce Committee, was in a unique position to change the law. In Magnuson he found a sympathetic response to the painful accounts of the human tragedies that daily seared his mind. Dr. Bergman became a constant and valued source of information, encouraging Senator Magnuson and the Senate Commerce Committee's staff.

His energetic and informed prodding were among the factors leading Senator Magnuson to introduce amendments to strengthen the Flammable Fabrics Act. In haughty response the chairman of the board of one of the largest textile firms in the nation, speaking for the textile manufacturers' trade association, vowed that "blood would run in the halls of Congress" before this "unneeded" and "punitive" legislation would pass. Nevertheless, in some measure due to Bergman's testimony and Magnuson's support, the Flammable Fabrics Act Amendments did become law in 1967.

It proved initially to be an empty victory. For the Department of

Commerce, which was to establish standards under the act, postponed their development by deferring in every imaginable way to the textile manufacturers' delays and obstructions. It was not the first time a congressional act had disappeared into a bureaucratic quicksand, and Dr. Bergman, unwilling to be satisfied with a "no-law" law, determined to rescue it from Commerce. To convey the intimate terror of a burn injury, he persuaded a local Seattle television station to run a half-hour film he had produced. The powerful documentary climaxed with gentle nurses and doctors changing the bandages of a scarred and frightened and suffering little girl. This film brought three thousand letters from the Seattle area to the secretary of commerce, insisting that he not delay or weaken the standard on children's sleepwear. At Senator Magnuson's request the film was flown to Washington, D.C., where the secretary of commerce and his close associates saw it for themselves. Within two weeks the secretary announced that a strict standard would take effect immediately and that proceedings would commence to raise the age limits of children protected from flammable sleepwear.

Then there was the example of folksinger Harry Chapin. Shocked by the mass starvation that followed the drought in sub-Saharan Africa, he founded a nonprofit educational group called World Hunger Year, supported by his concert earnings. Through the group (and his lyrics), Chapin proselytized on behalf of the need for major action to solve world hunger. But he wanted to do more than just inform. After his wife suggested a presidential commission to study hunger, Chapin began an intensive lobbying effort on Capitol Hill to pass a resolution calling for such a commission.

Chapin shed his jeans and work shirt for a proper suit and tie to lobby Representative Richard Nolan (D.-Minn.), Senator Patrick Leahy (D.-Vt.), and others. Building a core of committed congressional supporters ranging from liberal Senator George McGovern (D.-S.D.) to conservative Senator Bob Dole (R.-Kans.), Chapin's resolution won unanimous support in the Senate and a 368–34 victory in the House. He then sold President Carter on the proposal with an energetic five-minute rush of words in the White House, after which

Carter told him, "If this is the kind of energy that was brought to this resolution, I can see why it's reached my desk." Carter signed the bill in 1978 and appointed Chapin to the commission. Three years later the World Hunger Year was thriving, until Chapin was killed in a traffic accident in New York.

Or consider, finally, the case of Paul Reutershan. Reutershan was a young man, but he was dying of stomach cancer, an old man's disease. He had suffered health problems in the nine years since he had returned from Vietnam, where as a helicopter crew chief he often flew through what he described as a "fog" of the herbicide Agent Orange. Now Reutershan was convinced that his health problems and those of other Vietnam veterans were somehow related to his exposure to the chemical. When he went to a VA hospital to file a claim, they denied that there could be any link.

So he began to organize. In 1978 Reutershan contacted other veterans with similar problems and formed them into a group, Agent Orange Victims International. They filed a $10 million lawsuit against Dow Chemical, the defoliant's manufacturer. By December 1978, Agent Orange International had collected files on a thousand veterans from across the country who believed they had been similarly exposed. That month Paul Reutershan died. Frank McCarthy, a veteran who was to head the organization after its founder's death, described their final conversation. "The last time I saw him," McCarthy recalled, "he said, 'Please don't let it die, Frank,' and I told him, 'No way.' "

McCarthy and other veterans activists did not let it die. Instead, hundreds of small groups similar to Reutershan's, social service organizations, clinics, and churches continued to press for VA assistance for Agent Orange-related ailments. They were up against a formidable "iron triangle"—an alliance of the VA and the traditional veterans organizations and the congressional Veterans committees—which was determined to preserve the status quo. During the first year of the controversy the crucial House Veterans Committee, dominated by southern conservatives, held only one perfunctory hearing; only the Air Force, VA, and the traditional veterans groups testified.

So the Vietnam veteran advocates began working with the caucus of Vietnam Veterans in Congress rather than the committee. They demanded, first, that adequate scientific studies be done by an agency other than the Air Force and the VA; and second, that veterans be given full disability for their condition. Stymied in the congressional committees, they peppered the VA with lawsuits, held meetings and conferences, offered graphic testimony to the media and at increasingly frequent congressional inquiries. Vietnam Veterans of America, a nationwide membership organization led by Robert Muller, a paraplegic himself, set up a toll-free telephone number for veterans to call to receive information and a questionnaire on their condition.

Slowly but perceptibly the "iron triangle" began to budge. President Carter intervened in 1980 and removed most of the important policy and research decisions from the VA and gave it to experts from other agencies. And then came the return of the hostages—and the sudden rush of attention to the problems of Vietnam veterans. In June 1981 the House passed a bill ordering the VA to provide medical help for the veterans even though there was no watertight scientific proof that Agent Orange caused all their distress. The vote was unanimous; 388–0, and it passed the Senate and was signed into law by President Reagan. The government finally had come to see the wisdom of Paul Reutershan's deathbed assertion, "I got killed in Vietnam and didn't know it."

What Motivates Members?

However a case is presented, and whatever tactics are employed, it is advisable to understand initially that, above all else, *votes* on election day motivate congressmen. A large part of their job is staying in their job, and appeals which suggest their continued tenure—such as "labor has endorsed it" or "a poll showed consumers favor it"—will be favorably received by most members.

369

But pure politics is only one approach. Harry Chapin based his appeal, quite simply, on the homily that "it was right." Contrary to myth, appeals to justice and fairness can ignite some kindling among the wet logs of Congress. A related appeal can be made to a member's self-esteem—that by doing right, he'll do good. A congressman likes to be known as a good guy, as a defender of democracy, rather than as a "tool of special interests." Even those who service only corporate enterprise drape their arguments with appeals to the commonweal; it simply would not do for Exxon's management to argue that they need a reduction in the corporate income tax because they want to earn even *more* exorbitant profits.

If exhortations to morality and self-esteem are attempted without the prop of actual or potential publicity, they may fail. Congressmen respond to publicity—both adverse and complimentary. For example, when natural gas prices began to skyrocket in 1982 as a result of deregulation, the Iowa Citizens for Community Improvement (CCI) demanded that the Federal Energy Regulatory Commission (FERC) hold a hearing in Iowa on deregulation. At first Iowa Senator Roger Jepsen wasn't interested, telling CCI that the federal commission was too busy to travel there. The group then canvassed door to door and in a short time sent the senator nearly five-thousand postcards calling on him to ask FERC for the hearing. Also, on the same day and in five Iowa cities, activists scheduled appointments with Jepsen's aides at his regional offices; none of the aides showed. At the regional office in Council Bluff, CCI brought a live chicken, symbolic of a senator afraid to meet with his constituents. The gesture received front-page coverage in the city paper. Not long after, Jepsen had a change of heart. On the floor of the Senate he called on the FERC to hold hearings on gas decontrol in Iowa. The session was held in Des Moines on January 31, 1983—the first hearing on gas decontrol that FERC held for consumers.

If votes matter, then so do voter registration drives. They can galvanize people around an issue or candidate while at the same time bringing otherwise disenfranchised citizens into the system. In

1982–83, Operation PUSH and other groups registered an estimated 400,000 Chicago blacks with an eye toward the Democratic mayoral election. These new voters provided the margin of victory for Chicago's first black mayor, Harold Washington. Professors Richard Cloward and Frances Fox Piven have launched a drive to use social service workers to register people on unemployment lines, in welfare centers, and on cheese lines (created when the government began distributing surplus cheese to the poor). They write, "The conflict engendered by a registration movement will convert registering and voting into meaningful acts of collective protest." The ingenuity of their scheme, notes *The Nation* magazine, is that it is " a strategy which has the appeal of appearing (and being) as patriotic as the League of Women Voters and the Boy Scouts." Cloward and Piven have helped form a voter registration coalition in New York City that has won warm endorsement from state officials.

Campaign contributions. Votes and voter registration. Morality. Self-esteem. Publicity. What else motivates a congressman to act on an issue, or hide from it?

Congressmen, like most of us, also listen to reason—but they hear many reasons. One effective way to bolster your logical argument is to cite support from a "disinterested source"—another congressman, a respected columnist, or experts. Almost universally, congressmen refused to seriously consider hazards of smoking and the need to restrict cigarette advertising until the authoritative Surgeon General's Committee on Smoking and Health delivered its grim verdict, in 1964, that cigarette smoking was tied to lung cancer and other diseases.

Serious citizen action, with all these various approaches attempted in tandem, can succeed, even against the usual formidable odds.

How to Do It

1. LEARN ABOUT CONGRESS. You begin with a problem. Your daughter is seriously ill and you've discovered that hospital care costs $200 a day, and no person of your $15,000-a-year income

could possibly afford full medical coverage—unless Congress steps in. Or a gripe: Why are utility prices so high? Or an idea: Why not serve nutritional food instead of glop in your child's school lunch program? You're black, Chicano, or native American—and your state commission against discrimination drags it feet for two years before acting on complaints. Or you wonder why you can't buy a washing machine that works, or a safe car. You're a tenant in a neighborhood about to be run over by another highway or "rehabilitated" out of your price range by urban "renewal." Or you're a human being who breathes the foul exhaust of Chevrolets and Consolidated Edison plants ten miles away.

There are many ways to start acting to solve your problem. One is to write your senator or representative.

Your senator:

> The Honorable——
> United States Senate
> Washington, D.C. 20510

Your representative:

> The Honorable——
> House of Representatives
> Washington, D.C. 20515

Ask what laws Congress has passed or is considering to meet your community's needs. Ask which members of what congressional committees and which federal agencies handle such laws. In fact, ask your congressman what you can do to promote your point of view. If he or she doesn't have an adequate reply, perhaps your inquiry will prod the member of Congress to develop one. For example:

Dear Senator or Representative——,

We are two of your constituents who are concerned about hospital insurance, federal income taxes, and school lunch

372

programs. It is important that we learn better how to be assisted by the services of Congress and how to influence and participate in congressional decisions. Although we have been doing some thinking, it seems to us that you should have a great deal more knowledge, experience, and interchange with citizens on just these issues. Would you kindly give us *guidelines* and *details* on how we can more effectively present our concerns to you and to other legislators—local, state, and federal.

This request may take some of your time, but, if you have not already prepared such a package of advice, we are sure that many other citizens would similarly benefit from your insights and pointers. You're the expert on these matters. We look forward to your help.

> Sincerely,
> Fred and Martha

You don't need a "letter of introduction" from your congressman to "meet" Congress. You can begin with free government publications. For free copies of all House and Senate documents, including bills, resolutions, presidential messages to Congress, most committee reports, and public laws, write as follows.

For House documents:

> House Documents Room
> H 226
> United States Capitol
> Washington, D.C. 20515

For Senate documents.

> Senate Documents Room
> S 325
> United States Capitol
> Washington, D.C. 20510

Bills, resolutions, and laws are written in unfathomable legalese. But committee reports usually contain readable and informative descriptions of bills, presenting facts and arguments for and against, though often slanted toward the committee viewpoint.

Printed hearings contain copies of all testimony offered at committee hearings on a bill. Fact-filled and often even readable (but often a thousand pages thick), they also can be purchased by writing to the U.S. Government Printing Office.

The *Congressional Record* is printed daily while Congress is in session and purports to be a transcript of all speeches and proceedings on the floor of the House and Senate. It is the most useful source of congressional activity: of roll-call votes; of committee hearings and meetings; and of the floor and committee schedule for the following week, printed every Friday. It can also provide educational insight into congressional attitudes. The *Record* can be ordered for $218 a year from the Superintendent of Documents, Government Printing Office, Washington, D.C. 20402; it is also located at many public and university libraries.*

2. RESEARCH. The first response many congressmen make to any in-person citizen request is a barrage of questions: How much will it cost, next year and five years from now? What kind of tax do we use to raise the money? What does labor think about it? Who benefits? Couldn't the program be better run by the states, and wouldn't loan guarantees be more effective than subsidies? Have you talked to the Banking and Currency Committee? These can wither the unprepared citizen lobbyist. To avoid trouble, first be informed; then lobby.

You can begin, of course, with information from Congress: hearings and committee reports. You can ask your congressman for information from the Congressional Research Service on important issues. The CRS, drawing on the 60-million-piece collection of

---

*See appendix 1 for a list of groups and publications with information on Congress.

the Library of Congress, answers specific questions, compiles reading lists, and discusses the pros and cons of policy issues. You can also directly contact a governmental agency which administers federal programs that affect your community. If you seek information or help from it, your congressman can be of assistance: congressional inquiries to agencies are usually answered more promptly than your own unassisted letters, which may molder for months.

If your probing of an agency makes you question seriously its responsiveness or performance, you can ask your representative to call in the investigative branch of Congress, the General Accounting Office. With a staff of five thousand, led by accountants, lawyers, and other skilled professionals, the GAO has published revealing and authoritative reports on such topics as defense waste, nuclear power, energy policy, health care waste, inadequate enforcement of sanitary meat and poultry inspection, nonenforcement of pesticide safety regulations and state strip-mining laws, and the financial irregularities of national political parties. Single copies of these reports are provided free to the public. Potentially one of the greatest tools for citizens and Congress, the GAO is little known. It receives only a few hundred requests for action each year by members of Congress, who alone can request a GAO investigation on your behalf.

You should also be aware of the Freedom of Information Act, which requires public access to all "identifiable records" in federal agency files (but not Congress's), with certain listed exceptions. The exceptions—for national security, corporate trade secrets, internal agency memoranda, and six others—along with delaying tactics and duplicating charges, are often purposefully used by agencies to deny information that the public has a right to know. Amendments to the Freedom of Information Act, passed over President Gerald Ford's veto in 1974, strengthened the act and made it somewhat easier for citizens to obtain information; agencies must now respond to an information request within ten days, unresponsive bureaucrats can be sanctioned for their obstruction, and successful litigants can get attorney's fees from the government.*

Nor should you shrink from your own investigations, such as the one begun by the Connecticut Citizen Action Group's study of occupational health hazards, in the summer of 1971. During interviews at a Connecticut plant of Colt's Firearms, a student investigator was told by outraged workers that Colt was manufacturing bent-barreled M-16's, under contract with the Department of Defense, for use by GI's in Vietnam. Not only was Colt neglecting to straighten the barrels properly, but the company was also switching parts after performance tests of the rifles, inserting untested and perhaps defective equipment. The Citizen Action Group's headline-capturing report, including sworn affidavits from the workers, was turned over to the Justice Department for further investigation.

Congressmen can also help obtain information from the private sector, especially giant corporations, who are far more reluctant than even government agencies to let the public peer through this screen of secrecy. At the urging of a citizen, the late Representative Benjamin Rosenthal of New York sent out a letter to all domestic auto companies asking how they handle consumer complaints. The companies replied in some detail, and the letter may have stimulated them to formalize their complaint and review procedures; consumers can now at least point to these standards when they are violated. In 1966, when the information was treated like a trade secret, Connecticut Senator Abe Ribicoff successfully wrote the auto companies for a list of all models recalled for defects since 1960. A year or two later, when the National Highway Traffic Safety Administration neglected to continue gathering this data, Minnesota's Senator Walter Mondale wrote again and got more information about defective vehicle recalls

---

*If you cannot obtain the desired records, you can contact one of the groups which specializes in freedom of information problems. Among them are the Freedom of Information Clearing House, 2000 P St. N.W. Washington, D.C. 20036, and the Center for National Security Studies, 122 Maryland Ave. N.E., Washington, D.C. 20002. They will supply you with advice and information.

by the auto firms, and he in addition stimulated the agency to issue regulations and set up a complete information system open to the public.

3. ORGANIZE. There are several reasons why it is worth taking the time to organize a citizen action group. A group can commit more energy and resources than even the most dedicated individual. A group is more likely to have the resources and endurance to carry a seemingly interminable project through to completion; and the results of group projects are also usually more respected than an individual's efforts.

A highly successful organizing effort is the New York Public Interest Research Group's "Bank on Brooklyn" campaign, a well-coordinated drive attacking the red-lining practices of major New York banks.

The effort began in 1975 with a study by several Brooklyn College students—titled "Take the Money and Run"—which illustrated the failure of banks to reinvest in the communities of their depositors. Specifically, seven banks surveyed in Brooklyn had invested less than one half of one percent of their total assets in the communities where they received the bulk of their deposits.

Using this survey as an organizing tool, a NYPIRG staffer, in the fall of 1976, began organizing citizen groups in Brooklyn to oppose the banks' red-lining practices. Negative publicity campaigns, including picketing, leafleting, and rallies were aimed at recalcitrant banks. Throughout the campaign community groups have used data available under state and federal disclosure laws to determine how much of the depositors' money was going to depositors' credit needs. To date, the Bank on Brooklyn campaign has reached signed agreements with more than ten banks, who have agreed to reinvest specific amounts of money—in the form of mortgage and home improvement loans—in the communities.

If you decide to form a group, you should first draft a tentative but clear statement of the scope of the group's proposed activities (such as lobbying Congress) and your purpose (such as obtaining federal mass transit development funds). Next, bring together a number of friends, acquaintances, or people in the community known for involvement in civic affairs. They might include the president of your neighborhood association, the lawyer who headed the fund-raising drive for the reform candidate, or the ex-director of the free breakfast program.

The structure of your group is important. To be successful, you should emphasize *action* rather than organization. Minimize such typical club activities as regular meetings, titles, and minutes. Otherwise the purpose of the group becomes the group, rather than the substantive issue.

Funding is, of course, essential to organizing—and ultimate success. You can get by on little money by holding meetings in homes and similar skimping. Initial expenses can be paid by out-of-pocket $5 or $10 contributions from the organizers. Later, money can be raised by dues, if your membership is large, or by special fund-raising events.

But serious citizen lobbying of Congress can well drain your coffers faster than $2 dues or bake sales can fill them. The Coalition Against the SST in 1971 spent more than $20,000 for staff salaries, newspaper ads, research, phone calls, duplicating, and mailing—not counting expenses by individual member organizations. One way to raise necessary money is to appeal to sympathetic wealthy individuals who can underwrite you with thousands of dollars. For many years philanthropist Mary Lasker has been a one-woman bank for public health lobbyists. Her efforts deserve much of the credit for the bills which established the National Institutes of Health and Regional Medical Centers. But at the same time be careful not to be bought off: fit available funds to your goals, not your goals to the funds. Another way to raise money is by public subscription, as do the Center for Science in the Public Interest and Public Citizen. Finally, if your citizen effort involves merely research and organizing, not lobbying, you may be able to obtain the support of foundations, which typically dole out $5,000 to $20,000 per worthy project.*

---

*To learn about foundations, you can buy for $35 the *Foundation Directory*, published by the Russell Sage Foundation (most recently in 1977) for the Foundation Library Center, 444 Madison Avenue, New York, N.Y. 10022.

Once organized, your group's first project should be small, relatively easy to accomplish, cheap, and likely to arouse maximum interest and publicity.* In 1969, for example, after Senator Everett Dirksen appealed on television for congressional pay hikes by arguing that "senators have to eat, too," Mrs. George Cook of Idaho organized her friends to "send beans to the Senate," and received national press coverage. Other good projects are petition drives and preparing "congressional scoreboards," described below.

To be effective citizen lobbyists, group organizers should not stop at the local level. Whatever your interest, there is probably some national citizens' lobby in Washington that shares it.† Contacting, joining, or forming a nationwide citizens' lobby with a Washington office can help you in three ways.

First, it can serve as an early warning system to keep you informed well enough and quickly enough to make your lobbying in Congress timely and effective. Newsletters and word of mouth from Washington offices can give you a head start in developing personal contacts with congressmen and their staffs. The Environmental Policy Center has hosted lobbying conferences in Washington for citizens concerned about issues like strip mining; after in-depth briefings, the citizen lobbyists from "back home" fan out to communicate with their congressmen.

Second, these Washington offices can also speed the flow of information from you *to* Congress. Dealing daily with congressmen

---

Public Citizen's Action Manual (1973), by Donald Ross, provides illustrative consumer, environmental, and other projects that citizens can undertake. *For the People, a Consumer Action Handbook*, by Joanne Manning Anderson (1977, Addison-Wesley paperback), lists more than a dozen action-oriented consumer projects that citizens can carry out in their local communities—from health care and food marketing practices to energy use. *Fundraising in the Public Interest*, by David Grubb and David Zwick (1977, Public Citizen), and *The Grassroots Fundraising Book*, by Joan Flanagan (1977, The Youth Project), are valuable guides to activist fundraising, describing everything from canvassing and direct mail fundraising to marathons and benefits.

†See appendix 1 for list of national citizens' lobby groups.

and staff, Washington lobbyists can pass on the right information at the right time and become trusted advisers. This is hard to do from a purely local base.

Third, national affiliations give you at least the opportunity to lobby congressional committees. As a single local group, you can have some effect on your representative—or, if you are powerful enough, on your senators or entire state delegation. But the members of one committee come from districts all over the country. Without a base as wide as their own, your lobbying may be ineffectual. Some national organizations like Congress Watch help create "locals" dedicated to monitoring congressional activity from the home district itself.

As a last organizing step you may want to align your group or national affiliation with other sympathetic organizations. Coalition building is one of the most important tasks of citizen lobbyists, as long as it doesn't become a form of mutual, bureaucratic dependence. Coalitions increase the voters and geographic base represented, as well as improve the chances that at least some members of the coalition can command the congressman's attention. Look for allies in the home states and the districts of the congressmen—particularly the ranking ones—who sit on the committee you care about. A group from another state lobbying on a tax bill once startled then House Ways and Means chairman Wilbur Mills by encouraging picketing at his district office in Arkansas.

Thus, you have now moved from a person, to a group, to a network of groups. This path is the same progressive accumulation of citizen power that impressed Alexis de Tocqueville over a century ago. "As soon as several of the inhabitants of the United States have taken up an opinion or a feeling which they wish to promote in the world," he said, "they look out for mutual assistance; and as soon as they have found each other out, they combine; from that moment they are no longer isolated men, but a power seen from afar, whose actions serve for an example, and whose language is listened to."

*   *   *

4. LOBBYING. Whatever the connotation, to "lobby" means nothing more than to try to have an impact on the votes of lawmakers. You have a right to lobby under the Constitution, which guarantees "the right of the people peaceably . . . to petition the government for redress of grievances."

Facing you, of course, are the organized lobbies—from the Chamber of Commerce to the American Medical Association—discussed in Chapter 2. Citizen lobbyists, however, have often confounded the "pros" by breaking logjams of inertia and overcoming heavyweight opposition to achieve reform. Like Dr. Isadore Buff, who carried the bitter image of black lung from the coal fields of West Virginia to the corridors of Congress; Fred Lang, a solitary engineer who repeatedly protested the weakness of gas pipeline safety standards to no avail, until Congress listened and enacted the Gas Pipeline Safety Law. More recently there has been Dina Rasor who, only four years out of college, runs the Project on Military Procurement and educates the Congress and public about ineffective weapons systems.

Given such issues and such personal determination, a number of steps can be followed by the citizen lobbyist who is interested not only in making a stand but winning the point:*

• Planning. A serious lobbying organization working on a legislative effort begins with an analysis of the legislative forum in which it must do combat. Who are the key players? To answer this question the National Right to Life Committee, an antiabortion group, in 1973 began compiling what its newsletter called "an elaborate profile" on each member of the House and Senate. "We need . . . to know his position on human life issues, his voting record, his committees, his friends, his source of campaign funds, his basis of political

---

*For some, an initial, procedural step will be to file as a registered lobbyist under the 1946 Federal Registration of Lobbying Act. Registering should be as routine as renewing a driver's license. The reason for the act is not to prevent lobbying, but to keep track of who's doing it and how much is spent. (Since this is a technical area, with each situation turning on its particular facts, it is best to consult a lawyer.)

support, his family, his constituency, his district and anything else that will give us an advantage in influencing his vote."

What committee or subcommittee will consider the legislation? Who chairs it? Who are the important staff members? Are there legislative assistants on the staff of congressmen who have shown an interest in similar issues in the past? Early in the process, you should project a likely timetable of events, ranging from generating public support through introducing the bill, on to the hearing stage, committee markup sessions, floor consideration, Senate-House conference, and finally the possibility of veto by the President. Thoughtful consideration of substance and strategy at this early stage can avoid telling delays or outright failures later.

• Bill-drafting. Lobbying in Congress can pivot around someone else's bill *or* your own bill. Do not be surprised that you can ask your congressman to introduce a bill—that's part of his job.

Write up what you want to do in plain language. You can present your proposal directly to your congressman, who can refer it to the Office of Legislative Counsel for drafting. But it's better to have your bill drafted by an attorney who advocates your point of view. One good place to look is a law-student organization at a local law school. Even better may be one of the public interest law firms springing up around the country. Public Interest Research Groups, staffed by lawyers and other professionals, and funded by college students who guide overall policy, already exist in twenty-five states.

Your own congressman is probably not the best person to introduce your bill, for any bill introduced by a congressman not a member of the relevant committee is routinely passed over. Find out, therefore, which committee handles bills on your subject. And beware of the token bill, introduced by the congressman to get you off his back and then left to die in a committee he doesn't belong to. Most citizens are so excited by the introduction of their bill that they are easily fooled by this ploy. Ask your congressman to speak to members from your state on the committee; to write a letter to the chairman requesting hearings and to send you a copy; and to testify in favor of your bill at the hearings.

If the legislation concerning you doesn't get out of committee, chances are it will never be seriously considered. When Emanuel Celler, chairman of the House Judiciary Committee, was asked in 1958 for his stand on a certain bill, he replied, "I don't stand on it. I am sitting on it. It rests four-square under my fanny and will never see the light of day." Sometimes even the committee stage may be too late, because, as one committee staffer said, "Given an active subcommittee chairman, working in a specialized field with a staff of his own, the parent committee can do no more than change the grammar of a subcommittee report."

• Testimony and Hearings. Citizens have their best access to committees during the public hearings held on most major bills. When citizens are permitted through the large oaken doors into the hearing rooms, what they usually discover are plodding exercises in the compilation of information, views, and recommendations. Occasionally the hearings are extravaganzas staged for publicity and the press. In either case most experienced Capitol lobbyists find hearings serious enough—after all, they are making a public record that will last for years—so they rarely miss an opportunity to testify.

Testimony is an important way to educate committee members, committee staff, and the press. To ensure that your position gets a fair airing, you should help recruit relevant witnesses. One good pool to tap is experts. Many experts respond to calls from lay citizens, but a request from your congressman can help. Former Georgia Representative Jim Mackay once contacted fifty experts, many of whom peppered the House Commerce Committee with requests to testify on an auto safety bill, and the points of view they expressed prevented the hearings from being a mere whitewash. Witness recruiting is especially important on subjects so arcane—bank and tax bills, complicated housing finance laws—that only private interests directly affected know about the hearings. Only systematic monitoring and continuous presence in Washington can prevent defeat by default.

Yet one needn't be a professional "expert" in order to testify effectively. Often personal experience and passion count far more than learning or polish. An eleven-year-old Florida schoolgirl once testified before the Senate Commerce Committee on a study she had done of the impact of television advertising on her classmates. When Joseph (''Chip'') Yablonski, son of murdered United Mine Workers insurgent Jock Yablonski, testified on UMW election irregularities before a Senate Labor and Public Welfare subcommittee, his intense and touching manner etched his words onto everyone present. After the Farmington, West Virginia, mine disasters, the stricken widows of the victimized miners retained enough composure to convey the lesson of their sadness to a congressional committee. Union rank and file on a labor bill, migrant workers on a bill to give them minimum wages, mechanics on car repairability, housewives on consumer purchases: firsthand knowledge counts.

Dramatizing your testimony with personal narration may not only stave off committee members' boredom, but can also attract press attention. During hearings on the coal mine health and safety bill, miners with severe black lung gripped the attention of congressmen by showing how they collapsed from lack of breath after jumping up and down just a few times. In the underground natural-gas pipeline hearings, Tony Mazzocchi, then Washington lobbyist for the Oil, Chemical, and Atomic Workers Union, brought in the workers who repair and inspect underground pipelines in St. Louis. They showed the riddled pipe and demonstrated sloppy repairs to the members of Congress. During hearings on Agent Orange, Vietnam Veterans of America director Robert Muller sat at the witness table with a veteran who claimed he had been exposed to the herbicide; joining him were his wife and their brain damaged and crippled young daughter. Her heartbreaking presence was used to dramatize their assertion that Agent Orange's effects are felt for generations.

• The ''Markup'' Sessions. After official hearings are held, staff typically prepare a draft committee bill. Committee members then meet to go over the draft bill and to propose amendments. Because it is here that the contours and details of legislation are ironed out, markup sessions are crucial for citizen lobbyists. If one can gain a reputation for giving honest, informative, and accurate answers, staffers and congressmen may come to rely on your expertise. "The key point of contact is usually between a highly specialized lobbyist and the specialized staff people of the standing committee," said ex-Representative Bob Eckhardt of Texas. "Intimate friendships spring up there—it's the rivet point. Friendships that outlast terms. They probably have a greater influence on legislation, especially if it's technical."

• Lobbying for Votes. After all the legislative foreplay, legislation must come down to a simple head count. Eventually the interested citizen will attempt to persuade a member to vote a certain way. How can you personally sway votes?

You can try to *meet your congressman.* In 1965 congressmen interviewed said they spent 7 percent of their work week meeting with constituents. When you visit your congressman, write ahead to arrange an appointment. You then have a better chance of seeing him or her and it is a courtesy appreciated by busy members. Also, it can make your visit far more effective. If you state in your letter the precise issue you wish to discuss, the congressman can have his staff research the problem and "brief" him before your visit. Groups are even more welcome than individuals, for obvious electoral reasons.

You can also call the district office to find out when your representative will be in town, and try to arrange an appointment to see him or her then. Most representatives have full-time district offices, and most members are there during weekends or congressional recesses. Some eastern representatives, members of the so-called Tuesday–Thursday Club, are often in their districts Friday through Monday. Failing that, you should try to meet with a member of the representative's staff.

Or you can ask a congressman to *visit you and your group,* either in informal session or to give a speech followed by a question-and-answer session. Such gatherings can impress a member with your information, your issue, or your clout. Consider, for one example, Representative Dan Rostenkowski, (D.-Ill.). At one time in favor of U.S. involvement in the Vietnam War, he was persuaded by persistent and passionate high school students to break with President

Nixon's troop withdrawal approach. "I make a lot of speeches at high schools in my district," he explained, "and the kids ask damn penetrating questions about what useful purpose we are serving in Vietnam. As this thing has gone on, I've had more and more trouble answering them."

In personal lobbying it is also essential *to get exact commitments*. An experienced labor lobbyist tells of the citizen group which visited its local representative to solicit federal money for schools. The representative's response: "Why, yes, I've always been in favor of education and when the pending legislation comes up I'll certainly vote pro-education." They walked away satisfied they had a "firm commitment." In fact, the congressman was free to vote any way he pleased when the specific provisions of the education bill came up; each side could claim to be "pro" education. The lesson: spell out exactly what you want your congressman to do.

Even if you are specific, your request may be met by a smokescreen of diversionary actions. Don't be fooled by camouflages like a public yes vote on the floor after the member has already added a crippling amendment in the privacy of committee; the introduction of a token bill which will be safely tucked away in a committee of which your congressman is not a member; or a nice speech inserted in the extensions section of the *Congressional Record*.

Writing your congressman can have an impact. It is true that most letters from constituents never reach the congressman's desk, but they all reach his office. Although most mail gets little more than a glance from a busy clerk, there are letters that electrify, that counter false information, that change votes. These very often reach the congressman's attention. In the mid-sixties, when Congress had barely begun to look at unsafe automobiles, several members of the Senate Commerce Committee began to receive letters that shared common characteristics. They were written carefully, many by engineers and professional people. They were precise. Each told a similar story of the shoddy performance of tires. The committee members probably received, in all, fewer than fifty of these letters. But they had a profound impact on the members, whose staffs decided that they were unique enough and significant enough to be read by the senators themselves. Indeed, the committee cited these letters as a significant part of the evidence convincing it that tire safety legislation was needed.

Even letters which are not seen by policy-making staff or the congressman can have an important impact if there are enough of them. On important issues many members have their clerks count their mail the way geologists read seismographs. (Recall, for example, the labor law reform battle described in Chapter 2.) The sample may be statistically inaccurate, but it offers understandable and numerical guidance to a member who faces conflicting views and who wants to be reelected. Form letters flooding an office will not have this impact. Many individual letters will.

Letters which demonstrate familiarity with the congressman and his record immediately evoke respectful interest. "I strongly support your efforts to amend the Housing Act by requiring the FHA inspectors to be responsible for the quality as well as the value of housing, and I was pleased to see you vote for the Stokes Amendment which would have strengthened the voting rights bill. However, I am very much concerned . . ." This kind of opening is particularly effective because it conveys to the reader a number of facts. First, he is dealing with an informed voter, probably an opinion leader in his community. Second, this is a potential supporter, not an ideological opponent who would complain if the member voted for Washington's visage on the one-dollar bill.*

Two alternatives to direct mail are *telegrams* and *telephone calls*. Early in the legislative life of a bill, when there is time to write and mail a letter, telegrams make little sense. Telegrams are attention-getters, however, and can be effective when sent just before a vote: to ask a yea or nay, and to urge the member to be present for the vote. Ducking a vote is easier when the congressman thinks no one

---

*Representative Mo Udall has put together a useful summary on the fundamentals of writing a letter to a representative. It can be obtained by writing him to ask for a copy of "The Right to Write" (U.S. House of Representatives, Washington, D.C. 20515).

is watching. By calling Western Union, a fifteen-word "Public Opinion Message" can be sent to Congress from anywhere in the country for two dollars. It usually arrives one day after being sent.

The idea of sending something other than a letter, something symbolic of the issue that concerns you, can have a much greater impact in a congressional office than the hundreds of letters that are received every day. For example, over 40,000 citizens joined the "Consumer Nickel Brigade" in the summer of 1977. They mailed nickels to 83 wavering members of Congress urging them to support an Agency for Consumer Representation—a nickel representing the average cost per American to create the $15 million advocacy office. As a result of a "Cans to Carter" campaign organized by environmental groups seeking mandatory deposits on beverage containers, over 30,000 tin cans were received by the White House during the first two months of 1978. In a third campaign, people sent obituaries and automobile crash stories to their representatives to convince them to support passenger crash protection systems in automobiles. And in 1979 Congress Watch supporters sent play-money dollars with strings attached to lawmakers to dramatize the need for PAC reform.

On occasion, when an issue is emotional and well-publicized, great masses of telegrams flood into Washington. Within six days of former president Richard Nixon's firing of Special Prosecutor Archibald Cox in October 1973, a total of *350,000 telegrams* were sent to Capitol Hill and the White House from concerned citizens and groups across the country. This upwelling of public sentiment played a major role in persuading Majority Leader Carl Albert and House Judiciary Chairman Peter Rodino to initiate the dreaded impeachment process.

5. PUBLIC COMMUNICATIONS. The news media are the most visible and efficient voice to disseminate your purpose and activities. You may have appealed to the press in getting your bill introduced; or in the hearings; or before the markup session. At some point, however, before a floor vote, public support becomes essential.

The basic tool in your press kit is the *press release*. This is nothing more than a written statement by any person or group issued to the press—i.e., mailed or hand-delivered to every newspaper and broadcaster in your community. It should consist of accurate, newsworthy information. The photogenic, the unusual, an event, a charge, testimony—all may be newsworthy.

A second tool, the *press conference*, must be used with more restraint. It may involve a public reading of a statement, a question-and-answer session, or both. To make the immediate issue interesting and concrete, you might try to accompany it with some symbolic act, such as the presentation of your voting scorecard (described below) to the congressman. Because they take reporters' time, press conferences should be called only when there is important news. To help assure that the press will come to your conference, consider asking some community figure, such as a former elected official, to participate.

Your opponent's paid political advertisements on TV and radio may help you get *free broadcast time* to rebut them. Under the FCC's fairness doctrine, when a station presents commentary on one side of a "controversial issue of public importance," it must present the other side as well. The doctrine doesn't guarantee equal time, but it can give you free time if the station itself fails to broadcast your side. When you see materials you think require rebuttal, write the station manager, identify your group as having membership in the area, refer to the ads, and offer to provide or help the station prepare counterstatements. If you get no reply in a week, or if the station rejects your offer, you can send a written complaint to Chief, Complaints and Compliance Division, Federal Communications Commission, Room 322, 1919 M Street, N.W., Washington, D.C. 20036. Many radio stations (and some TV stations) devote program time for citizens to air their views. Whatever it is called—"Point of View" or "The Voice of the People"—local radio or television time is invaluable exposure.

The print media require a somewhat different approach. Letters to the editors of local newspapers can be effective. Studies have shown that the "Letters to the Editor" column is one of the most widely read sections of a newspaper.

A more direct press approach is also possible. Often citizens complain about press apathy or favoritism. Most people don't realize that it is possible if not helpful to visit unresponsive editors, look them in the eye, and ask them why they haven't covered an important story.* If you try to educate, rather than manipulate, and are candid and informed, you may well affect the policy of previously inattentive local media. Develop personal contacts and information exchanges with reporters, photographers, broadcasters, and editors, just as you might with congressional staff. They can be valuable sources of information to you, and you to them.

Recalcitrant local press may also be jarred into action by national media coverage of a problem in your community. With the exception of the *Louisville Courier*, Appalachian media in the coal mining states did little or no reporting (except for covering disasters) on unsafe mines and black lung disease, until miners' marches and work stoppages caught the attention of NBC, CBS, ABC, *The Washington Post*, and *The New York Times*. This technique of appealing to national press to stimulate local reporting can be important for citizens of one-company communities, like textile and paper mill towns around the country.

Finally, groups can communicate with the public by more *direct action*. Although some picketing and sit-ins aim more to intimidate than to inform their targets, most forms of public demonstrations are quite simply to demonstrate a point to the public. "The rich can buy advertisements in newspapers, purchase radio or television time, and rent billboard space," said Justice William O. Douglas in dissent to a Supreme Court decision involving Dr. Martin Luther King's 1963 marches through Birmingham, Alabama. "The less affluent are

---

*For an informative guide on how to prod local papers to be more accountable, see David Bollier's *How to Appraise and Improve Your Daily Newspaper: A Manual for Readers* (1978). (Copies can be obtained from Center for Study of Responsive Law, P.O. Box 19367, Washington, D.C. 20036; $5 for individuals and $10 for institutions.)

restricted to the use of handbills . . . or petitions, or parades, or mass meetings." Public demonstrations, often resorted to by those lacking formal access to the established media, can be a part of an overall campaign to awaken Congress to their concerns and convictions. It certainly helped stop the Vietnam War and limit U.S. military intervention in El Salvador. "Protest is a legitimate part of the operation of democracy," said Tom Downey (D.-N.Y.), an antiwar protestor in the sixties and a congressman in the eighties. "It is the steam valve for a boiler that has built up too much pressure."

Beyond Congress

Even getting a bill through Congress may be only the beginning.

First, the President may veto your bill.

Second, even if he signs it, he may refuse to spend all the money appropriated by Congress.

Finally, the federal agency that is supposed to carry out the program may write ineffective regulations within the broad congressional guidelines or may simply not enforce the law's provisions.

Ultimately, then, lobbying must focus on the agency and the White House. Tactics may have to change since, for example, appointed bureaucrats are generally less sensitive than elected congressmen to voters. Remember also that the agencies are beholden to the congressional committees which write laws governing their programs and which pass their annual budget. These committees (but not Appropriations committees) are now required by law to act as watchdogs over executive agencies, and, since in 1973, must issue reports every two years on their progress.

One important tactic beyond legislation is purely legal: going to court. NAACP lobbyists, for example, work arm in arm with their lawyer litigators, ready to file suit on the constitutionality of such bills as the antibusing act.

A different step beyond the Capitol corridors is to compete with Congress. For example, if you suspect that a bill you favor will not get a fair hearing in the official committee, hold your own hearings.

391

The National Welfare Rights Organization did just that, conducting hearings at the Capitol on President Nixon's welfare program two days before scheduled Senate Finance Committee action in November 1970. Senator Fred Harris, then a member of the Finance Committee, was so impressed by testimony at the hearings that when the "real" committee met shortly afterward, he gave NWRO a one-vote margin of victory over the Nixon plan.

You can also competitively stimulate Congress by getting a state law passed which it can imitate. Then Congress will have a proven model from which to build national legislation. After Massachusetts, for example, enacted a no-fault auto insurance plan, Congress gave serious consideration to a national no-fault plan for the first time. After California voters in 1978 approved Proposition 13, the property tax cutting measure, tax-cutting fever swept through Congress. And, of course, the nuclear freeze passed several state legislatures before it was even introduced in Congress.

Election Year

Your ultimate resort against unresponsive congressmen is to "throw the rascals out." But regardless of whether your congressman is vulnerable at the polls, election years and campaign months are the best times to press your issue upon congressmen, who seem not uncoincidentally more interested in their constituents at these moments of job insecurity. There exist, moreoever, several low-cost and little-used techniques by which citizens can change votes and views during critical campaign years.

A congressional scoreboard, to take a key approach, is a chart showing how your congressman has performed over the years on a specific issue—consumer protection, tax reform, civil rights, defense spending, environmental protection, or any other. Used creatively, this rating system can have a considerable impact in an election year. In 1982 the Council for a Livable World named twelve congressmen who had cast key votes against the Zablocki nuclear freeze the "Doomsday Dozen." Four of them lost, and the freeze was a major factor in two of the races (John LeBoutillier [R.-N.Y.] and James Coyne [R.-Pa.]).

In preparing your scorecards, it is best to concentrate on one area. Select perhaps ten votes in which the lines between support and opposition are clearly drawn, and make sure that you choose the important stage of the voting on each bill. (Sometimes a vote on an amendment or on a procedural motion may be more important than the vote on the final bill). Publicize the results as widely as possible within the district.

Interested citizens can go beyond a voting scorecard to do profiles of representatives. Utilizing library research and field interviews, writers could evaluate a local congressman's campaign contributions, campaign tactics, constituent services, committee and floor actions, and relationships to his or her colleagues.

In 1972 Ralph Nader's Congress Project compiled fifteen-to-twenty-page profiles of all members of Congress running for reelection, an achievement that has been emulated by citizens' groups at the local level. For example, in 1972, 1974, and 1976, the Connecticut Citizen Action Group did profiles of all state representatives running for reelection—approximately 150 in all.

What use can you make of campaign finance reports filed by candidates with the secretary of state in the home state and the clerk of the House or secretary of the Senate? Check especially for (1) failures to comply with the reporting requirements of the election laws, (2) potential conflicts of interest in the areas the candidate would cover as a legislator, (3) reported spending that is much greater than reported contributions—which suggests that some donors have secretly given cash, or (4) contributions "in kind," such as the loan of consultants, still on salary, from a corporation or labor union, or a free public opinion poll. The most important part of the laws to a citizen action group is the opportunity they provide—before the election—to find out who a candidate's supporters are, what interests they represent, and how much they are contributing. The laws provide one other "plus" for citizens' groups: any individual who believes the campaign finance laws have been violated may file a complaint with the Federal Election Commission.

Other areas of a candidate's background can also be investigated by the citizen. Members of Congress are required to file annual financial disclosure statements. These describe outside income and gifts over $100, and outside property and investments (excluding one's home) over $1,000 and liabilities over $10,000.* Other sources would include the public ownership files at television and radio stations showing if the candidate is affiliated with broadcasting interests, county property tax records showing what properties the candidate owns, reports on file at the Securities and Exchange Commission listing major ownership of stock (10 percent) in one company, and Standard and Poor's Register of Corporations for corporate directorships.

During an election year one of the most fruitful issues to raise with candidates is reform of Congress itself. Who goes to Congress is, of course, a critical question. But so is the question: What kind of institution should Congress be? Reform and creativity cannot flourish in an unresponsive institution, no matter how good its members. In letters, in visits, or during speeches, constituents can put their representatives on record about the rules which govern their work and our Congress. What follows are suggested questions, which can hopefully trigger a dialogue on congressional reform: each is merely a door to a roomful of detailed, follow-up inquiries. The candidate's replies to these questions (plus related newsletters, campaign literature, and newspaper clippings), should be kept handy so that the candidate can be reminded of his commitments if and when he or she wins the election and takes office. Will the candidate or congressman—

• Support public financing of a substantial portion of congressional campaign costs?

---

*House members' reports are available from the Office of Records and Registration, 1036 Longworth Building, Washington, D.C. 20515. Senators' reports are available from the Office of Public Records, 119 D Street N.E., Washington, D.C. 20510.

• Promote legislation to eliminate all existing loopholes (described in Chapter 1) in the campaign finance disclosure laws?

• Back legislation requiring the reasonable disclosure of organized lobbying activity, including disclosure of the major sources of funds used in lobbying, the amounts spent and received, and the specific issues involved?

• Support rules forbidding members to serve on committees having jurisdiction over any subjects affecting them financially?

• Support televised floor proceedings of the Senate?

Finally there is the election process itself. Interested citizens can turn their efforts to old-fashioned political organizing techniques to get out the vote. As a citizen action group organized for nonelectoral purposes—for conservation or child care—you can often rally many people who would ignore the normal appeals of the political parties. From the surprise showing of Eugene McCarthy in the 1968 New Hampshire presidential primary to Robert Mrazek's upset win over John LeBoutillier in 1982, congressional candidates have respected the power of citizen groups and their volunteer workers.

Especially in the primaries, where a challenger's main problem may be to battle his way out of obscurity, door-to-door canvassers and street-corner leafleters can make the margin of difference. Canvassers are also needed for the all-important voter registration drives. New voters, of all ages, often poor or from minority groups, usually lean against the status quo. Later, volunteers can help man telephones, staple newsletters, lick envelopes, and mail literature from campaign headquarters. On election day thousands of phone calls must go out to voters from sympathetic districts, to remind them to vote; car pools are needed to take housebound voters to the polls; and leafleters should be at every nearby polling location. All these are within the capacity of a well-organized citizen action group.

But don't consider winning the election as your only goal. Your chances of losing are too great to risk such single-mindedness. If a few losses seem to thoroughly discourage your members, remind them that your long-range objective is not superior numbers in

November, but favorable votes in Congress. If you gain new access to your representative or senator, or change his or her emphasis or views, your citizen action has won a victory. For the goal realistically is to obtain the attention and respect of those who represent you in Washington—and to give them conscience, which H. L. Mencken defined as ''the inner voice which warns us that someone may be looking.''

Appendix 1
Sources of Information on Congress

In addition to reading the government publications described in the epilogue, a good way for citizens to learn about current happenings is to draw on the research of Washington lobbies. Some distribute pocket-size directories listing members of Congress and their committee assignments: Common Cause, a leading citizens' lobby, at 2030 M Street, NW, Washington, D.C. 20036 (free); the Chamber of Commerce of the United States, Legislative Dept., 1615 H Street, N.W., Washington, D.C. 20006 ($3.00); the American Gas Association, 1515 Wilson Boulevard, Arlington, Virginia 22209 ($7.00); the American Medical Association, 1101 Vermont Avenue, N.W., Washington, D.C. 20005 (free).

Others publish scorecards on how every member of Congress voted on dozens of major bills, selected and scored from the political perspective of each organization. The most prominent are AFL-CIO, Legislative Department, 815 Sixteenth Street, N.W., Washington, D.C. 20006 (labor and social welfare votes); Americans for Constitutional Action, 955 L'Enfant Plaza North, S.W., Washington, D.C. 20024 ("conservative"); Americans for Democratic Action, 1411 K Street, N.W., Washington, D.C. 20005 ("liberal").

Groups with other perspectives which publish scorecards are Public Citizen, 215 Pennsylvania Ave., S.E., Washington, D.C. 20003 (consumer reform issues); Business-Industry PAC, 1747 Pennsylvania Ave., N.W., Suite 1250, Washington, D.C., 20006 (business); Consumer Federation of America, 1012 Fourteenth Street, N.W., Suite 901, Washington, D.C. 20005 (consumer); League of Conservation Voters, 317 Pennsylvania Avenue, S.E., Washington, D.C. 20003 (environmental); National Farmers Union, 600 Maryland Avenue S.W., Suite 202, Washington, D.C. 20024 (farming and agriculture); American Security Council, 499 South Capitol Street, S.W., Suite 500, Washington, D.C. 20003 (national security); Friends Committee on National Legislation, 245 Second Street, N.W., Washington, D.C. 20003 (peace issues).

Several sources offer more summarized, detailed, and comprehensive information. *Congressional Quarterly's Guide to the Congress of the United States* is an expensive ($90.00) but extremely thorough and fascinating tome on the history and workings of Congress, most recently published in 1982. *The Almanac of American Politics,* by Barone and Ujifusa (first published in 1972 and updated every two years), is a 1,200 page volume (one or two pages per member of Congress), available at bookstores for $16.95. *Congressional Quarterly's Politics in America: Members of Congress in Washington and at Home,* edited by Alan Ehrenhalt, is even more thorough and is available by mail from Congressional Quarterly, Inc., 1414 22nd Street, N.W., Washington, D.C. 20037 ($29.50). In-depth studies of major congressional committees, plus an examination of Senate and House rules, were published by Ralph Nader's Congress Project beginning in 1975. (Major libraries should have these materials.)

The rise of political action committees has spawned two hefty directories listing every PAC and its donations: *PACs Americana* by Edwin Roeder ($200.00, paperback) and *The PAC Directory* by Weinberger and Greevy ($185.00, hardback).

A map through the maze of the congressional budget process is provided by Stanley Collender's *The Guide to the Federal Budget,* published by the Northeast-Midwest Institute, publications office, P.O. Box 3729, Washington, D.C. 20013 ($8.00). Particularly useful for citizens interested in participating in budgetary politics are the legislative calendar and glossary of terms.

The *Congressional Directory*, often available free from your congressman, is otherwise a $13.00 paperback from the U.S. Government Printing Office, North Capitol Street, N.W., Washington, D.C. 20402; it lists all congressmen and their committee (but not subcommittee) assignments, and most congressional staff. More complete information about staff is contained in the *Congressional Staff Directory*, available at $22.00 from P.O. Box 62, Mount Vernon, Va. 22121.

By writing most committee offices (same address as your congressman), you can obtain at no cost their 100–300-page committee Legislative Calendars. They list every bill referred to the committee and what action has been taken, as well as descriptions of committee work, members, history, rules, etc. They are typically issued from one to six times a year, depending on the committee, and are therefore usually weeks or months out of date.

Two periodicals are especially informative on current legislation and, although expensive, are available in some large public and college libraries. The $726.00-per-year *Congressional Quarterly Weekly Report* is mailed every Saturday from 1414 Twenty-second Street, N.W., Washington, D.C. 20037, and is indexed by subject. The *National Journal*, a $455.00-per-year subscription, is published weekly by the Government Research Co., 1730 M Street, N.W., Washington, D.C. 20036. Each issue includes behind-the-scenes reports on legislative progress, pressures, and personal profiles, indexed every three months.

Finally, thousands of documents, directories, and reports can be obtained from the U.S. Government Printing Office. You can find out what may be helpful in the *Monthly Catalogue of U.S. Government Publications*, carried in many major public and university libraries; periodic GPO catalogues are mailed free on request.

* * *

As mentioned in the epilogue, there are numerous citizens' lobby groups with offices in Washington, D.C.—and many have local chapters. Each group centers its lobby on one or more related topics, so you should be able to find an organization which represents your specific interests. Groups include Consumer Federation of America (address above); League of Conservation Voters (address above) and Friends of the Earth, 620 C Street, S.E., Washington, D.C. 20003 (conservation/environmental issues); National Taxpayers' Union, 325 Pennsylvania Avenue S.E., Washington, D.C. 20003 (tax/libertarian); Citizens for Tax Justice, 2020 K Street N.W., Room 200, Washington, D.C. 20006 (tax reform); Common Cause (address above); National Women's Political Caucus, 1411 K Street, N.W., Washington, D.C. 20005 (women's issues); Public Citizen's Congress Watch (address above); Zero Population Growth, 1346 Connecticut Avenue, N.W., Washington, D.C. 20036 (population control); League of Women Voters, 1730 M Street, N.W., Washington, D.C. 20036 (women's issues, and election issues in general); National Association for the Advancement of Colored People (NAACP), 1025 Vermont Avenue, N.W., Suite 820, Washington, D.C. 20005 (racial issues); National Farmers Union (address above); American Association of Retired Persons, 1909 K Street, N.W., Washington, D.C. 20001 and National Council of Senior Citizens, 925 15th Street, N.W., Washington, D.C. 20005 (issues pertaining to the retired and elderly); Children's Defense Fund, 122 C Street, N.W., Washington, D.C. 20001 (issues pertaining to children); People for the American Way, 1015 18th Street, N.W., Suite 300, Washington, D.C. 20036 (religious and political freedom); and the American Civil Liberties Union, 600 Pennsylvania Avenue, S.E., Washington, D.C. 20003 (legal and civil liberties). Council for a Livable World, 100 Maryland Ave, N.E., Washington, D.C., 20002; SANE, 711 G Street, S.E., Washington, D.C. 20003; Union of Concerned Scientists, 1346 Connecticut Ave., N.W., Suite 1101, Washington, D.C. 20036; Common Cause's Nuclear Arms Alert Network (address above); and the Nuclear Weapons Freeze Campaign, 305 Massachusetts Ave., N.E., Washington, D.C. 20002 all deal with arms control and disarmament issues.

Appendix 2

Members of the House of Representatives (98th Congress)
(Democrats in roman; Republicans in *italic;* Resident Commisioner and Delegates in **boldface.**)

Ackerman, Gary (N.Y.)
Addabbo, Joseph P. (N.Y.)
Akaka, Daniel K. (Hawaii)
Albosta, Donald Joseph (Mich.)
Alexander, Bill (Ark.)
Anderson, Glenn M. (Calif.)
Andrews, Ike (N.C.)
Andrews, Michael A. (Tex.)
Annunzio, Frank (Ill.)
Anthony, Beryl, Jr. (Ark.)
Applegate, Douglas (Ohio)
Archer, Bill (Tex.)
Aspin, Les (Wis.)
AuCoin, Les (Oreg.)
Badham, Robert E. (Calif.)
Barnard, Doug, Jr. (Ga.)
Barnes, Michael D. (Md.)
Bartlett, Steve (Tex.)
Bateman, Herbert H. (Va.)
Bates, Jim (Calif.)
Bedell, Berkley (Iowa)

Beilenson, Anthony C. (Calif.)
Bennett, Charles E. (Fla.)
Bereuter, Douglas K. (Nebr.)
Berman, Howard L. (Calif.)
Bethune, Ed (Ark.)
Bevill, Tom (Ala.)
Biaggi, Mario (N.Y.)
Bilirakis, Michael (Fla.)
Bliley, Thomas J., Jr. (Va.)
Boehlert, Sherwood L. (N.Y.)
Boggs, Lindy (Mrs. Hale) (La.)
Boland, Edward P. (Mass.)
Boner, William Hill (Tenn.)
Bonior, David E. (Mich.)
Bonker, Don (Wash.)
Borski, Robert A. (Pa.)
Bosco, Douglas H. (Calif.)
Boucher, Frederick C. (Rick) (Va.)
Bouquard, Marilyn Lloyd (Tenn.)
Boxer, Barbara (Calif.)
Breaux, John B. (La.)

Britt, C. Robin (N.C.)
Brooks, Jack (Tex.)
Broomfield, Wm. S. (Mich)
Brown, George E., Jr. (Calif.)
Brown, Hank (Colo.)
Broyhill, James T. (N.C.)
Bryant, John (Tex.)
Burton, Dan (Ind.)
Burton, Sala (Calif.)
Byron, Beverly B. (Md.)
Campbell, Carroll A., Jr. (S.C.)
Carney, William (N.Y.)
Carper, Thomas R. (Del.)
Carr, Bob (Mich)
Chandler, Rod (Wash.)
Chappell, Bill, Jr. (Fla.)
Chappie, Gene (Calif.)
Cheney, Dick (Wyo.)
Clarke, James McClure (N.C.)
Clay, William (Bill) (Mo.)
Clinger, William F., Jr. (Pa.)
Coats, Dan (Ind.)
Coelho, Tony (Calif.)
Coleman, E. Thomas (Mo.)
Coleman, Ronald D. (Tex.)
Collins, Cardiss (Ill.)
Conable, Barber B., Jr. (N.Y.)
Conte, Silvio O. (Mass.)
Conyers, John, Jr. (Mich.)
Cooper, Jim (Tenn.)
Corcoran, Tom (Ill.)
Corrada, Baltasar (P.R.)
Coughlin, Lawrence (Pa.)
Courter, James A. (N.J.)
Coyne, William J. (Pa.)
Craig, Larry E. (Idaho)
Crane, Daniel B. (Ill.)
Crane, Philip M. (Ill.)

Crockett, Geo. W., Jr. (Mich.)
D'Amours, Norman E. (N.H.)
Daniel, Dan (Va.)
Dannemeyer, William E. (Calif.)
Daschle, Thomas A. (S. Dak.)
Daub, Hal (Nebr.)
Davis, Robert W. (Mich.)
de la Garza, E (Tex.)
Dellums, Ronald V. (Calif.)
de Lugo, Ron (V.I.)
Derrick, Butler (S.C.)
DeWine, Michael (Ohio)
Dickinson, William L. (Ala.)
Dicks, Norman D. (Wash.)
Dingell, John D. (Mich.)
Dixon, Julian C. (Calif.)
Donnelly, Brian J. (Mass.)
Dorgan, Byron L. (N. Dak.)
Dowdy, Wayne (Miss.)
Downey, Thomas J. (N.Y.)
Dreier, David (Calif.)
Duncan, John L. (Tenn.)
Durbin, Richard J. (Ill.)
Dwyer, Bernard J. (N.J.)
Dymally, Mervyn M. (Calif.)
Dyson, Roy (Md.)
Early, Joseph D. (Mass.)
Eckart, Dennis E. (Ohio)
Edgar, Bob (Pa.)
Edwards, Don (Calif.)
Edwards, Jack (Ala.)
Edwards, Mickey (Okla.)
Emerson, Bill (Mo.)
English, Glenn (Okla.)
Erdreich, Ben (Ala.)
Erlenborn, John N. (Ill.)
Evans, Cooper (Iowa)
Evans, Lane (Ill.)

Fascell, Dante B. (Fla.)

Fauntroy, Walter E. (D.C.)

Fazio, Vic (Calif.)

Feighan, Edward F. (Ohio)

Ferraro, Geraldine A. (N.Y.)

Fiedler, Bobbi (Calif.)

Fields, Jack (Tex.)

Fish, Hamilton, Jr. (N.Y.)

Flippo, Ronnie G. (Ala.)

Florio, James J. (N.J.)

Foglietta, Thomas M. (Pa.)

Foley, Thomas S. (Wash.)

Ford, Harold E. (Tenn.)

Ford, William D. (Mich.)

Forsythe, Edwin B. (N.J.)

Fowler, Wyche, Jr. (Ga.)

Frank, Barney (Mass.)

Franklin, Webb (Miss.)

Frenzel, Bill (Minn.)

Frost, Martin (Tex.)

Fuqua, Don (Fla.)

Garcia, Robert (N.Y.)

Gaydos, Joseph M. (Pa.)

Gejdenson, Sam (Conn.)

Gekas, George W. (Pa.)

Gephardt, Richard A. (Mo.)

Gibbons, Sam (Fla.)

Gilman, Benjamin A. (N.Y.)

Gingrich, Newt (Ga.)

Glickman, Dan (Kans.)

Gonzalez, Henry B. (Tex.)

Goodling, William F. (Pa.)

Gore, Albert, Jr. (Tenn.)

Gradison, Willis D., Jr. (Ohio)

Gramm, Phil (Tex.)

Gray, William H., III (Pa.)

Green, Bill (N.Y.)

Gregg, Judd (N.H.)

Guarini, Frank J. (N.J.)

Gunderson, Steve (Wis.)

Hall, Katie (Ind.)

Hall, Ralph M. (Tex.)

Hall, Sam B., Jr. (Tex.)

Hall, Tony P. (Ohio)

Hamilton, Lee H. (Ind.)

Hammerschmidt, John Paul (Ark.)

Hance, Kent (Tex.)

Hansen, George (Idaho)

Hansen, James V. (Utah)

Harkin, Tom (Iowa)

Harrison, Frank (Pa.)

Hartnett, Thomas F. (S.C.)

Hatcher, Charles (Ga.)

Hawkins, Augustus F. (Calif.)

Hefner, W.G. (Bill) (N.C.)

Heftel, Cecil (Cec) (Hawaii)

Hertel, Dennis M. (Mich.)

Hightower, Jack (Tex.)

Hiler, John (Ind.)

Hillis, Elwood (Ind.)

Holt, Marjorie S. (Md.)

Hopkins, Larry J. (Ky.)

Horton, Frank (N.Y.)

Howard, James J. (N.J.)

Hoyer, Steny H. (Md.)

Hubbard, Carroll, Jr. (Ky.)

Huckaby, Jerry (La.)

Hughes, William J. (N.J.)

Hunter, Duncan (Calif.)

Hutto, Earl (Fla.)

Hyde, Henry J. (Ill.)

Ireland, Andy (Fla.)

Jacobs, Andrew, Jr. (Ind.)

Jeffords, James M. (Vt.)

Jenkins, Ed (Ga.)

Johnson, Nancy L. (Conn.)

Jones, Ed (Tenn.)
Jones, James R. (Okla.)
Jones, Walter B. (N.C.)
Kaptur, Marcy (Ohio)
Kasich, John R. (Ohio)
Kastenmeier, Robert W. (Wis.)
Kazen, Abraham, Jr. (Tex.)
Kemp, Jack F. (N.Y.)
Kennelly, Barbara B. (Conn.)
Kildee, Dale E. (Mich.)
Kindness, Thomas N. (Ohio)
Kogovsek, Ray (Colo.)
Kolter, Joe (Pa.)
Kostmayer, Peter H. (Pa.)
Kramer, Ken (Colo.)
LaFalce, John J. (N.Y.)
Lagomarsino, Robert J. (Calif.)
Lantos, Tom (Calif.)
Latta, Delbert L. (Ohio)
Leach, Jim (Iowa)
Leath, Marvin (Tex.)
Lehman, Richard H. (Calif.)
Lehman, William (Fla.)
Leland, Mickey (Tex.)
Lent, Norman F. (N.Y.)
Levin, Sander M. (Mich.)
Levine, Mel (Calif.)
Levitas, Elliott H. (Ga.)
Lewis, Jerry (Calif.)
Lewis, Tom (Fla.)
Lipinski, William O. (Ill.)
Livingston, Bob (La.)
Loeffler, Tom (Tex.)
Long, Clarence D. (Md.)
Long, Gillis W. (La.)
Lott, Trent (Miss.)
Lowery, Bill (Calif.)
Lowry, Mike (Wash.)

Lujan, Manuel, Jr. (N. Mex.)
Luken, Thomas A. (Ohio)
Lundine, Stan (N.Y.)
Lungren, Dan (Calif.)
McCain, John (Ariz.)
McCandless, Alfred A. (Al) (Calif.)
McCloskey, Frank (Ind.)
McCollum, Bill (Fla.)
McCurdy, Dave (Okla.)
McDade, Joseph M. (Pa.)
McDonald, Larry (Ga.)
McEwen, Bob (Ohio)
McGrath, Raymond J. (N.Y.)
McHugh, Matthew F. (N.Y.)
McKernan, John R., Jr. (Maine)
McKinney, Stewart B. (Conn.)
McNulty, James F., Jr. (Ariz.)
Mack, Connie (Fla.)
MacKay, Buddy (Fla.)
Madigan, Edward R. (Ill.)
Markey, Edward J. (Mass.)
Marlenee, Ron (Mont.)
Marriott, Dan (Utah)
Martin, David O'B. (N.Y.)
Martin, James G. (N.C.)
Martin, Lynn (Ill.)
Martinez, Matthew G. (Calif.)
Matsui, Robert T. (Calif.)
Mavroules, Nicholas (Mass.)
Mazzoli, Romano L. (Ky.)
Mica, Dan (Fla.)
Michel, Robert H. (Ill.)
Mikulski, Barbara A. (Md.)
Miller, Clarence E. (Ohio)
Miller, George (Calif.)
Mineta, Norman Y. (Calif.)
Minish, Joseph G. (N.J.)
Mitchell, Parren J. (Md.)

Moakley, Joe (Mass.)
Molinari, Guy V. (N.Y.)
Mollohan, Alan B. (W. Va.)
Montgomery, G. V. (Sonny) (Miss.)
Moody, Jim (Wis.)
Moore, W. Henson (La.)
Moorhead, Carlos J. (Calif.)
Morrison, Bruce A. (Conn.)
Morrison, Sid (Wash.)
Mrazek, Robert J. (N.Y.)
Murphy, Austin J. (Pa.)
Murtha, John P. (Pa.)
Myers, John T. (Ind.)
Natcher, William H. (Ky.)
Neal, Stephen L. (N.C.)
Nelson, Bill (Fla.)
Nichols, Bill (Ala.)
Nielson, Howard C. (Utah)
Nowak, Henry J. (N.Y.)
Oakar, Mary Rose (Ohio)
Oberstar, James L. (Minn.)
Obey, David R. (Wis.)
O'Brien, George M. (Ill.)
Olin, James R. "Jim" (Va.)
O'Neill, Thomas P., Jr. (Mass.)
Ortiz, Solomon P. (Tex.)
Ottinger, Richard L. (N.Y.)
Owens, Major R. (N.Y.)
Oxley, Michael G. (Ohio)
Packard, Ronald C. (Calif.)
Panetta, Leon E. (Calif.)
Parris, Stan (Va.)
Pashayan, Charles, Jr. (Calif.)
Patman, Bill (Tex.)
Patterson, Jerry M. (Calif.)
Paul, Ron (Tex.)
Pease, Donald J. (Ohio)
Penny, Timothy J. (Minn.)

Pepper, Claude (Fla.)
Perkins, Carl D. (Ky.)
Petri, Thomas E. (Wis.)
Pickle, J. J. (Tex.)
Porter, John Edward (Ill.)
Price, Melvin (Ill.)
Pritchard, Joel (Wash.)
Pursell, Carl D. (Mich.)
Quillen, James H. (Jimmy) (Tenn.)
Rahall, Nick Joe, II (W. Va.)
Rangel, Charles B. (N.Y.)
Ratchford, William R. (Conn.)
Ray, Richard (Ga.)
Regula, Ralph (Ohio)
Reid, Harry M. (Nev.)
Richardson, Bill (N. Mex.)
Ridge, Thomas J. (Pa.)
Rinaldo, Matthew J. (N.J.)
Ritter, Don (Pa.)
Roberts, Pat (Kans.)
Robinson, J. Kenneth (Va.)
Rodino, Peter W., Jr. (N.J.)
Roe, Robert A. (N.J.)
Roemer, Buddy (La.)
Rogers, Harold (Ky.)
Rose, Charles (N.C.)
Rostenkowski, Dan (Ill.)
Roth, Toby (Wis.)
Roukema, Marge (N.J.)
Rowland, J. Roy (Ga.)
Roybal, Edward R. (Calif.)
Rudd, Eldon (Ariz.)
Russo, Marty (Ill.)
Sabo, Martin Olav (Minn.)
St. Germain, Fernand J. (R.I.)
Savage, Gus (Ill.)
Sawyer, Harold S. (Mich.)
Schaefer, Dan (Colo.)

Scheuer, James H. (N.Y.)

Schneider, Claudine (R.I.)

Schroeder, Patricia (Colo.)

Schulze, Richard T. (Pa.)

Schumer, Charles E. (N.Y.)

Seiberling, John F. (Ohio)

Sensenbrenner, F. James, Jr. (Wis.)

Shannon, James M. (Mass.)

Sharp, Philip R. (Ind.)

Shaw, E. Clay, Jr. (Fla.)

Shelby, Richard C. (Ala.)

Shumway, Norman D. (Calif.)

Shuster, Bud (Pa.)

Sikorski, Gerry (Minn.)

Siljander, Mark D. (Mich.)

Simon, Paul (Ill.)

Sisisky, Norman (Va.)

Skeen, Joe (N. Mex.)

Skelton, Ike (Mo.)

Slattery, Jim (Kans.)

Smith, Christopher H. (N.J.)

Smith, Denny (Oreg.)

Smith, Lawrence J. (Fla.)

Smith, Neal (Iowa)

Smith, Robert F. (Bob) (Oreg.)

Smith, Virginia (Nebr.)

Snowe, Olympia J. (Maine)

Snyder, Gene (Ky.)

Solarz, Stephen J. (N.Y.)

Solomon, Gerald B. H. (N.Y.)

Spence, Floyd (S.C.)

Spratt, John M., Jr. (S.C.)

Staggers, Harley O., Jr. (W. Va.)

Stangeland, Arlan (Minn.)

Stark, Fortney H. (Pete) (Calif.)

Stenholm, Charles W. (Tex.)

Stokes, Louis (Ohio)

Stratton, Samuel S. (N.Y.)

Studds, Gerry E. (Mass.)

Stump, Bob (Ariz.)

Sundquist, Don (Tenn.)

Sunia, Fofo I. F. (Am. Samoa)

Swift, Al (Wash.)

Synar, Mike (Okla.)

Tallon, Robin (S.C.)

Tauke, Thomas J. (Iowa)

Tauzin, W. J. (Billy) (La.)

Taylor, Gene (Mo.)

Thomas, Robert Lindsay (Ga.)

Thomas, William M. (Calif.)

Torres, Esteban Edward (Calif.)

Torricelli, Robert G. (N.J.)

Towns, Edolphus (N.Y.)

Traxler, Bob (Mich.)

Udall, Morris K. (Ariz.)

Valentine, Tim (N.C.)

Vandergriff, Tom (Tex.)

Vander Jagt, Guy (Mich.)

Vento, Bruce, F. (Minn.)

Volkmer, Harold L. (Mo.)

Vucanovich, Barbara F. (Nev.)

Walgren, Doug (Pa.)

Walker, Robert S. (Pa.)

Watkins, Wes (Okla.)

Waxman, Henry A. (Calif.)

Weaver, James (Oreg.)

Weber, Vin (Minn.)

Weiss, Ted (N.Y.)

Wheat, Alan (Mo.)

Whitehurst, G. William (Va.)

Whitley, Charles (N.C.)

Whittaker, Bob (Kans.)

Whitten, Jamie L. (Miss.)

Williams, Lyle (Ohio)

Williams, Pat (Mont.)

Wilson, Charles (Tex.)

Winn, *Larry, Jr.* (Kans.)
Wirth, Timothy E. (Colo.)
Wise, Robert E., Jr. (W. Va.)
Wolf, Frank R. (Va.)
Wolpe, Howard (Mich.)
Won Pat, Antonio Borja (Guam)
Wortley, George C. (N.Y.)
Wright, Jim (Tex.)
Wyden, Ron (Oreg.)

Wylie, Chalmers P. (Ohio)
Yates, Sidney R. (Ill.)
Yatron, Gus (Pa.)
Young, C. W. Bill (Fla.)
Young, Don (Alaska)
Young, Robert A. (Mo.)
Zablocki, Clement J. (Wis.)
Zschau, Ed (Calif.)

Members of the Senate (98th Congress)

(Democrats in roman; Republicans in *italic*.)

Vice Pres. *Bush, George* (Tex.)
Abdnor, James (S. Dak.)
Andrews, Mark (N. Dak.)
Armstrong, William L. (Colo)
Baker, Howard H., Jr. (Tenn.)
Baucus, Max (Mont.)
Bentsen, Lloyd (Tex.)
Biden, Joseph R., Jr. (Del.)
Bingaman, Jeff (N. Mex.)
Boren, David L. (Okla.)
Boschwitz, Rudy (Minn.)
Bradley, Bill (N.J.)
Bumpers, Dale (Ark.)
Burdick, Quentin N. (N. Dak.)
Byrd, Robert C. (W. Va.)
Chafee, John H. (R.I.)
Chiles, Lawton (Fla.)
Cochran, Thad (Miss.)
Cohen, William S. (Maine)
Cranston, Alan (Calif.)
D'Amato, Alfonse M. (N.Y.)
Danforth, John C. (Mo.)
DeConcini, Dennis (Ariz.)
Denton, Jeremiah (Ala.)

Dixon, Alan J. (Ill.)
Dodd, Christopher J. (Conn.)
Dole, Robert (Kans.)
Domenici, Pete V. (N. Mex.)
Durenberger, Dave (Minn.)
Eagleton, Thomas F. (Mo.)
East, John P. (N.C.)
Exon, J. James (Nebr.)
Ford, Wendell H. (Ky.)
Garn, Jake (Utah)
Glenn, John (Ohio)
Goldwater, Barry (Ariz.)
Gorton, Slade (Wash.)
Grassley, Charles E. (Iowa)
Hart, Gary (Colo.)
Hatch, Orrin G. (Utah)
Hatfield, Mark O. (Oreg.)
Hawkins, Paula (Fla.)
Hecht, Chic (Nev.)
Heflin, Howell (Ala.)
Heinz, John (Pa.)
Helms, Jesse (N.C.)
Hollings, Ernest F. (S.C.)
Huddleston, Walter D. (Ky.)

407

Humphrey, Gordon J. (N.H.)
Inouye, Daniel K. (Hawaii)
Jackson, Henry M. (Wash.)
Jepsen, Roger W. (Iowa)
Johnston, J. Bennett (La.)
Kassebaum, Nancy Landon (Kans.)
Kasten, Bob (Wis.)
Kennedy, Edward M. (Mass.)
Lautenberg, Frank R. (N.J.)
Laxalt, Paul (Nev.)
Leahy, Patrick J. (Vt.)
Levin, Carl (Mich)
Long, Russell B. (La.)
Lugar, Richard G. (Ind.)
McClure, James A. (Idaho)
Mathias, Charles McC., Jr. (Md.)
Matsunaga, Spark M. (Hawaii)
Mattingly, Mack (Ga.)
Melcher, John (Mont.)
Metzenbaum, Howard M. (Ohio)
Mitchell, George J. (Maine)
Moynihan, Daniel Patrick (N.Y.)
Murkowski, Frank H. (Alaska)
Nickles, Don (Okla.)
Nunn, Sam (Ga.)
Packwood, Bob (Oreg.)
Pell, Claiborne (R.I.)

Percy, Charles H. (Ill.)
Pressler, Larry (S. Dak.)
Proxmire, William (Wis.)
Pryor, David (Ark.)
Quayle, Dan (Ind.)
Randolph, Jennings (W. Va.)
Riegle, Donald W., Jr. (Mich.)
Roth, William V., Jr. (Del.)
Rudman, Warren (N.H.)
Sarbanes, Paul S. (Md.)
Sasser, Jim (Tenn.)
Simpson, Alan K. (Wyo)
Specter, Arlen (Pa.)
Stafford, Robert T. (Vt.)
Stennis, John C. (Miss.)
Stevens, Ted (Alaska)
Symms, Steven D. (Idaho)
Thurmond, Strom (S.C.)
Tower, John (Tex.)
Trible, Paul S., Jr. (Va.)
Tsongas, Paul E. (Mass.)
Wallop, Malcolm (Wyo.)
Warner, John W. (Va.)
Weicker, Lowell P., Jr. (Conn.)
Wilson, Pete (Calif.)
Zorinsky, Edward (Nebr.)

INDEX

409

INDEX

415

ABOUT THE AUTHORS

MARK GREEN is a lawyer and the president of the Democracy Project, a public-policy institute with offices in New York City and Washington, D.C. He has written and edited several books on government and business, including *The Other Government: The Unseen Power of Washington Lawyers* (1975), *Taming the Giant Corporation* (1976, with Ralph Nader and Joel Seligman), and *Winning Back America* (1982), which was nominated for an American Book Award.

MICHAEL WALDMAN is the research director of the Democracy Project. He is a 1982 graduate of Columbia College, where he was an editor of the *Columbia Daily Spectator* and won the Charles A. Beard prize in political science.

CONTRIBUTORS
TO EARLIER EDITIONS

MICHAEL CALABRESE is a 1979 graduate of Harvard College, where he was a reporter for the *Harvard Crimson*. He is currently getting a joint degree from the Stanford Law and Business Schools.

LYNN DARLING is a reporter with *The Washington Post*.

JAMES FALLOWS was President Carter's speechwriter from 1976 to 1978. He is the author of *National Defense* (1981) and is currently the Washington editor of *The Atlantic Monthly*.

BRUCE ROSENTHAL was the editor of *Critical Mass Journal* and is now communications director for the National Association of Towns and Townships.

DAVID ZWICK is the author of *Water Wasteland* and is director of the Clean Water Action Project.